the Last Step

The American Ascent of K2

RICK RIDGEWAY

Prelude by
James W. Whittaker

THE
MOUNTAINEERS

Published by
The Mountaineers
1001 SW Klickitat Way, Suite 201
Seattle, WA 98134

Cloth edition: first printing 1980. Paper edition: first printing 1999, second printing 2001, third printing 2003.

Published simultaneously in Great Britian by Cordee, 3a DeMontfort Street, Leicester, England, LE1 7HD

Manufactured in Canada
Edited by Rebecca Earnest
Cover design by Helen Cherullo

Library of Congress Cataloging in Publicatino Data

Ridgeway, Rick.
    The last step.

    1. Mountaineering — Pakistan — K2 (Mountain)
2. K2 (Mountain), Pakistan — Description   I. Title.
GV199.44.P182K184 1980   915.49'1   80-19395
ISBN 0-89886-007-5 (cloth)
ISBN 0-89666-632-4 (paper)

♻ Printed on recycled paper

In memory of
Chris Chandler

Keep your eye fixed on
the path to the top,
but don't forget to look
in front of you.
The last step depends
on the first.
Don't think you're there
just because
you see the summit.
Watch your footing,
be sure of the step,
but don't let that
distract you from
the highest goal.
The first step
depends on the last.

— Rene Daumal,
   Mount Analogue

Contents

Introduction to the New Edition

K2, THE SECOND HIGHEST PEAK ON EARTH, continues to live up to its reputation: the Mountain of Mountains, the Savage Mountain, the Mountaineer's Mountain. It may be lower than Everest by 230 meters, but to mountaineers it measures significantly higher in difficulty.

Steep and four-sided, like the Great Pyramid of the Himalayas, K2 has become the testpiece of high-altitude mountaineering. Year after year expeditions, counting among their members the world's most accomplished high-altitude climbers, make the pilgrimage into the heart of Central Asia's Karakoram mountains to attempt the Mountain of Mountains. Today K2 has seen nearly two hundred ascents, but at the same time it continues to justify its other reputation as the Savage Mountain: nearly fifty climbers have died either trying to get to the top, or trying to get back down alive.

Twenty years ago it would have been hard to predict K2 would gain such popularity—and notoriety—not only among climbers but also with the broad public. In 1978, when we walked those 110 miles from the end of the road to the base of the mountain, K2 had been climbed only twice, and the second ascent (by an army of fifty-plus Japanese climbers) had been staged less than twelve months before. In those days, a survey on Main Street, America, would probably have revealed as many people who thought K2 was a new brand of dog food as those who knew it as the ultimate high-altitude peak in the world.

All that changed in 1986. K2's popularity among mountaineers, coupled with a reversal of the Pakistan government's former reticence in allowing more than one expedition at a time on the peak, resulted in nine expeditions arriving at the same time. As with the notorious tragedy on Everest that was to happen ten years later, it seemed almost inevitable that something would go wrong. And as on Everest, the set-up to tragedy in 1986 began when a large number of climbers were caught in a storm at the 8000-meter high camp. The wind-whipped snow pinned them in their tents without food, oxygen, or fuel, and hour by hour they deteriorated from the combined effects of hypoxia and de-hydration. Two of them fell into torpor, delirium, and finally death. When the storm abated five days later, those still alive began their descent, but more either collapsed, unable to stand back up, or stumbled and fell to their deaths. When it was over, of the seven climbers who had been trapped, only three got down alive.

In 1986 alone, twenty-seven people reached the summit, but thirteen died from exposure, high altitude illness, slipping and falling, or falling into a cre-vasse. Unlike the novice climbers led by professional guides who were the majority of victims in the Everest tragedy in 1996, the fallen K2 climbers were some of the best in the world. Then, as though to further confirm K2's reputa-tion, in the following three years, sixteen expeditions in a row failed to reach the summit. It wasn't until 1990 that climbers again stood on top of the second highest point on earth.

From the perspective of hindsight on our own climb in 1978, it is easy to conclude that we were lucky. It can also be said, I think, that luck is less a matter of chance than an ability to recognize opportunity. We had two days of flawless weather when we made our summit bids, but by then we had paid our dues. We had worked hard above our advance base camp for over sixty days, and by the time we started our descent, those of us on the summit teams had stayed at 8000 meters or higher for five days and four nights. We had waited long and patiently for our window of good weather and also had chosen to back off when conditions were questionable, as they were when John Roskelley and I attempted to make a direct finish up the northeast side of the summit pyramid.

When at last I did find myself standing on top of K2, my oxygen-starved brain had just enough presence of mind to remind me that the day would no doubt be one that would stand out for the rest of my life. While it would be an exaggeration to say that when I returned home the experience changed the direction of my life, it did give me a new yardstick against which to measure my more prosaic day-to-day challenges. I learned on K2 what another moun-taineering friend had once told me was the way you go about eating an el-ephant: you do it one bite at a time.

Tenacity isn't the only lesson I brought down from K2. Looking back with perhaps a more mature perspective, the arguments and squabbles that colored our expedition—and are predominant in this book—seem sometimes petty. They make me wish we could go back and approach our differences with more mutual empathy, and also with the knowledge that in the long run those differences seem minor alongside the memories not only of the summit day but also of the day on the ridge at 22,000 feet when I saw the butterflies; or the day the low afternoon sun cast our rainbow-rimmed shadows over the glacier a vertical mile below; or the day when we returned safely to base camp and received from our teammates a series of hugs and shoulder-slaps, despite our differences.

Such sentiments perhaps aren't surprising considering that all of us on the K2 team are now somewhere between fifty and seventy years old. One thing that hasn't changed in the last twenty years, however, is the mountain itself. Its immutability reminds me of a scene in Joseph Conrad's *Nigger of the Narcissus,* when Old Singleton, the most experienced hand on the crew, has to take the helm for four days to bring the ship safely through a hurricane. When his long watch is over the old seaman stumbles down the companionway, pausing at a porthole to gaze at the sea. In front of him he sees his hand, weathered and veined, arthritic from the hours and days of gripping the wheel, and he thinks back to when he first went to sea as a youth, and how then his body was lean and strong. Then he looks back to the sea, the immutable sea—the same as our immutable mountain—and it looks exactly as it did when he first saw it, exactly as it will when he is gone.

Rick Ridgeway

Prelude

THIS STORY TAKES PLACE IN THE HEART OF
Central Asia—the border between Pakistan and China—on the second
highest mountain in the world. Called K2, it soars 28,250 feet above the
sea, and it is one of nature's most spectacular architectural achievements.
Rising four-sided in perfect symmetry, like the Great Pyramid, it reaches
such altitude that when viewed from an airplane even a hundred miles distant, it dominates the horizon.

K2 is so remote that the Balti hillspeople, whose villages are the human
habitations nearest the mountain, don't even have a name for it. It was
first sighted by Westerners, from a survey point more than a hundred
miles away, in 1856. In that first mapping all the peaks of the Karakoram
—the range in which K2 is located—were named by labeling each one
with a "k" followed by a number in the order in which they were sur-
veyed. Later, most of these labels were dropped in favor of names that had
currency among the local Baltis: Masherbrum, Gasherbrum, Chogolisa.
But when asked their name for the peak that was most distant and highest,
the Baltis only shrugged. Some of them were aware the great mountain
existed, but since it was so far away and so seldom seen, they just called it
"Big Mountain"—Chogori. The surveyors, hesitant to name the mountain
after their own kin, such as they had with Everest, kept their field-note
designation. Although a glacier at the foot of the mountain was named
Godwin-Austen, the mountain has since been known as K2. It is a name
that, even with its brevity, is oddly suitable: it conveys the arcane majesty
of this great peak.

Because of its steepness and extreme altitude, its difficult approach, its
harsh weather, because of the lack of Sherpas to help ferry loads at high

3

altitudes, K2 is the hardest of the world's high mountains to climb. It was first attempted in 1902 when the art of mountaineering was being weaned beyond the Alps of Europe, but that expedition failed low on the mountain. Most of the subsequent attempts were made by Americans—in 1938, in 1939, and again in 1953. Like Everest, which was called a "British" mountain because Britons had made most of the early attempts to climb it, K2 was an "American" mountain. But unlike the British, who in 1953 became the first to climb Everest, the Americans missed their chance: in 1954, an Italian team made the first ascent of K2.

My own personal high point in mountaineering was on May 1, 1963, when I became the first American to climb Everest. It was only the third time that the world's highest mountain had been climbed by anyone. Then ten years later, in 1973, I got a call from Jim Wickwire, an attorney and well-known climber from my hometown of Seattle, saying he was seriously planning an expedition to K2 and wondered if I would be willing to sign on as leader. Even though by then Everest had been climbed a dozen times, K2 had only had that one ascent by the Italians in 1954. "Wick" was looking for a leader who not only had the climbing experience, but who could also manage the organization of tons of food and equipment and design a fund-raising program to cover expenses.

The human mind has an uncanny ability, when remembering past experiences, to winnow the disagreeable and allow recollection only of that which was fun, exciting, and enjoyable. The memory of my climb up Everest was much like that. Only if I thought hard could I recall the extreme winds and numbing cold, the continual struggle to suck enough oxygen into the lungs, the loss of appetite that always comes with altitude, and the weeks and weeks of risk and effort necessary to climb a really big mountain. Instead I usually remembered the fantastic scenery on days so clear you could see for hundreds of miles; I remembered the incomparable excitement of making those last steps when I finally reached the highest point on earth. I hadn't been back to the Himalaya since the Everest climb, and I had often wanted to return. But I had let the years slip without making any definite climbing plans. By the time I received that phone call I was forty-four and I knew that if we did manage to get a permit, by the time we organized an expedition and got to the mountain, I would probably be forty-six. But I was still in good shape, and the Himalaya beckoned. Without much hesitation I told Wick I would be happy to lead the expedition to K2 and would apply to the Pakistan government for permission.

To organize an expedition to a big peak in the Himalaya, you don't simply get on a plane, fly over there, hike to the mountain, and start climbing. First there is a mountain of red tape—the paperwork necessary to get a climbing permit from the foreign government. Then you must raise the money, organize the equipment, purchase the food—usually weighted in tons—then pack everything and see that it is shipped and doesn't end up impounded in some distant customs warehouse. It is then time to transport the tons of gear to the base of the mountain, and this normally involves hundreds of local porters. With everything assembled at the base camp, the climb can begin.

The most critical task, however, is choosing the team members. Each one must be more than a competent mountaineer; it is equally if not more important that he or she be even-tempered and companionable. This is often the attribute most difficult to judge when considering a climber for an expedition, because every person who at sea level seems to be affable and clear-thinking can change—when exposed to the rigors of living at high altitudes—from a Dr. Jekyll to a real Mr. Hyde.

After we had the permit in our hands, we rounded out the team. In addition to Wickwire and me there were already two other climbers with us: Rob Schaller, a climber and pediatric surgeon who would also function as team doctor, and Leif-Norman Patterson, a Norwegian mathematics instructor living in British Columbia who not only had an outstanding climbing record in Peru and Alaska, but a reputation as friendly and even-tempered, even under the strain of high-altitude climbing. After careful consideration we finally chose four more climbers; in addition, we would be accompanied by a filmmaker, Steve Marts, and also by my wife, Dianne Roberts. She hadn't had much climbing experience, and her main role would be photojournalist.

Using my experience on Everest, I planned every step of the way as diligently as possible. We carefully packed the food and gear in individual fifty-five-pound porter loads and shipped four months in advance. We ourselves left for Pakistan in April so we could arrive at the mountain early in the season to take advantage of any good weather. We arranged to hire porters in advance of our arrival and pay them good wages. With such careful planning we felt confident nothing could go wrong; we were soon to learn that confidence was based on complete naivete.

All of us had read accounts of how porter strikes had crippled many past expeditions in this area, but we all hoped that if we simply paid the porters good wages we would arrive in Base Camp trouble free. It was a false hope. Because it had been so many years since a major expedition had been in the area, there were no set rules for either side to follow. The result was misunderstanding that led to several strikes, which severely delayed the expedition.

We finally reached Base Camp, but it had taken almost two months since leaving the United States—many weeks more than we had expected. Much worse than just being behind schedule, the delays had eroded our spirit, we had picked up local "bugs," and there were the beginnings of schisms among the climbers, some already disgusted with our progress and wanting to go home.

We had chosen as our route the great unclimbed, unattempted north-west ridge of K2. It was a bold undertaking. The very steep rock and ice ridge descended over six thousand vertical feet from the summit to a col above our camp. We began to climb and established Camp I and Camp II before the first storm, in early June. Before the disappointing end of our expedition, we would experience many more. One of the major difficulties of climbing in the Karakoram is the unpredictable weather. Often June and July have predominantly good weather, but it is never possible to predict with any certainty. Our first storm hit at sixty miles an hour, covering fixed ropes and tents and driving us off the mountain. After that storm we managed to carry several loads above Camp I, but no sooner had we finished than new problems developed. Two climbers were seriously ill with pneumonia, which left only four of us able to work with full strength. In addition, several of the team were disenchanted with the way things were going, and the resulting schism further weakened us. It was then I doubted that we could climb the mountain.

Some of us felt that even if we couldn't get to the top we still owed it to ourselves to get as high on the mountain as possible. In early July three of the team set off to push the route along the knife-ridge. They managed to reach the top of the first gendarme—a sharp pinnacle that rose as part of the larger northwest ridge—but what they saw from there was both exhilarating and disheartening. Behind them, they could make out our camp at the pass, and then the Karakoram spreading westward to the Hunza region. Nanga Parbat, over twenty-six thousand feet and the citadel of the Hunza Valley, rose dominant on the horizon. Straight below them, almost seven thousand feet down, they saw the north glacier of K2 running into the parched-brown hills of the Sinkiang Province of China. But the view in front of them was awesome. Even though they were then at twenty-two thousand feet, the main pyramidal mass of K2 still rose sharply before them for over a vertical mile. Their eyes followed the difficulties they would have to cross in order to reach the summit, and it was obvious the task was impossible. The top of that gendarme would be the high point reached by our 1975 expedition.

Our retreat and hike out to civilization was uneventful; despite the exhilarating scenery of granite spires and snow peaks, there was no overcoming our disappointment and failure. The years of preparation seemed for naught; we hadn't even reached the halfway point on our dream mountain.

But going out, a few of us began to think about coming back. Maybe if we had a more feasible route, maybe if we selected a stronger, larger team, maybe if we could get the Pakistan government to somehow ensure better performance of the porters. . . . With all these "maybes" would we have a chance of coming back and actually pulling it off? I had doubts—there were so many obstacles—yet the more I pondered, the more I realized it was possible. I had set out to lead a successful expedition to the second highest mountain in the world, and I wouldn't feel satisfied until we completed what Americans had first set out to do in 1938. There now had been five American failures in a row (including a joint German-

American expedition in 1960). But what if we did all that work, only to be once again turned back, to become the sixth failure? We were still in debt: I didn't want to think about that possibility.

But it was unfinished business. Shortly after returning to Seattle, several of us from the 1975 expedition got together to discuss the possibility of going back. Jim Wickwire was all for it, and it seemed his enthusiasm was indefatigable; I felt that if for no other reason his energy would *have* to result in our climbing K2. Rob Schaller was up for another try, and Leif-Norman Patterson also wanted to be counted in. Leif, more than any of us, had been the neutral mediator during our disputes: he was a very strong climber and a close friend. It was a good start. We knew most of the problems, and my optimism began to build.

I wrote a long letter to the Pakistan government explaining all the difficulties we had experienced and made dozens of suggestions that would help future expeditions to the Karakoram. I stressed how good this would be for the porters and the government as well. Two months later they replied that they were implementing all of my recommendations and hoped my next visit would be more pleasant.

The procedure was by now familiar. The first thing was getting another permit. We thought about approaching through China. That would add a fascinating dimension to the expedition, and through satellite photographs it appeared the Chinese had built a road within forty miles of the North Ridge of K2. I contacted our Washington state Senator Henry "Scoop" Jackson, who agreed to help. He wrote a letter on my behalf to the Chinese Liaison Office in Washington, but the answer was negative; the time was not right to open Sinkiang.

So we were back to approaching K2 through Pakistan. The problem was that use of the Kashmir approach to the Karakoram was now in full swing. The Japanese already had a permit to try K2, with fifty climbers, in 1977;the Polish would be on the mountain in 1976; it looked like others were vying for 1978. Would we have to wait until 1979, or longer? I wrote letters directly to Pakistan and submitted our application to the Pakistan Embassy in Washington, D.C. And then waited. I had applied in March of 1976; finally, in October, I received an answer from the Pakistan Embassy: "Dear Mr. Whittaker, Your application was forwarded to the Government of Pakistan who have regretted their inability to approve it for leading an expedition to K2 in 1978. However, you may apply for the same in 1977 to attempt the peak in 1979."

It was a hard blow to accept. I also learned that the 1978 permit had been given to Chris Bonington, the well-known British leader of major expeditions to the Himalaya, including Everest. We were on the verge of giving up, but I decided to make one last try. For years I had been friends with the Kennedy family, and I asked Senator Ted Kennedy for help. He said he would write Prime Minister Bhutto and see if there was anything that could be done.

On New Year's Day, 1977, I received a letter from the Pakistan Embassy saying their government, as a special case, had allotted our expedition, as well as the British, permission to try K2 in 1978. The only condition was that we agree to follow the British by a few weeks to avoid logjamming on the approach march. We were on for 1978!

If I had learned one lesson in 1975, it was the supreme importance of choosing the team members. I decided to pick only climbers who had experience over twenty thousand feet, who were highly motivated, and who were willing to accept the high risk. I also decided we should choose from a large pool of people, so I put the word out that we were open for applicants who wanted to climb K2. The response was immense. Within a couple of months I had resumes from over a hundred climbers. We had so many qualified applicants that the only way to choose was to pick those either personally known or who had strong references from people personally known. It was mandatory that each member be 100 percent committed to the idea of working hard to get *anyone* to the top of K2. I wanted the best, toughest, meanest climbers in the United States.

Before we could complete the team, however, we had a tragic setback. Leif Patterson and his son, climbing on a Sunday afternoon by their home in Golden, B.C., were killed in an avalanche. It was a terrible loss to his family and friends.

Leif's death left a vacancy I knew couldn't be filled. It would be impossible to find anyone with his combination of climbing ability, determination, and camaraderie. I continued the search, spending hours discussing the pros and cons of this climber or that until finally we had our team:

Craig Anderson, 30. A zoologist whose climbing experience in Nepal included the 1973 Dhaulagiri expedition.

Cheri Bech, 32. A nurse who held the altitude record for American women when she reached 24,700 feet on Dhaulagiri with her husband Terry.

Terry Bech, 38. An anthropologist who had lived nine years in Nepal and had done considerable mountaineering over 20,000 feet.

Chris Chandler, 29. A Seattle physician who had reached the summit of Everest in 1976 on the American Bicentennial Expedition.

Skip Edmonds, 30. Another physician, who had also climbed in the Nepal Himalaya.

Al Givler, 30. Known to always have a smile for everyone; he had an outstanding climbing record in Alaska and North America.

Dusan Jagersky, 37. An immigrant from Czechoslovakia who had dozens of first ascents in Europe and an impressive record in Alaska.

Lou Reichardt, 34. A neurobiologist from San Francisco who had climbed to the summit of Dhaulagiri in Nepal and Nanda Devi in India.

Rick Ridgeway, 28. A writer and filmmaker from Malibu, California; he had reached 26,200 feet on Everest in 1976.

Dianne Roberts, 29. A photojournalist and my wife; she was with us on the 1975 K2 expedition and had reached 22,000 feet.

John Roskelley, 28. Considered one of the best high-altitude climbers in the country, he had stood on top of Dhaulagiri and Nanda Devi.

Bill Sumner, 35. A former nuclear physicist who turned to producing tents at his home in Index, Washington. He had an outstanding climbing record in the Northwest United States and had climbed above 20,000 feet in Nepal.

Rob Schaller, 42. A Seattle physician, he had also been on the 1975 K2 trip.

Jim Wickwire, 37. A Seattle attorney who had ice-climbing experience in the Cascades and Alaska.

I felt it was the strongest team of American climbers that had ever been assembled to climb in the Himalaya. (Later, we added *Diana Jagersky* as Base Camp manager.) Again, my job was only starting: I still had the wearisome task of food and equipment preparation, the quest to dredge enough funds to pay for everything—all so the real effort could begin. Again, I had confidence we could get the mountain.

The story of any mountain climb is only in small part about finding routes, fixing ropes, establishing camps, fighting storms, and gaining summits. The real story is the people who do these things. The American Ascent of K2 is a story about people. It is about a team that leaves the United States dedicated to victory on K2; about individuals who have to overcome their fears, desires, and disappointments to achieve that victory. There is love, hatred, tears, laughter, even defeat. I will always remember that day the summit teams were turned back by soft snow and avalanches from their last-ditch effort to reach the top, when I said to Dianne, "I guess that's it. It looks like it won't go; we'll probably go home with another defeat."

It is also a story of tragedy. The summer before we were scheduled to leave for Pakistan, Al Givler and Dusan Jagersky, after making the first ascent of a remote and difficult peak in Alaska, fell on the descent and were both killed. We decided that rather than replace them with other climbers we would try K2 with a smaller group. Yet it was only physically smaller; spiritually they were there with us all the way, and when, despite all odds, and at the eleventh hour of the expedition, four of our team made those last steps to the summit, Leif, Al, and Dusan were there with us all, gazing across the mountains from the top of the second highest point on earth. This book is dedicated to their memory.

—James W. Whittaker

1

Dust from the Road

THE DESERT AIR BLEW IN OUR FACES, DRY-
ing our skin and chapping our lips. We were standing in the back of an
open jeep, and our Pakistani driver hit holes in the road with such speed we
bounced off our feet and had to hold on to keep from flying out. An
enormous dust cloud rose off the powder-dry road, and only now and again
could we glimpse the two jeeps behind us. There were five of us in the lead
jeep. The other nine climbers, our Pakistani liaison officer, and the four
strong, good-looking men from Hunza we had hired to help carry loads on
the mountain were in the rear jeeps. Together we were the 1978 American
K2 Expedition.

Jim Wickwire, with us in the lead jeep, was the first to raise the
question.

"Those guys back there are eating some dust," he said. "Since it is such a
sensitive subject, it might be diplomatic to pull over and let Whittaker take
the lead."

The rest of us immediately agreed. When we left Shigar that morning,
we had intended to pull up rear position, but our driver, still seeing checkered flags after his daredevil drive the day before from Skardu, had bolted
out in front. It was the departure from Skardu that had raised the ire of Jim
Whittaker and caused his reprimand. He was not mad that we had sped off
to avoid eating dust, but because our leaving without warning disrupted
plans of the town's officials to give us a farewell send-off. Jim had been left
standing in the street with the officials as we roared by, shifting gears and

yelling and hooting and spewing up clouds of dust. The officials were also left holding the souvenir postcards we were supposed to sign. The photographer, who was to take the team photo with the officials standing next to us, slowly packed his camera.

But Jim's embarrassment was only part of the problem. Our liaison officer—a Pakistani Army sergeant-major assigned to escort our expedition —had threatened to quit the expedition on the spot. Having set up the meeting, he had lost credibility. "If you cannot control your own team members, I will not be a part of this expedition," he announced, and he reminded Jim that the bridges they were crossing were military installations. Since he would not be along to see that no pictures were taken of them, he would have to confiscate all our film.

Jim had had to plead with him—and pleading is not necessarily something Whittaker likes to do—telling Saleem, "It's only the way Americans do things. It doesn't mean they won't obey me—it was just that they didn't want to stay behind in the dust from the other jeeps. It was kind of a joke," he said, sheepishly.

Jim had managed to pacify Saleem and persuaded him not to abandon the expedition, something that would have effectively stopped us before we started. No expedition is permitted to climb in Pakistan without a military liaison officer, and without Saleem to control the porters who would haul our equipment to the base of K2, we wouldn't have had a prayer of reaching the mountain anyway. Jim was really angry. What we thought was innocent tomfoolery (we didn't know about the bank officials and the autographs and the photographs) ended that night in Shigar with Jim lecturing us on team unity, on individuals thinking only of themselves, on how could we possibly expect to make one of the world's most difficult climbs if we weren't willing to work together? So, when Jim Wickwire suggested we show contrition and let the others pass, we all heartily agreed. We yelled up to the driver to pull over.

John Roskelley, who had been over this road before when he came to the Karakoram Mountains on another climbing expedition, had already learned the hazards of desert travel. He wet his bandana from his drinking bottle and tied it around his mouth and nose bandit-style.

The other two jeeps passed and Whittaker waved; we could see he was smiling. Apparently, he was willing to forget our peccadillo, and we all felt the problem had been worked out. Each of us knew that in the early stages of climbing expeditions, rancor and gall are like blisters that have to be aired and dried, lest they fester to crippling wounds; we had all seen how, on the 1975 K2 Expedition, arguing and bickering had contributed to an early defeat, and we resolved not to let that happen this time.

That morning when we left Shigar I had still felt uneasy, but my optimism was returning. The climb had to be a collaborative effort if we had any dreams of success, and it seemed that everyone was well aware of that. There was no doubt we had bitten off a big hunk—and a dangerous one, too. That fact had been laid bare before us two days back when we learned of a tragedy on Chris Bonington's expedition; they had been trying a new route on K2, but now they were on their way home. Nevertheless, our team had a positive air. I remembered the pact we had made before leaving the States: we would work together, giving as much as we could, to get somebody—anybody—to the top of K2.

The road climbed along the foothills flanking the broad alluvial plain of the Shigar River. Behind, we could see the even broader valley where the Shigar joins the mighty Indus, which flows from the distant plains of Tibet. Above us, a ridge bordering the valley rose to such a height that it supported glaciers, glistening brightly against the cobalt blue sky. Below, in the plain, we could see oases outlined by tall Lombardy poplars, and here and there big, bushy mulberries, ripe with red berries. The poplars formed borders around fields of wheat, green in early summer. It was only in such oases, irrigated by water flowing from the high, perpetual snows, that the Baltis—the people who inhabit these valleys of Baltistan—could survive against the desert.

It seemed odd, traveling through desert, that we were on our way to try to climb the second highest mountain in the world. All of us except Diana Jagersky, our Base Camp manager, had climbed at least once before in the Himalaya. But except for Rob Schaller, Jim Wickwire, Dianne Roberts, and Jim Whittaker, who had been on the 1975 K2 climb, and John Roskelley, who had been in the Karakoram the year before, all our experience had been in the Himalaya of Nepal. In Nepal, the seasonal monsoon brings thick, warm rain from the Bay of Bengal and turns the foothills into jungles. The Karakoram, however, are in the lee of the northwest end of the Himalaya proper, and therefore are sheltered far inland from most of the rain that comes up from Pakistan, creating desert conditions in the lower valleys. Nevertheless, at high altitudes there are still many storms.

Our jeep downshifted as it crested a small hill and began a steep descent to an arroyo bottom. We had left the area of trees and villages; the floor of the desert was covered with stones the size of soccer balls, washed down from the bordering hills, with desert sage sparsely and boldly rooted between the rocks. The smell of sage blossoms was strong. The stream had been bridged by two sturdy planks, but the planks had washed out and now we had to detour downstream to a suitable ford. Our jeep's suspension strained as it moved across the larger wash-bottom rocks, and water swirled up to the top of our tires. We climbed steeply up the other side—all of us still holding on so we wouldn't bounce out. Once up the opposite bank, we could see ahead the long line of tractors, each pulling a trailer, that had left Skardu ahead of us. The tractors carried our food and equip-ment—all 19,250 pounds of it.

In all, there were fourteen tractors, and we could see most of them stopped behind one that appeared to be broken down. We pulled up to the rear and walked over to it. Most of them were nearly new Massey-Fergusons, probably from some aid program, and each pulled a homemade trailer filled with the sturdy cardboard boxes containing our gear. We had been apprehensive about sending our equipment ahead of us. But since the tractors only traveled at twenty miles an hour, it was either that or have them arrive a day behind us at the end of the road.

Subadar-Major Mohammed Saleem Khan, our robust liaison officer, had assured us our gear would be safe: he had personally told the tractor drivers to make certain each item arrived intact. Saleem was six feet tall and, at the beginning of the trek, a sturdy two hundred pounds. He wore a camouflage field shirt, a camouflage hat with one brim folded up Aussi style, and khaki pants. He had short, thick fingers, and the habit of officiously holding up his index finger when he made a point. When he spoke, it was with much bombast, as a lord might speak to a servant. Though we did not understand Urdu, we sensed that those to whom he spoke, listened. We were never too concerned about our equipment. We were also happy he was our liaison officer because we knew his firm manner was our best hope against crippling porter strikes—an important factor in the failure of the 1975 K2 expedition.

As it turned out, the tractor was not broken. Its trailer had lost a keeper-washer on the wheel bearing, and the driver was fashioning another one from a tin can. It looked like the operation might take some time, so we moved a few boulders to open a detour, motioned the waiting tractors and jeeps around, and continued on. We had less than an hour's travel to the end of the road.

There were dozens upon dozens of Baltis walking along the road, all porters we had contracted with earlier in Skardu, and all of whom had walked for two days and nights to meet us at the roadhead where the trek to Base Camp would start. They were dressed ragamuffin in homespun trousers and coats, and each wore a wool cap rolled at the sides and flat on top—the Gilgit cap, as it is called. Each carried a hiking stick the length of a cane, but with a crossbar carefully jointed across the top, forming a T-shape.

We had hired from among the people of Skardu 100 of the total 365 porters we would need to carry our gear to Base Camp. On an appointed day, hundreds of them had lined up in an open square of the village; Rob Schaller, our team's chief physician, had to sort through the lot and choose the healthiest. Their names were recorded in an accounting book, and each man pressed his inked thumb next to his name, sealing the contract. Packing the few belongings they would take on the long approach march in cloth satchels tied around their backs, they set out that afternoon hiking toward the end of the jeep road. There, the tractors would dump the loads: loads that would be carried on foot, across deserts, through narrow canyons dangerous with falling rock, and over long glaciers, 110 miles to Base Camp.

It was at the trailhead that we planned to hire the remaining number of our army of porters. In total, we had 280 loads to be carried. But we would need more porters than we had loads, because most of the country we were about to march through was uninhabited; unlike Nepal, where porters each night procure their own food in local villages, here it would have to be hauled with us. We would need 70 porters to carry food for the 280, and another 15 to carry food for the 70 carrying food for the 280. Special couriers had been dispatched from Skardu to send word to the villages that on that day, June 22, we would be hiring at the trailhead. If the number of people who had shown up for jobs in Skardu was any indication, we would find more than enough porters waiting for us a few minutes up the road.

Ahead, we could see the main Shigar Valley continuing several miles until it narrowed and disappeared in a turn behind high mountains. Some distance up the valley, there were summits of impressive peaks certainly over twenty thousand feet high. Rob Schaller pointed out another valley that breached the Shigar just a mile or so beyond our jeep. It was the valley of the Braldu River; the Braldu we would follow some sixty miles, hiking along its bank, across alluvium cut by deep wash gullies called nullahs that we would endlessly descend and ascend, over cliffs that sometimes narrowed and bottlenecked the river, fording icewater tributaries and, at one place, building a rope crossing over a river—too swollen to ford— whose bridge had fallen down. All the way to the Baltoro Glacier. Then, for some fifty miles, we would hike on one of the largest temperate-zone glaciers in the world—a glacier covered with rock debris fallen from the bordering slopes of the most awesome mountains on earth. At the end of this glacier we would find K2.

Farther up the road we could see hundreds of Baltis trying to crowd under the shade of a single tree growing in an expanse of otherwise barren desert, covered only with sage. When they heard our jeeps, they waved and cheered, running toward us. There were obviously many more of them —several hundred, at least—than there were available jobs; we suspected it might be a task keeping order when they learned there was not enough work for everyone.

On the 1975 expedition the team had had no control over the selection of porters, and as a result, they ended up with many weak men who became seriously ill later on the approach march. Rob Schaller remembered well what it was like:

"There was so much sickness I had two hospital tents set up all the time," he said, "with as many as thirty people at once in them. I was so busy with the sick and injured, I didn't even feel like I was part of the expedition, especially with the other climbers so afraid of contracting a sickness from the porters or from me since I was working so close to them. I remember graphically once having a guy in the tent who was stuperous with spinal meningitis, and I had just done a lumbar puncture on him. There were a couple of other guys with pneumonia and shaking chills and high fever, and Dianne came to the tent with my dinner. She set the meal in front of the tent, and from a distance yelled, 'Your dinner is ready.' "

To avoid such problems we had three doctors this time, and Rob decided to give each porter a brief physical before he was hired. To speed up the process, the two other doctors on our team, Skip Edmonds and Chris Chandler, helped examine the porters. Jim Wickwire and John Roskelley milled through the crowds selecting those who looked strongest and fittest, or those with commendation papers certifying good performance on previous expeditions, and sent them over to line up in front of the doctors. If they passed the physical, they were directed to another group where their names were recorded.

The rest of us tried to keep order. Many porters tried to sneak across to join the group of men already selected. John Roskelley and I each had hiking sticks commandeered from a porter; when any of them tried to break ranks we would soundly whap them—not injuring anybody, but using enough force to keep them in line. It was reminiscent of a scene from the days of the British Raj.

Jim Wickwire was conscious of the power he wielded over these people. "I stood on a rock looking at this sea of humanity," he said, "playing the role of god. I would look out over the crowd, pick out a guy who looked strong, and point at him. The two or three people next to him would think they were the one being singled out until I made the right gestures to indicate the guy I meant. Then he would walk over to the medical line, ebullient, while the others stood there in the heat, dejected. I didn't particularly like the job, but there was no other way of doing it."

Wick didn't need to feel guilty; our method of handling the porters was enlightened empathy compared with early expeditions visiting the Karakoram. On the first attempt to climb K2, in 1902, all porters were carefully watched during the day's march and, at evening, any stragglers or troublemakers were publicly whipped. Saleem, our liaison officer, was much harder on the porters than any of us, knocking them around with a big stick with more force than we used. At first I thought Saleem had a superior and colonial attitude. Later I discovered that he had a deep-hearted regard for their welfare and felt a genuine camaraderie with the porters. Hitting them was simply the way both sides expected porters to be handled. With any less force, there would be undisciplined chaos.

By the time we had selected about two hundred men, the others hoping for jobs became restless, realizing their chances were dimming. It became more difficult to control them. Sometimes John and I had to hold our staffs across five or six, pushing for all we were worth. Eventually, we hired the number of men we needed and the others began to wander off, walking back god knows how far to their villages. Others lingered, hoping for a miracle.

Finally, the tractors with our equipment arrived. The next job was unloading, inventorying, and issuing loads. It was hot work in the direct noon sun, with no shade for shelter. By early afternoon, however, the job was finished. We could shoulder our own packs. We planned to hike only as far as the village of Dasso, about four miles away. The approach march was beginning.

THE APPROACH MARCH WAS BEGINNING BUT many of us were still no more than barely acquainted with one another. For most of us, however, there was at least one or two other people we had known before: Terry Bech had been with John Roskelley, Lou Reichardt, and Craig Anderson in 1973 on Dhaulagiri. Lou and John had reached the summit together on that climb, and together, three years later, had made the summit of Nanda Devi, the highest mountain in India, by a very difficult unclimbed ridge. Skip Edmonds and Bill Sumner were good friends from the Seattle area and had been together on a small climbing and trekking trip to Nepal. Chris Chandler and I had been together in 1976 on Mount Everest; Rob Schaller, Jim Wickwire, Dianne Roberts, and Jim Whittaker had been, of course, together in 1975 on K2. Diana Jagersky had not been on a climbing expedition with any of the others, but she had known several of the Scattleites for a number of years. Only Cherie Bech, Terry's wife, had the job of getting to know everyone.

One of the attractions of big expeditions is the opportunity of meeting people and being intimately close to them for months, people who, as often as not, have varied and fascinating backgrounds. The assortment on our trip was even more eclectic than usual. For one thing, it was a highly educated group: four doctors of philosophy, three doctors of medicine, and a lawyer, and everyone else with a college degree of some sort.

For several days after arriving in Pakistan we stayed in Rawalpindi and the neighboring capital, Islamabad, making last-minute preparations. We were courteously hosted by several families from the American Embassy, but were scattered around town in twos, each pair staying in a different house. It was not until we flew to Skardu that we began to know one another.

On that flight, we followed the Indus up through the Himalayan foothills, leaving behind the humid heat of the Punjab, flying north until the great river made its turn east toward Tibet, bending around the immense massif of Nanga Parbat, 26,660 feet above sea level. At last we were in the mountains. Our little Fokker F-27 flew at an altitude well below Nanga Parbat's summit, and from the windows we saw at horizon-level glaciers spilling from the flanks of the mountain. Smaller summits passed under our wing, breathlessly close. After so many months and years of writing letters to obtain government permits, of raising support and money, of purchasing food and seeking donations of equipment, of packing and shipping, of planning strategies on how best to place and supply camps, of daydreaming about summits, it was an exciting moment.

When the plane began its descent sunlight reflected off the Indus and, in one nearby area of flat flood plain, it glimmered off the tributaries and oxbows. Next to the river was Skardu, a town of about ten thousand people. Surrounding the houses and bazaars were green fields of wheat, poplars, mulberries, and apricots, and beyond the fields, dry, barren hills.

The plane touched down and in a few minutes we were gathering our luggage. The bulk of gear had been shipped to Pakistan weeks before and trucked to Skardu on a long, circuitous road through the Himalayan foothills. All we had to bother with was our duffels of personal equipment. So far, we were on, if not slightly ahead of, our most optimistic schedule—something that was a very important consideration, since we had been forced to begin our trip late in what is normally the season of best weather for climbing in the Karakoram.

The British, led by well-known expedition leader Chris Bonington, had originally been given permission to climb K2 in 1978. To ensure enough porters for both groups, we had been required to begin our own approach march almost a month behind his team. That decision made, the only question left unresolved concerned routes on the mountain: we must choose one other than Bonington's.

K2 is the most remarkable of all the world's highest mountains in that it is nearly a perfect pyramid, much as most people would imagine the ideal mountain. Unlike Everest, there is no "easy" way to get up K2. Both previous ascents of the mountain had been via the Abruzzi Ridge on the southeast side of the peak, and although that is the easiest access to the top, it is still a difficult and demanding climb. Of all the unclimbed ridges of K2, two were of most interest both to Bonington's group and to us. The West Ridge looked like a handsome route—steep, and direct to the top. It would have difficult sections all along, but the hardest parts of all would most likely be encountered near the summit. Scarcity of oxygen would make the climbing there even more difficult. The other possibility was the Northeast Ridge. The Poles had nearly reached the summit on this ridge in 1976, but had been turned back only 700 feet from the top when threatening weather and pending nightfall forced them to retreat. It was no doubt a less steep route than the West Ridge but it had the disadvantage of being very long. At one point, the ridge maintains the same altitude for nearly half a mile, and because it is knife-sharp, it would be a problem to haul equipment across to the upper camps.

At the time of our meeting in Seattle eight months before we left the States, Bonington's group still had not chosen their route, and we discussed our own preferences. Most of us thought the West Ridge superior because it was such an aesthetic line to the summit; the rest thought the Northeast Ridge offered a better chance of reaching the top. A few weeks later the decision was made for us: Bonington had chosen the West Ridge. We would have the Northeast Ridge.

We had stayed in touch with Bonington during preparation. He helped us by filling our oxygen bottles in England; we helped by supplying him with oxygen bottles and regulators manufactured in the States. We had radios with compatible frequencies, so we could stay in contact during the climbs. While in Rawalpindi, we learned that his group had successfully reached the base of K2 and were beginning their ascent. With our own expedition moving along well, who could tell? Maybe we could make rapid progress and meet Bonington on the summit! Even though such thoughts were flights of fantasy, we did look forward to hiking to their base camp and passing the grog bottle.

THERE WERE THREE jeeps waiting when we landed in Skardu to take us to the government-run rest house. Leaving the airport, we ran into four Americans on another climbing expedition. I knew one—Jim Donini, a famous climber with whom I had been on a trip to the Amazon a year before. It is one of the more amazing aspects of climbing to be in such a remote corner of Central Asia and run into pals you last saw in South America. Jim was part of a four-person team attempting an extremely difficult twenty-four-thousand-foot unclimbed peak called Latok (they surmounted nearly all its difficulties, but failed a few hundred feet short of the summit). Since they would use the same approach trail as we would, they hoped to leave Skardu at least a day ahead of our much larger group to avoid congestion on the trail. But they were still waiting for the arrival of some of their goods being air shipped from Rawalpindi and, so far, nothing had shown. It looked like both our groups would be in Skardu for a few days, so they promised to drop by our hotel.

We loaded our gear into the jeeps, crawled in the back, and were ready to drive the five or six miles into town. I hopped in a jeep with John Roskelley and a few others; immediately John told the driver to step on it and pass the jeep in front of us, so we wouldn't eat dust. The driver hesitated, but John and the rest of us assured him it was O.K. So he threw it in gear and spun around the jeep carrying Jim Whittaker and Dianne Roberts. I heard Jim yell at us as we passed, "O.K. you guys, we go first." Our driver heard the order and pulled over, allowing Jim's jeep out in front. John pulled out his bandana and tied it around his mouth to filter dust. I heard him mutter under his breath, "What a bunch of bull—pulling rank. This whole expedition better not be that way."

We drove down the half-mile-long main street lined with small shops and bazaars. Standing in the back of the jeep, we had to keep a weather eye for low-hanging power lines. The streets were crowded with an assortment of Baltis dressed traditionally in homespun and Gilgit caps, mixed with taller, more swarthy men—probably from the lowlands—wearing shalwarcamise, the national costume of baggy pajama pants and a pullover shirt that drops below the waist. As could be expected in a Moslem country, few women were to be seen except those working in the wheatfields. If the women caught you looking at them, they either turned away

or covered their faces with their scarves, revealing only their eyes. Purdah
—the tradition of isolating women—though not as strong as in the lowlands, still prevailed.

The government rest house was a new, concrete, one-story building,
built in an effort to increase tourism in Baltistan, the province around
Skardu. There were no trees or bushes on the premises, and mortar was still
splashed on the bathroom tiles. It was spartan but clean and far and away
the best accommodation in Skardu.

Not wasting time, we began to sort through the duffels of personal
equipment that had been issued to each climber, including the four Hunza
high-altitude porters and, by government regulation, Saleem the liaison
officer. Although he wouldn't go above Base Camp, it was required of
expeditions to outfit their L.O. with ice axes, crampons, double boots, and
every other item of gear the climbers received. Each person had quite a
pile: two sleeping bags (a lightweight one for the approach march and a
heavier one for high altitude), pack, goggles, balaclava, several types of
mittens, down booties, parka, down vest, a specially made jumpsuit of
Gore-Tex material, many pairs of socks, special underwear made with
angora rabbit wool, pile coats and pants, down pants, water bottles, headlamp, knife, climbing knickers. Each climber had brought a personal ice
hammer, ice axe, and double boots.

I was bunking in a room with Jim Wickwire, Saleem, and Chris
Chandler, a close friend with whom I had been to Everest in 1976. Once
we had our equipment, Saleem came over to my bed to inspect my gear; he
noticed I had a type of sock that he, apparently, had not been issued. He
picked them up.

"I don't receive this type of sock," he said in stentorian voice, a hint of
British accent in his English.

"Well, I'm sure we can find you a pair somewhere."

"Yes. *You* must go now and find this type of sock for me," he ordered.

I could see we had to get things straightened out right away. Saleem
hadn't yet left the army barracks.

"No, Saleem. *You* must go and find your own socks."

He looked taken aback, but did not appear to be insulted. After a few
seconds, he smiled and said, "O.K. I go and see if Leader has socks."

Before we would have time to finish sorting and initialing our gear with
a marking pencil, we had an appointment: afternoon tea with the district
commissioner of Baltistan. It was important to be on good terms with the
D.C., as he was to help us hire porters, facilitate the transfer of funds
through the local bank to pay porters, arrange for a radio operator who
would monitor our broadcasts from Base Camp and pass on any news to
the outside world, and generally troubleshoot any problems we might
have.

We entered through a gate to a lawn and flower garden courtyard with a
modest-sized one-story whitewashed stucco house. On the lawn were a

couple of dozen chairs arranged in a semicircle, and we all took seats while servants served tea and biscuits and Balti musicians and dancers performed for us. We were a motley crew; I wondered what was the commissioner's real opinion of us, behind his outward politeness. But when he brought out his guest book for us to sign, I learned he was used to hosting mountaineering expeditions and, therefore, perhaps didn't take any offense at our appearance. The book was a compendium of climbing history in the Karakoram for the past twenty-five years. There were names of the early American climbers in the Karakoram: Bates, Houston, Bell, Schoening; the famous Italian alpinists Carlo Mauri and Walter Bonatti as well as the Italian anthropologist-climber Fosco Maraini; perhaps most interesting of all, the great German climber Hermann Buhl, who in 1953 startled the climbing world with his bold solo push from his expedition's high camp to the summit of Nanga Parbat. For twenty-one years Germans had been trying to climb Nanga Parbat, and after four defeats that had claimed thirty-one lives, Buhl was instantly a national hero. It was haunting to read his name, signed in the guest book in 1957. He had been on his way to make the first ascent of Broad Peak, a 26,400-foot neighbor of K2. He and his climbing companion made that climb with so little trouble, they decided to make a first-ascent of nearby Chogolisa. On the descent, Buhl broke through a cornice. His body is still up there somewhere, frozen in the ice.

We walked back to the rest house and spent most of the evening packing our personal gear. With any luck, the next day we would pack the extra food we had purchased into porter loads, sort through all the boxes that had been shipped in advance, and send the loads ahead on the tractors. Jim Wickwire, who was bunking next to me, had all his gear heaped, like the rest of us, in a big pile that he was sorting through, packing everything into duffels, trying to keep handy the items he would need on the approach march.

Perhaps more than any of us, Wick felt confident that not only would someone on our team reach the summit, but in all probability, that someone would include him. After the 1975 failure, it was his commitment to climbing K2 that, more than anything, resulted in the effort to return in 1978. Wick had worked closely with Jim Whittaker to obtain the permit, and it was Wick's opinion that was heard the strongest when it came to deciding who should be invited on the 1978 team. Wick had done the most research on our proposed route; he had written to the Polish team that had attempted the Northeast Ridge in 1976 and had obtained valuable information on the details of the route and the placement of the camps, along with a set of instructive black and white photos of the ridge. He was thirty-eight years old, five foot eight inches, with short-trimmed black hair graying on the edges. He was strongly built, and although in good shape he sensed this expedition could very well be the high-water mark of his climbing career. He was a senior partner in a successful Seattle-based law firm and was married to a striking woman who gave him unfailing support in all his endeavors. They had five children and were a close-knit family. You could almost hear them rooting their support, twelve thousand miles away.

Wick, Chris Chandler, and I sorted through our gear and talked about our proposed route.

"It took the Poles ten days to get across the traverse from Camp Three to Camp Four. They were some pretty tough dudes, too, so I don't imagine we'll make it much easier," Wick said.

"Tough dudes is probably an understatement," I said.

"They had nineteen climbers," Chris added. "Each one was handpicked from the best in Poland, and they've got some hot climbers. There are only fourteen of us."

"It's the headwall below the summit that will be the crux," Wick said. "I think the secret of getting to the top will be putting Camp Six as high as we can get it. That is, if we can find a ledge for a tent—it's pretty steep up there."

We had been through these discussions many times before: How many carries would it take to stock each camp? How high could we carry before we needed oxygen? Where would we place each camp? We were still talking, packing our gear at the same time, when Jim Donini—my friend from the Latok expedition—walked in. With him were the three other climbers from his group. We thought they had just come over to chew the fat; however, they were bringing electrifying news.

"How's it going?" we said.

They nodded, not saying anything. Two of them sat on a bed; Donini stood for a few seconds watching us pack. He had a serious look on his face but I did not, at first, sense anything wrong.

"We just came from the rest house where we're staying," Donini said. He paused, then added, "Bonington's there. So is Doug Scott."

The room suddenly went quiet. We looked up at Donini.

"What the hell is Bonington doing back here..." Wick asked. I glanced at Wick, and for a second our eyes held. I could tell we both had the same thought: Bonington is back in Skardu; something must have gone wrong. Very wrong.

"It was Estcourt," Donini said. "Avalanche just above Camp Three. A big slab broke off. I guess they never found the body."

Wick and I still held each other's eyes. We both looked surprised, serious, eyebrows twisted. It was taking several seconds to sink in, but already I felt nausea rising in my guts.

"Did anybody else get the chop?" Chris asked.

"Just Estcourt," Donini said. "He and Scott were coming out of Camp Two when the slab broke off. I guess they were roped up and Estcourt pulled Scott off but somehow the rope caught on a rock or something and broke. Scott looks shook up—it was another close call for him. Bonington looks pretty bad too. I think he and Estcourt were close. They've been hiking at full speed, five days down from Base Camp, so they could call Estcourt's wife before the news gets out."

"Where is everybody else?"

"They stayed to break camp, and I guess they're on their way down now, moving slower with porters."

The news spread from room to room and, in a minute, the others were coming in to hear the details.

"Oh Christ, that's horrible," Whittaker said. He was a personal friend of Bonington, and he knew he should go over to see him before Chris and Scott left for Rawalpindi on the morning's flight.

"Is Bonington over at the other rest house?" Whittaker asked.

"No, I think he's at the district commissioner's house," Donini said. "Filling in the officials on what happened."

Whittaker left immediately and covered the mile to the district commissioner's house at a fast clip. There was a full moon. The valley and the surrounding hills were beautiful in silver light and dark moonshadows, but Jim had a hard time appreciating it. His thoughts ran first to how hard it was going to be for Bonington. Jim knew that he and Estcourt had been close friends. But there would also be the hassles of returning to England without having even climbed much above Base Camp, and there would be Nick's loved ones to face.

Jim could not help thinking how the West Ridge had been our own first choice of routes, and we had decided to try the Northeast Ridge only because Bonington had picked the West Ridge. That was getting awfully close to home.

He found Bonington and Scott in a living room with the district commissioner and two other officials. Bonington looked terrible. His eyes were bloodshot and he had a sad, wornout look. He was still dirty from the trail, his hair was full of dust, his voice was hoarse and haggard. He and Scott had walked the 110 grueling miles from Base Camp to the roadhead in five days. Whittaker could sense, from Bonington's eyes, the strain of the ordeal.

They greeted each other. Bonington related to Jim how Estcourt had been killed in the slab avalanche. "It was an unbelievably big slab," Bonington said. "Maybe eight feet thick, and when it came off it roared clear across the glacier floor." They talked for some time, and before Jim left, Bonington said, "Good luck on your climb. I have a good feeling you'll make it without incident. Somebody has got to climb K2 in style, and I think it will be your expedition."

Jim bid everyone good night and started toward the rest house. This time he noted the full-moon glory of the Indus valley. His thoughts were on the vicissitudes of living and dying. He thought how lucky had been his own immediate family, in which no one had died. But he had so many friends who had died young. He thought of Bobby Kennedy, and then of Jake Breitenbach, who had died on the '63 Everest expedition. Jake had been killed by an ice avalanche just the second climbing day into the expedition, but the team had decided to keep going, as if they had to climb the mountain for Jake's sake. He thought of Leif and Al and Dusan, who should have been with him on this expedition. But instead of being fearful of the outcome of our own climb, Jim felt that, somehow, we had paid our dues. There had been enough deaths; the gods should be appeased. We should get to the top of K2 and down again safely. He was more than ever committed to that goal, and he hoped the rest of the team felt the same way.

That night Jim and Dianne shared a room with the other married couple on the team—Terry and Cherie Bech. Sometime in the middle of the night, Terry awoke the others in the room talking in his sleep. In a strange voice that sounded like it was coming from another person, he kept saying, "No, no, don't do that. Don't do that. Be careful, you'll cause an accident. Be careful. We'll all be killed."

ON THE MORNING OF JUNE 21, TWO DAYS later, we loaded the fourteen tractors and trailers and sent them on their way. We would leave later that same afternoon, riding in jeeps as far as Shigar, a town somewhat smaller than Skardu, and about four hours' travel in the jeeps. The tractors would drive into the night and arrive at Baha, the place where the road ends and the trail to K2 begins, about noon the next day—more or less the same time we would arrive in the jeeps.

The departure from Skardu was chaotic. Lou Reichardt was still at the bazaar buying last-minute supplies. Whittaker had to see the district commissioner and an official from the bank before leaving, so he and Dianne left the rest house early. John Roskelley, Rob Schaller, Skip Edmonds, Jim Wickwire, Craig Anderson, and I loaded into the back of a jeep and sped off. We drove first toward the center of town and on a corner saw Jim and Dianne talking to the bank official and the commissioner; a few of the other team members were parked nearby. Someone in our jeep had the idea of speeding by instead of stopping, waving as we passed and getting out in front. No more eating dust; we would be the lead jeep. We all had mischievous twinkles in our eyes—it would be a good way to get back at Whittaker for the episode a few days earlier.

From the back of the jeep John leaned over to the driver, yelling, "Shigar! Shigar! Don't stop, go, go, fast!" as I yelled "Rapido! Rapido!"

Jim was standing with the officials and Saleem the L.O., towering above the Pakistanis, on his head a distinctive Gilgit cap. Our jeep roared by and he looked up, not taking much notice, expecting us to stop. But we were waving and laughing. The jeep kept going. Just as we rounded the corner, I glanced behind and saw Jim with an incredulous look, motioning us to stop and come back. It was too late; the driver was possessed with the demon look of a racer entering the straightaway, and none of us really wanted him to slow down. I thought to myself, "I wonder if Jim is going to be upset?" and a second later Jim Wickwire said, "I know one thing for sure. Jim is going to be pretty upset." But none of us suspected the flare-up that was to follow; none of us suspected there were reasons we should have stopped.

The jeep sped through the afternoon, first traveling along the bank of the Indus. The river was swollen in spring thaw, muddy with silt and glacial flour carried from the remote and secret corners of the Himalaya. Behind us, the sun had dropped below the high mountain ridge bordering the valley and cast great shadows across the valley floor. Puffs of clouds added different shadows to the enchanting design. Across the river, a flat region of several hundred acres had trapped drifting dunes, forming crescent patterns like giant scimitars of sand. The road dropped to the river, crossed a large suspension bridge, and switchbacked up a steep, narrow defile, perfect for ambush from roving bands of Pathan warriors crazed with "jihad," the celestial call to Holy War against infidels. Nothing happened, of course. We arrived at the top of the pass, sped over a flat section, and emerged along the bank of the Shigar River. About an hour before dusk we entered the village.

The jeep pulled into a large, grassy courtyard. We had made arrangements to stay in a small rest house across the street. But since we would all have to squeeze into a single small room and the sky was cloudless, it seemed the best idea to sleep outside under the stars. We had time before the other jeeps would arrive, so we grabbed our cameras and explored the town. The one main street made several odd bends around giant sycamore trees, and the two-story houses with balconies overhanging made it too narrow for anything much larger than a jeep to pass. We were walking back to the rest house when the other jeeps arrived. Instead of stopping, they went right past us and, through the windshield, I glimpsed Jim's face, tightjawed, staring ahead. Obviously, he wasn't happy.

Jim got out of his jeep and walked straight to the porch in front of the rest house. I couldn't imagine why he was so upset—we had only sped by him as a joke—but Diana Jagersky supplied the answer.

"He had some sort of ceremony planned with the bank officials and the district commissioner," she said. "We were all supposed to get our picture taken together, and when you guys went by it blew the whole thing. Saleem asked why Jim didn't have more control over his own team—it was a bad scene, and Jim is pretty upset."

Jim came back out of the rest house. I thought it a good idea to confront the problem right away instead of letting it smolder. I walked over to him and said, "Jim, I heard we blew the scene with the bank officials when we sped off. I guess you're a little upset."

"No," he said. "I'm a lot upset."

"Jim, we didn't know you had arranged to have photographs taken with them. It was only a joke."

"We'll talk about it later. I want to talk to everybody together."

That evening we crowded into the small room of the guest house. Jim began the discussion.

"First, I want all of you to know I'm very upset. I had to stand there in front of those people in Skardu today and explain why I didn't have any control over the team. Saleem asked me if I couldn't control my own climbers, how could I expect him to control the porters? We lost face and we lost respect—something we can't afford to lose. If none of you are willing to work together on this thing, we might as well go home now."

Wickwire apologized, saying we weren't aware of any reason to stay behind. Our intentions hadn't been malicious.

"I know," Jim said, "and I suppose in time I'll forget about it, but for now I'm mad and nothing you say can change that. One thing we've got to do on this climb is work together. We can't have individuals running off half-cocked and doing what they want."

"We couldn't agree more," Wick said. "Nothing has changed since that first meeting in Seattle. We agreed to work together—work as hard as we can—and we're all still committed to that."

We had reached that agreement eight months before departure. Though some of the team had not before been on a big expedition to climb a very high-altitude peak, everyone knew that with fourteen climbers and such an extremely difficult peak as K2, we would be lucky if two got to the top. And to get even two up would take total effort from every person. Each would have to stock camps. We all realized that, on big climbs, the glory usually goes to the few who make the summit, while those who work hard to put them there go unnoticed. For that reason, among others, many climbers go with just a few close friends and climb smaller peaks that do not require the load-carrying logistics of extreme altitude. Our four friends on their way to try Latok were such climbers.

But K2 would take more work than other big peaks—even Everest. On Everest, expeditions normally hire small armies of Sherpas to help carry loads to the upper camps, allowing more climbers to reach the summit. But in the Karakoram there are no Sherpas. We had four Hunzas with some climbing ability and a little experience, but by and large, the job of hauling loads would be ours alone.

We all knew that more than a few expeditions have fallen apart before attaining their goal because of quarreling and an inability to work together. That is understandable when one considers the stresses on people in expedition situations: stress from climbing at high altitudes and natural irritability from being without oxygen; stress from constant exposure to danger; stress from confinement in small tents during frequent storms, often for days or weeks, with the same people. The sort of people who go on such expeditions are usually strong-willed, dominant and persuasive, achievement oriented. It is not surprising that with a tent full of such people, sometimes penned together during storms for days on end at twenty thousand feet and higher, tempers often flare.

Finally, it is difficult, no matter how much you understand the necessity, to accept—after working hard for weeks or even months—a decision of who will go to the summit, if that decision does not include you. But we had all pledged to try to overcome this problem—to work as a team. Jim worried that, by taking off in the jeep, some of us had disregarded this need to work cohesively. Most of us felt he had overreacted—that there wasn't cause for him to be as upset as he was—but we were all glad he had got it off his chest. We felt optimistic that night as we drifted off to sleep. A lot of little earthquakes are better than one big one.

The next morning was bright and cloudless. We left Shigar at first light, so we would arrive at the roadhead before noon. There were still porters to hire, loads to issue, and if enough time remained, four miles to walk to Dasso, the first village on the trail to K2. Rob, John, Wick, Craig, and I again piled in the same jeep; our driver again blasted off in the lead. Wick suggested that this time we pull over and let the others pass. As I saw Jim Whittaker drive by, waving and smiling, I thought, We're going to work together as much as we can to get somebody—anybody—to the top of K2.

2

Bridge over the Dumordo

June 23. ONE HUNDRED AND TWENTY-SIX IN the shade. I had made the mistake of leaving camp that morning with only one quart bottle of water, doctored with iodine and Wyler's lemonade mix, and already it was empty. On our first full day's march, we were moving from Dasso to Chakpo, a distance requiring a hike of about six hours. It was distance without shade or village. We had left early—getting up well before five o'clock—and for the first two hours, while the sun was behind the ridge bordering the valley, the hiking was pleasant. When the sun popped over the ridge, we immediately felt the heat from its direct rays.

For some distance, the trail followed a flat alluvial terrace only a hundred feet or so above the Braldu, but soon the swollen river forced us up a steep bank to gain a higher, older terrace left from the river's younger days. It was a hot, sweaty, switchbacking trail, a trail of mindless monotony. I watched drops of sweat twinkle in direct sun as they beaded on my forehead and fell to the burning sand. Above us, far away but tantalizing, we could see snowfields gleaming on high-altitude glaciers.

We reached the upper terrace where it seemed we would have nothing more than a flat walk for two or three miles. We could see a fork in the valley ahead where another drainage joined the Braldu, and we knew that was where the village of Chakpo lay. Another village was below us, on the other side of the river, on another terrace at a lower altitude. A small canal flowing from a diverted lateral stream a mile or so upriver irrigated the

30

village, bright green with early summer wheat. The fields wore patch-work, each square bordered by stone walls to discourage grazing cows and goats. The outermost squares of the village, wheat-green perimeters, con-trasted sharply with the desert gray and brown. Because we had to camp near drinkable water—the Braldu water would not do, since it contained a thick suspension of glacial flour—we planned our marches to end each afternoon in such a village. On the fourth day we would reach Askole, the last village before entering the high mountains.

What we thought would be a flat walk of a couple of miles became more a trial of endurance when we encountered our first nullah— a Hindi word describing a deep cut by a lateral stream in a river's alluvial terrace, a word that could also be used accurately to mean: "to drive crazy" or "to cause torture to." A nullah surprises. You are hiking along perfectly level ground, not expecting any change. The nullah cuts sharply into the terrace, and is not visible until you are perched on the edge. Suddenly, you find yourself facing a steep descent—often hundreds of feet—and then a steep ascent up the other side. The one we encountered that first day of approach turned out to be the deepest; we had to drop well over five hundred feet.

By midafternoon, we were a mile out of Chakpo. We walked through an open expanse of burnt ground, bare except for dwarf desert scrub growing in bunches. In the middle of the expanse was a single thorny-leaved tree, under which all our porters were tightly packed, resting in the only avail-able shade. We passed the tree and the porters waved, laughing and smiling. Two urchins no more than three years old ran up, offering us large, fresh radishes. They were scantily clothed in torn, holed homespun, their skin was dirt brown, their cheeks red and chapped. They smiled shyly; we paid them with a few small brass coins. They handed us the radishes and scurried away. From a safe distance, they stopped to examine their coins.

For the afternoon we had been without water. It was a relief to reach the cool air floating over the first wheatfields, and to soak our feet in irrigation ditches. In another half hour, we reached our campsite: a terraced field gone fallow, cropped short by grazing animals, a lawn per-fect for lazing away the remaining hours of sunlight. The sky was cloud-less. There was no need to set up a tent, since no one would want to sleep in one anyway. The porters had piled their boxes in neat rows in a neigh-boring field, and they would sleep there. Our boxes of cookware and food for the evening's meal had not yet arrived. Porters carrying those loads were still on the trail. Meanwhile, there wasn't much to do.

Two of our Hunza high altitude porters (we referred to them as HAPS) had gone to fetch water in five-gallon plastic jerry cans from a spring on the other side of town. This spring was also a watering hole for animals but, after a thorough search, we realized it was the only local water source not containing glacial flour. Apart from its foul taste, drinking silt-laden water can cause diarrhea and intestinal disorder. The HAPS came back with two full water jugs.

"Where did they find water?" John Roskelley asked. John was an old hand in the Himalaya—he had been on six previous expeditions and he, more than any of us, knew the danger of contracting dysentery on approaches—one of his expeditions, to Jannu in eastern Nepal had been thwarted by dysentery. John had suffered all sorts of ailments contracted in the Asian outback—giardia, ear infections, schagella, worms, spinal meningitis—and he was very sensitive about hygienic precautions.

"In that spring we passed on the way into town," someone answered. "It's the only waterhole around."

"Good Christ!" John said, "I just saw a Balti taking a pee in that place."

Dianne, who was taking a swig from her water bottle, quickly set it down and spit a mouthful on the grass.

Diana Jagersky asked, "What should we do? There's no other water around. I put a heavy dose of iodine in it—should kill anything."

"It will kill most everything," Skip Edmonds said. "And beyond that, there's not much we can do."

So we drank the water, though thinking of the Balti peeing seemed to give it a different flavor. While Diana was busy with dinner, the rest of us wrote in our journals, read books, played Frisbee, or napped on the grass. Terry and Cherie Bech washed their clothes in a nearby irrigation ditch. In Skardu, both had purchased the Pakistani shalwarcamise—the loose-fitting cotton trousers and shirt comfortable in the desert, fully covering the skin from sun, but loose enough to be reasonably cool. Cherie's outfit was wine red with white and yellow embroidery. In that, and the dangling gold earrings she had bought in the bazaar, she looked very handsome.

A young boy from the village came over and offered for sale a half-dozen hardboiled eggs. We bought them; the yokes were bright yellow and fresh. The boy stayed, sitting across from us cross-legged, staring. He had sharp features, medium dark hair, and dark, bright, intelligent eyes. His smile showed even white teeth. We offered him a handful of M&M's. He took a few, set them in his lap, then picked one up and examined it. Very carefully, he peeled off the hard candy coating, again examined the chocolate core, then tasted it. He smiled and looked at us. Laughing, we taught him how to eat M&M's whole. A few days later, Craig Anderson had a similar experience: he gave some young girls a packet of bright-colored lifesavers, then saw the same kids wearing necklaces made of the candy.

The boxes arrived with kitchenware and food, and Diana Jagersky, somehow still showing vitality after the day's enervating hike, tackled the job of preparing dinner. It would be Diana's job each day to arise before the rest of us, prepare breakfast, issue our lunch ration, then pack the cookware and food back in their boxes for the day's carry. Then, in each new camp, she would again unpack the boxes and prepare dinner. Once on the mountain, she would have the same job of preparing meals in the lower camps. It was a duty she always met with élan, even when she had hiked as far, and carried the same loads, as the rest of us.

Diana—born Diana Chiarelli—grew up in Seattle, the daughter of a respected architect emigrated from Italy. Like many Seattle kids, she developed an early interest in skiing. During and after college she worked as a buyer for Recreational Equipment, Inc. There she met two people who were to affect her life: Jim Whittaker, the general manager, and Dusan Jagersky, a climbing guide who worked part time as a ski repairman, and who became her husband.

Dusan had come to the United States from Czechoslovakia. He was five foot six inches, stockily built, with a muscle-rippling upper body, and his life revolved around a passion for mountains and climbing. In Czechoslovakia he had worked as an avalanche patrolman, climbing instructor, and guide in the beautiful Tatra Mountains. The government supplied him with room and board, so he was more or less subsidized to climb. It was a perfect job; perfect until the summer of 1968 when Russian tanks rolled across the border. Dusan, knowing there could be no compromise between the Russian oppression and his free spirit in the mountains, arranged a false passport and escaped. He arrived in New York penniless, but with a conviction that he could start a new life.

He landed a job in Harlem in a sweatshop, working with other immigrants. He saved every possible nickel and resolved to get out of the city as soon as possible. Every morning, he rode the subway from the Bronx downtown; every morning, he stared at a cigarette advertisement in the subway's headliner that featured a photo of a beautiful mountain, snow and glacier covered, surrounded by green forests and bright alpine flowers. Every morning for six months that photo was inspiration.

One of those mornings, Dusan was reading the paper in the subway when he saw another picture of another mountain. The caption said: "Mt. Rainier, State of Washington." Dusan couldn't stand it any longer. He had to get out of New York. He got a map, traced the highway system west, bought an old VW, and started driving. Two weeks later, he had not only climbed Rainier, but had landed a job instructing for the Mount Rainier guide service.

He was back in the mountains, making new friends. One day, he piled into the old VW with several other climbers and headed north with a plan to climb Mount Baker, near the Canadian border. Coming round a bend in the road, Dusan suddenly jammed on the brakes, throwing his friends forward. The car skidded to the side of the road. He got out and for several minutes, while his friends thought he had lost his marbles, he stared at the vista in front of him. There were forests of hemlock and fir, wildflowers, and in the background, a magnificent mountain covered with snow and glaciers. It was Mount Shuksan. Before him was the advertisement, the

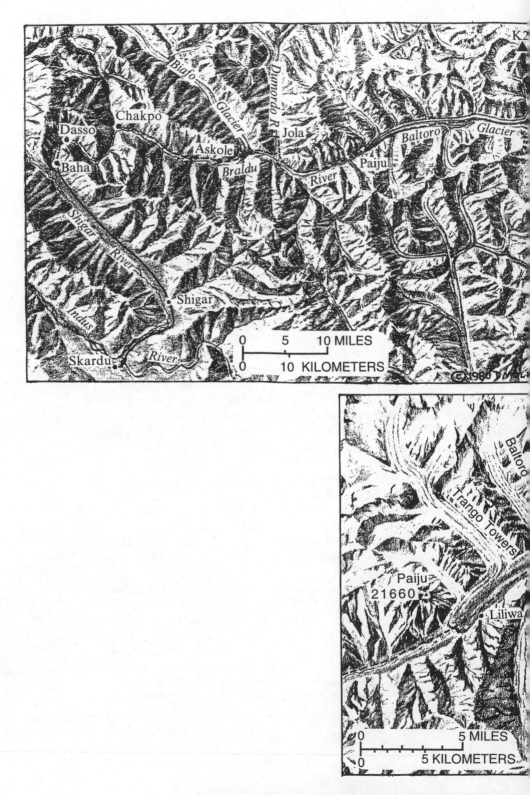

The route to K2, inset at
left, in detail below

panorama that every morning for six months had called to him from the New York subway.

After the guiding season, Dusan got a part time job at REI, where he met a pretty, twenty-five-year-old, dark-haired woman who seemed always to smile and laugh, and they fell in love. The main problem was that she did not know how to climb. After he had given a couple of basic lessons, they were ready for their first ascent. There was only one suitable objective: Mount Shuksan. The romance flowered and they were soon married.

For Dusan, it was the American dream. He met another ambitious young climber who was not unlike his wife, in that he was always laughing and smiling, optimistic and affable. Al Givler was nearly thirty years old and married; he had grown up in Seattle and was known locally as one of the area's better alpinists. Al and Dusan started a service offering individual guided climbs, as well as classes, in the Pacific Northwest, and through hard work and good promotion it became a success.

Apart from their business, both of them had a desire to make new and hard ascents. They had a desire for big mountains. They heard a rumor that Jim Whittaker was gathering a team to go back to K2. There were hundreds of climbers hungry for the few available spots, but Al and Dusan hoped they had a better chance than most. They arranged a meeting with Jim Wickwire and Whittaker, who were recruiting the team. Soon the reply came. They were going to K2.

For Al and Dusan, it was more than just a chance to realize the dream of climbing in the Himalaya; it was a chance at one of the world's greatest mountaineering objectives. No other high-altitude mountain in the world had such allure, such magnitude, such beauty. They were determined to be in top shape, and that meant plenty of climbing. A year before the expedition was to leave, they decided to go to Alaska with Wick to make the first ascent of a beautiful unnamed peak in the Fairweather Range. They traveled up fjords in inflatable rubber boats, pushing leads through the pack ice, then snowshoed up a glacier, man-hauling sledges. Arriving at the base of their peak, they chose a direct route up a prominent, steep, rock and ice buttress that lead straight to the summit. The climbing was superb, the rock in perfect condition. They made rapid progress and, in the afternoon of the second day, they stood on the summit.

There is a picture of Dusan on the summit that Diana keeps in her living room. He has on a white English sports hat—the kind sportscar drivers wear—with ear flaps hanging down, like ears on a springer spaniel. His eyes are sharp and sparkle in the near midnight arctic sun; the orange light has painted his face with a warm glow. He is looking at the horizon. He is pensive, but pleased. A satisfied look. It is the last photo of Dusan. A few minutes later, he and Al began their descent. No one will ever know which of them slipped. But they were roped together, and they fell four thousand feet.

WE ASKED DIANA if we could help prepare supper, but she had it under control. Jim Whittaker was lighting the stove, and Dianne was unpacking boxes and sorting lunch for the next day. Months earlier, when we had had that big meeting in Seattle to work out expedition logistics, the first question was: Who could replace Al and Dusan? After much discussion, the answer finally came: nobody. We would keep the team small. We knew Al and Dusan would be climbing beside us, in spirit if not in body. But we did decide we needed a person to manage Base Camp, organize the food, and cook. Jim said he had long considered Diana for the job. He could not think of anyone who was a harder worker with as cheerful a disposition. But would Diana want to go? Would there be, for her, too many shadows and emotions? We agreed that Jim should, at any rate, invite her. She thought about it for a week or two, then accepted. She needed a diversion, to get away from Seattle. "I've got a lot of time to fill," she said.

Diana had the dinner ready. We each received a portion of freeze dried porkchops and mushroom gravy. I leaned against a rock backrest, lying on my sleeping bag, and watched the last sunrays inch to the tips of the peaks above the valley walls, then disappear. I pulled out the radishes we had bought from the two children and bit into one. It snapped fresh and juicy, and tasted good with dinner. It was the end of the first day on the trail.

ON THE FOURTH DAY WE REACHED ASKOLE, A village of perhaps a hundred houses. This is the last human habitation on the way to K2, still almost eighty miles away. We entered the outskirts of town walking between stone walls lined with poplars and apricot trees. The shade, cooled by irrigation water in the fields, created a feeling of hiking in a park.

Small huts built over irrigation streams housed old granite grindstones, powered by paddle wheels and used for milling wheat. The women were, as usual, shy. Those working in fields turned away if we looked at them. Occasionally, we would spot a female face on a rooftop, but it would disappear as soon as we made eye contact. The men were out to welcome us, however. All greeted us with, "Salaam!" as we walked to a dusty lot enclosed by stone walls. There we made camp.

Instead of leaving in the morning we would stay an extra rest day: our schedule had been set by the Pakistan government in new regulations covering approach marches for climbing expeditions. It gave the porters time to buy the wheat flour they would need for the rest of the march and, for those who lived in Askole, there would be a chance to visit their families. The regulations also required that we pay the first installment of wages to the porters.

By Balti standards, Askole is a medium-sized village, and like all such places with no roads for automobiles, no electricity, no telephones, it has a medieval ambience. The streets are narrow, made for people. Animals grange in courtyards, roosters call from rooftops, and the smell of manure prevails. The people cook over open fires, and like people who cook this way the world over, they smell of smoke. It is easy to imagine their lives have not changed for the last thousand years, but actually this is not true. While the influences of modern times are certainly felt, and the passage each year of dozens of climbing expeditions is accelerating this influence, the more distant past has seen other significant contacts with outside cultures whose imprint is still evident today. Everything about the Baltis—their language, religion, architecture, even their physical features—reflects the waxing and waning of centuries of empires across Central Asia. Here it is possible to find people representing nearly the gamut of human physiotypes: among our porters were men with the Asian epicanthic fold; Mongolian men with thick black hair and swarthy skin, looking yet like Tartar horsemen from the Steppes; Southern European men who could easily have come from a peasant village in Sicily; even men with blond hair and blue eyes.

Originally, the Balti people were dominated by Tibetan culture. The language they speak is derived from ancient Tibetàn; its similarity to that parent tongue is thought by some linguists to be even closer than is today's modern Tibetese. The architecture also reflects this influence: beams and joists are T-barred on upright posts, construction is typically two-story, and overhanging eaves are seen on some buildings.

By the 1500s, the Mongol invasion was sweeping across the Indian subcontinent, and one of its outmost arms touched the remote Braldu valley in the Karakoram. Today, the Baltis kneel several times a day (five times for the most orthodox) and pray toward Mecca: "There is no god but Allah, and Mohammed is his prophet." In Islam the whole world is a mosque, and prayer can take place anywhere. On the approach march it was common to see Baltis, their carpets spread at the side of the trail or the outskirts of camp, bowed in prayer.

Our retainment of each Balti porter took the form of a signed contract designed by the Pakistan government. For our part, we agreed to pay each of them 45 rupees ($4.50) a day, with half pay for rest days and days spent returning from Base Camp to their villages; to pay a stipend for food; to buy insurance covering each porter for up to $1000 in event of death; to guarantee that each load weighed no more than fifty-five pounds, to provide each man with footwear and rainwear; and to provide the group with stoves for cooking dinner and tarps for constructing shelters. Each day's hiking distance, referred to as a "stage," was precalculated, and if we asked the porters to hike more than that distance in one day, we paid them accordingly. In return, this contract obliged each Balti to faithfully deliver his load to the base of K2 as long as we met our half of the agreement, and prevented him (at least in writing) from going on strike.

Most of the details and enforcement of this contract grew out of the failure of the 1975 K2 Expedition. Although the porters on that expedition had also agreed to wages predetermined by the government, there had been no way to prevent the porters, once they were above the last villages and away from civilization, from striking.

To prevent the same thing from happening in 1978, Jim made some recommendations in a report to the Pakistan government. To his pleasure, they agreed with his suggestions; the contract was designed. All porters were hired through the district commissioner's office in Skardu, where efforts could be made to see that the Baltis understood the contract and pressure applied to ensure they would not strike. Furthermore, the Pakistan government decided to assign our expedition an older, experienced liaison officer who would make certain that the Baltis, as well as the Sahibs, honored their respective halves of the contract.

Subadar-Major Mohammed Saleem Khan was better than we had ever hoped. He exuded authority. Each day, he made grandiloquent speeches to the porters, underlining their duty to Pakistan and to God to carry their loads to the base of K2. He made certain loads were weighed so each man would carry fifty-five pounds, and no more. And he made certain we paid each his correct wage. The porters seemed pleased, and we were pleased. But it cost us a king's ransom.

That first day in Askole, we pulled out our money bag and began the laborious job of counting out hundreds of stacks of rupee notes. The money was laid on a plastic tarp and each man was called forward to receive his pay and ink his thumbprint in a ledger. Jim shook each man's hand, thanking him for his good work. Saleem oversaw the payment, and everybody was happy. But the total cost for just the first four days' march tallied a whopping $10,000; despite our advance knowledge of the wage agreement, we had underestimated the expense of delivering our loads to Base Camp. Jim realized he would have to arrange for more money to be sent up from Skardu by mail runner.

The underestimation of porter expenses and the temporary shortage of cash notwithstanding, Jim had done a remarkable job of financing the expedition. It is no easy task raising money for mountaineering ventures, especially in the United States where there are no government funds available as there are in many countries. The bill for a big Himalayan expedition can total a quarter-million dollars, or more. There are expenses for food and equipment, oxygen bottles and regulators, shipping freight, airline tickets, porters, and an infinity of smaller items that rapidly eat up an expedition's budget. For example, we learned in Askole that just to have more money sent up from the Skardu bank, we would have to hire two guards—they were reluctant to travel alone—and pay them full porters' salaries to escort the porter who would actually carry the money, plus three more porters to carry food for the two guards. It was an unforeseen expense that, in the end, came to $450.

Past expeditions have raised money in many ways. Members of the 1975 K2 expedition—which was still in debt $8000 when we left the States on the 1978 trip—had solicited donations from private individuals, made a film (which was never sold), given innumerable slide shows and lectures, and written a book (*In the Throne Room of the Mountain Gods*, by 1975 team member Galen Rowell). For the 1976 American Bicentennial Everest Expedition, which Chris Chandler and I were on, the major source of money was CBS, which bought both the rights to film a documentary TV special, and my book *The Boldest Dream*.

We considered a television film to underwrite our K2 expenses, but there were two problems. First, it was difficult to interest the networks. Most producers had never even heard of the mountain: we called one who thought K2 was a brand of dog food. "What would you want to climb the second highest mountain for?" was a frequent question. "If you're going to all that trouble and spending all that money how come you're not climbing Everest?" The second problem was that making a film would drastically increase the logistical complexity of the expedition. Adding a film crew would mean adding more porters, more food, more supplies up the mountain—more everything. It could conceivably make the difference between reaching or not reaching the summit. We decided that, if at all possible, we would avoid television.

Jim's idea was to finance our expedition by appealing to the general public for support. He persuaded Seattle advertising agency Hinton, Steele and Nelson to design, free of charge, a poster-brochure explaining the background of our proposed attempt on K2 and why reaching the top would be a milestone in American mountaineering, then persuaded Craftsman Press to print it for us free. The brochure asked for a $20 donation—tax deductible—in return for a postcard signed by each team member, carried by runner from Base Camp and postmarked in Skardu, Pakistan. In addition, each contributor's name would be included on a microfilm list that would be buried on the summit of K2. Jim talked three magazines—*Summit*, *Mariah*, and *Wilderness Camping*—into running advertisements, free of charge, to plead for donations. Then he lined up Nike shoes, who ran another ad in several national magazines, asking people to support the expedition. It was a clever ad. There was a large aerial photo of K2, and under it the caption, "Because it's not there." What was not there, of course, was the cash to make our dream a reality.

WHEN WE LEFT the States we were about $30,000 short of our estimated budget of $125,000, and the contributions were still pouring in as we boarded the plane in New York. Jim knew, however, that with the support of so many people, the pressure was on to get to the summit. If he returned this time with an unsuccessful climb, there would be no chance of raising money for another try. It had been hard enough this time. Many had asked, "If you didn't make it in '75, what makes you think you can make it in '78?"

Jim replied that he had learned from his mistakes. With the new Pakistan regulations, there should be no problem with porter strikes. The route we would attempt was, for the most part, a known quantity, having been nearly climbed by a Polish team in 1976. He had been very careful to pick team members who were not only good climbers with considerable high-altitude experience, but also (presumably) mature people who knew how to get along with others on expeditions. He had resolved to include all the climbers equally in decision making, so no one would feel left out. On the '75 trip, two climbers had threatened to quit the expedition because they felt they were mere pawns, being used as porters to ferry loads between camps so the "lead" climbers could try for the summit. To avoid such problems, Jim intended to divide lead climbing equally, and he vowed not to choose the summit team until late in the climb. "The mountain will decide who goes to the summit," he told us. "When the time comes, I think it will be obvious to all of us who is still in the best condition, and who has the most drive to get that summit."

Still, even with the lessons of the '75 failure, Jim knew there was no guarantee of success. It had taken considerable courage to decide to go back in '78. For him, it was a big gamble: there was a lot to win, but perhaps even more to lose. He was almost fifty years old; he felt this would be his last big expedition.

Jim had been climbing since his childhood in Seattle. He was born in 1929 and raised by a family conscious of outdoor activities. At age twelve, he joined the Boy Scouts. Many of the hiking trails in the Cascades lead to the base of bigger mountains; since he and his troop often found themselves at the end of a trail and the beginning of a mountain ridge, they started scrambling up to the heights. The scrambling led to more serious climbing with the Explorer Scouts, and later the Mountaineers. By the time he finished high school, he had climbed all the major peaks in the Cascades; in his first year of college he started and ran a guide service on Rainier.

Working with his twin brother, Lou, he put himself through college guiding clients to the top of Rainier. The two Whittakers gained a lot of experience climbing on ice and snow and traveling on glaciers. After they graduated, both were drafted, but instead of overseas duty in the Korean War, they were sent to Colorado to teach for the Mountain and Cold Weather Command. In the summer, they taught rock climbing and, in the winter, cross-country skiing. It wasn't a bad way to fight a war.

When he was discharged, Jim returned to Seattle, guided one more summer, then was hired as the first full-time employee of a co-op selling mountain climbing and outdoor gear. Recreational Equipment, Inc.,— REI Co-op—was started in 1939 by a group of climbing pals looking for an inexpensive way to import climbing gear (at that time it was all imported from Europe) and their first outlet was the storage room of a gas station. When Jim took over, they expanded to the second floor of a decaying office building, sharing the store space with an accountant who doubled as the store's clerk. That first year, 1955, they grossed $80,000. Jim retired as REI's president and general manager in 1979; that fiscal year, total sales were nearly $50 million, making REI the biggest specialty retailer of backpacking, climbing, and outdoor gear in the world.

The turning point in Jim's life, however, was not REI, but a phone call one day in 1960 from well-known climber and explorer Norman Dyhrenfurth. Jim had recently returned from an ascent of Mount McKinley, and combined with his years on Rainier, had considerable accumulated experience climbing. Dyhrenfurth wanted to know if Jim would be interested in going to Mt. Everest in 1963.

At that time, Everest had been climbed only twice; first by Hillary and Tenzing in 1953, then by the Swiss in 1956. The American expedition was planned as a paramilitary operation on the grandest scale: 19 climbers, 37 Sherpas, and 909 porters to carry 29 tons of gear 180 miles from Kathmandu to the base of Everest. Originally, Dyhrenfurth planned a mountaineering grand slam: to climb not just Everest, but also its two satellite peaks, Nuptse and Lhotse, on the same expedition. Gradually that plan was scuttled and replaced by an even more ambitious goal: to climb two sides of Everest simultaneously. One team would ascend the southeast ridge (South Col) route used by Hillary and by the Swiss, and another would attempt the unclimbed West Ridge; the two parties would meet on the summit and together descend the southeast ridge, thus completing a traverse of the summit. If successful, it would rival the greatest ascents in mountaineering history.

Dyhrenfurth was unwilling, however, to gamble all on one bold plan. Dividing the expedition into two groups would divide the strength of the team. It was decided first to concentrate their unified strength on the goal of getting one team to the top via the southeast ridge. Having accomplished that, they would try the simultaneous ascent, with the assurance that the expedition was already a "success"—something necessary to pay their expedition debt of nearly half a million dollars.

For the first attempt, Dyhrenfurth chose two of his strongest climbers: Sherpa Nawang Gombu and Big Jim Whittaker. They were a Mutt and Jeff team—Gombu five foot four, Big Jim six foot five—but together they reached the summit on May 1, 1963. Three weeks later, the other team completed its objective—a traverse of Everest by the West Ridge. The traverse was an astounding and outstanding achievement, but the man who came away with the most recognition was the one who stood on the summit first. May first was a day that forever changed the life of Jim Whittaker. From then on, his name was affixed with the cognomen, "The First American to Climb Everest."

Jim came home a hero. The National Geographic Society, which had in part sponsored the expedition, awarded to each member its Hubbard Medal; a few weeks after returning from the Himalaya, Big Jim stood in the Rose Garden, next to Nawang Gombu, relating their experiences to an attentive John Kennedy. Five months later Kennedy was shot—an event that was to have an indirect but marked influence on Whittaker's life. The Canadian government decided to name the highest unclimbed mountain in their territory after their neighbor's slain president, and the National Geographic Society contacted Jim to ask if he would be interested in making the first climb of the mountain.

Jim accepted the offer and, in 1965, made preparations for the ascent. He called a few friends, signed them up, and thought he had a complete team. Then came a telegram from Washington, from Senator Bobby Kennedy's office: the senator, and possibly his brother Teddy, wanted to know if they could join the climb.

At first Jim was hesitant. The Kennedys had little experience mountaineering. But he greatly admired the family, and it would be a once-in-a-lifetime chance to climb with them. Teddy Kennedy had to withdraw his application because of a back injury suffered in a small plane crash, but it was agreed that Bobby could come along. Jim picked him up at the airport, outfitted him, and they left for Canada. Kennedy picked up climbing technique rapidly. He was in good shape, and he made the first steps onto the summit. There is a photograph in Jim's living room of the two of them, leaning on each other on the summit, with a hand-scrawled inscription: "I am the one helping him. RFK."

After the climb, Jim had to go back to Washington to write the story for the *Geographic*, and Bobby insisted he stay with the family at Hickory Hill, their home in McLean, Virginia. It was a pleasant two weeks and the beginning of a close friendship. They made plans for future adventures. Each summer, they floated a wild river and, each winter, they skied at Sun Valley. Jim had joined the jet set and found himself sitting in rubber rafts with Andy Williams, George Plimpton, Claudine Longet, skiing with Jackie Kennedy, sailing with Aristotle Onassis. It was on one of the float trips that Jim had a conversation with Bobby Kennedy he will never forget:

"We were floating along having a great time," Jim recalls, "when Bobby suddenly asked me the strangest question. He said, 'Jim, have you ever thought who you would have as pallbearers for your funeral?' "

"No, I haven't," Jim told him. "Why do you ask?"

"Oh, I don't know . . . I was just wondering."

"Why? Have you thought about it?"

"Yes. I would want my best friends."

Not long after, Jim listened to Ethel Kennedy tell him, "You've got to do it. There's no choice. That's the way Bobby wanted it." Jim was a pallbearer at Bobby Kennedy's funeral.

"Even then," Jim now says, "I think Bobby realized he was living on the edge, and it was one of those things he had to think about. So I guess he had told Ethel who he wanted for pallbearers. He was the most incredible man I've ever known. I think what I admired about him most—and maybe what I've tried to pattern myself after—was his ability to always grow, to assess each situation, absorb each experience, and in some way learn something new. He was always pushing himself, always moving forward, always testing. I remember on the climb up Mount Kennedy he was constantly asking me questions about this or that, always quizzing me about what it was like on Everest. And on that climb, he was in fantastic shape. Some of the experienced climbers were holding *him* back. I really grew to love the guy."

After the assassination, Jim's life centered mostly around his three sons and running the outdoor equipment store. He was having trouble at home. In 1972, he was divorced from his wife, and at age forty-three almost had to start over again. But, a year later, he was married to a talented, pretty, twenty-five-year-old Canadian, Dianne Roberts. For Jim, life blossomed again. It was the beginning of the better years. He was again interested in climbing, too, and the following year agreed to lead the 1975 K2 Expedition. After that expedition failed, it was not long before Jim knew he had to go back. He saw Ethel Kennedy a short time after the '75 defeat, and she asked, as if there could be only one answer, "You *are* going back, aren't you?"

Jim also knew that, if the 1978 K2 Expedition were successful, it would be the capstone of a successful career and an interesting, exciting life. If it failed, though, it would be a lackluster finish to his career as a climber; he felt he wouldn't have it in him for another attempt on a major peak, and he knew he would be left with the feeling he should have quit while he was ahead. But there was not really a choice. Jim is a person who likes to quote famous people and, of his repertoire, his favorite is from Goethe: "Whatever you can do, or dream you can, begin it. Boldness has genius, power and magic in it."

HIKING IN CRISP MORNING AIR WAS AN INVIGorating contrast to the usual midday heat. The mile out of Askole was the most pleasant of the approach march. Willows lined the trail that followed irrigation canals gurgling with crystal water from a nearby artesian well. There were sounds of footsteps and low-voiced chitchatting from porters both behind and in front, and the song of finches in the apricot trees. Overhead, a lone vulture—a big one, perhaps the lammergeier—wheeled in widening gyres, carried aloft on a rising air cell heated by morning light now glowing on the upper rim of the valley.

We left the shaded lanes and wheatfields and once again entered the desert. Soon the morning sun changed to noon sun, and we climbed a switchbacking trail up a rocky promontory to avoid a narrow in the river gorge. On top of the promontory, the trail traversed the cliff before again descending to the river bank. In places it was hair-raising. Poles of eucalyptus braced against the cliff, supporting a frame of other poles on which was laid a ramp of heavy flagstones. The exposure was dizzying; below the scaffolding, the cliff dropped away to the whirlpools, sinks, and standing waves in the ice-cold Braldu.

Alpinist Reinhold Messner, generally agreed to be the foremost climber in the world today, has described this approach to the Baltoro Glacier as more dangerous than the climbs at the end of the march. On his approach to Hidden Peak in 1975, he had a close call on a particularly treacherous section of trail between Chakpo and Chango (an area we had traversed four days earlier) when a landslide broke loose above him, sending him perilously close to the edge of the rushing Braldu.

Later in the summer, while we were climbing, we learned that the leader of a British Latok expedition had been swept to his death in this same section when part of the trail sloughed away, throwing him in the freezing water. A few weeks after that incident, an American trekking party on their way to visit our Base Camp suffered a near-fatality on the same section. The trail broke away, throwing a fifty-seven-year-old woman into the water. Shelby Scates, a newspaper correspondent coming in to cover the last part of our climb, jumped down to the river's edge. As the woman swept by, he swung his ice axe and stabbed her pack. Just as the axe began to slip from his grasp, another man in the party scrambled down and helped drag the woman to shore, saving her from icy death.

By midafternoon we had reached the confluence with the Dumordo River, one of the biggest tributaries flowing into the Braldu. Normally, the river is either forded—when the water level is low during spring or fall—or crossed by a suspension bridge two miles upstream. We found the river swollen with early summer thaw, much too high to ford. We could hear, below the roar of the turbid water, the deeper sound of big boulders grinding beneath the torrent sweeping them downriver. The Burmatype suspension bridge, made of vines woven into thick hawsers suspended over a narrow in the river, was gone; sometime in the past year it had broken and been swept away, and the people of Askole, who usually maintain such bridges, had not bothered to replace it.

As I turned up the Dumordo to hike the two miles to Jola, the place where the bridge usually spans the river, I was by myself. It is difficult, on big expeditions, to find solitary time; when it occurs, it is something to enjoy. Wild roses covered the hillside, and their small pink flowers added color to a backdrop of sharp, glacier-covered peaks rising above the canyon walls. I heard rocks falling from the steep hill above me. Looking up, I spotted Jim Wickwire and Jim Whittaker, following a small goat trail they apparently thought was the main hiking trail. I could see that their trail—what there was of it—soon ended in a cliff; I yelled to them they would have to descend. I watched as they carefully downclimbed the cliff—even one slip could mean a long fall. A half hour later, they joined me on the river bottom, a much better place to hike.

"Another mile or so and we'll be to Jola," Jim said. "I hope John has the bridge rigged. If everything is set up, we should get across without losing too much time."

"Waste time or not," Wick added, "I sure as hell prefer to go over on our own rope bridge than cross that woven weed contraption we had to go over in '75."

Soon, we could see the narrow at Jola and, as we had hoped, a rope spanned the river where the bridge used to be; we could see a T-bar seat, hanging from a pulley rigged to pull people and loads across. On the far side, John Roskelley was securing a rope anchor.

We had learned the bridge was out before we started the approach march. While in Askole, we had met the rest of Bonington's team on their way home; they confirmed there was not even a temporary rope crossing. They had hiked up the Dumordo River to cross at the terminus of the Panmah Glacier, where the river originated, and then back down the other bank. The detour had taken two full days. Jim started thinking about rigging a Tyrolean rope traverse to ferry the loads. While we were busy ferrying loads, the porters could move up to the glacier and down the other side. Unladen, they should be able to make it in one long day and, consequently, we would lose only that much hiking time.

While working out the details, Jim learned that John Roskelley had already considered the situation and devised a similar solution. The obvious problem was how to get a rope across to the other side. John suggested that, while the expedition laid over in Askole for the rest day, he would go in advance, equipped with several lengths of rope and carabiner snap links, and simply wait for someone to show up on the other side. He speculated that since there was considerable traffic in the area from other expeditions, it should not be long before someone passed on the opposite shore, detouring up to the glacier. He would hail them, toss a line weighted at the end with a rock, and have it hauled across with the span rope attached. Once the span rope was secured, he could cross the river and rig a proper bridge. Jim agreed to the plan. The evening of the first day we arrived in Askole, John set out for Jola.

JOHN ROSKELLEY WAS twenty-nine years old, wore a neatly trimmed, brindle-colored beard, and at five foot ten inches was a handsome, trim, 145 pounds. He was raised in Spokane, Washington, east of the Cascades, and spoke with a barely perceptible midwestern accent. He loved puns and jokes, liked to laugh. His childhood was full of bird-hunting and trout-fishing with his father, who was outdoors editor for a local newspaper. Spokane is a conservative place; John grew up unaffected by the politics and drugs that changed the lives of so many other people his age. During his college years at Washington State he spent most of his free time hunting, drinking beer with the boys, chasing girls, and to an ever-increasing degree, climbing.

The climbing started when he was fifteen; from the beginning, he sensed that was what he most wanted to do. While in college, he made a trip to California's Yosemite Valley with the dream of climbing the North American Wall of the famous El Capitan. Three thousand feet high, it is absolutely plumb-bob vertical, and at that time, 1971, it was considered the hardest rock climb in the world. Normally, a climber attempting it would have had years of preparatory experience climbing "big walls," but for John it was going to be his first try. Several hundred feet off the ground he watched his partner rip out a series of small pitons and fall eighty feet. Undaunted, John aided his unnerved companion down, hiked back to the climbers' camp, found another partner, and finished the climb. John wanted to be one of the best.

His big break came in 1973. An American expedition to Dhaulagiri—at 26,795 feet the sixth highest mountain in the world—was being formed, and the team would include the best high-altitude climbers in the country. John submitted an application but was turned down because of lack of Himalayan experience. Refusing to be caught by this Catch-22, he continued to lobby for a position; just before the expedition was to leave, he was added on. At twenty-three he was the youngest member of the team, and he became one of the three climbers to reach the summit. (The others were Lou Reichardt and a Sherpa, Nawang Samden.) It was the start of an amazing career in the Himalaya.

John had pushed to his limits on Dhaulagiri, suffering frostbite that cost him the ends of a few toes. But he was not intimidated. In 1974 he joined the American contingent of an international convention of climbers in the Pamir mountains of Russia. Other expeditions followed in rapid succession: 1976-Nanda Devi, India; 1977-Makalu, Nepal; 1977-Trango Towers, Karakoram, Pakistan; 1978-Jannu, Nepal. John had just returned from the Jannu expedition a month before he left for K2. His future schedule would be equally formidable: he would return from K2 to spend the winter climbing frozen waterfalls in Canada; in early March 1979, he would attempt Gauri Shankar, a beautiful unclimbed peak in Nepal; from there, in June 1979, he would head to the Uli Biaho Tower in the Karakoram. And he was already making plans for other peaks after that: Makalu, Masherbrum, Everest. John was realizing his dream. He had the best record of any Himalayan climber in the United States. But it wasn't without cost.

He was married to an attractive schoolteacher from a Mormon family. John, when he was home, did what he could to make money writing and lecturing. But it wasn't paying all the bills, and it wasn't covering the costs of his expeditions—now averaging two a year. Not to mention the fact that he was hardly home. He felt pressure, but he also had to keep climbing: "It's not something I want to go out and do *every* day," he said. "But it sits in the back of my mind, and I *have* to go. I don't think many athletes can tell you why they do what they do. They know they are drawn, but not why." If he stuck it out, he thought, he would eventually make enough on his lecture tours to give his wife a decent living. But it became obvious as the expedition progressed, as I got to know him better, that it was not easy. Every time the mail came, he first arranged his wife's letters in chronological sequence, then before opening them said: "Well, let's see if I'm still married."

John was showing his determination to work hard, and everyone had the feeling he was a likely candidate for the summit. The first day of the approach march, when after dinner everyone relaxed after the hard day's work hiring porters, and the hard day's hike, John had stayed up several hours documenting the names and villages of each porter we had hired—paperwork required by the government. When we learned the bridge at Jola was down, he was the first to volunteer to go ahead and jury-rig a new one.

JOHN HAD HAD HELP in building the bridge from Sadiq Ali, one of our sirdars, or porter chiefs; now we would have a chance to inspect their handiwork. I saw John on the other side of the river. He yelled for me to cross. Sadiq lashed me to an upside-down T-bar, with my legs over the crosspiece, and with a retrieval line, John hauled me to the other bank.

"I think we can get all the loads across tonight if we work late," he said, optimistically.

"Good job on the bridge," I replied. "Kind of fun swinging over that torrent."

Our voices were raised above the roar of the river. The others arrived and were ferried across, then as the first porters appeared, we began the lengthy task of clipping each of the more than 300 fifty-five pound boxes to a pulley and man-hauling them across.

Meanwhile, the porters were instructed to set out up the valley to the river's origin—the snout of the glacier—cross it, and return by the far bank. They left in a big, cheering crowd, apparently not minding the extra day's hike. That they were getting paid full salary for the extra day, without having to carry a full load, no doubt added to the merrymaking. As the porters disappeared up the river valley, we continued ferrying loads. In spite of the hundred-degree heat, it was fun working together, pulling on the rope in time to a heave-ho, heave-ho. We had managed about a quarter of the loads, in two hours' work, when someone looked up and said, "I hate to say it, but I think our work is just starting."

Upriver, we could see all 350 porters coming back, along the same bank they had left that morning. They had encountered a lateral tributary swollen in the thaw and had been unable to get across it. Now the only choice was to haul each of them, one at a time, over on the T-bar.

There is a story in the Koran that says all men who die must cross a tenuous bridge before they may enter heaven. Those who fail the test fall off the bridge and plunge into the abyss of hell, condemned forever. Many of our porters were deep in prayer as we tied them to the T-bar and launched them, bobbing madly on the stretchy nylon rope, across the roaring water. A few panicked and grabbed the stationary span rope; we had to yank hard to break loose their hands. At least one porter started jerking and flipped upside down. But the safety belt held him to the T-bar.

We worked late into the night.

The next morning, after just a few hours' sleep and before first light, John Roskelley and Sadiq Ali were back at work. Through the second day we hauled men and gear; by that night the job was finished. All the porters were on the far shore, huddled around small fires, cooking chapatties and brewing salt tea. The rest of us scattered, spread our bags on the sand, and spent another night under the bright canopy of Karakoram stars. The next day we would trek to Paiju camp, beneath the shadows of the first "big" peaks, and within eyesight of the snout of the Baltoro Glacier.

IT WAS A STAGE AND A HALF FROM JOLA TO Paiju, and by noon we still had some five miles to go. We hiked across the broad alluvium of boulders and rocks, cut by nullahs, with granite peaks and glaciers above the valley walls. Though we were entering the region of high mountains and hiking at about ten thousand feet, it was still desert. Sage, wild rose, and a scant, stubby grass clung to the dry hillsides. We stopped occasionally to scan the bordering hills for signs of Siberian ibex or shapu (a mountain sheep), both said to frequent the area, but we saw only the remains of one of these big sheep, next to the trail. Perhaps it was the kill of a snow leopard, also said to occur here, but so elusive and rare a species that only a handful of Westerners have had the privilege of seeing this blue-eyed big cat.

The sky was still clear overhead but clouds were forming down the valley. In the other direction, toward the head of the Baltoro Glacier, there were lenticular clouds, looking like alien flying saucers. That morning we had noticed the air darkening with a high, windblown dust, yellowish and ominous, apparently carried aloft from the endless deserts of China's Sinkiang. Up high, there was strong wind, but at the valley floor the air was still and warm.

We crested the border of a nullah and walked a ridge that afforded a view of the valley both forward and behind. Now a few clouds gathered above. The first wisp of wind from the high mountains cooled our skin. We stopped to admire the view, and someone pointed to the head of the valley, many miles beyond. In the distance, we could see a large peak with a lenticular cloud suspended above and to leeward. A white plume trailed from its summit. The mountain looked different from the others; it had the unmistakable look of one of the earth's great ones, the look of an eight-thousand-meter peak. We checked our map and determined it to be Broad Peak, 26,400 feet. Five of us were gathered: Diana Jagersky, Skip Edmonds, Jim Wickwire, Chris Chandler, and me. Together we stared at the giant. There is magic in the first glimpse of a major mountain, a feeling of awe before the most powerful architecture on the earth's surface.

The wind from a darkening squall brought drops of rain, raising from the desert floor the musky aroma of sage. We hiked on, but not for half an hour before we were again brought to stop. Now we had another view up the valley, and we could see another mountain next to Broad Peak. It did not seem possible, but this great pyramid dwarfed its neighbor. We were fifty miles away: even that distance did not diminish its grandeur. It stood alone, lording over its domain, rising singular to an altitude that seemed mythical. It was our first glimpse of the mountain for which we had traveled so far: K2.

We unshouldered packs, sat on stones, and stared. There was an air of reverence. The only words were a few whispered comments:

"I can't believe anything could be so big."

"Look at that high cirrus cloud girdling the peak at about eight thousand meters—and the summit rises well above it."

"It's so impressive standing alone. It isn't surrounded by satellite peaks like Everest."

The feeling common to all was humility mixed with, perhaps, not a little apprehension.

We opened our lunch sacks and snacked on kippers and crackers and cheese spread. My thoughts drifted to an evening three days before, in Askole. We had camped with part of Bonington's team, on their way home. To climbers, their names had household familiarity: Tut Braithwaite, Pete Boardman, Joe Tasker. Together, they were the most peripatetic climbing group in the world, with a long list of major accomplishments: Annapurna, Changabang, the Ogre, and Everest. The first ascent of the huge southwest face of Everest, in 1975, had been their foremost achievement. Tut Braithwaite and Nick Estcourt had led the difficult rock band, the key to the summit that had thwarted all previous attempts; Doug Scott and Dougal Haston had first reached the summit, followed by Pete Boardman. Pete was only twenty-three at the time, the youngest member of Bonington's team.

It was one of Boardman's comments that I remembered now. We had been around the campfire drinking coffee, smoking hash, and swapping stories. Conversation had wandered from Patagonia to the Orinoco Jungle to New Guinea, but eventually we had landed on the subject that was most on our minds: K2. (The British are known for laconic understatement, and British climbers practice this to a fine art. The most horrendous climb in the Alps or in the Himalaya—when the story comes out—is nothing more than "a bit of a nasty climb, but a fine outing." The most hair-raising scene imaginable—a climber out a hundred feet on a lead rope, unable to find protection with his pitons, legs starting to shake and knuckles white—is dismissed with: "Oh, yes, it was a bit gripping that, but I was doing fine until I dropped me matches and couldn't light me fag. Then it got a bit nasty.")

We had listened to Bonington's group describe K2; for those of us who had not been on the 1975 team, it was our first close-hand knowledge of what we were getting into. Boardman said, "I think we were all a bit surprised. Didn't quite expect it, you know, to be such a bloody big climb. I think we probably underestimated it a little, there just weren't enough of us, and we realized right off there was no way we could get up it. Too much hard climbing too high. Tut was laid up with some nastiness in his lungs, then with the avalanche we had to pack it in. That's quite a hill; I don't think any of us have ever seen anything quite like it. It's a phenomenal hill...."

Looking up at K2, so enormous even from fifty miles away, and thinking of Boardman's description, "a phenomenal hill," combined to give that feeling of humility: there was no room for conceit before a mountain such as K2. It was also the meeting with Bonington's group that, more than anything, gave us the feeling of apprehension: Before learning of Estcourt's death we had all commented that K2, for a big mountain, should be a relatively safe climb. Unlike Everest there would be no icefall —a dangerous section of glacier where the ice moves over steep underlying bedrock, causing blocks to break and shift and sometimes squash climbers —and since we would most of the time be on a ridge, there should not be any danger of avalanches falling from above. But it was not an avalanche from above that killed Estcourt, it was a slab from a snowfield that broke under his feet. Now, there was no way we could rationalize away the dangers of K2.

I squeezed the last of a tube of cheese spread on a cracker. The cirrus around K2 were lowering and the mountain was almost gone, enveloped in the clouds. I wondered what our chances were of reaching the summit. I remembered how hard it had been three years before, on Everest, to climb at twenty-six thousand feet, even with oxygen. There, we had had help from Sherpas to carry the oxygen and other equipment to the upper camps. The climbing was less steep, too, with no real technical sections on the upper reaches. On K2, there would be hard ground the whole distance.

The mountain disappeared from view. "That was quite a sight," Jim

Wickwire said. "That mountain is just as impressive as the first time I saw it in '75. It's going to be interesting to see how we do."

I shouldered my pack and started hiking. I thought about the Poles, who had attempted the ridge we were going to try back in 1976. Nineteen extremely strong, tough climbers had turned back. I would not admit it to the others, but I could not imagine how we could expect to do much better. It just seemed too high and too steep. And without Sherpas.... I put the thoughts out of mind. I recalled a pithy statement attributed to the famous woman climber, Beverly Johnson: "Climbing mountains is like eating an elephant. You have do it one bite at a time." We would just have to keep taking bites and see how far we could get. Ahead, about two miles away, I could see a grove of trees and grass. It was Paiju camp, the destination of that day's march.

3

The Book of Marvels

ONE OF THE WORLD'S GREATEST BOOKS IS AN illustrated work not found on any list of classics, and it is never included in any college lit course. But it has inspired several generations of young boys and girls with a feeling of magic and mystery, a vision of secret places in the far corners of the earth where it might still be possible, in a distant oriental bazaar, or a secluded caravansery, to purchase an old, greening lamp that, if rubbed in just the right way, combined with just the right incantation, will produce a genie. Today, when I thumb through Richard Halliburton's *Book of Marvels*, I am struck with those same childhood lusts for travel, those same visions of Petra and Samarkand and Baalbek, of genies and flying carpets and the stone eyes of the sphinx staring across the deserts of time.

The trek into the inner sanctum of the Karakoram, into the icy upper reaches of the Baltoro, was a trek into the pages of the *Book of Marvels*. The Baltoro Glacier began two miles above Paiju camp, a tongue of ice hundreds of feet thick, sticking out into the valley floor. On the tip of the tongue was a large hole, also hundreds of feet across, and from this hole sprang full-born the Braldu River. It was a mammoth spout of water gushing from the guts of the glacier, meltwater beginning its journey down the Braldu to the Shigar to the Indus to the Arabian Sea. On top of the glacier, the ice was covered with a layer of gray and black and brown rocks fallen from centuries of landslides off the bordering slopes—glacial moraine—and there were few places of exposed ice. Had we had an aerial view of the glacier (as we would in the weeks ahead from the upper flanks of K2) we would have seen the rocks arranged in stripes that ran parallel lanes down the glacier, like dividers on a giant ice highway; the stripes of lateral glaciers would merge with the stripes of the bigger Baltoro Glacier, and each stripe would be a geological fingerprint of the origin of each glacier. Together, they would suggest slow, inexorable movement.

The trail through the moraine was at times thin and indistinct, and if we did not watch closely for slight footprints on occasional mats of soil, it was easy to lose the way. Often we hopped from boulder to boulder, then up steep, rock-covered ice flanks and down the other side. There were crevasses, but on this lower end of the long glacier they were infrequent, and the ones we did see were never covered or hidden; there was little danger of falling in one and no need to wear ropes. If I found myself alone, I would stop to listen. The only sound would be occasional rocks falling down ice banks and ridges, and now and again a pop or groan from pressure building and releasing deep in the glacier.

The magnificence of the peaks on all points of the Baltoro Glacier evokes storybook fantasies. Paiju Peak, 21,654 feet, rises in columns of joined spires connected by gulleys and ramps, and each feature is fringed in snow. The next group of peaks—the Trango Towers—dominates the area above the snout of the Baltoro. The Trangos are distinct from other peaks: granite towers boldly lined with massive joints, vertical walls of rock, 4000 feet high. One of these peaks, appropriately called Nameless Tower, is a pipedream image of the perfect mountain spire—a shaft of granite, vertical on all sides, rising in an unbroken twenty-five-hundred-foot column to an altitude of twenty thousand feet. It has been climbed but once and no doubt will be the focus of many more attempts in the future.

Even on the glacier we still hiked in heat, and most continued to wear short pants and loose cotton shirts. Skip Edmonds had brought a laundry bushel of pressed blue surgeons' shirts stamped "University of Washington Hospital"; most found them comfortable in the heat, but they gave us the look of interns on a hiking trip. On the second day on the glacier, we crossed an area of hard, blue ice for some reason not covered by rocks, and the chilled air radiated up and cooled our legs. We found a freshet of meltwater running in an ice channel; this sweet water was the first we considered safe to drink without adding bitter iodine purification tablets. Since the iodine went into even cooking water, its taste permeated everything, and it was great pleasure to be rid of it.

That afternoon we would reach Urdukas—a Balti word meaning "split rock," after a huge broken boulder overlooking the campsite. I was hiking that afternoon with Jim Whittaker and Dianne Roberts. Jim still wore his Gilgit cap and yachting pants. Like most of us, he hiked with an aluminum ski pole (donated by K2 Skis) that functioned as a hiking stick. He carried a bright red Kelty pack, usually loaded with most of his personal gear. Although he could have given all his gear to porters, Jim, like most of us, wanted to carry a few pounds every day to keep his legs honed. Dianne hoped to stay light so she could dart off the trail after good photos, but her assortment of cameras and lenses filled her pack.

Dianne was thirty years old, round-faced and rosy-cheeked. She had smartly trimmed short brown hair and hiked each day in khaki shorts and a print blouse covered with a bird-hunter's vest—the type with small pockets for shotgun shells. She carried film in the shell pockets, though, and the vest's larger pouches were perfect for lenses. Dianne was a photo-journalist, and one of her dreams was to come back with coffee-table-book-quality photos of our expedition and the Karakoram.

Jim mentioned an incident that morning with one of our five porter group leaders who had had the audacity to ask Dianne for one of her two ski poles. To Jim, it seemed like bad form, especially since the porter already had one ski pole.

"And there I was," he said, "with only one ski pole myself—I'd given the other away to another porter—*and* I have a much heavier load than this guy's carrying. Just because he is a boss among the porters, he thinks he doesn't have to carry anything. I really got ticked off, and I gave him the business. He can't understand English, but he got my point.

"I can't believe these people, I guess it's because they're so poor, but they constantly expect you to give them things. There's no end to it. And if you don't comply they go on strike. I know we've been lucky on that so far —Saleem has been a big help. He's done a good job of keeping them honest, and I know in those speeches he makes to them every day, he tells them if they're not honest, if they don't live up to their part of the agree-ment and get our loads to Base Camp, they'll pay for it in the next life. Saleem says they're basically children—no sophistication at all—and you've got to treat them like children."

"I don't think that's exactly fair, Jim," Dianne said. "Sure, they're not educated, and maybe not sophisticated, but you can't blame them for wanting to get all they can out of us. They're so miserably poor, and they see us come here surrounded by unbelievable wealth.... They're just people, and how can you blame them? Besides, we haven't really had any problems at all—nothing like '75."

"Knock on wood," Jim said. "We've still got several days to Base Camp. If there are no strikes."

"Oh, I don't think there is anything to worry about, Jim," Dianne said. "If the porters were going to strike, they would have done it by now."

Jim, necessarily, had to look at the Baltis from the point of view of an employer who had hired them to complete a job; because of the enormous difficulties encountered on the '75 expedition, it was understandable that at times he would be skeptical of their performance. Dianne, on the other hand, looked at the Baltis with a photographer's eye. She saw them as visually fascinating and viewed the display of their culture as might an anthropologist. Where Jim saw possible strikes, wage negotiations, and delays, Dianne saw two-page spreads in *National Geographic*.

Not to say that Jim was, in any way, a pessimist. He was not necessarily an optimist, either, but more a realist. While he knew there was a good chance we would have a porter strike, he never lost any sleep worrying about it. If it happened, he would deal with it then. He accepted things as they came, and when things went well, that was fine; if they were not so well, he would do what he could to make them right. "Jim just kind of loves life in its entirety," Dianne once said. "The good, the bad, and the ugly. I guess I'm more of an optimist—I just prefer to see the good."

Whatever characteristics were different in the personalities of Jim and Dianne, they were certainly less than the similarities, and as a couple, Jim and Dianne radiated the impression of two people with gears meshing well.

Jim, Dianne, and I caught up with Jim Wickwire, who had stopped to snack on his lunch rations. He was sitting on a peculiar flat stone, supported on a column of ice maybe three feet high and as thick, with the rock mushrooming over all sides. The sun had melted the glacial snow around the rock, leaving it balanced and looking like a Toadstool from Wonderland.

The four of us had a pleasant stop, munching, watching the porters hike by, and gazing across the valley at the incomparable granite spires rising everywhere. Jim and Wick got up and resumed hiking, and Dianne and I walked on by ourselves. It was a good chance for me to chat with her and learn more about her background, how she became a photographer and how she met Jim. All I really knew was that she had been born and raised in Calgary, Canada, and had been married to Jim about six years.

"After college I left home, worked in Toronto awhile in research psychology, saved all my money, got interested in photography, vagabonded to Europe. I couldn't yet support myself with photography, so I got a job with the Canadian National Park Service. That's when I met Jim. He was on a fact-finding tour—he is on a board that advises the Secretary of the Interior on policy for national parks—and they were visiting some of the western Canadian parks. I was in charge of showing them around. I kind of expected a group of eighty-year-old fuddy-duddies, but boy, was I surprised. It was a great electric love-at-first-sight romance. He went back to the States and I started getting these huge, funeral bouquets of flowers sent to my office. Then we started meeting in various halfway spots like Vancouver, until the travel tickets and phone bills got too high so we got married.

"I had no idea, at the time, that a few years later, I would be on two major expeditions to try and climb the second highest mountain in the world. I had grown up in Calgary, I had hiked in the Rockies all my life, and done a little skiing, but I didn't know anything about technical climbing."

"Didn't you have any premonitions this kind of thing might happen," I asked, "when you married Jim?"

"No, I think if I thought about the Himalaya at all, it was maybe as a neat place to go hiking. But I did have a premonition about one thing—it wasn't just a premonition, more a certain knowledge—that whatever happened, life with Jim would never be boring."

I did know that Dianne had had some problem keeping her own last name after she was married.

"It was U.S. Immigration. I told them I wanted to keep my own last name, but they kept sending resident alien 'green cards' made out to Dianne Whittaker. Finally, I ranted and raved enough that their lawyers decided if it did go to court, they would lose. So one day I received an envelope in the mail and inside, with no accompanying note or letter, was a green card made out to 'Dianne Roberts.' "

From reading accounts of the '75 K2 expedition, I also knew Dianne had had some trouble being the only woman on that trip. She had wanted to be considered one of the team, and she had worked as hard as anyone during the preparation. Her problems were not only the result of being a woman in what is mostly a man's sport, however. She also was a novice climber, and many of the members of that expedition resented her presence because they knew the only reason she was there was that she was Jim's wife.

"I think if we could have communicated better, things wouldn't have fallen apart as they did," she said. "Things got passed around among the climbers, but no one came directly to me. I just hope none of that happens this time."

Dianne still had not had much climbing experience by the time of the '78 expedition, but she nevertheless hoped to climb high on K2. As on the '75 trip, she had again shouldered much of the work during the preparation, and she felt she had earned her place. She saw her role of photographer as a serious one, and she had commitments to Nikon to produce the best set of expedition photographs possible. In order to get good photographs, she had to be where the action was, and that meant climbing. Still, a number of the team were not so sure she should go high on the mountain, and even as late as the final stage of the approach march, it was not clear what would be Dianne's exact role.

"I just hope that if people have any feelings about what I'm doing one way or the other, they speak up in front of me so we can clear them up."

We caught a glimpse of Jim and Wick ahead, and Dianne sped up to catch them. I continued to walk alone up the glacier. I could hear the sounds of my steps, and of rocks falling here and there off the debris-covered ice as the glacier imperceptibly quivered and moved another fraction of an inch, down toward the desert.

URDUKAS IS A GRASSY HILLSIDE OASIS, greened by several small springs percolating through the gravelly soil. Small bushes grow around the springwater, and rosy finches hop in the branches and sing songs. The grass is colored by small purple flowers and some yellow ones that look like buttercups; white butterflies—the kind common in summer fields back home—visit the flowers. Below this oasis, the gray Baltoro Glacier fills the valley floor like a turbulent sea, frozen in geological time. Across the glacier, behind the opposite hillside, are two groups of twenty-thousand-foot granite peaks, the Baltoro Cathedrals and Lobsang Towers, that rise like a painted backdrop for a theatrical stage. One of these spires is a perfect triangle, with a rock face as smooth as sheet metal. Down the valley is Paiju, and across, the Trango Towers. Urdukas, the oasis, is the last place—as one continues up the Baltoro—of green, living things; realizing this, it was important for us to savor the time spent there. It would be months before we returned.

The grass slopes were peppered with large, protruding granite boulders, and under leaning walls and in small caves and holes some of the porters prepared shelters while others ranged the slopes, hunting for scarce firewood. With more and more expeditions each year visiting this place, firewood was difficult to find. Although we provided dozens of kerosene-burning stoves, they would be used primarily for brewing tea in the upper zones of no wood. Now, the porters needed fires to cook hundreds of chapatties to be eaten during the remaining four days' march to Base Camp. It was for this time to cook that they required a rest day at Urdukas, and none of us objected. It would be hard to imagine a more dramatic rest station.

While the scenery was incomparable, there were two drawbacks: flies and fierce heat. To protect against both, we erected two big tents of the sort used for car camping. We spent the hottest part of the afternoon inside with the covers over the large mosquito-netted windows furled and trussed to allow entry of the slightest breeze that might cool the inside, and also to expose the view across the valley. As the sun lowered to the valley's rim, horizontal lines of clouds were drawn like venetian blinds over Paiju Peak, and the eerie light cast heraldic rays across the walls of the Trango Towers.

When the air cooled and the flies went to rest, we ventured out; while Diana Jagersky prepared dinner, Chris Chandler and Cherie Bech held clinic for the porters. Each evening, the doctors (Rob Schaller most often took this responsibility) held a clinic and, each evening, long lines of porters queued up to seek treatment. Probably the majority of the complaints were legitimate—bronchial ailments, some tuberculosis, worms, trachoma and conjunctivitis, giardia and schagella—but a percentage of them were trivial, and Rob had a jar of Good and Plenty placebos, in addition to the ubiquitous aspirin, which he handed out. Cherie Bech had another technique for the dozens of porters who complained of minor blisters: when a porter would point to a sore spot on his foot, Cherie would take off her own shoe and point at a raw spot the size of a half dollar. Usually, the porter would stare at her wound, perplexed, and walk away.

The doctors realized that for most of the many porters who had legitimate complaints, there was little they could do. Unless the porters had worms, which could be treated with a single administration of medicine, it was impossible to follow up a multi-day medication program. The doctors knew what would happen if a porter were given a vial of pills and told to take-one-four-times-a-day-for-a-week: besides the danger of his taking them all at once, the pills were often sold or traded. After each clinic, there was brisk barter in aspirin and Good and Plenty. The Good and Plentys had more value than aspirins because they were not only bigger, but more brightly colored.

The next day the main task, before the heat of the day drove us to the tents or under recesses behind the large boulders, was to dismiss fifty porters who had eaten themselves out of a job. Each day the main body of porters consumed many loads of food—mostly ground wheat flour called "atta"—and each day we sent that number of porters back home. Now the porters were cooking up most of the remaining flour in preparation for the remaining miles to Base Camp. Our army of load carriers dwindled each day.

Jim Whittaker and Jim Wickwire spent most of the morning in the tent counting rupees. Then the money was stacked in separate piles, each man was paid, and with a handshake and thank you, he was sent on his way. There was still the problem of how the porters would cross the swollen Dumordo River. After calculating how long it would take, and consequently how much it would cost, to send the porters up to the head of the valley to detour down the far side, we decided it would be cheaper to send a team of porters to rerig the rope crossing, then pay two of them to guard the bridge (or certainly someone would steal the ropes) for the duration of the expedition, so our mail runners could make regular trips between Base Camp and Skardu.

With the fifty porters paid there was little to do but find shade and spend the day reading, writing, or chatting. Terry and Cherie Bech had rigged a shade awning by snapping together two rain ponchos, supporting them on ski poles. The two Bechs, Bill Sumner, Chris Chandler and I lounged on the grass, spending several hours swapping stories and getting to know one another better. It was the first chance I had had to spend any time talking to the Bechs.

Cherie Bech was thirty-three years old, of medium height and lean build, and wore her straight, light brown hair shoulder-length. Her face was sharp-featured, skin drawn tight over high cheekbones, mouth wide and capable of changing quickly from an open sensual smile to a pursed-lipped seriousness. From her ears dangled ornate gold earrings she had purchased in the Skardu bazaar. She often used strong, unabashed language, and she thought of herself as a decisive, strong woman. Ambitious, a good climber, and a good nurse, she was the mother of two children, one of whom was named Annapurna—her namesake not only the famous mountain in Nepal, but also the Nepalese midwife who had delivered her. Mountains were a big part of Cherie's life, and she very much wanted to be the first woman to climb K2.

Cherie was born in Australia at the end of World War II, went to nursing school in Sydney, and at age twenty-one started climbing in Australia's Blue Mountains. Soon she graduated to the New Zealand Alps; after a two-year apprenticeship, she started thinking about the Himalaya, packed her rucksack, and vagabonded to Kathmandu. That was where she met Terry Bech, and after a three-week romance, they were married.

At that time, 1971, Terry had already been in Nepal for six years, working first as a Peace Corps volunteer then, supported by a Ford Foundation grant, undertaking a survey of the music of the various ethnic groups of Nepal. He was considered one of the world's authorities on Nepalese ethnomusicology. Terry was an unusual-looking man. He was thirty-nine years old, had a broad, balding forehead, dark, wispy hair, black eyebrows, and dark, intense eyes. His high forehead gave him a cerebral look, and with his habit of staring at you, eyes wide when he talked to you, he had an aura of a scientist deep in intellectual thought or, perhaps, a slightly wild musician with symphonies no one else could hear playing in his head. Terry was, in fact, a professional violist and made his living playing in orchestras.

Terry grew up in Spokane, Washington, and was introduced to mountaineering in the Cascades. He had been on several treks over high passes, had climbed some smaller peaks during his years in Nepal, and had attempted Dhaulagiri in 1969. He was invited on another attempt of Dhaulagiri—the same expedition that John Roskelley, Lou Reichardt, and Craig Anderson were on—in the spring of 1973. Since Terry was in Nepal, the expedition asked him to reconnoiter the mountain, so in 1972 he and Cherie set out with six hundred pounds of gear and a few Sherpas to climb as high as they could on the flanks of Dhaulagiri. I had heard parts of the story of this "reconnaissance" from other climbers, but sitting under the awning in Urdukas, I was anxious to hear the details firsthand. They both related the story:

"We only had a trekking permit to make a reconnaissance of the peak," Cherie began. "But right off we decided we would go as high as we could, and see—who knows?—if we could get to the top. But then the porters quit on us, leaving us stranded at about eleven thousand feet with six hundred pounds of supplies. So we began the long process of hauling everything to Base Camp. We were carrying huge loads, and it took almost three weeks just to get everything ferried to Base Camp."

"Then the work really began," Terry continued. "We not only had to scout the route to each new camp, but we had to haul all the supplies too—all with just the two of us. We carried huge loads—some up to a hundred pounds—but we kept at it. Finally, after about seven weeks, we had a tent at the high camp, and a few supplies in it, and we thought we just might have a chance of making the summit. But before we could try, a fierce storm hit us, and without enough supplies up high to wait it out, we had to abandon the climb."

"But we did reach a high point of over twenty-four thousand feet," Cherie added. "Which isn't bad for just the two of us with no Sherpa support."

"And what was really incredible," Terry said, glancing at Cherie with a look that suggested both pride and respect, "was that Cherie had been carrying a double load the whole time. She was five and a half months pregnant."

Despite Cherie's accomplishment on Dhaulagiri, it was not enough to gain her a position on the bigger American expedition the following year, so she bid Terry good luck as he left Kathmandu for the long approach trek and the Kali Gandaki Valley between Annapurna and Dhaulagiri. The expedition was a success—three climbers reached the summit, including one Sherpa—but Terry was not among them. A sharp ear infection forced him down from the high camp, although he worked hard to assist the two members who did reach the summit. Because there have been relatively few American expeditions to the big Himalayan peaks, and because the fraternity of high-altitude climbers in this country is small, it was no surprise that those two summit climbers, Lou Reichardt and John Roskelley, were also on our K2 team.

Cherie and Terry had lived in Nepal for three more years before moving to Bloomington, Indiana, so Terry could complete his Ph.D. in the University of Indiana's Department of Tibetan Studies. It was hard for two people in love with mountains to stick it out in the corn belt. When they heard Jim Whittaker was forming a team to try K2, they drafted resumes and sent in their applications.

Jim was looking not only for climbers with high-altitude experience, but, being interested in providing women a chance to break into the men's world of mountain climbing, he wanted to have at least one woman as a full climbing member of the team. Dianne had been the only female on the '75 trip, and he knew how lonely she had been for another woman to talk to. So, with Dianne's encouragement, the Bechs were invited to join up. For the Bechs, it was to be a drastic, but welcome, contrast—from the horizontal world of Indiana to the vertical world of the Karakoram.

IN THE MIDAFTERNOON, four British climbers, on their way home from an unsuccessful attempt on the fabulously beautiful Gasherbrum IV, shambled into camp. They were a strong team of well-known alpinists, but they had chosen an extremely difficult route that proved too dangerous from rockfall to justify continuing the climb. The leader was Martin Boysen, famous as one of Bonington's strongest colleagues. He had twice been on Everest, including the 1975 expedition that had successfully made that first ascent of the huge southwest face. After Tut Braithwaite and

Nick Estcourt had managed to find a passage through the difficult rock band, allowing Doug Scott and Dougal Haston to push to the summit, Martin and his close friend Mick Burke set out for the high camp to make their own summit bid. They got an early start, but partway up, Boysen's regulator malfunctioned, and he did not want to continue without oxygen. Burke went on by himself. In the afternoon, a cloud covered the summit area. Burke was never seen again. It was presumed he stepped through a cornice. His companions hoped it was on the way down—after making the first solo climb to the summit of Everest.

That afternoon, Jim Wickwire and Boysen walked up a hill behind camp so they could see Gasherbrum IV and Martin could point out his attempted route. They had first met in '75, when Boysen was in the Kara-koram on an attempt to climb the formidable Nameless Tower, and it was good to catch up with what each had been doing in the intervening years. This led naturally to K2, and to the tragedy on Bonington's trip. Having been on earlier Bonington trips, Boysen had known Nick Estcourt well.

"I heard the news first on the radio about three weeks back," Boysen said. "They didn't say who it was—simply that someone on the British K2 Expedition had been killed. But I knew right then who it was. Nick had been having troubles with his personal life—split up with his wife—and he'd been a bit moody and depressed and I knew it was him."

"But it was an avalanche," Wick said. "It could have happened to any-body. He was in the wrong place at the wrong time."

"He had his guard down," Boysen said. "He shouldn't have been on the mountain. You just don't go on a big climb if there are any doubts."

Wick found interesting Boysen's idea of a connection between Estcourt's personal problems and his death, which ordinarily would have been con-sidered a random accident. Maybe Estcourt was not as perceptive as he should have been; perhaps, had he been in a more positive frame of mind, he would have smelled danger before he stepped out onto that slope and broke loose that big slab. Wick was not sure there was a valid connection. But it led to further discussion of death in the mountains, and of that ever-present specter that one writer of mountaineering literature has referred to as "the background noise of climbing."

"The one that hit me hardest was Mick's death on Everest," Boysen said. With a tone of bitterness, he added, "If it hadn't been for a faulty part in an oxygen regulator, we both would have made the summit, and Mick would still be alive."

"I've lost some close friends in the last year myself," Wick said. He told Boysen about his climb the year before in Alaska, when Al and Dusan had died, and how it had felt to have—in just a few minutes—the elation of victory change to meaningless void.

"What about your wife?" Wick asked. "What's her feeling about you going on these trips every year?"

"When I got married, sixteen years ago, I was a climber already," he said. "She worries, of course, but she has accepted the risk. She's very supportive."

"That's just about how mine is," Wick said, "and God knows how much I depend on that."

The heavy conversation was getting to both of them, so they wandered back to the campsite and joined some of the others making short practice climbs on the nearby boulders. It was late afternoon, and a pleasant breeze blew from the upper Baltoro, thinning the hordes of flies and gnats. The three women, Dianne, Diana, and Cherie, were back after a short hike above camp, where they had discovered a small waterfall and a rare moment of privacy to shower under brisk water in bright sun. The rest of the group sat on the grass, writing in their journals and reading books or chatting; there was a picnic atmosphere that day.

There are some days on long expeditions, days that are warm and memorable, days when you not only spend hours reading a book, or talking to friends, but when you realize better how important it is—in the grander view—to do such things. You look at mountains and valleys and glaciers and flowers with crisp perspective. You find yourself in the thick of conversations on religion, politics, and personal philosophies. It is more than just having time to read and think and talk, more than just being away from bills and phone calls and freeways. What gives rise to these times of reflection, often times of lucidity, is that you are involved in a hazardous enterprise. Sitting at Urdukas that day in the bright Karakoram sun was not like sitting on the beach in California. There was danger in the project that we were about to begin. It is not that we dwelt on the danger—on the contrary, most of us rarely even thought consciously about it—but it added to the picnic atmosphere in our camp that day (or any day of our approach march) that crystal quality that is part of the intangible stuff that makes people climb mountains.

I HEARD DIANA JAGERSKY UP FIRST, TRYING to get the stove started to heat the brew water, and cursing under her breath when it would not prime properly. Beyond her, not far away, rose the lonely song of a Balti calling to Mecca in his own dialect: "There is no god but Allah, and Mohammed is his prophet." It was a singular, haunting call, a beautiful, clear, melodic voice, a song that drifted over the rocks and the wasteland to the mountain walls, was reflected, and came back to us.

I lay for a moment with my eyes closed. For the first time in weeks the air felt brisk, enough so that I wanted to pull the down lip of my sleeping bag around my neck and not get up. But there was an excitement to the morning, a slight electric tingle that urged me to open my eyes and sit up, get out of my bag, pack, and get under way. When I managed, at last, to sit up, the reasons for that tingle became evident: we were in Concordia, the heart of the Karakoram, and at every point of the compass were the greatest peaks on earth. By afternoon, the approach march would be over. We would be in Base Camp.

All of us had, again, slept that night under the stars. By sitting upright in my bag and leaning against a rock backrest, I could see up the Godwin-Austen Glacier. Eight miles away, directly up this glacier, was K2. It rose two vertical miles above the glacier, pyramid-shaped, cloudless in the morning air. From that viewpoint, it was perhaps the most magnificent mountain on earth.

Concordia, so named by Conway in 1892, is the confluence of two major glaciers. From K2 to the north, the Godwin-Austen Glacier, bordered by Broad Peak, flows to Concordia, where it joins another glacier coming from the south: the Upper Baltoro, which is actually a separate glacier from the larger Baltoro on which we had been hiking. The Upper Baltoro spills off the slopes of Chogolisa, the Golden Throne, and the Gasherbrums. These glaciers unite as the main artery of the Baltoro, which leaves Concordia and flows west, forty miles back to Paiju camp. Standing at Concordia, one is at the center, a hub with glaciers radiating from it like spokes: in all directions from this hub rise enormous peaks. Directly behind Concordia is Gasherbrum, shaped like a shark's tooth: to the south is the snow-mantled Golden Throne and nearby, Chogolisa, sometimes called Bride Peak. The names of these magnificent peaks bespeak the poetry of the place.

I wormed out of my bag and dressed in my surgeon's shirt and pants. It was the second week of hiking. By now, morning packing was routine and took only a few minutes. I walked over to Diana's makeshift kitchen for a brew of coffee and cocoa and a hearty helping of mushy oatmeal. Most of the others were up and, as usual, Lou Reichardt was already about to leave camp. Most days, Lou and John Roskelley were the first on the trail and first into camp, moving much faster than the others (although for the last two days Lou had been slowed by a sprained ankle). Jim Wickwire and Jim Whittaker were frequently just behind them, and the rest of us dribbled into each day's camp somewhere in the middle. Bill Sumner and Craig Anderson almost always arrived last, often just before dusk.

Although it was difficult, at the time, to recognize it, this pattern reflected in no small degree the personalities of the team members: in retrospect, it portended a lot of what happened later on the climb. John and Lou were very competitive, anxious to get to the mountain, and wanted to demonstrate their willingness to work hard and move fast. Wick would have been right with them, first into camp every day, except that he was carrying a heavier load to further strengthen his leg muscles. In contrast, Bill Sumner and Craig Anderson hiked slowly. Craig spent considerable time each day composing photographs with his three cameras (including a wide-format panorama Linhof) and Bill seemed not so much to look at the surrounding scenery as to meditate upon it. He was of the disposition to go slow, more a religious pilgrim to the mountain than a climber come to conquer the great peak.

Lou Reichardt shouldered his pack and left camp, with Jim Wickwire on his heels. I was anxious to get an early start myself so I could make that last day into Base hiking with John Roskelley. I had two reasons for wanting to hike with John: he was without doubt the best technical climber on the expedition, and I wanted a chance to talk with him and get to know him better. I even thought we might get a chance to do some lead climbing together, although I knew he usually climbed with Lou. Besides, he had the expedition's cassette stereo in his pack, with speakers strapped to each side, and I wanted to listen to Eric Clapton blasting rock-'n'-roll as we made those last steps to the base of K2.

It was always desirable to leave each morning before the porters took off. Hiking behind a string of them on a narrow part of the trail could be very slow. They had a disconcerting habit of suddenly stopping to rest, in the middle of the trail, about every ten minutes. The leader of the pack would call a halt, and each porter would take his T-stick, place it behind him, and rest his load on it. In order to pass, it was usually necessary to scramble up around the trail to the front of the line, often over loose rocks and talus, and often to the amusement of the porters. Even if berated, they never seemed to rest off the trail as, from our point of view, courtesy would dictate. After thinking about it, however, it became obvious that, from *their* point of view, it was easier to rest in the middle of the trail. Besides, since they knew they would get to the next campsite in plenty of time, why should anyone want to pass? A number of our crew realized this early on, and knew it was just as easy to rest behind the Baltis when they rested. That morning, however, John and I were out in front.

The Godwin-Austen Glacier is laned with wide bands of rock and adjacent bands of ice pinnacles—called "neve penitentes"—caused by the melting and freezing action of the temperate-zone sun. These are the features that, when viewed from an airplane or from the top of a mountain, are the parallel stripes of a glacier you may have seen in geography or geology books. They gave us the choice of hiking either on lanes of rock or on lanes of ice pinnacles that we had to weave through, and it seemed a toss-up which was faster.

The sky was still hazed with the strange smoglike dust blown in from China; in addition, there were other portents of bad weather. It had seemed near-miraculous, after all the tales of bad weather on the '75 expedition, that we had slept out under the stars nearly every night of the approach march. On only one day had it rained, and even that had been light. But now there was a telltale lenticular forming over Broad Peak. These saucer-shaped clouds are caused by moisture-laden air blown up the windward side of a mountain and condensing in discs on the lee side of the summit; they usually mean bad weather will soon arrive. Still, we could not complain. We would arrive at Base Camp after a mere thirteen and a half days on the trail—faster than we had ever hoped in the light of the thirty-six-day approach march in 1975.

After less than four hours of hiking, John and I could see Wick ahead at a flat, rocky area. We guessed that must be Base Camp. We knew the Japanese K2 Expedition the year before had used the same spot. Theirs had been an enormous, paramilitary operation, with 56 climbers (including two young Pakistani climbers) and 908 Baltis to porter their equipment to Base Camp. They had had predominantly good weather, and it was no surprise that they placed seven climbers on the summit. It was only the second ascent of K2, made via the same route the Italians had used in 1954 on their first ascent, but given the size and complexity of the Japanese siege, most climbers the world over dismissed their expedition as having achieved little of significance in mountaineering history. We were reasonably certain the location of their base would still show signs of Japanese garbage.

John and I arrived a few minutes past ten. Wick had already been there more than half an hour. Lou was out scouting a nearby campsite. Wick admitted that, especially with his heavier pack, he had had to "suck it up" and push himself to keep up with Lou. We scouted around for the best tent sites, identified the bundles containing our two "car-camping" tents, and set them up. We also set up two smaller tents, one for the four Hunza high-altitude porters and another for Saleem. We had another huge tent about twenty feet long and ten feet wide, which we pitched to house some of the porters, though most of them would have to construct shelters by stacking boxes and covering the enclosure with plastic tarps. Kerosene stoves were issued so the porters could brew tea. It would be a cold night, and we had to sympathize with them, shivering in their shantytown shelters while we would be bundled in down bags in our fancy tents.

Base Camp was fully established before noon, and a good many of the porters wanted to be paid immediately so they could leave and return as far as Concordia before nightfall. But we had not yet received the extra money we had sent for from Askole, days before, when Jim had calculated a pending cash shortage. We needed it to meet the final payment for the porters. By our estimation, the porter carrying the money should have left Skardu over a week before, and since he would be able to travel fast, he should arrive anytime. Fortunately, only 81 of the total 220 porters who had made it to Base Camp wanted to return that afternoon, and we had just enough money left to pay each his salary of 740 rupees—about 74 dollars. We considered it no small coup that, with Saleem's encouragement, we had persuaded the remaining 139 to stay a little longer to help ferry loads partway around the mountain toward our goal, the northeast ridge.

We had discussed this idea two days before at Concordia. It had seemed almost a miracle that we would reach Base Camp so soon. This improved our chances of reaching the summit, but it was still very late in the season and we wanted to do everything possible to speed the climb along. Up to that point the porters had been amazingly cooperative and hard-working. For the past few days, Saleem had gathered the porters each morning before leaving camp to thank them for their help and encourage them on; even along the trail he would stop to make grandiloquent speeches to much cheering and applause. There was an amazing esprit de corps.

Considering the élan the porters had shown as far as Base Camp, we thought perhaps we could persuade at least part of the group to stay one or two days more. It would be a difficult carry to an altitude of about 17,500 feet. The feasibility of the plan depended on finding a safe route free of crevasse danger, since none of the porters would be roped up. Unfortunately, few of them wore adequate footgear. In Askole, we had issued Vibram-soled hiking boots, but we discovered to our chagrin that most of the porters had left them behind so they would not scuff such a pretty pair of new boots; also, they could later use them for trade or barter. Saleem nevertheless seemed to think he could talk many of them into going the extra distance. We were thrilled when 139 agreed to the plan. Since we had about 125 loads to carry around the mountain, our good fortune seemed heaven-sent.

But there was a problem with keeping the porters even one extra day: we were nearly out of atta, staple of the Balti diet. We had just enough for their return to Askole. Staying that extra day would create a serious shortage.

There was one possible solution. After Bonington abandoned his West Ridge attempt, his team scuttled their Base Camp with haste, leaving most of their food supply behind. There was a good chance we could find a cache of atta there. We knew the camp had already been raided by Askole men, but we reasoned they would have rummaged for valuables such as rope and climbing gear and would have left behind heavier, less valuable food bags. We decided that the next day some of our team would go to Bonington's camp on a food scavenge; Lou and Wick volunteered to take five porters and hike around to see what they could find.

Meanwhile, it was going to be important to move as fast and as efficiently as possible—while we still had the porters—to scout a route around to the east side of the mountain. The Godwin-Austen Glacier turns at Base Camp and continues up between the east side of K2 and the back side of Broad Peak, forming a small icefall at a constriction in the glacial valley where the southeast ridge of K2—the famous Abruzzi Ridge—joins the glacier. We thought we could find a safe passage, free of crevasses, if we stayed at the edge of the glacier, close to the foot of the Abruzzi Ridge. We had been told, by a Pakistani climber who had been on the Japanese expedition the year before, that just around the Abruzzi Ridge, off the glacier, was a campsite free of rockfall from the heights above. We hoped the porters could carry the loads as far as that campsite.

If we ourselves had to carry those 125 boxes, each weighing fifty-five pounds, it would take at least ten days.

Chris Chandler and I volunteered to scout the route early the next morning. We would be accompanied by one of our Hunzas—Honar Baig—who had been with the Japanese the year before and thus would know the most likely place to find a safe passage. It would be necessary to work fast and make few mistakes because the porters—each carrying a load—would be only an hour behind us. Ideally, we would have had at least one day to scout the route, but we felt we could not afford the extra time: there was not enough food for the porters, they might not want to bivouac for another cold night, and of even more concern, it looked like bad weather was coming.

By early afternoon a lenticular cloud had formed over K2; then high-altitude cirrus began to move in. By dusk, clouds were swirling about the summits of both K2 and Broad Peak. It was an awesome spectacle; all of us sat outside the tents, cameras poised, trying to capture the scene. The clouds would periodically open, allowing glimpses of the upper reaches of the two mountains colored orange by the low sun, contrasting vividly with the steel-blue clouds. We had a good view of most of the south face of K2. Several of the team had for some time discussed this face as a possible alternative route to the northeast ridge. It had two advantages: it was close to our present campsite and therefore would eliminate the lengthy carries to the other side of the mountain; and it provided a more direct line to the summit, with no lengthy traverses such as those we would have on the northeast ridge. The principal disadvantage was that it appeared unsafe. As if to dramatize this point and congeal our thoughts, a large avalanche thundered off the face, sweeping close to where we would climb if we picked that route. It was unanimous that we proceed to the northeast ridge.

On the morning of July 6 we awoke at 5:10. After several brews of tea and cocoa, Bill Sumner, Wick, and Craig Anderson left with five porters for the abandoned British Camp to recover food for the Baltis. Lou Reichardt, who was supposed to go with Wick, stayed in camp because of a cough and sore throat that he did not want to aggravate. Chris Chandler and I left at 6:15, with the Hunza, Honar Baig, to scout the route to "Advance Base Camp."

It was cloudy, misty, and drizzling as we walked up the moraine in the light of early morning, but despite the dreary sky it was fun to be with Chris. It brought to mind the early mornings when together we had scouted the route through the notorious Khumbu Icefall on the Bicentennial Everest Expedition. We could see the porters about an hour behind us; we knew we had to be quick finding a route through to Advance Base. If there were any delay, the porters would be unlikely to stand around in the rain and sleet waiting for us to locate a safe passage.

We wandered through a maze of seracs—ice blocks formed when

glaciers moved over steep, underlying bedrock—and it was difficult to guess where the best route would be. Twice we hiked up passageways between the blocks only to be stopped by cul-de-sacs. The best strategy seemed to be to divide, with each of us scouting different directions. Occasional broken bamboo marker wands indicated the Japanese had used portions of this route the year before. Honar Baig went directly up while Chris and I explored more toward the center of the glacier. We could not go too close to the middle, however, because there we would find crevasses too dangerous to travel over with the porters.

We were getting nervous. It was snowing lightly—though the cloud ceiling was still a thousand feet above us, and there was enough visibility to navigate—and we could not find a passage the porters could easily follow. They were less than ten minutes away, a long line of small men dressed in homespun rags, brown against the snow and gray sky, each with boxes tied with goat-hair ropes slung over their shoulders. Chris and I rapidly considered the alternatives and decided we had to try to climb out of one of the cul-de-sacs. We would fix a few lengths of rope, using ice screws and pickets, cut steps in the steeper ice with our ice axes, and motion the porters up. Then we would just have to hope the rest of the route of Advance Base Camp would be straightforward.

While Chris stretched out the rope I hammered in the pickets—aluminum stakes driven in snow—and anchored them. The porters would use the rope as a handline. Then I quickly cut a few steps. I could see the porters only two hundred yards away; they had stopped, presumably to wait until we finished rigging. In a few minutes, one of the sirdars came ahead to see how we were doing. I told him to go back and tell the porters to start up—we were ready. I tied a few more knots, then headed back to help guide the porters through the seracs while Chris and Honar Baig finished making last-minute adjustments to the handline.

I wound my way back down among the ice blocks. Despite the bad weather, things were going like clockwork. If we could get those loads to Advance Base today, we could be climbing on our ridge in five days. It was too good to be true. I turned the last corner, around the ice block, and stopped. Below me were our boxes, all 125 of them. And not one porter. In the distance, I spotted long lines of them marching back toward Base Camp. They had not waited for us to finish the handlines.

I sat down on the boxes to wait for Chris and Honar Baig. I could not blame the porters; it was cold and sleeting, they did not have proper clothing, and they were no doubt apprehensive about going higher on the glacier. At least, I thought, they had got the boxes a few miles beyond Base. Still, it would be an enormous job to carry them the remaining distance to Advance Base. We would just have to grin and bear it—an added week of hard work.

We arrived back to Base amid a bleak drizzle of rain and slush. Most of the team had spent the day sorting gear, and the news of our failure to get the loads to Advance Base was taken with equanimity. Wick, Bill, and Craig had fared better at the British Camp. They had not located a great deal of porter food, but they had managed to bring thirty pounds of dahl (dried peas) and some rice, tea, sugar, and biscuits, along with twelve oxygen bottles from the British supply. Best of all, they had located the oxygen cached in 1975, and to their surprise, most of the bottles were still full pressure, registering between 3700 and 3900 psi. They had been afraid the bottles would be frozen in hard ice, but they found them stacked neatly, clean of snow, and in excellent condition.

The next morning we awoke early to begin the long job of ferrying loads to Advance Base. The sky was slate gray. Diana made breakfast, and as we sat around drinking tea, Saleem came over to tell us that nearly a hundred porters had agreed to stay that morning to carry for three hours up the glacier before heading home. That would leave them enough time to return to Concordia that day—and us enough time to get to Advance Base. It was incredible luck. We all felt a warm thanks for these people who were going out of their way to help.

Chris said he was tired and wanted to take a rest day, so John Roskelley, Jim Wickwire, and I raced ahead to finish putting in the route to Advance Base. Above the seracs and the ropes we had placed the previous day, there was easy walking on the rock moraine fringing the glacier. We found the campsite and in a few minutes saw Jim Whittaker approaching. Following Jim, in a long line, were all the porters.

The campsite was filled with cheering and backslapping. Jim opened a couple of food boxes, passing out cookies and candy to the porters. They all had big, toothy smiles: for them the job was finished and they would soon begin the trek home, taking with them all our blessings.

Back in Base Camp the porters packed their few belongings and prepared to leave. But the runner had not yet arrived from Skardu with the money. We managed to establish radio contact with Skardu and learned the runner's departure had been delayed; he would not arrive for another two or three days. There was no choice but to send someone with the porters to pay them when the runner was intercepted. Jim felt that as expedition leader it was his responsibility to go, and Terry volunteered to accompany him. It was an unenviable task—they would not only leave the climb at its beginning, but also lose valuable acclimatization at the lower elevations.

Before Jim, Terry, and the porters left, Saleem had to make a farewell speech. From the top of a rock he told the porters what a terrific job they had done, and that the Americans, the Pakistanis, and Allah were proud of them. It was an emotional moment seeing them go, and to express our appreciation, Jim climbed the rock next to Saleem to thank the porters on behalf of our team.

Jim addressed the porters, who stood in a large semicircle before the rock, in a strong booming voice:

"I want everyone here to know, that carried up to our American Advance Base Camp, you have done something you can be very proud of." Jim paused while Saleem translated. "It will go down in history that you have done this thing. Your sons and daughters, and their sons and daughters, shall know what you have done." Again Saleem translated, and a murmur of approval passed through the crowd. "Our expedition is very proud of you!"

A great cheer arose from the porters, and someone yelled, "Islam!"

The crowd thundered back, "Zinabad!" (long live).

"Saleem Sahib!"

And the crowd roared, "Zinabad!"

"Leader Sahib!" (referring to Jim).

Again, "Zinabad!"

The cheering continued, and over the noise Jim yelled the finish to his speech: "From this day forward until the end of time, it will be known what you have done, and we thank you!" Saleem translated, to thunderous applause. The rest of us, who had been listening from the sidelines, went to shake hands with the porters. It was a farewell with much goodwill on both sides.

Once they had left, Base Camp suddenly had a quiet, almost lonely air. But our spirits were high. Diana Jagersky was busy cooking dinner— freeze-dried porkchops, mushroom gravy, and green beans, with cheese-cake for dessert. Bill Sumner helped Saleem fine-tune the single-sideband radio with which Saleem would make daily calls to Skardu while we were high on the mountain. Wick listened to a Beethoven symphony on the cassette machine and wrote in his voluminous journal. The rest of us read, wrote, or simply sat under the awning erected above the kitchen area, drinking tea and eating biscuits.

Everyone was happy with the progress of the expedition; we had done remarkably well in only two weeks. Everyone except Rob, who suffered from a bronchial infection, was more or less healthy. Almost always, on expeditions to remote areas, a good part of the team gets knocked out for at least a few days from viruses, bronchial infections, or dysentery. A few of us had sore throats, coughs, and hoarse voices, and some decided to rest for a day or two to prevent these from developing into more serious problems, but for a group of Westerners into their third week in Central Asia, we were amazingly healthy.

Everyone was also getting along well. The only flare-up of tempers had been the jeep incident in Skardu, which Jim seemed to have forgotten entirely. Most of us had come to realize that his show of anger had been, for the most part, to save face with Saleem. We were about to begin the climb and it seemed that each of us was still committed to the goal we had set almost a year before in Seattle: to get *somebody* to the top of K2.

We stayed up a little later than usual that night, joking, laughing, reading, and writing. Wick noted in his journal that there was a marked difference between the '75 trip and the '78 expedition at this stage of the climb. He wrote how much better everyone seemed to be getting along, and how much more resolved they were to make the expedition a success. For Wick, personally, it was the beginning of the final act in a drama he had been living and dreaming for six years: to climb K2. That evening he wrote:

> I am absolutely convinced that I am better fit at this stage of the expedition than I was in '75. And today I have had a strong feeling of certainty that this time we will be successful —stronger than at any time since the '75 failure, and I've had a stronger feeling of certainty than any time before that I will get to the top.

4

The Crystal Ball

July 11. LOU REICHARDT PROBED THE SNOW with his ski pole, like a basset hound sniffing something suspicious.

"I think there may be a crevasse here," he said, turning to us while continuing to test the snow with his pole. "I'm going to move up a few yards. It looks like a better crossing."

From my point of view fifty feet behind Lou, it looked as if there were nothing in front of him but solid glacial snow. Crevasses are like that; wind and new snow can keep them hidden. The deep cracks in the glacier will continue to widen and grow, and so will the trapdoor lids that cover them. Sometimes it is almost impossible to tell there is a hundred-foot-deep pit under what looks like perfectly stable snow—until you try to cross it. Then your body weight breaks through the cover, and in you go.

Lou moved up fifty feet, paralleling what he suspected was a hidden crevasse, until he thought he was at a place where the fissure would be narrow. I jammed my ice axe into the snow and belayed the rope around it and over my boot top while Lou crawled across. If he did go through, I could quickly hold the rope over my boot top and stop his fall.

John Roskelley, leading another rope team, saw the area Lou was trying to avoid, and he thought there would be a better crossing in the opposite direction.

"I'm going down this way," he called over, and started probing while Craig Anderson belayed his rope.

Lou safely reached the other side; I took the rope off belay and started across myself. I reached the suspected crevasse. It was possible to tell there might be a hole below the snow only by carefully studying the surface—there was a slight difference in the texture. I began to cross, and that was when I made my mistake. Lou's track made a wide detour to avoid what he sensed was the most dangerous spot; instead of following, I cut the corner. If I had had a vantage from down in the deep pit, I would have seen the snow bridge was much thinner where I was about to step.

Skip said I looked like a cartoon roadrunner. The snow all around me gave away, and I stood there for a split second suspended over a black void, with a dumb look on my face. Then, pfft! I was gone.

It happened too fast to remember falling. One moment I was on the Godwin-Austen Glacier, beneath the enormous east face of K2, hiking up to establish Camp I at the base of the northeast ridge. The next moment I was hanging from a rope, ten feet down in an ice pit. Fortunately I hadn't fallen far. Skip had kept the rope tight as I crossed and I had fallen only a few feet before the slack was taken up, stopping me. I cursed my own stupidity, then prepared to get myself out. I took out two jumars—special clamps with a cam device that allows them to slide up a rope but locks in place when the pull is downward. With foot loops attached to the jumars, you can easily climb up even a free-hanging rope. My heavy pack was a hindrance so I took it off, tying it to the end of the rope. I could pull it up later.

Before starting up I looked around inside the crevasse. It dropped away below me into blackness. Above, through the trapdoor hole I created when I fell in, light illuminated the surrounding blue-white ice. Some distance along the crevasse I saw another hole. It looked like a dark room with a single bare bulb hanging from the ceiling. Then I took a second look. At the bottom of the cone of light was John Roskelley, hanging upside down from his rope about thirty feet deep in the crevasse.

Diana Jagersky said it had looked like slapstick comedy. Both John and I were crossing the crevasse simultaneously, and at the same instant, both of us fell in. "One second you were both there," she said. "And the next there were just two holes with ropes disappearing in them. It really cracked me up."

I saw John struggling to right himself against the weight of his pack, and my first concern was that he might be injured.

"John!" I yelled. He looked around, bewildered. "Hey, over here. It's me, Rick. You O.K.?"

He glanced over and spotted me, about a hundred feet away. I could see he was trying to put the pieces together.

In a second he yelled back, "Yeah, I'm O.K. You O.K.?"

"Fine. I'm getting ready to jumar out. This has got to be a first. Two in a crevasse at the same time."

John struggled to get himself upright while I worked my way up. Just then Chris popped his head over the lip. I was about five feet below him.

"Oh, there you are," he said. "I expected to look over and see you fifty feet down or something."

He helped me over the edge, then John. Both John and I were chagrined. We were supposed to know better how to detect crevasses and were lucky we had not been injured. We hauled our packs up and continued on toward camp.

The weather was still overcast, snowing on and off, but it showed signs of improving. The day before, July 10, we had been weathered in. Those of us who were to carry the first loads to Camp I, at the base of our ridge, had spent the day in a twenty-foot-long tent at Advance Base Camp, or "ABC," as we had started calling it. But by this morning at eleven, the storm had started to break up, and we decided to try to get a carry to Camp I. We crossed the upper Godwin-Austen Glacier under the east face of K2, an eleven-thousand-foot wall frequently swept by avalanches calving off ice cliffs just below the summit. We tried to stay close to the center of the glacier to avoid the avalanche zone, but unfortunately the center had the most hidden crevasses. After falling in, John and I were more careful. We made the last distance to our campsite without incident.

The place we chose for Camp I was directly at the foot of the northeast ridge. It was an ideal location, protected from rockfall and snow avalanches, and also free of hazardous crevasses. On Everest it had been necessary to place one of our camps in the middle of a glacier because there had been no other site safe from avalanches; we had had to be careful not to leave the immediate camp area, which we had probed for crevasses. On the 1976 British Everest Expedition, one of the climbers—in that same camp—stepped behind his tent and broke through a crevasse; he was dead by the time they got him out.

We cached our loads, then took a rest and snacked on lunch before beginning the trek back to ABC. We also made sure to drink plenty of water. We were at about eighteen thousand feet, and it is very important at altitude to drink fluids. Much body water is lost through the rapid inhalation and exhalation of cold, dry air. High fluid intake also washes from the blood bicarbonates that concentrate in reaction to this heavy breathing. But everyone seemed to be adjusting to the altitude very well— nobody reported nausea or bad headaches. We had already been above sixteen thousand feet for a week, so we'd had enough time to acclimatize to that altitude.

It was a quick hike back to ABC, moving slightly downhill along the glacier following our uphill tracks. On the way up, the surface had been softened so much by the sun that we sank up to our calves, but it was firmer now. We had less concern about hidden crevasses, too, since we had an established trail. But we realized it had been an oversight not to bring a bundle of marker wands; the next snowfall would cover our tracks and without wands to mark the way we would once again have to probe through the minefield of hidden crevasses.

Back at ABC, we were greeted by the other team members who had come up from Base Camp. Jim Whittaker and Terry Bech were there, after making a one-day marathon trip from Urdukas to Base Camp—a distance that had taken us three days to cover on the way in. They had staggered in late at night, navigating the last section of moraine with head-lamps and following the shouts of Saleem and the porters to find the camp. They had intercepted the money runner a short distance below Urdukas and had paid the porters. It was good to have them back, and from the smiles on their faces, the feeling was mutual. They had brought mail carried up from Skardu by the runner, and as soon as the letters were handed out, people wandered off to their tents to catch up on loved ones back home. On long expeditions, it seems there are two main diversions: eating, and receiving mail. Of the two, mail is by far the more important.

The only members of the team not present were Rob Schaller and Bill Sumner. Rob had not yet recovered from his bronchial infection, and Bill wanted to rest a day before coming up to higher elevations. Bill had seemed reserved over the past couple of days, but it was not apparent whether his reticence was simply his normal demeanor or whether something else was bothering him. He had not participated in any of the route-finding as far as Camp I; most of his work had been carrying loads from the abandoned British Camp, and from the '75 oxygen dump, to Base Camp. He had spent a lot of time teaching Saleem how to use the wireless, and of all of us, he seemed to enjoy talking with Saleem, the HAPS, and the porters the most. He considered what he learned from them as valuable as the experiences climbing the mountain.

Spirits were high that night in our big caravan tent at ABC. We had stacked equipment boxes inside along the tent walls, and they made comfortable benches to sit on while speculating on what lay ahead. Diana again cooked dinner, after having made a full carry to Camp I—a scenario that was to become a common pattern in the weeks ahead. She would get up before everyone, make breakfast, see everybody off, then pick up a load herself and carry it to an upper camp, getting back down in time to prepare dinner for the gang. She seemed indefatigable. And if that were not enough, she always smiled and laughed; no one on the trip appreciated a good joke more than she did.

The cassette stereo blasted out an old Beatles tune—we had brought along several hundred batteries—and with a pot of tea brewing, we gathered to discuss future strategy.

"We've got a terrific place for Camp One," Lou Reichardt said. "Safe from avalanches and crevasses. I think just around the base of the ridge from the camp, we can find reasonable access to the crest of the ridge, and then on to Camp Two. I've studied the photos from the Polish attempt [Wick had corresponded with the Poles and obtained several pictures from their unsuccessful attempt to climb the northeast ridge in 1976]. We've got a choice of two snowfields to go up. The Poles chose the farther one, but I think we should at least have a look at the closer one, and then decide."

It was typical of Lou to analyze strategies. He had a scientific mind, plus considerable experience on big expeditions, and in the weeks ahead Jim would rely on Lou's calculations and suggestions on load-carrying logistics, and later, on summit strategies.

Lou continued, "It also seems to me we will eventually want to abandon Base Camp, except for Saleem, who can stay there with his cook, and probably this camp as well, then move our base of operations to Camp One. It's just too far from here to the base of the ridge."

If we abandoned ABC—the camp we were in that night—it would be fine with everyone. When we first arrived there, we thought it reasonably safe. But every so often a rock would come crashing into camp, sending everyone diving for cover. In one of the tents one night, there had been a particularly close-sounding whistle as a rock flew by; in the morning, the occupants had seen a hole neatly punctured through the top of the tent, with a matching hole on the other side where the rock had exited.

"Yeah, I've been thinking we should move everything to Camp One," Jim Whittaker said. "There's a lot of stuff here we'll have to carry up, but I think it's the best strategy. We should have four guys leave tomorrow who will stay and occupy Camp One, then the next day start to put the route in to Camp Two. The rest of us can carry loads from here and start to get Camp One ready as our new base."

"I've done some thinking on who should go up to put in Camp Two," he continued. There was silence in the tent. This would be important. Most of us wanted a chance to get out in the lead. In addition, it was the beginning of what would inevitably turn into endless jockeying for position. It was much too early to guess who would end up in position to try for the summit. An infinite number of things—sickness, injury, fatigue, despair—could happen to any of us between now and then, but it was not too early to start playing leapfrog mathematics to see who might be chosen to lead from Camp III to Camp IV—a very long, very steep traverse at twenty-three thousand feet. We knew that would be some of the most tricky and difficult climbing on the trip, and there were several of us eager to have the chance to lead across it.

"The four I've been thinking about for the job are Lou, Skip, Chris, and Craig. Jim looked at everyone, checking for differing opinions. Lou nodded. He would be pleased to get out in the lead. Skip said it sounded O.K. to him, and Chris was agreeable too. But Craig said he would rather stay behind and carry loads—he was not quite ready to do any leading.

Jim studied his notes and thought for a while, then looked at me.

"How do you feel, Rick? Want to have a go at putting in Two?"

I had been leaning with my arms on my knees, staring at the tent floor, while Jim announced his first choice for the Camp II team. As soon as he mentioned the names—Lou, Skip, Chris, Craig—I realized an important implication of Jim's choice: he was trying to separate people who might naturally pair up as rope teams because of their experience climbing together on previous expeditions. Of the strongest climbers on the team, those who had climbed together before were Lou Reichardt and John Roskelley, on Dhaulagiri in 1973 and Nanda Devi in 1976, and Chris Chandler and me, on Everest in 1976, as well as on many other climbs in the United States, Canada, and Peru. Jim Wickwire, obviously among the strongest climbers, was odd man out. He had not, in the past, been a consistent rope partner with any other team member. There were other pairings that seemed natural: Bill Sumner and Skip Edmonds had been on many climbs together; and Terry and Cherie Bech, as husband and wife, would have seemed a logical pair had they not made it clear they wanted to be treated as separate individuals on the climb, and thus preferred not to be roped together.

Before we left the States, all of us had talked at length about the problem of climbing pairs forming early in the expedition. It was considered a problem because we all felt that much of the feuding, the quarreling, and the schisms that all of us had observed on big expeditions were often the result of cliques forming early in the climb.

We hoped to avoid this. For one thing, on the approach march and later at Base Camp, instead of separating people in small, two-person tents, we slept in two big tents. Also, people rotated between the big tents, so we would all spend time with everyone on the team, rather than just a select person or two.

To prevent cliques from forming during the climb—or at least during the initial stage of the climb—Jim had decided (with the approval of us all) to avoid, whenever possible, pairing people simply because they had in the past been rope partners. But there was a trade-off in this strategy: while it might forestall cliques, it is nevertheless more comfortable to climb with an old pal whose judgment can be trusted, whose actions are predictable. When your partner leads, sets anchors, and fixes the rope for you to climb, it is nice to know the anchors will be well placed and solid, and when you are leading, to know your partner has a trustworthy belay to secure the rope should you fall.

But Jim, like most of us, felt this advantage was overshadowed by the danger of locking into fixed pairs. Everyone realized that it would be inevitable, even unavoidable, for people to pair up later in the climb. During the final stages, when we would prepare for the summit assault, Jim would have to choose who would be first to try for the top. That choice, we all knew, would be based on how well each of us had performed up so far, how much strength we had left, and how much desire we had to push all the way. And the choice, inevitably, would be made in pairs, since climbing would be slow on the technical sections below the summit, with three or more people on one rope. But we hoped that by that stage of the expedition we would all know one another well enough, that we would all be committed to working together to get the first climbers to the summit, and that there would be no resultant disharmony from the pairings.

So when Jim announced his first choice for the Camp II team, it was no surprise that he had not picked both Chris and me. Chris and I had been climbing together since 1973, when we had both been invited to try a new route on a twenty-thousand-foot peak in Peru. We had hit it off very well and together had reached the summit. Several other climbs followed, including another trip to Peru the following year, and then, in 1976, the Bicentennial Everest Expedition. From the start of that trip Chris and I were an inseparable rope team, and we did a major part of the route scouting up to the twenty-four-thousand-foot level. Once in position for the summit, however, a last-minute shuffle put Chris on the first assault and me on the second. It was disappointing not to be on the same summit team, but seemed likely both teams would get a chance to go all the way. As it turned out, Chris and his climbing partner reached the summit, narrowly escaping a bivouac, and safely descended. The Sherpas, however, were reluctant to carry more oxygen to the high camp to support a second assault, and when the weather closed in we abandoned the mountain, happy to have had two reach the top.

In the two years between Everest and K2, Chris and I had seen each other often, and we were still good pals. We had hiked together several days on the approach march; a week before, we had scouted the route through the icefall to ABC. When Craig declined to join the lead team to Camp II and Jim asked if I would take the position, I realized I would again be paired with Chris. I was a little surprised, but Jim explained his reasoning.

"I know you and Chris are old-time climbing partners, but I think we all know each other well enough now, that we're not risking any splits in the team."

"Who do you have in mind to put in Camp Three?" Lou asked.

"It's still a little early," Jim said, "but I'm thinking of Wick and me. Just the two of us could do it—it's one of the least technical sections of the climb—and if we did need help, I could ask another climber or two to come up. I would like to get a little lead climbing myself, you know—we would all like a stab at putting in some of the route. But I realize my main responsibility is being the leader, working out logistics. Still, I think Wick and I could do it in a few days. I would get it out of my system, then spend the rest of the time helping to haul loads and work out the supply lines."

"That sounds reasonable," Lou said.

"I know there are still a lot of people left out," Jim went on, "but it's going to be a big climb, and everybody will get a chance to do some leading. I've said before, on the '75 expedition it was a mistake to leave some people out of the lead climbing. I don't intend to do that this time."

"Have you thought about what supplies should first be carried to Camp One?" Lou asked.

"I have a list of a few things," Jim said, "but maybe we should make a more detailed one." Jim, Lou, and several of the others started to discuss the load priorities. Instead of joining in the conversation, I sat for a few minutes thinking how, in its initial stages, the climb might unfold. There had been a name noticeably unmentioned for the lead teams up to Camp III—John Roskelley—and it was clear what Jim had in mind. He was saving John for the difficult section from Camp III to Camp IV, the traverse. But who would John team up with? The only climber with skill in hard technical climbing (something certainly needed on the traverse) who was not on one of the initial teams was Bill Sumner. Perhaps they would pair up. But somehow that seemed unlikely. Bill and John were such opposite types. Bill was quiet, introspective, and approached most things in life—climbing, physics, making tents and equipment—in a slow, thorough manner. He was a complex, contemplative person. John, on the other hand, usually said whatever was on his mind, giving no consideration to the consequences of his statements. "I've never been one to beat around the bush," he said, describing himself. "I tell people exactly what I'm thinking. I know I'm kind of brusque, but at least you know where I stand."

But if Bill did not climb with John, who would? It was doubtful either Terry or Cherie Bech was technically qualified for the hard leading to Camp IV. Craig had turned down the lead to Camp II, and again, it was questionable whether he had the technical ability for the much more difficult traverse. Jim and Wick would need a rest after working to Camp III. That left the Camp II team: Lou, Skip, Chris, or me.

Skip had done some good technical rock climbing, but it was not clear whether he would be interested in leading the traverse. Like Bill, his close friend, he was introspective and had a slow, methodical approach to climbing. It did not seem likely John would pair up well with Skip. That left Lou, Chris, and me.

It was impossible to predict which of us might go with John. In any case, it had taken the strong Poles ten days to complete the nearly one-mile length of the traverse, and we had little hope of doing it much faster. That meant it could take two or even three teams, rotating every couple of days, to fix ropes along the traverse so we could haul supplies to Camp IV. By then, Wick would be rested. Maybe he could form a team with Bill. That seemed only natural—they got along well together. Which again left John, Lou, Chris, and me. I wondered how Jim might sort us out. If he wished to avoid old cliques, he would have to put Chris with either Lou or John. Again, as with Bill, I was not sure John would be compatible with Chris. A few days earlier, John had privately voiced to me his concern about getting along with Chris the rest of the expedition.

"Chris is a good friend of yours," John told me, "and I thought maybe you could clear something up—maybe talk to Chris. I have a suspicion he thinks I'm down on him because he thinks I'm a straight redneck conservative. I know we're different, but I don't give a damn if he smokes hash."

"I don't think Chris dislikes you at all," I told John. "I guess he thinks you're a little outspoken, and obviously you guys don't see eye to eye on a lot of things, but he doesn't have any animosity."

Chris wore shoulder-length hair and a beard and liked to finish off each day with a pipeload of hash from a stash he had purchased in Rawalpindi. He was not the only one who smoked hash on the trip—even Jim Wickwire, the straight-laced lawyer, got loaded with several of us one evening at Urdukas—but Chris, more than any of us, still lived the freewheeling life of the sixties. I had always been impressed that his style had never been cramped by his medical career. But more than one patient, in the emergency room of the Seattle hospital where he worked, had refused to be examined by Chris, not believing he could possibly be a doctor.

I went on staring at the tent floor, working out the future. It seemed most likely that Lou would again team with John, as he had done on previous climbs. Wick would probably be with Bill Sumner, and I would once again climb with Chris. It was all right, I thought, but I was a little disappointed. Although I had not told anyone, I had a strong ambition to climb with John. I had several reasons; most of them, I admitted to myself, were selfish. I was getting along with John very well, and I sensed in him a future friend. I also felt he was the best climber on the team, and therefore the one most likely to reach the top; if I teamed with him, I would also be in an excellent position. I knew we would make a very strong pair. Still, I felt if I made any overt move to team up with John, I would be abandoning my friend Chris. I was a bit ashamed of my ambitions.

Gradually, I realized how ridiculous it was, mapping all these scenarios of who would climb with whom. Time and again, all of us had told each other we would avoid the jockeying-for-position, the game-playing that happens on big expeditions, and here I was indulging in it already, at that early stage. It was ludicrous. I had to laugh at my own gullibility. Anything could happen—sickness, injury, storms—to change any sequence of events planned in advance. But one thing was certain: with an assortment of people as talented, as goal-oriented, as heterogeneous as this group, there was no doubt that whatever the crystal ball held in store, it was going to be interesting.

July 12. IT WAS A BRILLIANT MORNING, THE best day since we had arrived at Base Camp the week before. Eight of us were scheduled to carry more loads to Camp I, and this time, Lou, Chris, Skip, and I would stay to occupy the camp. The next morning we would leave early and begin to scout the route to Camp II.

Fresh snow had, in places, covered our footprints; at times, it was difficult to follow the track winding through the maze of crevasses that we had worked out the previous day. I was leading a rope with Chris in the middle and Cherie on the end. There was a second rope with Lou, Skip, and John. Wick and Jim would make their carry later in the day.

We were in the same area where, the day before, John and I had fallen into the crevasse; I was being more cautious. I carefully probed with my ski pole, working it down through the snow. Suddenly it broke through. I pulled the pole out and craned my neck—nothing but blackness through the hole.

"Crevasses here," I called back to Chris. "I'm going down a ways to look for a better crossing."

I paralleled the crevasse edge for a couple of hundred feet, then again tested snow. It seemed much harder—possibly the crevasse was narrower, or there was a snow bridge I could not see spanning it. Taking no chances, I had Chris belay me while I belly-crawled over the suspicious area, commando style, spreading my weight evenly over the snow lid covering the crevasse.

I got to the other side, stood up, and continued on, keeping the rope between Chris and me taut. When he got to the crevasse, he decided to walk across. It was a repeat of my performance the day before: one second he was there, the next there was nothing but a hole with the rope disappearing into it. Cherie gave a little scream, and the rope went tight. I fell on all fours, digging my axe in the snow so I could stop the fall as the rope pulled on my waist harness.

That's the third plunge in only two days, I thought. We're going to have to establish a safe route through here and make wands out of tent poles, or somebody will get hurt sooner or later.

Lou crawled to the edge of the crevasse, planting a ski pole under Chris's rope to prevent it from cutting farther into the edge and making it more difficult for Chris to climb out. After a few minutes Chris had jumared up the rope and crawled out, unhurt.

We moved slowly, carefully probing each crevasse crossing. Most were narrow enough to jump across. With ski poles, we could break through the snow that covered the crevasse, widening the hole until we located its true sides, and then, knowing its width, jump across.

At one crevasse I hesitated for a moment, judging whether it was too wide to jump. I am only five foot five—and at that I have short legs—so I am not a very good broad jumper, especially with a fifty-pound pack. But this one seemed feasible.

"Watch me," I told Chris. "I'm going to jump. It's a real leg-stretcher."

I held my axe with both hands so I could whack it into the far side if I fell short, then cocked my legs and jumped, just making the far side. Chris followed me across, then Cherie approached the hole. She hesitated for a minute, looking down into the crevasse.

"Just stand on the edge and jump," Chris said. "It's easy."

Chris was getting ready to belay her. He had not finished planting his ice axe to anchor the rope when Cherie, getting ready to jump, stepped too close to the lip of the crevasse. The snow caved in, and she disappeared. The rope wound out. In a second Chris was pulled off balance and onto his knees. The rope went taut between him and me, as both of us planted our ice axes, to break Cherie's fall. John, on the other rope, quickly moved to the crevasse edge and looked down.

"She's down a good thirty feet," he reported. "Way down there."

He cupped his hands and yelled, "Cherie, you O.K.?"

We couldn't hear her reply, but John looked up and relayed the message.

"She seems O.K.," he said. "She's probably shook up but I don't think hurt. She's really down there."

John looked back down the crevasse and yelled to Cherie, "I'll lower another rope. Tie your pack to it, then get your jumars and come up on your own rope."

John lowered the rope and in a few minutes had Cherie's pack out of the crevasse. We waited for Cherie.

"What's she doing?" Lou asked impatiently. "She's been down there ten minutes. She should have been out by now."

John again yelled down the crevasse, "Cherie, can you get out?"

"She's having some kind of trouble," he reported. "She's been in quite a while—might be getting cold. Looks like we'll have to pull her out."

Lou anchored the rope leading to Cherie with his ice axe, freeing Chris and me to join John at the edge of the crevasse. I peeked over the edge; she was barely visible beneath the thin shaft of light entering through the hole in the snow.

We rigged our jumars to make a ratchet device to keep the rope from slipping back, and the four of us began hauling Cherie in time to a heave-ho, heave-ho, gaining a quick five feet with each tug. In less than a minute we had her up.

Except for a minor cut on her nose she was uninjured, but she was shaken by the fall. She brushed the incident off with a laugh, telling us it looked pretty inside the crevasse with all the smooth blue ice walls, but she admitted she was a little cold and glad to be out. We rested for a few minutes, sitting on our packs, to give Cherie time to recover before getting under way again.

"I had trouble with my slings," she said. "I couldn't get them adjusted right so I could jumar up."

"Yeah, it's hard if you're not set up just right," Chris said. "I'll help you get things adjusted later."

Nobody else said anything. Chris was sympathetic; like the rest of us, he realized Cherie had probably had very little experience with jumars, but unlike us, he wanted to help her learn. John, Lou, and I thought that if she did not know by now, K2 was no place to learn. But Chris got along with Cherie much better; during the approach march, and for the past week, they had spent hours together talking, comparing their experiences in Nepal, their experiences raising kids (Chris had three children, although they were in the custody of his divorced wife), and their careers in medicine. They had a lot in common. Chris was finding that Cherie, more than anyone else on the trip, shared many of his own attitudes, beliefs, and values.

Some of the rest of us were skeptical, and among ourselves we quietly questioned Cherie's ability as a mountaineer. It was still too early in the expedition to pass any judgment, but so far she seemed unsure of herself. Later that day, back in ABC, she would explain that her fall had been due to several inches of snow that had covered the previous track, hiding the true edge of the crevasse. Wick noted in his journal that evening:

> To my observing eye the route hadn't changed a bit. Despite the Dhaulagiri performance of seven years ago, I'll be surprised if she goes very high on the mountain. People say she's a good climber, better than Terry, but I want to see.

I had first questioned Cherie's judgment five days earlier when we carried our first loads to Advance Base Camp. Terry Bech and Jim Whittaker were still down the glacier, hiking to intercept the money-runner. Most of us carried packs filled with personal equipment so we could stay at ABC that night. Because Terry was away, Cherie wanted to help carry some of his personal gear, as well as her own, to ABC; she left Base Camp with a huge pack weighing easily ninety pounds. My pack weighed nearly fifty pounds, and I thought that was on the heavy side. From my experience climbing big mountains, I had learned it is very important to pace yourself. We would be on K2 for at least a month and a half, and it demanded caution not to burn out early. So I was surprised to see Cherie with such a behemoth load. As it turned out, people helped her carry part of the pack to ABC, although she did manage to deliver most of the load. That afternoon I expressed to John my doubts on her sagacity.

"I'm afraid she's trying to prove herself, to show us she's capable of carrying as much, if not more, than the men on the trip," I told John. "Cherie has a strong desire to be the first woman to climb K2, but I've got a suspicion she might push herself too hard to do it."

"I'm afraid it might be a repeat of what I've seen on other trips," John said. "Every time I go on one of these big climbs with women it's the same story. Every single time—I swear to God, this is the last time I'm climbing with any of them. I've seen them kill themselves trying to prove they are as strong as men. Eight of them in the Pamirs, then Devi. People always criticize me for being down on women on expeditions, but I've never yet been on a big mountain with one that's worth a damn."

On two of John's previous expeditions, women had died. In 1974 he was part of an international convention of climbers hosted by the Russians in the Pamir mountains. A group of eight Russian women had died tragically, caught in a storm on an ascent of 23,400-foot Peak Lenin. Perhaps they should have turned back at the first sign of the pending storm, but they were close to the top and pressed on until the blizzard stopped their advance—and their retreat. In 1976 John was on Nanda Devi with Willi Unsoeld and his daughter Nanda Devi, whom he had named after this beautiful mountain in India. Devi fell ill from a strange stomach ailment high on the mountain, and before she could be evacuated, she died.

"Anyway, I think I'll talk to Cherie about it," I had said. "Just to let her know she doesn't have to prove anything."

The next day I found myself alone for a few minutes with Cherie, in the cook tent, and I broached the subject. As I had expected, she reacted defensively.

"I'm used to carrying heavy," she said. "We did it week after week on Dhaulagiri. Hell, man, we had to shuttle hundred-pound loads with just two of us. I would get into camp each night sweaty and sick, and I'd upchuck, and then do it again the next day."

I decided if I said any more it would only end in argument. Perhaps she was super strong and could carry heavy every day without burning out early. I just hoped she did not get herself in trouble higher on the mountain, when things would, without doubt, get a lot tougher.

AFTER CHERIE RECOVERED from her crevasse fall we shouldered our packs and finished the hike to Camp I. It was turning into a marvelous day. We were beneath the awesome east face of K2, with our northeast ridge forming the right skyline. We eyeballed the route up to the place where Camp III would eventually be placed, then along the difficult traverse to Camp IV. It looked spooky. Above IV, we could see that we would have to make a long climb to the top of a rounded dome, where the ridge joined the summit pyramid. Camp V would go there. The summit itself was concealed by a cloud—the only cloud in the sky.

We arrived at Camp I, dumped our loads, then began chopping platforms for our tents out of the ice. John and Cherie unloaded and started back to ABC. In the distance, out on the glacier, we could see Wick and Jim slowly hiking toward us in the heat of the afternoon sun.

FROM WICK'S JOURNAL

> July 12. A brilliant day, a joy to be in the midst of the great mountains. Not the joy of route pioneering that Rick, Chris, Lou, and Skip will have tomorrow in moving up to establish Camp II. But the joy of feeling strong, full of life, the sheer exuberance of moving up the glacier beneath mighty K2. This is what Jim and I had this afternoon in making a late carry to Camp I. The heavy load didn't matter; we were in close

proximity to the commencement of our route, the magnificent northeast ridge. Hidden by clouds at the start, the upper ridge gradually revealed itself. A large avalanche down the eastern wall of K2, sending the telltale white cloud spreading out across the glacier in front of us, did not disturb our feeling of confidence.

Jim wanted to move fast, and fast we did, making the carry to Camp I in under two and half hours. Once there, it was good to see the guys had put in a very nice campsite against the buttress terminating the northeast ridge; the setting is superb. We stayed long enough to help erect another tent, then walked back out on the glacier.

As we left, the entire route, except for the final summit rise, unfolded, and as afternoon sun filtered through wispy clouds, we could see the stretch to the dome at twenty-five thousand feet. The difficult traverse was foreshortened, but we could see each pinnacle, each dip, each facet of this stretch from Camp III to Camp IV.

At that moment, the feeling of certainty that we would climb this mountain became almost overwhelming. We were in high spirits. Weren't we Pacific Northwesterners, after all, from the Land of Ice and Snow, and wasn't this our kind of mountain? An ice and snow behemoth on this east side. It wasn't overconfidence, but rather a feeling that we would without doubt overcome the difficulties—the storms and the rest—and reach that highest crest. As surely as we threaded our way through the crevasse field without mishap, we would climb to the summit of K2—the mountain of my dreams.

Then for me there would be other mountains and summits —those of the everyday world. Renewed closeness to a woman a man has been so fortunate to meet, to love, to have children with, and finally, to grow old together.

It's surprising how these good days can magically occur. Tonight I am a happy man, blessed with a wonderful wife and children, good and true friends, and the opportunity to reach the high and lonely summit of K2.

I ROLLED OVER IN MY SLEEPING BAG TO AD-just an arm that had fallen asleep. I felt the blood run back into the tissue and the numb and prickly feeling give way to warmth. Without opening my eyes, I fluffed the down parka under my head and snuggled in to re-capture the last thread of that pleasant dream before the arm woke me up. The only thing distracting me from complete comfort was the urge to pee. But that meant getting up and going out on the ice—wearing just my long-john underwear. Out of the question.

I had nearly regained the sweetness of that lovely dream when a sharp pop sounded from deep in the glacier. That is one of the fun parts of sleeping on glaciers—listening, and feeling the ice move, waiting for the occasional groans and sharp cracks from down in the bowels of the ice. In a second I heard another one. I could not feel any movement, as you sometimes can when there is a major split in the glacier. There was only the deep-down Pop!

I realized that I was, unfortunately, waking up. Somehow I knew if I opened my eyes it would be getting light outside. I hesitated, then cracked one eye open. Sure enough, I could see the pastel yellow of the tent fabric over my head. The first light of dawn.

I lay for a few more minutes before getting up. I thought, Today we start the route up to Camp II. It was exciting to think about getting out in the lead, exploring new ground. I sat up in my bag and put my pile jacket over the angora wool underwear I slept in. Then I leaned over, keeping my legs in the warm bag, and peeked out the tent door. The sky was deep indigo in the early morning light, made richer by the high altitude. There were still a few first-magnitude stars visible. And not one cloud. I pulled back into the tent and thought how lucky we had been with the weather. There had been only one day, a few back, when we had had to wait out a snowstorm in the tents. And almost every day of the approach march had been flawless. I knew it could not last. But again, perhaps it was a good sign, perhaps this was to be a year of exceptionally fine weather in the Karakoram. I knew a break like that, more than anything, would give us the luck we would need to reach the summit.

"Chris, you have the time?"

I was sharing a spacious four-person tent with Chris; Lou and Skip were in another one next door. I had drowned my watch in one of the rivers on the approach march, so I was always asking the time. Seiko had given us all those new alarm-buzzer, digital readout, calendar models, with a light to see in the dark. Chris stirred a little, but did not reply.

"Hey, I think it's time to get up. What's your watch say?"

He again stirred, half rolled over, and opened an eye.

"Five forty-six and twenty seconds. July twelve." He rolled back over, paused, and then added, "Oh yeah. It's Thursday."

Chris stayed in his bag as I began to get dressed. I could hear mumbling from the tent next door, and in a minute came the blow torch sound of the kerosene stove. Lou and Skip were heating water for the morning brew.

I thought, It will be warm today, unless the wind comes up, so I'll just wear my angora woolies and my Gore-Tex jumpsuit. I weasled into the jumpsuit, then put my felt boot liners inside the outer boots, worked my feet in, and zipped up the knee-high gaiters. My toes were cold in the icy boot, but I knew they would soon warm.

I smeared PABA lotion on my face, cleaned my goggles, and loaded my camera. Other than packing the rope and climbing hardware we would need for the day, I was ready to go. Chris was still snoozing.

"You ought to get ready. We'll be leaving soon," I said to him.

From the next tent I heard Lou call, "Brew water is ready, you guys."

"Be right there," I called back.

Chris sat up in his bag. "O.K.," he said. "Guess that means it's time to do it."

We sat in front of Lou's and Skip's tent drinking tea or coffee and munching a breakfast of candy bars, Slim Jim pepperoni sticks, and freeze-dried beef stroganoff leftover from the previous night's dinner. After breakfast, we loaded our packs with about two thousand feet of six- and eight-millimeter rope, a dozen snow pickets, several deadmen (aluminum plates about eight inches wide and a foot long that set themselves to make anchors when placed in the snow and tugged), ice screws, pitons, aluminum chocks to jam in rock cracks, and carabiner snap-links to fasten the rope. With a little lunch packed, and a quart bottle of water apiece, we were ready.

We left camp at 6:30 and climbed along the base of the ridge until we reached a snow gully dividing two rock promontories. There was more rock above the gully, and one concern was avoiding, as much as possible, rockfall from above.

"The Poles went up the next gully around the corner," I said. "But I think this one is faster and no more dangerous. Let's give it a go, and we won't fix any ropes. That way we can always come down the Polish gully if this has too much rockfall."

We reached the top of the gully about 8:30, Lou breaking trail, kicking steps in the snow almost the whole way. A few rocks had hurtled down as the morning sun loosened the frozen debris above the gully, and we would definitely want to investigate the Polish gully when we came back down later in the afternoon. The sky was still cloudless; it looked like it would be a perfect day. For the first time, we were high enough to see a magnificent twenty-four-thousand-foot peak that adjoins K2 on the northeastern side —Skyang Kangri, also called Staircase Peak, after a series of huge steps on its eastern ridge. At the foot of Skyang Kangri, the head of the Godwin-Austen Glacier, was a nineteen-thousand-foot pass known as Windy Gap. We could just see over the top of Windy Gap, and on the other side the beginnings of the burnt-sienna hills of China's great Sinkiang Province. There was considerable magic in that first view into China.

Above, the route steepened and the snow changed to ice. We cut a platform, placing two ice-screw anchors, and began to belay the rope to the lead climber. Lou led the first section, then I took over, then it was Chris's turn. Just below the crest of the ridge, it appeared that the ice stopped, and we would be forced to climb up rock to reach the top of the ridge. We tried to avoid rock, when possible, because it was loose and frost-shattered. There was danger the lead climber would knock loose rocks on those below.

Chris worked up the ice by planting his axe, pick first, then kicking into the ice with his front points—two spikes on the crampons that stick out from the toe of the boot. It is not a particularly difficult technique, but Chris had not been climbing for almost a year before the expedition, and it was easy to see he was uncomfortable. He climbed off the ice and onto the bordering rock, carefully continuing up. Skip and I were together on a small platform cut in the ice and Lou was a few feet above. We watched Chris cautiously take each step. He was about sixty feet above us. As we had feared, he loosened a few rocks, which zinged by, just missing Skip and me; Lou was better protected under a rock outcrop. We yelled to Chris to be more careful, but another barrage of rocks came down. Skip and I tucked, covering our heads and backs with our packs. Rocks hit all around, but amazingly I was not touched. I heard Skip cursing—he must have been hit.

"Skip, you O.K.?"

"No. I got a couple in my arm and shoulder."

He was feeling his arm and rolling back his sleeve.

"I don't think it's broken," he said. "But it hurts like hell."

There was a big bruise already rising on his forearm. Some of the skin was cut and bleeding, but not badly. His shoulder seemed bruised but otherwise O.K.

Chris yelled down, "Sorry. There's lots of loose stuff. You guys O.K.?"

"Be careful," I yelled. "Skip got hit in the arm and shoulder. I think he'll be able to climb up, but I don't know about leading."

Chris went on, and in a minute another barrage of rocks came down. Again, we ducked. This time, I felt several good-sized ones thump into the padded pack covering my head.

Suddenly I flew into a rage, screaming at Chris, "Get back on the ice! You trying to kill us?"

Chris yelled back, also upset but more contained than me, "Look, the ice doesn't go much higher than this anyway. I've got to be on rock from here up. I'm *being* careful—it's loose up here."

I realized losing my temper was not making things any better. But it seemed to me he could have climbed farther on the ice, minimizing the time on the rotten rock. Chris continued up and traversed so that any other rocks would roll down another gully, missing us. Ten minutes more and he was at the crest of the ridge, ready to belay us up. As I climbed the rock, I realized it was impossible not to knock a few down. When I got to Chris I apologized.

"Sorry I yelled at you that way. I know it was loose—it was just scary being on the wrong end of a bowling alley."

"Forget it," Chris said, but I could see he was still miffed.

Lou followed me up. Although he did not say much, it was clear he had not been impressed with Chris's lead. We rested awhile, and from our new perch on the ridge crest we were able to see down the glacier to ABC and across the valley to Broad Peak. Two rope teams of antlike figures were moving up the glacier—that would be the rest of the team including our four Hunza porters, carrying loads from ABC to Camp I. From our vantage point it was easy to make out the hidden crevasses. The snow covering them had a unique texture and contrasted clearly with the surrounding white. Thus, the crevasses formed long zebra stripes that split the glacier side to side, and it was fun to watch the climbers below approach one, stop, and move along it to find a suitable crossing. Had we been in radio contact, we could have coached them across the glacier; it seemed odd how hard it was to detect a crevasse when standing on the edge of one.

The next several hundred feet up the ridge was easy, then it steepened and our pace slowed. We discovered a section of white eleven-millimeter rope buried under a few inches of ice, obviously left from the 1976 Polish attempt. Foolishly, Lou and I went up and started hacking it out, thinking we might be able to reuse it and save our own rope; we should have realized that after two years it would not be trustworthy. Chopping it out of the ice was an arduous task, and since Skip and Chris were idle, Lou suggested they go back to the steep section where Chris had knocked down the rocks and reroute the rope to a safer location.

Lou and I eventually scuttled the idea of using the Polish rope and continued up, fixing our own line as we went. About 3:30 P.M. we were only a few hundred feet below a level spot on the ridge, the spot that would be our Camp II site. We decided to retreat and come back early the next morning to finish fixing ropes into the new campsite.

We headed back to the ridge crest, above the spot where Chris had knocked down the rocks. Below, we could see Chris and Skip rappelling the ropes. It had been four hours since they had left Lou and me higher on the ridge.

"They should have had those ropes finished by now," Lou said. "There's been more than enough time."

"Yeah," I agreed. "It's taking them awhile."

"Those guys weren't too impressive this morning, either. I know Skip isn't acclimatizing well, but Chris could be doing better. If they don't hurry, we'll be out here tonight bivouacking. Seriously."

"I'm not sure it will come to that, but they sure as hell could be moving faster," I agreed.

At the same time as I agreed with Lou, I felt guilty criticizing Skip and Chris behind their backs. Skip had mentioned he did not feel he was acclimatizing very well; we were at twenty thousand feet, and if he felt sluggish it was understandable. And while Chris had lacked zest the last couple of weeks, it seemed rather extreme to charge him with indolence. But there were the small things—like being slow getting up in the morning. Perhaps he thought of this trip more as a vacation than as an arduous ascent that would take all the energy and effort any of us could muster. Maybe, for him, it was an escape from the problems he faced back home. He was having trouble with his ex-wife—divorce, alimony, child custody. Or perhaps these problems had followed him to K2 and were weighing heavy even as he began the climb on the ridge.

There was one thing I knew for sure, one thing I thought the others probably realized, too: Those who would finally be picked to go to the summit would be the ones who had not just worked the hardest and climbed the best, but those who had demonstrated the most gusto, those who had not just climbed hard but had climbed with relish. It was that kind of person Jim Whittaker liked, and it was that kind he would pick to go to the top. I knew Chris had to show some spark and verve if he were going to make it.

I thought, Maybe that's why I feel a little guilty when I criticize Chris for being slow—because I know he is not going to be chosen if he doesn't put out that little extra distance. That's the core of the problem right there, isn't it. That's the guilt. If Chris and I are climbing together as a rope team, chances are Jim will pick another pair over us. It's almost a simple choice—a choice of staying with Chris, your friend, and probably not getting to the top, or going with Roskelley and almost certainly reaching the summit if anybody at all makes it.

That's what you want, Ridgeway, I thought. And you know that's what you're going to do. You'll go with Roskelley even if it means abandoning Chris. You want the summit so bad. You missed it on Everest, and you're not going to let it happen this time. But is it worth it? Ask yourself that. Chris is having a lot of trouble now, trying to figure out his personal life, and shouldn't you be with him, giving your support? You should be, but you won't. Because you want that summit too bad.

I had been intending to talk to Chris about it for some time, but whenever I was alone with him and started to mention it, I always got distracted onto something else. I always thought, Well, I'll bring it up soon. Only I never did. It is funny how things like that work; it happens so often with people you care about. You want to tell them something, something that is important because they are your friend, but you can't quite bring it out. And so you end up discussing the weather, or the climb, or what equipment you should haul next to which camp, and all the while you're thinking, Yes, I'll bring it up. And all the while you know you probably won't.

Chris and Skip had the rope ready.

"About time," Lou said, as he got ready to rappel. I followed Lou down the rope, giving him enough time to get out of the gully in case I should loosen any rocks, and I thought, Yeah, I'll have to talk to Chris about it.

July 14. ANOTHER BRILLIANT, CLOUDLESS DAY.
The gods of the weather are still favoring us. If it keeps up, we could climb the mountain in only a month. The thought is intoxicating, and too attractive; I know that will not happen. There will be the inevitable storms, the delays, the illnesses. But it is still a possibility, and good grist for those daydreams while I stand on the snow, anchored to pickets,

belaying the rope out around my waist, watching Lou climb higher. One more rope length and we'll reach Camp Two, I think.

Lou, Chris, Skip, and I had again left camp early in the morning, a little tired from the long day before, but fired with the knowledge we would get to Camp II and firmly establish the route with fixed ropes. It would be ready for the others—who meanwhile were carrying more loads from ABC to Camp I—to start stocking Camp II. Then Jim and Wick could begin immediately the push to Camp III. Yes, I thought, it was very fast, very rapid progress. The four of us agreed to divide into two groups: Skip and Chris would stay lower on the route to exchange the less secure six-millimeter rope we had put in the day before for eight-millimeter, and in addition move the rappel from the dangerous gully where Chris had dislodged the rocks to another one farther up the ridge that had less rock around it; Lou and I would go to the campsite, fixing ropes that far. If time allowed, we would prepare a few tent platforms as well.

It was still noon as we made the last distance to Camp II; we would have plenty of time to work on the campsite. There was no doubt we were at the "right" spot. There were aluminum poles, with tatters of orange nylon fabric hanging like debris from a past war, the remnants of the 1976 Polish camp. We took off our packs, laying them in a pocket between the poles—it was steep enough that we could not set our packs on the slope without fear of their rolling away. It would take time to chop the tent platforms in the hard, icy slope.

Before we started, Lou and I relaxed and nibbled on our lunch ration. The view was supurb. Skyang Kangri was to our left, behind were the hills of Sinkiang, brown in the rain shadow of the Karakoram. Across the Godwin-Austen were the massive ramparts and hanging glaciers coming off the north side of Broad Peak, forming a wall along the glacier and hiding from view the peaks beyond. But we knew we would see them soon enough from the higher camps: Gasherbrum II, III, IV, Hidden Peak, Chogolisa.

Lou and I sat quietly, gazing. Below, we could see small figures making their way up the glacier, carrying to Camp I. Tomorrow many of them would be coming up to stay, to begin the carries to Camp II.

Lou turned around and looked at the slope above Camp II. It was only visible for about five hundred feet—above, a hump in the ridge hid the rest of the route to Camp III. It would be a long, though relatively easy, climb.

"We're here early with still a lot of time," Lou said. "And a little extra rope and a few anchors. Maybe I'll run out a few hundred feet more above camp."

"You'd be poaching on Jim and Wick's territory," I said, thinking it more important to use the time preparing the site here. "It's their lead from here to Three."

"It's all for the good of the expedition," Lou said, laughing mischievously. "They probably won't like it, but there's not much they can say if they come up here and the rope is already in."

"OK, but stick around long enough to help me chop a tent platform," I said with a chastizing tone.

We continued to nibble lunch, and I thought that Lou was going to be perhaps the hardest person on the trip to get to know. In fact, it might be impossible. It was easy to tell he was highly motivated, driven to accomplishment, and that he had as likely a chance as any of reaching the top of this peak. If anyone would go that little extra distance—the extra I thought would make the difference when Whittaker picked the summit climbers—it would be Lou. It was typical of him, for example, to decide to go up and fix a few hundred feet more rope, even though we had already done our job and it would be just as useful to stay at the campsite and cut tent platforms. But I believed it was also a gesture to spite Wick and Jim—especially Wick—and I thought I knew Lou's motivation. John Roskelley had tipped me off a few days earlier.

It was a small incident—outwardly small—back when we first arrived at Base Camp and half the team had gone off to search for porter food at the abandoned British camp. Chris and I had gone up toward Advanced Base Camp. Originally Lou had volunteered, saying Wick would go with him to the Brits' camp to get the extra food. Lou wanted to see that side of the mountain anyway, and he felt that finding extra food for the porters was the most important task at hand. That evening he took Wick aside and said, "I hope you didn't mind me volunteering you for the job, but I know you and I are about the strongest guys here, and we could do the best job." Wick had been complimented.

The next day, however, Lou woke up with a sore throat and cough and decided he would be better resting a day than risk having the illness develop into something more serious. When Wick went to Lou's tent to see if he was ready to go, Lou said, "I've still got a sore throat this morning, and also a new cough. I'd better stay here and rest." Wick left the tent, but as he did he grumbled, "Yeah, and I've got an old cough."

A small thing, but Lou had fumed, and I suspected he was still fuming now, more than a week later. I also suspected stringing out three hundred feet of rope across Wick's territory was Lou's way of showing Wick he was no slouch and not one to shrink from a job. Lou was an odd-looking sort. He appeared to be about his thirty-five years, no more or less. Sitting next to me, he had the unconsciously disheveled appearance of an academic, or a scientist. I did not know much about his research in neurobiology, but I did know he was highly respected in his field. Of course, he was as serious about his career in science as he was about his career in climbing. I had heard an amusing story that when Lou returned with John Roskelley from the summit of Dhaulagiri in 1973, his colleagues played a trick on him. Lou had climbed the 26,795-foot mountain without oxygen, and in retrospect he remembered how difficult it had been to think coherently at that altitude. As a neurobiologist, he was very much aware of the permanent damage that hypoxia—lack of oxygen—can cause to brain cells. It is a common joke among climbers that you come back from high-altitude trips acting like someone fresh from fifteen thousand volts of shock therapy.

With this in mind, Lou's colleagues began calling him up and saying things like, "Lou, where were you this morning?"

"I was right here in my lab," Lou would reply.

"Why weren't you at the meeting? Remember, we had an important meeting this morning. Nine o'clock. You were supposed to be there."

"I didn't know about any meeting. There was a meeting?"

"Lou, we told you five times there was a meeting. You feeling O.K. these days?"

Lou eventually figured out the joke, but apparently not without worrying he might be suffering from brain damage.

Sitting next to him, I noted his brown-black hair sticking out in tufts from around his ski goggles, the lenses of which were smudged with sun-cream. He also had sunscreen smeared in blotches on his face and lips, and big blobs of the stuff stuck in his month-old beard. He was wearing his angora wool top, and his pile underwear for pants. I sat watching him out of the corner of my eye. His nose was running, and I watched with amusement as he blew his nose in his hand and sat for a moment wondering what to do with it. He glanced around for a few moments looking for something to wipe it on, and not finding anything suitable, smeared the mess on his trousers, leaving white patches stringing across the wool pile.

I thought, Boy, this guy sure is weird.

There was one other story I knew about Lou, one that shed a little more light on his personality but at the same time made him seem even more enigmatic. It was one of the more incredible—and tragic—stories in the history of American climbing. The year was 1969, the scene the first American attempt to climb Dhaulagiri, and by a new and difficult route. The team was a selection of some of America's best mountaineers.

Eight of the team were pushing the route up a glacier at the base of the east ridge. A fog settled, minimizing visibility, and suddenly in a distance they heard the unmistakable roar of an avalanche. Everyone took shelter; Lou found only a change in the slope—a hummock—to hide behind. The avalanche hit, and he felt his back pelted with ice debris. Then it cleared, and all was quiet. Lou looked around, and slowly he realized the extent of the tragedy. He was the only one alive; all seven of his companions had been killed.

It seems safe to say most climbers would have hung up their ice axes and considered such miraculous escape as divine intervention, a celestial message to give up climbing. Lou not only continued, but his next major expedition took him back to Dhaulagiri, to take care of unfinished business. After reaching the summit, his first eight-thousand-meter peak, he went to the summit of Nanda Devi in 1976 and was now on K2 in 1978. Lou was no ordinary man with ordinary drives; he had some kind of devils running around inside, which apparently were exorcized—and then, I suspected, only temporarily—by brilliant accomplishment.

WE FINISHED LUNCH, and Lou helped to chop the tent platform before stringing rope up the icy slope above Camp II. After he left, I continued chopping. It was laborious work. Under a few inches of snow, the slope turned to hard ice and progress was slow. It was fascinating work, though, since I kept uncovering remnants from the Polish expedition —old hardhats, unused packets of fruit juice mix, candy wrappers, even a can of sausage that I opened and found to be tasty. I felt as archaeologists must during digs, stopping to wonder about the people who had left these mementos. What were their hopes, their frustrations, their fears? There had been nineteen of them, the best climbers in their country, and they had given this route everything they had. And missed. Only five hundred feet from the summit, and turned back. But they had got down safely, at least. I wondered what our own story would be few months hence.

Lou finished the ropes and came down to give me a hand. It was now late afternoon, time to head back to Camp I. The trip down would be easier than yesterday, we thought, with the ropes rearranged and safely secured. We began the long series of rappels. Skip and Chris were way down the slope, near the bottom. It was satisfying to see the ropes secured well, the ice screws well placed and tied off with nylon webbing to save carabiners. It was a much better job than Lou and I had done when we first placed the anchors; it gave me a warm feeling to know Chris and Skip had done it. Lou seemed pleased, too.

We called ABC on the walkie-talkie that evening to report that Camp II was established, with fixed ropes in place.

"Terrific," Jim replied. "That's wonderful news. Great job, you guys. I guess you'll be coming back down to ABC tomorrow for a rest? You deserve it."

We looked at each other, and winked. "Rest?" Lou said. "What for? No, we're going up in the morning to carry the first loads to Camp Two."

Back at ABC, everyone sitting around the radio looked at each other, surprised by the reply, but smiling and laughing.

"O.K., you tigers," Jim said over the radio. "We'll see you up there tomorrow. Most of us will be moving up to stay. Then in Urdu he added the word that meant Good Job! "Botacha!" he said.

FROM WICK'S JOURNAL

> July 17. A good day. Jim and I weren't able to get all the way to Camp III, although we didn't expect to. Got away about 8:00 A.M. and headed up the steep section of rope Lou had

fixed a few days before. Steeper than it appeared. Jim led the first pitch up very steep snow, to a corner where a small ice cliff forced us right. Then across a crevassed section, then a steep 150-foot pitch of snow and ice. This took us to the crest of the ridge and the bulk of the day's work.

Hot day. Sapped our energy. The upper mountain kept inching closer, however, and even the traverse didn't seem as long or foreboding. But make no mistake! This ridge is long and without letup in difficulty. The absolutely superb weather is enabling us to steadily move up the mountain. The storm days are coming; it is just uncertain when.

Tomorrow we should make it to the site of Camp III. It will be another long day. After that I'm not sure what. Descend to Camp I for a rest day, or hump loads from II to III. Glad Lou will be with us tomorrow. Spread the weight. Today packing two thousand feet of rope, numerous ice screws, pickets, and deadmen, while leading up steep ice, was hard work.

Jim is asleep. He dropped off right away when we got back; he's tired from the day's exertions. Being forty-nine years old and pushing the way he does is remarkable. There's not many like him. Lou is by himself in the dome tent next to ours. He apparently talks to himself as there are strange noises and mumblings emanating from his tent. He is undeniably strong, but his personality is somewhat different.

Sunlight still on the peaks. Thinking of you this minute Mary Lou.

July 18. What you might call another long day. But it was worth it. Camp III is ours at the foot of the formation the Poles called the Keystone. Roughly 22,300 feet. We reached the campsite at 4:45 P.M., and now we're back in Camp II just before dark. Must say I feel as though I've been pulled through a wringer. Getting dark, my headlamp batteries are low.

FOR SEVERAL DAYS, WHILE LOU, SKIP, CHRIS, and I had worked to Camp II, and then Jim and Wick and later Lou had pushed to Camp III, John Roskelley had been in ABC, sick. Rob had diagnosed a bronchial infection and had suggested strongly that John lay low, lest it develop into pneumonia. We had all been concerned for his health; if he did not get better, we would lose our strongest climber—the one we were counting on to do most of the leading across the traverse.

In the afternoon of July 17, while Jim and Wick pushed the first half of the route to Camp III and the rest of us humped loads to Camp II, John decided he felt good enough to start heading up the mountain. Rob advised otherwise, but John had had enough of ABC; he was itching to start leading and to help with the load carrying.

With John were Dianne Roberts, Diana Jagersky, and Terry Bech. Terry had also been out, with a sprained ankle he had suffered on the marathon trip to Urkudas with Jim, but now he too was feeling fit enough to start climbing. Dianne and Diana had been busy every day with the boring job of transporting food and gear up the glacier from ABC to Camp I. We now had enough confidence in our four Hunza porters, however, that we would let them continue that job while everyone else tackled the ridge. Except for Rob, who was still in ABC not feeling well, all of us would at last be in Camp I or above.

We heard John, Dianne, Diana, and Terry coming into camp before we saw them. They were carrying the stereo—or rather John was carrying it —and he again had the two speakers strapped to the outside of his pack. He discoed into camp, ice axe overhead, with the cut "Stayin' Alive," from the Bee Gees' *Saturday Night Fever*, playing at full volume. Over the next several weeks that was to become our theme song.

There was a party atmosphere in Camp I that afternoon. We mounted the stereo in the cook tent, and with a selection of more than fifty tapes we had everything from Chopin to Clapton, Bach to the Stones. Everybody was back early from the day's carry to Camp II, and with John and the rest in from ABC, we all lay in the afternoon sun swapping stories. Nobody was sure who threw the first snowball.

We immediately divided into two sides—the north side of the camp versus the south side. Snowballs flew everywhere; strategies formed. One side charged, then formed an invincible British Square. It fell like Khartoum, and they retreated to the equipment tent, or fort as it were. Lou, who had been quietly reading in the cook tent, walked out to see what the ruckus was all about and immediately caught a dozen snowballs from both sides.

Exhausted from the attacks and counterattacks at eighteen thousand feet, we all retreated into the cook tent for an afternoon snack. Dianne Roberts commented that we had to start thinking about product photographs for all the sponsors who had donated equipment for the climb.

"You don't have to worry about any for REI," somebody said. "Their logo will be seen in every shot." Most of our tents came from REI and had enormous REI logos stencilled on the rain flies, which would be prominent in every photograph of every camp.

Lou, who had quietly returned to his book, looked up and cracked, "Yes, I can see next year's REI catalogue now. 'Jim Whittaker says, We climbed K2 with equipment anyone can afford.' "

We all chuckled. John, who was obviously happy to be up with everyone, had a roguish look in his eye as he asked Dianne, "How about those gauze masks we use to keep the cold air out of our lungs? Need any product shots of those?"

He was referring to a mask many of us wore while climbing, particularly when it was cold, that looked like a painter's dust mask, but was designed to humidify and warm air as one breathed. Breathing so much cold, dry air is a common cause of coughs at high altitude.

"Oh, I suppose," Dianne answered. "Why, do you have some particular shot in mind?"

John left the tent, still with a twinkle in his eye. We continued talking, and in a few minutes Diana Jagersky groaned, "Oh no. I knew he was up to something."

We looked outside the tent and saw John approaching. Except for his boots, overboots, ice axe, and a breathing mask covering his privates—but just barely covering them—he was naked. Dianne shot a few quick photos.

"The *National Geographic* will love these," she said.

LOU LEFT THAT afternoon to join Jim and Wick at Camp II. By now, the trip from I to II was a milkrun with all the ropes properly adjusted and much of the snow stamped into a good trail. Jim and Wick had radioed earlier that they might need help, and we all agreed Lou should be the one to go. The next day he would help Jim and Wick push the remainder of the way to Camp III.

We also thought he might be able to deliver a message. While everyone was in a good mood, and there was that party atmosphere, there had been some earlier grievances. The principal one was that Jim was not doing a proper job with logistics, that instead of leading the route he should be down overseeing the load carrying. That morning, everyone had left camp to carry up the ridge, grabbing whatever equipment came to hand. It was obvious we needed a detailed plan specifying equipment priorities and earmarking which gear was destined for what camp. Each camp should have a "camp kit" of equipment, as Lou called it, and we agreed he should be the one to help Jim devise a suitable plan.

Other than that, things were going very well—almost too well. On big mountains it is easy to become overconfident, especially during spells of good weather when rapid progress is made. Over the next three days Camp III was established, almost all the supplies we would need on the upper mountain were carried to Camp II, and most of the team was healthy and strong.

On July 19, Jim announced the strategy for the next stage of the climb—an announcement we had been anxiously awaiting: the push to Camp IV. His decision was what most expected. The first team to lead would be John Roskelley, Bill Sumner, and Jim Wickwire. They would have two days to push the route. Then Chris Chandler and I would take over for two days and see if we could reach the Camp IV site.

Over the next two days, several of the team moved up to Camp II to begin ferrying equipment to Camp III, and later to support John, Bill, and Wick when they began the traverse. It was incredible to think that in less than a week we could be in Camp IV, having accomplished the most technically difficult part of the climb.

I was satisfied with the idea of climbing with Chris. I still harbored a secret desire to team up with Roskelley but Chris seemed to be going better, and he was excited about the chance to get out in the lead, especially on the steep ground of the traverse. I still had not had my talk with him, but by then I had convinced myself it really wasn't necessary. If we would just work as hard as we could, we might make a position for ourselves on the summit team. It was looking like we could get up the mountain by the middle of August, or even sooner. I started to think about being back in California for the fall surfing season, or maybe spending time traveling after the climb. The porters had invited us to their homes in Hunza . . . .

Everything was looking good. Everything, that is, except the wisps of high cirrus clouds moving in from the southwest, moving rapidly overhead at about forty thousand feet, darkening the afternoon sky, portending the first of many storms.

5

The Snow Butterfly

FROM THE FOGGY RECESSES OF HIS SUBCON-
scious, Jim Wickwire tried to piece together the disjointed scenes. He was
in his living room, in Seattle, arguing with Jim Whittaker.

"We can't just give up," he told Whittaker. "We can't just abandon the
mountain like that. We have to go back. We have to..."

The doorbell rang, and Wick answered. There was a messenger; he had
a telegram. Wick read it, and looked at Jim.

"There, you see. This does it. It says here there is another group this
very minute on K2, another American group, trying to climb the
mountain, and they're using *our* fixed ropes."

Wick said the last sentence with emphasis. Jim was convinced; they did
have to go back. Together they scurried around the house, quickly packing
gear and making plans for a lightning-quick return.

"But the permit," Jim said. "We've got to get the permit."

"We'll figure out something to tell the Pakistanis," Wick said. "They'll
have to give us the permit. We've got to go back now. Everybody is saying
we abandoned the mountain. I don't know why we left in the first place,
but we've got to go back. We can't let them climb the mountain. They're
using our fixed ropes. We shouldn't have left..."

Wick awoke to the voice of John Roskelley, poking his head through the
tent door. Lou, lying in his sleeping bag next to Wick, was already awake.
It was 5:30 A.M., July 22, the first day of our first major storm.

"It's snowing pretty heavy," John said. "There's quite a bit of accumula-

104

tion. Doesn't look like we'll be able to move today."

"Well, we can't expect to make progress every day," Lou said.

There were seven of us at Camp II; the rest of the team was at Camp I. Lou and Wick were in one tent, Bill Sumner was with Cherie Bech, John and I bunked together, and Chris Chandler was in the equipment tent, by himself.

"We've done pretty good so far," John agreed. "I guess we could all use a rest day. It's not a severe storm—yet, anyway. Still warm, and so far no wind. But on the other hand, there's a lot of new snow already."

"Fingers crossed it's a short one," Wick said, still groggy and still thinking about his dream, relieved it had been only that. The same one had been recurring lately, but usually he had awaken from it with a quiet satisfaction when he realized he had returned to K2, and was on its slopes. That morning however, the dream had left him with an unfathomable uneasiness.

We can't possibly have abandoned the mountain, Wick thought, wondering about the dream's meaning.

"I'm going back to the tent," John said, "and brew up some breakfast with my good-looking tent-partner."

"He couldn't be any worse than waking up and looking at this mug," Wick said, gesturing at Lou and laughing. He forgot his dream and began thinking about how to cope with the first storm. There were really only two alternatives: go down to Camp I and wait for weather to improve, or stay at Camp II and wait for weather to improve. There were a few trade-offs. On the one hand, it might speed acclimatization to spend a few days at Camp II, at about twenty thousand feet. It was not so high that the effects would be debilitating; on the contrary, it would probably speed the physiological adjustments that help the body work more efficiently with less oxygen. Also, if the storm lasted only a day or two, we would not have to reclimb the section to Camp II and could thus move quickly to Camp III and start the traverse. On the other hand, each one who stayed high would be eating food and burning fuel that had been carried to that level with much sweat and toil. Since more supplies were stockpiled a relatively short distance below, at Camp I, this was not as critical as it would be later in the trip at the higher camps, but it was still worth thinking about.

After a leisurely breakfast and a radio call to the others in Camp I, it was agreed we should stay in Camp II for at least another day to see if the weather would improve. In truth, we all welcomed the rest day; some of us had not really had a day off since arriving at the mountain. There was little to do but lie in the tents, nap, read, write in our journals, and talk. Wick and Lou spent the morning discussing the politics of the American Alpine Club, Lou's tragic trip to Dhaulagiri in 1969, and Wick's involvement in the 1975 K2 expedition that had led to the present trip. But by afternoon, they had decided their time would be better used devising a logistic plan for the later stages of the climb. Lou worked out a basic scheme; Wick provided a critique. Essentially, it was designed around an initial summit attempt by three people, with two backup teams. There would be minimal equipment carried to the upper camps, and most important, very little oxygen. Oxygen would be used only above Camp VI— on the way to the summit. Lou estimated that, with any luck with the weather, we could be in position for the first summit attempt as early as three weeks hence.

While we all agreed we should resist using oxygen until we absolutely had to, there was considerable disagreement on just what that point might be. Lou argued, with much logic, that if we were to use oxygen for anything but the summit attempt above Camp VI—that is, if it were used in hauling loads from Camp V to VI—the exponential increase in the number of bottles required at Camp V would, in all likelihood, take so much time to haul up as to prevent us from reaching the top. I realized what a luxury it had been on Everest, two years before, to have had forty-five Sherpas to haul oxygen up the mountain. There, we had started breathing "O's" at what now seemed the extravagantly low altitude of 24,500 feet.

Lou and Wick's initial plan was only one of many schemes that would come and go over the next several weeks; as their ideas were radioed down to those at Camp I, the only consensus seemed to be that we would have to wait and see. Meanwhile, John and I passed the day in our tent, talking less about the expedition and more about ourselves, getting to know one another better.

"Your wife has to be one of the more amazing people on earth," I told John, "to put up with you. You're never at home. You were on Jannu from February until May, then home for just a month before you left on this trip."

"And after this I'll be ice climbing in Canada," John reminded me. "Then in February, I leave again for Gauri Shankar, and after that directly to Uli Biaho without going home."

"How can you afford it?"

"Most trips don't cost me much—at least I've come that far. We'll probably get the fifteen hundred dollars back on this, for example." (We had each contributed $1500, to be paid back when and if the expedition recovered its debts, through magazine articles, lectures, and other revenues.*)

"But you still need some money for the trips. And then you have a house, a wife, a daughter . . ."

"She's a schoolteacher, and most of the burden is on her. I give some lectures when I'm home—as many as I can put together—and then do some odd-jobbing. If I could only sell that book it would help."

John had written a book on the Nanda Devi expedition, the one on which Devi Unsoeld had died. So far he had not found a publisher.

---

* Such as royalties from this book you're reading, the knowledge of which, I hope, takes some of the sting out of what you paid for it.

Knowing how much time and work went into writing a book, I sympathized with his frustration.

"You're one of the best climbers in the country, and as far as Himalayan-type climbing goes, you're far and away the best in the United States," I told him. "There ought to be some way you can make a living off that. Look at Messner. He's doing fine—house, plenty of dough, goes on trips all the time."

Reinhold Messner is generally considered the world's top mountain climber; he makes a very comfortable living writing books, lecturing, guiding, and endorsing products.

"Yeah, don't remind me. I keep telling Joyce that it's just around the corner, that this whole thing will start paying off. Sometimes I don't blame her for getting down, but I just know it will work out. Besides, there's no way I could stop climbing. It's just something I have to do."

There was a long pause as both of us lay on our sleeping bags, staring at the checkered pattern of the rip-stop nylon tent fabric. Then a smile broke over John's pensive face.

"Look what I'd be missing," he said, gesturing around. "Lying in this tent at twenty thousand feet, looking forward to a dinner of freeze-dried shrimp creole, cut with dehydrated margarine that tastes like sock squeezings, in a tent with a leaky roof. You'd have to be crazy to pass this up."

We both laughed; it was true. We would not have given it up for anything. At least not on the first day of the storm.

The second day was another matter. Both John and I had finished reading *Holocaust*, and the only other paperback around was a water-logged copy of *Don Quixote*. After the windmill scene I lost interest, despite Sancho Panza, and even with absolutely nothing else to do, I could not finish it. We lay there, staring at the tent walls, occasionally mumbling to each other. By using our radios, we did not have to leave our tent to talk with Lou and Wick, whose tent was about a hundred fifty feet away. We did not even have to go outside to pee; we had solved that one by cutting the mosquito netting away from the tent window and simply bellied up to it to relieve ourselves.

Fortunately we stayed in good humor, spending much of the time laughing at each other's rude jokes. That afternoon, still staring at the tent walls and listening to snow patter on the nylon, I looked over and saw John grinning to himself. He propped up on one arm, and looked at me.

"I'm sorry Rick—I apologize, for your sake."

"Sorry? About what?"

"Well, I'm sorry that I'm not a woman."

He lay back down, chuckling. John and I were getting along very well; in spite of his jokes, we both sensed a new friendship in the making, even if he were not a woman.

By the third day, the wind had picked up and it seemed colder. Frigid gusts buffeted the tents, making it necessary to go outside more frequently —two or three times a day—to shovel accumulated snow from the tent walls to prevent their collapsing. About three feet of new snow had built up. We knew that even if the storm ended soon, it would be an additional day or two—until the new snow either consolidated or avalanched —before we could resume climbing. It was clear the delay would last at least a week; we realized then it made the most sense to retreat to Camp I, thereby conserving supplies at Camp II.

We thought, however, that two people should stay to keep the tents free of snow and the camp open. Any of us would gladly have stayed—because of the advantage of more rapid acclimatization at the higher altitude—but to most of us, it did not matter much one way or the other. In fact, Bill Sumner had already rappeled back to Camp I the day before. John and I walked down to Lou and Wick's tent to have tea and discuss how best to retreat to Camp I.

"Whoever goes down should be able to help with the logistics planning," Lou said.

"That obviously includes you," Wick agreed, looking at Lou.

"Actually, both of us should go down," Lou replied, "although I would prefer staying up. Chris should also go down since he is supposed to be the oxygen expert. He should be included in any talks about when we should start using it, and consequently how many bottles we haul up."

"I'll go down, too," John said. "I don't mind adding my two cents to any discussions."

I did not feel I was instrumental in any logistics planning, so I mentioned I would not mind remaining at Camp II.

"Then you and Cherie should stay," Lou said.

"And that will split Chris and Cherie," I said, "which might not be a bad idea, considering all the rumors." I had brought up a delicate subject some of us had been surreptitiously discussing for over a week: a suspicion about the growing friendship between Chris and Cherie. During the approach march, before we reached Base Camp, Chris and Cherie were together a lot, though at the time no one thought much about it one way or the other. Once on the mountain, they usually climbed together. Soon after we reached Camp II, Cherie moved into the cramped equipment tent with Chris; the two of them ultimately switched to the larger dome tent after Bill Sumner went back to Camp I. We speculated that Bill was embarrassed sleeping by himself in the larger tent, but instead of making the logical but equally embarrassing suggestion that they swap tents, he chose to bail out to Camp I on only the second day of the storm.

John had been the first to mention the subject to me, shortly after we reached the site of Camp I, although I had been aware of the possibility before then. In a private moment, John had asked me what I thought.

"You're his best friend," he said; "you know him better than any of us."

"They're certainly becoming close friends," I said. "But I don't know any more than that."

"I wouldn't care myself," John said, "one way or the other, if I didn't think it would have an adverse effect on the climb. But look, there are only fourteen of us on this team, counting the four Hunzas. If Chris has something going with Cherie, and Terry finds out—which he has to—and gets upset, and all three end up leaving, that's twenty-five percent of our strength. It could very easily make the difference whether we get to the top. Not to mention the depressing effect it would have on the rest of the team. There just isn't any place on a climb like this for that sort of thing. I can't believe it. It's just like on the Nanda Devi expedition, before Devi died. Two of the team fell in love with her, and it almost finished the climb. It happens every time—I guess it's being up here in this snow and ice for months without any companionship—but if people can't handle themselves better, they shouldn't come. At least Devi was single and didn't have a husband along on the climb. If my wife ever did anything like that I'd shoot her, not to mention what I'd do to the guy."

"Maybe I should talk to Chris about it," I had suggested.

"That's a good idea. You're in the best position to do something."

But I never had. It was the same as my earlier intention to talk with Chris about my wanting to team up with John, instead of with him: every time I was alone with Chris and had the chance to bring it up, I waffled and swallowed the words.

"Maybe there's nothing to it," I tried to convince myself. "And maybe it really isn't any of my business, anyway." But I knew better. I was avoiding my obligation, as Chris's friend, to talk to him.

SO WHEN THE DISCUSSION SURFACED AT Camp II, it was not an entirely new subject.

"Do you really think something is going on?" Wick asked.

"It seems likely," I replied.

"Having suspicions like this on a climb can't be any good for any of us," Wick said.

"Hell," John added, "three people out of fourteen—that's nearly a quarter of our strength."

"If I had to put the blame on anyone," Lou said, "it would be Chris. But we still don't know if there's anything to this."

Again I felt guilt from not speaking to Chris earlier—perhaps that could have cleared this mess up before it progressed so far. But it probably would not have repaired the disappointment Lou was feeling toward Chris. Ever since we had first put in the Camp II route, when Chris knocked the rocks down on Skip and me, Lou's respect for Chris had been diminishing. He was less concerned about a clique of Chris and Cherie, thinking John's and my concern was sensationalistic, than about what he considered to be Chris's dawdling. Lou felt that Chris was not doing his share of the work; he thought Chris had been carrying light loads and taking too many rest days.

The day before the storm began, several of us had set out on the first major carry to Camp III, but Chris had stayed behind, as had Cherie and Bill Sumner. At high camp, after the long, difficult carry in increasingly thin air, we criticized all of them for not doing their share of the load carrying. It started to snow and John and I headed back for Camp II while Lou and Wick stayed to inventory the equipment. I was pleasantly surprised, on my way down, to see Chris, Cherie, and Bill heading toward me, carrying loads. Except for Bill, they were not carrying very much, but it was better than nothing. We greeted each other, then continued on. Later, they ran into Lou and Wick.

"Hello," Bill cheerfully called when seeing Lou and Wick approach. "Nice day to be in the mountains."

It was snowing harder. The white, colorless sky was like a thin solution of the snow, and the climbers floated in the amorphous white.

Lou was surprised to see them. "It's a little late to be out in this weather," he said.

He then inspected their loads so he could add the contents to the inventory list, and noted that Chris carried only one oxygen bottle and a few fuel cartridges—about twenty pounds in all. Cherie had even less.

"You guys aren't carrying too much today," Lou said. He had noticed both Chris and Cherie seemed defensive.

"We had a late start," Chris replied.

"You should get moving a little sooner."

"I guess we all can't be supermen."

"I suppose I should tell you we have been talking about you at Camp Three and your names have been taken in vain."

This was too much for Cherie; she started crying. Lou had not meant to be so critical, but he realized his words had caused more injury than he intended. Lou had not known Chris had been sick that day and had forced himself to carry anyway, even though his load was light. Chris was taken aback at Lou's criticism: he had expected people to be pleased that he was carrying at all. Whatever the merits of each side of the story, the fact remained that a schism between Lou and Chris was growing.

"LET'S GO BACK to the tent," I said to John, "and tell Chris it will be best if he goes down with the three of you."

John and I scampered back along the seventy-foot handline that connected Lou and Wick's tent with our own. The tent that Chris and Cherie occupied was within calling distance of ours; I shouted over, and Chris poked his head out the door.

"Listen, we've been discussing what to do with Wick and Lou, and everybody agrees four should go down, and two stay. It seems best that those who go down be the ones who could add most to the logistics planning that needs to be done at Camp I. Since you're the oxygen officer, we figured you should be there. Cherie and I can stay up here and shovel snow."

"I don't want to go down," Chris yelled back. "I just got up here."

"But we need you down there—you're in charge of the oxygen."

"Big deal. I couldn't tell them anything they don't already know. Besides, I want to stay up and acclimatize."

I pulled my head back in the tent and looked at John.

"Well, we can't *make* him go back down," I said.

Chris was probably right in thinking he could not tell anybody anything they did not already know about the oxygen systems, but I sensed he resented our deciding—without consulting him at all—that he should descend. John and I radioed Lou and Wick.

"He doesn't want to go down," I told Lou.

"That's it," Lou said. "Wick and I are heading down in a few minutes with or without anybody else. You guys do what you want." They left that evening. John and I decided to stay one more day, partly in the hope that the weather would improve, but also to determine whether Chris would change his mind about going down. But the following morning, the weather continued bad with even more snow and wind. John and I descended to Camp I.

WE CROWDED INTO THE CARAVAN TENT AT Camp I. Except for Chris and Cherie, all of us were there, including the four Hunzas. The stereo, with speakers hanging in the tent corners, played an old Joan Baez album of Dylan tunes. In another corner, Diana Jagersky cooked dinner. After so many days of skimpy high-altitude rations, it was wonderful to dine on what we considered "home cooking": dried split-pea soup with chopped canned ham and, best of all, freeze-dried jumbo shrimp with cocktail sauce.

It was much more comfortable waiting out the storm at Camp I. The cook tent was more a community center. We could sit inside, drink tea, read, listen to the stereo, or gossip; even sleeping tents were not so small and crowded as those at Camp II. And there were useful projects to do.

Lou and Jim compared notes on strategies for the upper part of the climb; fortunately, even though they had developed their plans independent of one another, they agreed on many crucial points.

They felt we should carry only a minimal supply of oxygen high on the mountain and try to avoid using it at all below Camp VI. For the first time, there was also detailed discussion of alternative routes near the summit. Unlike most other ridges on K2, whose crests continued to the very summit of the peak, our ridge—the northeast—terminated in a broad snow dome more than three thousand feet below the top, at the foot of the great summit pyramid. That suggested two options: we could either climb directly up the face of the summit pyramid, as the Poles had tried, but failed, to do in 1976; or traverse left under the pyramid headwall until we joined the Abruzzi Ridge route, following that to the summit. The first option, the "Polish finish," as we started calling it, was a direct line to the summit, and therefore—from an aesthetic point of view—more attractive. In addition, it had never been completely climbed. The second option, the Abruzzi, except for the traverse to reach it, was known territory, having been climbed to the summit by two previous expeditions. There was little doubt we could get to the summit on this Abruzzi route, provided we could successfully traverse from our ridge over to it.

Whether that would be true of the Polish finish was another question. At about twenty-seven thousand feet, there was a very steep ice and rock section—in one place it was near-vertical for at least a hundred feet—and we knew we would have to fix ropes. This meant, in all probability, that one team would have to climb up and fix the section—a job that would take all day—then come back down, sacrificing their chances of reaching the summit; a second team would follow the next day, using the fixed ropes, and go on to the top. Sitting around sipping tea, we considered the merits of each strategy. We concluded, at least for the time being, that we should try to pursue the Polish finish if at all possible. It would, quite simply, be the grandest way to complete the climb.

While the rest of us kicked more ideas around, Bill Sumner began teaching climbing techniques to the four Hunza porters. Of all of us, Bill spent the most time with the HAPS, and along with Diana was becoming their good friend. Bill immensely enjoyed hearing about their life in Hunza, about their experiences on other expeditions, about their religion (unlike the majority of Pakistanis, they were Ismaili moslems, followers of the Aga Khan).

Bill found that the HAPS, especially Honar Baig and Gohar Shah, possessed considerable natural climbing ability; they quickly caught on to technical ice climbing techniques, learning to use crampons and ice axes to climb the steep ice blocks around camp. We hoped they would be able to help carry loads higher on the mountain. It was clear, however, that even with Bill's excellent lessons, they had limited experience and would have to be closely watched.

An incident a few days earlier had dramatically emphasized this; only luck had prevented an injury, or worse. During the storm, the four HAPS slept at Advance Base Camp, and when visibility permitted they carried loads up to Camp I. The third day of the storm was particularly bad; no one on the upper part of the mountain moved. The team at Camp I radioed the Hunzas at ABC, telling them there was no need to come to

Camp I if they did not want to. But it was a matter of pride; they were trying to impress us with their efforts to do their share of the work. Despite foggy conditions on the glacier, they decided to make the carry.

Later that morning we heard distant shouts. Visibility on the glacier was less than a hundred yards. Diana Jagersky took a radio and walked out a short distance from Camp I, yelling as loud as she could, "Radio! Radio!" In a minute the HAPS turned on their walkie-talkie, and Gohar Shah's voice came over the air.

"Hello. This is Gohar Shah."

"Gohar Shah, this is Diana. Are you O.K.?"

"Hello. This is Gohar Shah."

"This is Diana. Are you O.K.?"

"Hello, this is Gohar Shah. Yes. Yes. No. I mean no."

Gohar was having trouble transmitting with his walkie-talkie. The trouble was compounded by his barely comprehensible English.

"Gohar. What is wrong? Are you O.K.?"

"Hello? This is Gohar Shah. We have small problem. Honar Baig in crevasse."

"Oh no. Is he O.K. Is he hurt? Call to him and see if he is O.K."

"Yes," replied Gohar. "Honar Baig in crevasse."

"Call to Honar Baig," Diana repeated, with growing frustration. "Ask him if he is O.K."

The radio crackled with static, and Diana was afraid they had improperly adjusted the squelch control. But in a minute another voice came over the air.

"Hello, this is Honar Baig. I am in crevasse."

"You mean you are out of the crevasse, or in it?" Diana asked.

"This is Honar Baig. Have problem. In crevasse."

"Honar Baig, are you hurt?" Diana persisted.

"In crevasse, upside down."

Diana listened incredulously. The HAPS had lowered the walkie-talkie on a rope to Honar Baig, who was talking from the bottom of the crevasse thirty feet down, where he was wedged, nearly upside down, between two ice walls. In the background of their transmission, Diana heard, very very faintly, the voices of the other three HAPS, who must have been leaning over the lip of the crevasse, yelling frantically, "Honar Baig in crevasse! Honar Baig in crevasse!"

"Hold on, Honar Baig," Diana urged. "We will come and help you. Don't move."

A rescue party went out for them. When they arrived they found Honar sitting on the edge of the crevasse. He had managed to climb out using his jumar clamps, but instead of attaching his leg loops, he had grasped the rope ascenders and somehow pulled himself all the way out using only his arms. His injuries were relatively minor—a sprained wrist, sore shoulder, cut nose; he was lucky they were not more serious. But we realized we would have to be more careful with the HAPS. We could not depend on them to get themselves out of trouble in case of accident.

ON JULY 26, the fifth day of the storm, Saleem announced, via radio from Base Camp, the arrival of a group of porters carrying food rations for the HAPS, and most important to us, the mailbag from Skardu. It had been several weeks since any of the team had had news from home. Saleem told us there were ninety-five letters in the bag. Four climbers volunteered to go down and return the next day with the mail. About midmorning, Jim Whittaker, Jim Wickwire, Rob Schaller, and Dianne Roberts roped together and began the long descent to Base Camp. Despite the continuing storm, all four of them had a wonderful trip. Although nothing particularly unusual had happened, for Dianne Roberts it was one of those rare times when perceptions crystalize to a sharp lucidity, when somehow all the elements seem to fit just right, leaving one with an experience that is mystical, perhaps even religious. In a letter written to Susanne and Jake Page, close friends back home, Dianne described the journey:

> During the last storm that prevented us from working high on the mountain, Jim, Wick, Rob, and I made a trip from Camp I to Base Camp (a *very* long walk) to pick up the mail. On the way down it was snowy and foggy—a total whiteout. Walking on the glacier is rather dicey at the best of times—lots of hidden crevasses—but on this day it was downright dangerous. Jim was leading and he couldn't even tell if he was walking in a straight line. Wick and I, roped behind him, kept guiding him left or right as he probed for crevasses. It took two and a half hours to reach Advance Base (normally a fifty-minute trip) then another two hours to Base. But Jim, Wick, and I felt great—we are all very close anyway—and even Rob, whose normal mood is morose, admitted it was a good trip even though he had felt the weather had been too bad to leave camp that morning.
>   Returning to Base Camp, after a couple of weeks on the ice and snow, was wonderful. That miserable heap of rocks at the base of K2 seemed like heaven. All the colors of the rocks and the sky had an intensity I had never seen before. The grubby Askole porters, who had carried up loads of flour and rice and sugar—and our mail—greeted us with open arms, and Saleem, our liaison officer who (bless his soul) is stuck down there tending the radio, was so happy to see us he embraced us and treated us to a feast of goat meat and chapatties. We spent the night there in the thick air at 16,500 feet (you can't believe how heavy the air at 16,000 feet seems after being up around 20,000 for awhile) and the following morning we trekked back up the glacier to Camp I. On the way up, the wind abruptly shifted 180 degrees, coming from China instead of Concordia, and the sun shone through for the first time in eight days. Jim

again led the way (our tracks from the previous day were covered). It was very slow going; we all had very heavy packs; we were plowing through deep snow; we had to beware of hidden crevasses. But for some reason I felt calm and very happy. The pace was perfect for daydreaming, and my thoughts drifted back home. I thought of Annie Dillard (she lives, I think, in the San Juan Islands), and how beautifully she writes, and how I wished I could write like that, and how I somehow knew, intuitively, we would like each other, and that perhaps, when I got home, I should write her a letter, and maybe, somehow, meet her. But of course I won't. I remember I felt the same way about Joni Mitchell—that instinctive kinship—and I never wrote her either.

Anyway, it was one of those days in the mountains—the days one wishes all days were like—when all the rhythms matched up, when even the hard work flowed, effortlessly, without pain; one of those days when I knew my companions felt exactly the same, when there was no need to talk because there was everything to say but no way of saying it, when even the sun beating down, burning my face, was somehow welcome and the heaviest load sat on my back like a feather. It was the sort of day I wish could happen more often, but that I am thankful happened even once.

The 180 degree shift in the wind Dianne had mentioned was indeed the herald of improved weather—the long-awaited end of the storm. We made plans to return to Camp II. We radioed Chris and Cherie, who said they would descend the next morning to pull the fixed ropes from beneath the new snow, and more important, to kick down the fresh accumulation —which would help minimize the danger of avalanches hitting those climbing up.

Everyone was up early. After breakfast we prepared our loads for the carry to Camp II. Four of us planned to spend the night there: John Roskelley, Bill Sumner, Jim Wickwire and me. Over the previous few days we had designed a new strategy for the next stage of the climb—moving back up to Camp III, then negotiating the difficult traverse to Camp IV. Instead of Wick, Bill, and John taking the first crack at it with Chris and me the second, as we had originally planned, Jim had decided to have John and me spend the first two days fixing ropes. Then Bill and Wick would take over. With any luck, we would reach Camp IV in one push.

There were several reasons for the change. Bill, feeling he was not climbing very fast at the higher altitudes, preferred to be on the second team. And, since Wick had put in the route to Camp III, it was felt the next lead should go to someone else. That John should be among those to lead across the knife-edged ridge was never questioned: not only had he not yet done any lead climbing, but he was the most proficient technical ice climber in the group. Needless to say, I was delighted to have the chance not only to climb with John, but to climb with him across the most difficult terrain on our route. For me, it was the major turning point in the expedition.

The person most obviously left out was Chris. During the days he and Cherie had stayed at Camp II, there had been much secretive discussion in Camp I, and nearly everyone there felt that the two should descend. I cared less about the actual friendship developing between Chris and Cherie than about how it might injure Terry, weaken Chris's chance of being on a summit team, or in general create disharmony that could possibly jeopardize the expedition's chances of success.

Unfortunately neither I nor anyone else brought our concerns directly to Terry. If we had, we might have prevented many future problems, for Terry was in no way worried. He knew Chris and Cherie were becoming close friends, and he himself saw in Chris a future friend. But he felt they were being selfish by staying high so they could better acclimatize, eating food all of us had worked hard to deliver to that altitude, while everyone else waited out the storm in Camp I. The rest of us assumed Terry's increasing moroseness, as the storm continued, was from other concerns.

Jim Whittaker had been keeping a low profile. As a person who himself values his private moments, he was inclined to let others do the same— unless, of course, it began to have an adverse effect on the expedition as a whole. Apparently, he had not seen Chris's and Cherie's friendship as any problem. No doubt his attitude was influenced by Dianne; she grumbled that Cherie was being victimized by male chauvinists, particularly John Roskelley. Dianne felt a sharp repugnance for John's attitude that he would never "permit" his own wife to behave in such a manner; in fact, she thought John's marital mores—and for that matter many of his other beliefs and values—smacked of some medieval code of ethics designed to maintain male supremacy.

But regardless of Jim's personal attitude, the team had asked him to do something. His only action, however, was to call Chris midway through the storm and tell him it would be "politically expedient" to descend. To the bewilderment of nearly everyone Chris chose to stay at Camp II. Finally, Jim realized that, at a minimum, Chris would have to come back to Camp I after the storm to at least discuss the problem, and that if Chris were to be put in the lead as we worked toward Camp IV, it would be only in support of Bill and Wick.

Many of the team believed it had been a mistake for Jim not to order Chris to descend earlier, that he had not recognized, in this ignoble affair, the seeds of future disharmony. Perhaps had we all better communicated our concerns; perhaps, had Jim been more forceful in asking Chris and Cherie to descend, we could have forestalled the acrimony and animosity, the poison, that were to divide our team.

I CAUGHT UP WITH LOU AND JOHN ABOUT
half an hour out of Camp I, where the fixed ropes started up the steep
slopes to Camp II. They were stopped at the bottom of the first rope,
staring up the thousand feet of snow, ice, and rock that led to the crest of
the ridge. My first thought was that they were waiting for Chris, who
must be somewhere above, clearing the ropes and kicking loose the
avalanche-prone snow. That morning Lou had talked to Chris on the radio
and told him we would meet him partway down the lower ropes. But
Chris was not in sight.

"I'm reluctant to start up the ropes," John said. "It just smells funny.
Too much new snow. It looks very unstable."

"I think we should definitely wait for Chris to come down and clear the
way," Lou said.

We decided to dig a test pit and study the snow. Looking down the hole,
we could see three layers, the bottom of which seemed to be resting on
hard ice spread with a coating of little ice ball-bearings—good conditions
for a slab avalanche. We waited for Chris.

"Maybe he thinks we are climbing higher," I suggested, "and will rendezvous with him farther up."

"Maybe," John said. "But it's not worth going up just to deliver a few
loads of food and oxygen."

"You've survived more climbs than any of us," I agreed.

"Yeah, and I've backed off a hell of a lot of them, too," John added.
"That may be one reason I'm still around."

"I think there's a ninety-five percent chance it's O.K.," Lou said. "But
let's not forget one thing: about five miles from here a friend of ours is
buried right now. Nick Estcourt landed on the five percent."

Saying no more, we cached our packs under a rock and returned to
Camp I. It was frustrating to lose yet another day after being penned up
for so long, but none of us doubted we had made the right decision. There
was more than one person in camp, later that afternoon, who cursed Chris
for not descending all the way and clearing the ropes.

On the radio that evening Chris said he had descended three hundred
feet down the gully below the ridge, but he had not seen anyone. He
thought we had decided not to come up.

"Of course he didn't see anyone," Wick commented, somewhat acerbi-
cally. "If his job is to knock down avalanches, does he think we would be
standing in the middle of an avalanche gully where he could see us?"

Jim "ordered" Chris to come down the next morning.

"Why don't you plan on meeting us here in Camp One for breakfast,"
Jim told Chris, "nice and early, say about seven."

Lou left camp first the following morning and met Chris near the base
of the ridge. Cherie was a distance behind, descending more slowly.

"Basically there are three things we're upset about," Lou said to Chris.
"One is that you didn't come down earlier when Whittaker made several

suggestions that it would be a good idea. The other is that you didn't come down at all yesterday to break trail for us as you said you would, causing us to lose an entire day. And finally, because it seems your friendship with Cherie is upsetting Terry, and that is affecting the whole team."

"Let me take these one at a time," Chris replied. "First, Jim never ordered us down. He said something like it would be nice if we came down, but he never ordered us. He made it sound like we could come down if we wanted to—and we didn't want to. But I did come down yesterday."

"Funny we didn't see you. What time was it?"

"Well, after we got the call from you—about seven—we made breakfast, got our gear in order, and left about ten."

"It seems you could have left a little earlier than that. We had given up by ten and were back in camp."

"I came down the ridge and looked over and didn't see anybody. The weather was still questionable, and I wasn't sure you were coming up . . ."

"You should have come down all the way to camp. But there's nothing to do about it now—the day has been lost. What about you and Cherie?"

"Do I have to clear it with you, Lou, before I choose who my friends are on this trip? That's my business—not yours."

"It's my business—it's everybody's business—when it affects the team."

"Then I'll talk to Terry when we get to camp. I really doubt he considers it to be the problem you guys seem to think it is."

Lou went on up. Chris passed John and me at the bottom of the ropes. John more or less said the same thing Lou had. I told Chris I thought it might be a good idea if he talked with Jim and apologized for not coming down.

"Whittaker's not mad at anybody," I said. "All you've got to do is start working hard and you'll have as good a chance as anybody to make the summit. You know how he's going to choose the summit team. He'll pick whoever is out there doing the most, working the hardest. That's the kind of climber Jim likes."

"O.K.," Chris promised. "I'll talk to him."

"There's one other thing," I said. "I feel kind of bad—I think I should have talked to you earlier. That's what friends are supposed to be for. I just never brought it up. Sorry."

Chris continued down. We met Cherie a few minutes later.

"We should tell you that people are a little upset back in camp," John said.

"I just talked to Lou," Cherie said acidly. "I'm tired of hearing all this stuff about Terry being upset. Everyone whispering behind our backs. You're all bastards. Bastards, bastards, bastards."

"Look, we could care less what goes on as long as it doesn't affect the team and the climb," John said.

"What do you mean what goes on? I'm sick of all this gossiping," Cherie started to cry.

"It's not that big a problem," I told her. "I'm sure it will be easy to clear up."

"O.K.," Cherie said. "I'll talk to Terry and the others in camp." She worked her way down the ropes.

John and I made Camp II about ten-thirty. We moved back into the tent we had left several days before, finding much of our gear wet, but knowing it would dry in the afternoon heat. There were still a few clouds in the sky, and haze hung over the summits of Broad Peak and K2. It seemed, however, as if the storm were clearing. We felt confident we would have good weather for the trip to Camp IV. I was excited with the anticipation of going out on the traverse, of exploring new territory, of doing some hard climbing with John. And I looked forward to leaving behind, for a few days anyway, the wrangling and squabbling and bickering. Gazing up at the great summit pyramid peeking through the clouds after so many days of storm, our little contentions seemed so petty. I only hoped that, in the weeks ahead, we would be able to measure up to the majesty of such a mountain.

July 30. CRYSTAL AIR. NO CLOUDS, NO WIND. A summer feeling, the earth falling away before us to a distant, curved horizon, an indigo sky. It was the sky of a day after a long storm: a sky with no dust or pollution, no opaqueness; a sky that was a vacuum, like a sky on the moon. A mountain a hundred miles away appeared in minute detail, as if it could be touched.

I moved with deliberate, even steps, kicking the toe of my boot into the surface snow, feeling my crampons bite the ice underneath, then moving my axe, then my other foot. Pace. In our packs we had twelve hundred feet of rope, which we intended to string all that day; so far, we had a good start, but we had much ground to cover and would make it only if we kept up an exact, deliberate pace. I regulated my breathing to harmonize with the movements of my feet—I knew this would conserve energy, allowing me to maintain a better pace, all day, without stopping.

I turned around to see John belaying me, standing on a snow platform cut in the steep slope about two hundred feet away. We had worked out a system for rapidly fixing the ropes: for this first section I would lead out, tied to the end of the rope, while John progressively fed it out, belaying through the anchors we had placed at this station. Every so often, I would put in another anchor—an ice screw, a picket, a deadman, or a piton—clipping the rope through it to decrease the length of a fall in case I should slip. When I got to the end of a two-hundred- or three-hundred-foot section (the rope was cut in varying lengths), I would anchor it, and while

John jumared across, I would rearrange the next sling of climbing hardware and uncoil a new section of rope. When John reached me he would immediately tie in to the new rope, pick up the already organized hardware sling, and start along the next section. I would rest while belaying John on his lead, then the cycle would repeat. On the extremely steep sections with loose rock—where a fall was a very real possibility—we would add an extra, heavier, belay rope.

I continued my lead, keeping to a steady, even pace. The altitude was 22,600 feet. I felt strong, very strong; I knew I could go all day without stopping, not even for lunch. I knew we could string the twelve hundred feet. This was my chance: if I put in a good performance climbing with John here, I might possibly earn my place on the summit team.

I stopped, examined a large rock that looked ideal for looping with a sling to provide a protection point, then climb up to the top of it. There was an old piece of white rope frozen partway under the rock—the Poles had also used it for an anchor. At the top of the rock I was on the knife's edge and could gaze down the Pakistan side of the ridge. As if mounting a horse, I threw one leg over the crest and straddled it while I worked the sling into place. With the rope clipped through, I moved on, soon reaching its end. I placed another anchor and tied off the rope. John started up and joined me at the belay stance.

We were climbing on the edge of a knife. The slope dropped away on both sides, steeply, dramatically, to glaciers thousands of feet below. We had crossed the ridge and dropped a few feet below its crest, traversing. For the first time, we were in China.

"I'm not sure I remembered to get my visa," John quipped.

"I don't think there's anyone around to check our passports," I replied.

There was an excitement in working so precisely, so efficiently, and a satisfaction in seeing the years of practice and honing of skills, the years of climbing on lesser peaks, paying dividends in such a grand manner.

John's first lead was steeper, across rocks and ice, then up a pointed gendarme—a pinnacle—rising out of the ridge. Once over the gendarme, he disappeared. Presently, I heard him call me. The rope was anchored; I could climb up. My rest had been very short. I traversed, then climbed up the gendarme to his station. Again the hardware was ready, a fresh rope uncoiled. I tied in to the rope and was off on the next lead, carefully dusting snow from the rocks, delicately placing my steel-spiked crampons on the stone. I felt superb, climbing catlike. We were still traversing—not gaining altitude, but moving horizontally along the edge of the knife. One hundred feet, one hundred fifty, then the end of the rope. I anchored it and John came across. He tied in to the next one and was gone. Precision. Efficiency. Twelve noon and we had already fixed more than seven hundred feet of rope. I knew we could finish the twelve hundred by the end of the day.

It was my turn to belay, my turn to rest. My only duty was to feed out the rope around my waist to John while he climbed. For the first time that morning, I studied the terrain to the north—the remote, uninhabited Shaksgam district of China's Sinkiang Province. Visibility was extraordinary: it was possible to see for distances that must have been much more than a hundred miles. The sere mountains stretched away, into foothills, punctuated occasionally by glacier-covered peaks. One peak about thirty miles inside China, to the west of K2's north glacier, rose white and black out of a sea of brown hills like the dorsal of an Orca.

We could also see the lower section of K2's north ridge. Entirely on the Chinese side of the mountain, this ridge is one of the most outstanding features of mountain architecture of earth. It rises at a continuous angle of forty-five to fifty degrees, uninterrupted by any major steps or irregularities in its crest, from the head of the north glacier to the summit, a vertical rise of nearly fifteen thousand feet. It is the longest uninterrupted mountain ridge on earth. No one has ever attempted to climb it, though there was a rumor a group of Chinese tried to reconnoitre it a few years ago. It is, without doubt, one of the most awesome challenges remaining for tomorrow's mountaineers.

I carefully studied the hills beyond the north glacier, wondering if perhaps I could see a road or other sign of human passage. When Jim, Wick, Rob, and the others had been planning the 1975 K2 attempt, they had studied satellite photographs that appeared to show Chinese roads within forty miles of K2. But all I could see was unmarked, barren hills, burnt brown in the rain shadow of the Karakoram.

Despite the loneliness of that wild place, we were within a few hundred miles of Lop Nor, the Chinese test site for nuclear bombs; in a radio call a few days before, Saleem had said he heard on a Radio Pakistan broadcast that the Chinese had just exploded another bomb in an above-ground test. The winds were blowing lightly from that direction. Standing on a snow platform cut in a ridge at twenty-two thousand feet, looking over one of the most vast, remote areas on earth, I wondered if I was being dangerously exposed to radioactive fallout. I laughed—cautiously—at the absurdity of the idea.

John was halfway out on his rope. It would soon be my turn again. I paid out the line, watching the bright red coils contrasting with the snow crystals as they looped off. If I moved my head just right, I could see light refractions in the crystals; I stared fixedly at these miniature rainbows. My mind drifted, hypnotized by sharp colors and thin air and warm sun. A butterfly landed near the rope. It was a beautiful butterfly, about three inches across, piebald orange and black like the painted lady butterfly back home. I remembered how I used to catch butterflies just like that one when I was a kid. With my butterfly net made out of cheesecloth. What a collection I had . . .

A butterfly? At twenty-two thousand feet?

I came out of my trance, blinked, and looked again. It was still there, sitting on the rope, slowly unfolding, then closing, its wings.

"John," I yelled. "You'll never believe this. There's a butterfly here sitting on the rope."

"Yeah, there's more over here. They're flying in all around."

I spotted two, three, four more. In no time there were a dozen, then twenty, then I counted thirty, a cloud of them flying up from some unknown place in China, rising on air currents up the mountain ridge. I noticed many of them landing in the snow, sticking to the ice crystals, dying. What could have been the reason for this lemming migration? I was still much affected by the spectacle as I jumared up to John and took the next lead.

We continued leapfrogging leads until, at 5:00 p.m., we had stretched out and anchored the last section of rope. Twelve hundred feet of steep ridge was behind us, fixed with rope. We were twelve hundred feet closer to the summit of K2. With the steep ridges and faces of nearby Skyang Kangri orange with alpenglow, we turned and retreated toward the shelter of our tent at Camp III, still silent, absorbed in the magic of a perfect day. We moved with a slower, relaxed tempo, looking over the wilds of China and Pakistan like evening eagles soaring in the rare air of high places. We came to a section where we walked the narrow ridge crest, balancing on the edge of the knife—the exact border between China and Pakistan. The sun was setting behind K2. The low light caused a rare and dramatic phenomenon: our shadows were cast across the Godwin-Austen Glacier below, and as we moved our arms the shadows swept across miles of snow and rock. There was even more witchery, a rainbow halo around the shadow of our heads. Like Gods of Valhalla we ruled—for the few minutes the sun hovered at that acute angle—a land of ice and snow.

We got back to the tent at last twilight. It was an effort to unstrap our crampons, store our harnesses, ice axes, and packs, and crawl into the tent, not to rest but to start melting snow to cook dinner on our little stove. Tomorrow would be another long, long day. Again, we would have to rise at 4:00 a.m., climb back over the ropes we had just fixed, and start stringing more. But we were confident we would reach the camp site.

"We're most of the way there," we radioed the others. "Tomorrow we should make it to Camp Four. From where we stopped today, it looked like there's another section of very steep ice, then a large gendarme to pass one way or another. But we'll get around it, and that should put us very close to Four."

"Unbelievable!" Jim radioed back. "You guys are real tigers."

But not everyone below was as sanguine as we were. Knowing it had taken the Poles ten days to cover the same distance, here were John and I claiming we would fix it in two. Several of the others took a wait-and-see attitude. But there was no denying we had made terrific progress.

We finished our scant meal of an anonymous flavor of freeze-dried food. We had been too tired even to cook it. We had added hot water, waited a minute, and eaten the meal. By the time we finished melting water for breakfast and for the next day's climbing, it was 11:00 P.M. Before falling asleep I made a few notes, writing by headlamp, in my journal:

> When I'm next asked that frequent question, "Why do you climb?" the answer will be easy. All I will have to do is tell them what it was like climbing on K2 on July 30, 1978. That is if, with words, I can possibly come close to conveying a day so full of magic.

July 31. BY 7:30 ON THE SECOND DAY OF OUR efforts to complete the traverse, John and I had reached the end of the ropes that marked the high point of the previous day's climb. Aided by the Polish ropes that were still usable in a few places, we were moving very fast. John took the first lead, then we alternated until 3:30, when we decided to return to Camp III. But we had not reached Camp IV. We realized our previous day's optimistic appraisal had been premature when we came to the large gendarme that, from our vantage point the day before, we had only partially been able to see. It turned out to be more difficult than we had expected, but we climbed it. John led the steepest section; we felt we were only a short distance from Camp IV, and that we could have made it that day had we only had a little more rope and a little more time. Again, our optimism would be short-lived.

We arrived back at Camp III earlier than we had the previous day, extremely tired. This time, at least, we did not have to cook dinner. Bill Sumner and Jim Wickwire had arrived. They greeted us, as we climbed into camp, with steaming mugs of hot chocolate. I wrapped my cold fingers around the warm cup and slowly let the hot liquid run down my throat and spread its warmth through my body. One of the lessons one learns from hard climbing is how satisfying something simple can be. It is a valuable lesson; for the rest of your life, hot chocolate will have a special quality you will never forget. When I drink hot chocolate now, even if I am otherwise warm, I wrap my fingers tightly around the mug.

That evening, there were low clouds down toward Concordia. Worse were the lenticulars over both Broad Peak and K2. We refused to believe that, after such a long storm, we could have only two days of clear skies before more bad weather; we hoped the lenticulars were only false warnings. Our hopes were unfulfilled. By morning it was snowing lightly, just as it had been the first day of the last storm.

It was not so bad, however, that we could not climb, so we were up before first light at 4:45 A.M. As usual, John was the first to stir. He lit the stove and began the hour-long job of melting snow. I knew I would soon have to unzip my bag and let in the cold air, then begin to pack my gear in my rucksack—my fingers would go numb—then work into my insulated boots, still frost-covered—my toes would also go numb for at least half an hour, until feeling came back in razor jabs of pain. I did not want to open my eyes; I did not want to move. My leg muscles ached from the hard climbing the day before. I felt enervated.

Maybe I could tell the others I needed a rest day. According to the original plan, Wick and Bill were to take over the lead. But John and I had volunteered to carry ropes and equipment behind them to speed things up, and I knew our assistance would be useful.

I heard Wick stir in his bag and say something about "time to get ready." Bill, perhaps feeling as I did, was not moving.

I lay still, seeking the motivation to get up. I tried not to lose sight of the overall picture: think about the summit and how important it is; maybe it hurts to get up this one morning, and you have to fight with yourself to do it, but months and even years from now it will all seem worth it. Think of the overall picture.

John was busy with breakfast; Wick was starting to get dressed. Then the feeling that was my single best motivator on such mornings began to creep over me: guilt.

I thought, So you're going to let your mates do all the work while you laze away the morning in the sack. Let John do all the cooking. Let Wick organize all the gear.

That was enough. I could not stand myself any longer. I rose up on one arm, sighed good morning to everyone, and prepared to get under way.

We were confident we could reach Camp IV that day. Bill and Wick left first, as planned, to climb to our previous high point and then start onto new ground. John and I followed, pausing every now and then to retie anchors or adjust rope tensions, improving the route. We caught up with Bill and Wick around nine. They were moving slowly, especially Bill. John and I sat on our packs, watching snowflakes gently settle and stick to our clothing, patiently waiting while Bill very slowly led out on the ridge. Realizing there was little we could do, John and I decided to return to Camp III. We also realized we would not that day reach our new campsite. But when Bill and Wick returned later that afternoon, they said they had got to within a couple hundred yards, and unless the snow increased, there was no doubt we would make it the next day.

Meanwhile, the rest of the team had been busy ferrying loads to Camps II and III. Lou Reichardt, for two days straight, had carried heavy loads from Camp I direct to Camp III, descending to Camp I in a single day. That was twice the distance the others were carrying. The lower camps were consolidating rapidly. If the weather held, and we could get a few loads across the traverse to Camp IV, we would be in position to strike at the upper part of the mountain. Three days earlier (before the clouds again moved in) Jim Whittaker had dictated to his tape-recorded "journal":

We only have a few more carries to go to Camp II, and most of the carrying is now to Camp III. We've got a full complement of people staying at Camp II to carry up to III. With the route going so well to IV, we could start up to Camp V within a few days. The weather today and yesterday has been beautiful. Maybe we'll have a spell of ten days of good weather. That would put us close—well, with fifteen days of good weather, we would be on the summit.

The following day we again awoke early. Conditions were the same: snowing, but light enough to allow movement on the mountain. We were just ready to leave camp when Bill announced he was tired and preferred to stay behind to rest.

"I'm feeling weak," he explained. "I know I would slow you guys down. Maybe if I had a rest day I could recoup my strength."

Bill had been having trouble adjusting to the altitude; he also had seemed to lack enthusiasm, which perhaps was a result of his poor acclimatization. The previous day he had climbed very slowly. When John and I had caught up with Wick and him, Bill had quietly asked John if he would take over his job so he could go back down.

"I was tired, too," John told me later. "And besides that just isn't how I like to do things."

John, Wick, and I left camp at 7:00. We were so confident we would reach Camp IV that we loaded our packs with extra supplies so we could cache equipment there and properly establish the camp. We took with us two tents, an oxygen bottle, 750 feet of rope, assorted climbing hardware, stoves, fuel, pots and pans, and fourteen man-days of food. The packs were heavy but not unreasonable.

By 9:30, we had reached the high point. Visibility was poor. It was still snowing lightly, but tackling the first lead, I made reasonable speed to the base of a fifty-foot-high pinnacle rising on the ridge crest. Remembering the Polish accounts, we knew the campsite would be on the other side of this pinnacle, perhaps only two hundred feet away. John started up. But his pack was too heavy for the steep lead, so he cached his load and continued on. Soon, he had the rope fixed and Wick and I followed.

It was difficult to see any distance through the snowfall, but we followed the ridge, dropping fifty feet below its crest on the Chinese side, hoping we might find a flat spot large enough for a campsite.

"I thought the Poles had their campsite here," I said to Wick.

"They did," he replied. "There's no doubt. We're at the end of the traverse—it's the same spot. But there's no place for the camp."

"Maybe there's a place on the crest—a flat spot."

John moved up, disappearing into the fog.

"I'm at the top," he yelled back. "It's still a knife edge. No place for any tents."

VI
Direct
VI
V
IV
III
Sinkiang China
© 1978 DM
Kashmir
Pakistan
Northeast Ridge
1978

It was 3:30. We knew we would soon have to turn back if we were to make it to Camp III before dark.

"I wish John and I hadn't been so optimistic after that first day when we told everyone we were nearly at Camp Four," I said.

We waited a few minutes. The clouds thinned, slightly improving the visibility.

"I can see a little more," John shouted down. "There might be something on the crest in back of us. I'll check it out."

We waited a few more minutes.

"It looks O.K.," he yelled. "We can level a spot big enough for three tents, anyway."

"We got it after all," Wick said. "Camp Four is ours."

Wearily, we shook hands and smiled broadly, as big snowflakes began to fall around us.

WE AWOKE THE NEXT MORNING AT CAMP III to the barely perceptible sound of snowflakes falling on the nylon tent fly and gently sliding, with a slight scratching sound, to the growing rim of fresh snow around the tent. None of us moved in our sleeping bags. Without speaking a word, we knew it was to be a rest day. For six days we had climbed hard without stop. Now it was time to give our bodies a chance to recover. With great pleasure, I burrowed into the down comfort of my warm bag and lazily passed the morning drifting in and out of sleep.

As on the two previous days, the snow was light. We learned that Lou and Jim were carrying loads from Camp II to Camp III. Lou was first to arrive with, as usual, a heavy load. He was in a very bad mood.

"I would have thought if you guys weren't carrying to Camp Four you could at least break trail down to Two for those of us still working," he grumbled.

Expecting to be congratulated for our quick push to Camp IV, we were taken aback.

"We've been breaking our backs for six days, and if anybody has earned a day off it's us," I told Lou.

Lou calmed down. It seemed his grousing was mainly disappointment over being excluded from the push to Camp IV; he was impatient with the lackluster task of ferrying loads from Camp I to Camp III. He was also simply exhausted after breaking trail for five and a half hours.

Jim soon arrived and, also in a sensitive frame of mind, launched into Bill for taking two rest days in a row.

"Some of us around here have to work for our keep," he said. "How do you expect to climb this mountain unless we get some loads up?"

Bill was surprised at Jim's outburst. He thought both Lou and Jim were suffering from what he called "storm panic" at the thought of another delay from bad weather, and that, even when we were pinned down, they expected people to "run in place."

With half the team present (the others were resting in Camp II, except for Chris, who had descended to Camp I with a sore throat) we gathered in one of the tents for a strategy meeting. Jim opened the discussion with a reaffirmation of his intention to give everyone a chance to do some lead climbing.

"I don't want to repeat the mistake we made on the '75 trip," he said, "by excluding part of the team from the lead climbing, to the point where they said, 'Why should I carry so somebody else can get to the top?' So I want *everyone* to have a chance to carry to Camp Four, and I want to give at least Terry, Craig, and possibly Skip a stab at leading to Camp Five. If any of them can't make it, I'll put them back on the lower carries, but at least they'll have had a chance."

Each of us heard the special meaning in Jim's emphasis. Earlier that morning, those of us in Camp III had discussed the topic. John had felt most strongly, and Wick and I had more or less agreed, that Dianne would jeopardize her own safety and everyone else's if she was allowed to attempt the steep traverse.

"I don't want to have to go out and rescue anybody and risk my own neck just because they shouldn't have been allowed to cross in the first place," John said to Jim. "Dianne, for example, should not be allowed to go to Camp Four."

"Look, dammit," Jim said, "Dianne came on this trip to climb as high as she can. She has worked as hard as anyone, deserves the chance to go, and I'm taking her across regardless of your opinion. You don't have to risk *your* neck in any way."

"I was under the impression Dianne was supposed to be the photographer on this trip, not a climber," John fired back. "Everybody here knows the only reason she's along is because she's your wife."

He paused, then added, "Look, I'm not trying to hit below the belt. It's only that I've been on too many of these things where people don't come back alive, and I'm just not the kind of person who can sit back and not say anything when I can see the writing on the wall."

The last comment was a sideswipe at Wick and me who, in private, had agreed with John. But both of us realized there was no way to change Jim's mind. On all other points regarding strategy on the climb Jim had been flexible, listening to everyone's opinions, but when it came to Dianne he was intractable. Dianne herself knew she was the least experienced of us, but she felt she had worked as hard as anyone—if not harder—to make the dream of a K2 summit a reality; she had carried many loads to Camps I, II, and III and she felt she had earned the right to go as high as she could.

The subject was dropped. The discussion continued for ten minutes, with Jim mentioning that, after Camp V was established, it would be time to start thinking about summit teams. Jim said he would pick those who had worked the hardest and who retained the most drive. He looked at Lou when he said it, clearly dangling a carrot to help Lou through the boredom of carrying loads lower on the mountain, letting him know his efforts carrying heavy packs and double-staging from Camp I to Camp III were being noticed. The question of Dianne's going to Camp IV was not brought up again. It was apparent John's opinion would be overshadowed by Jim's desire to see her get as high as she could.

Jim and Lou returned to Camp II. The plan, weather permitting, was for those of us in Camp III to carry more loads across the traverse the next morning. We spent the afternoon chatting, and the subject again was whether Dianne should be permitted to cross to Camp IV.

"I just wouldn't risk my neck," John said. "That goes for anybody else not qualified, too. If I've warned somebody they shouldn't cross, why should I go after them?"

Both Wick and I agreed with John.

"I don't know," Bill replied. "I think I would have a hard time sitting in this tent knowing somebody was out there dying."

"But we couldn't do much anyway," Wick said. "There's no way to carry people across these ropes."

"I know," Bill said, "but I would still have to try."

"It would be like that guy from India on the International Everest Expedition a few years back who got stuck on the traverse up to the West Ridge," John said. "Wolfgang Axt got criticized for leaving him there to die, but there was nothing he could do to save him. It was a classic example of saving your own neck."

The discussion petered out as everyone lay thinking about the future of the climb. It was snowing heavily. After fifteen minutes John broke the silence.

"I'd like to be able to do everything I say," he said. "Hell, I'd be out there—we all would—if anybody on the team was in trouble. Whether we risked our necks or not. I'd never be able to live with myself otherwise."

"This mountain is going to tell us who can get across that ridge and who can't," Bill said.

"Yeah," John replied, "but sometimes the mountain gets to have her word when the climber should have spoken up first."

THE SNOW CONTINUED through the night. By morning there was no doubt we were in for another multiday storm. Jim called on the radio, requesting that two of us go down and two stay at Camp III. That would mean fewer people using supplies up high, but still would leave a couple to excavate tents during the storm and to break trail down when the weather improved.

Bill and I volunteered to descend; despite the heavy snow, several people would be carrying loads to III, using the path Bill and I would break on our way down. I left first, sliding down the ropes, enjoying the solitude. Soon I ran into Lou heading up with another heavy packload. Then I saw Diana Jagersky, away from her job as Base Camp manager to carry a few loads to the higher camps. She filled me in on the Camp I scuttlebutt we had missed during our week's push to Camp IV.

"The biggest and sharpest rock still in our shoe is the Chris and Cherie thing," Diana said. "A lot has happened while you were gone. I should warn you, Terry blames the whole thing on you and John. He is only a short distance behind me, and no doubt he'll have something to say."

"Blames me?"

"Yeah, and Jim more or less supports him. Terry claims that Chris is a good friend of his, and that he—along with Cherie—is being badmouthed by others, especially you and John."

"Things have certainly taken an unexpected twist. I thought Terry would be mad at Chris, and at Cherie. Now he's bummed at John and me? I was only trying to help."

"Don't look at me," Diana said. "The rest of us are trying to stay as far away from this thing as we can. It's too weird."

"Good luck," she said, and went on up. In a few minutes I saw Terry. I was again impressed by his intense, cerebral facial demeanor, and I realized how very little I knew about this strange and complex man.

We exchanged pleasantries, formally and politely discussing the weather. Then I brought it out into the open.

"I suppose there are a few things you and I should discuss," I began.

"Yes," he replied. "I think you and John are trying to malign Chris and Cherie. I'm not sure why—perhaps you want to keep them from the competition on the summit teams. I don't know. But I've talked at great length with Chris, I consider him to be a good friend, and I will support him as one of the climbers who deserves to go to the top."

Terry spoke quietly and very analytically, looking at me the whole time with his dark, penetrating eyes. It was more than a little disconcerting.

"Look, Terry, I honestly thought—when this whole thing started—you would be hurt by it. In retrospect I sure wish I had minded my own business. But I was only trying to help."

I was getting emotional, and those last words came with a quiver. Terry resumed in his precise voice.

"Cherie and I have been married for eight years. She wouldn't do anything to hurt me. She's the finest, strongest woman I know, and if you took the trouble to learn anything about her, I'm sure you would agree."

I apologized to Terry for having meddled in what was none of my business. Again I told him I had been thinking only of his welfare, and that I did not want Chris to fall out of favor with the rest of the team. Terry's formality loosened; with a warmer look in his eyes he accepted my apologies and we gave each other a bear hug.

"We're going to get to the top of this thing one way or the other," I grinned.

"We've still got a hell of a team," he agreed. "It's the strongest group of climbers I've ever seen."

We went our separate directions. Feeling much better, I continued alone to Camp I. I knew Chris was there, and I learned that Cherie, having also succumbed to a sore throat, had descended earlier that morning. I felt if I could iron things out with them, the cracks in the rampart of the 1978 American K2 Expedition might be repaired before the dam broke. I found them sitting together in the cook tent.

"Welcome to Camp I," Cherie said sardonically. Chris offered me a cup of tea.

"Let's get it over with," I said.

Cherie looked up. "We just feel that you and John are to blame for the whole thing. If you had minded your own business there wouldn't be any problem at all."

"What really bothered me," Chris broke in, "was when I passed you that morning coming down from Camp Two, and you told me I should come back here with my tail between my legs and apologize to Whittaker. As if it was my fault. Apologize for what? And you were trying to be my friend?"

"I only thought I was helping," I said. The weeks of guilt I had been holding, the feeling of having betrayed my friendship with Chris—first by not discussing the problem at its very beginning, then by joining up with Roskelley to put myself in the best position for the summit—these feelings focused to an emotional upwelling and tears ran down my cheeks. I sat down next to Chris and put my arm around him.

"I'm sorry pal," I said. "I hope we can be friends after all this."

Chris stared at his feet, and Cherie also seemed embarrassed.

Cherie said, "Rick, I still like you. We've got our differences to be sure, but we can put them aside. It's not your fault alone. Roskelley is no doubt the main culprit, but we can all get along well enough to see this thing through."

I felt Chris's arm tighten around my shoulder. It was the first time I had seen a breach in Cherie's armor, and it was good to discover a regular, vulnerable human, just like the rest of us, beneath the mail. I also thought that laying myself bare, despite how difficult it was, might help heal past wounds. Once again I felt close to Chris.

There were still problems—now they blamed the whole thing on John. But I was, by then, feeling a growing kinship with the guy I had climbed to Camp IV with, and consequently a loyalty toward him. And how, I wondered, did Lou and Wick fit into all this? Jim and Dianne apparently leaned toward Terry, Chris, and Cherie, but I suspected Jim, as leader, would have the diplomacy to stay in the middle. The others seemed to stand on the sidelines, but they were really as involved as any of us. They had to be: we were in too close proximity, we depended too much on one another—even for our lives—to stay on the sidelines.

Maybe, I thought, it was not as big a problem as it seemed. I had been able to talk frankly with Terry, Chris, and Cherie and repair the rift that had been growing. Perhaps John could do the same. I was not sure. But I knew one thing for certain: we had reached Camp IV, another week had gone by, and it looked like another storm might delay us yet another week. And one more garment had fallen off each of our bodies, and we were each becoming, week by week, a little more naked.

BIG HIMALAYAN CLIMBING EXPEDITIONS seem to breed contention; it is almost as predictable as the monsoon storms that swell from the Indian Ocean. Except for Diana, all of us had climbed before in the Himalaya, and most of us had been on big expeditions. We had all seen it happen—the slight difference, the sly comment, the oblique criticism—small barbs that make small scratches that eventually grow to big wounds, which infect and poison the team. We had been aware of the potential problem before leaving the United States and had agreed to do everything possible to avoid the schisms. Ours would be an open expedition; we would voice our grievances; Jim would listen carefully to all opinions.

We had all come with the hope we would work closely as a team, to have fun, to have an adventure, and to bring a successful conclusion to the forty-year American dream to climb to the summit of K2. It seemed, however, that if we were to reach the summit of K2, it would not be without dissension.

I have a few ideas why long climbing expeditions so frequently end in acrimony. The first has to do with the type of people usually attracted to Himalayan climbing, and the second with the circumstances in which—on big expeditions—these people find themselves. Mountain climbing is, above all, an individual endeavor; an individual's reasons for such extraordinary effort and sacrifice to reach a summit are often complex, eluding simple explanation. Taken by itself, standing on top of a peak—usually too exhausted to appreciate the view (if you even have one past the clouds that, as often as not, shroud high mountains)—is about as useless as any final achievement in any sport. And if the summit happens to be one of the eight-thousand-meter peaks in the Himalaya—one of the fourteen mountains on the "Grand Prix circuit" of high-altitude climbing—you are not only exhausted, but also physically debilitated from hypoxia, loss of muscle tissue, and grey matter; you have a reasonable chance of losing your fingers and toes to frostbite; and there is a frighteningly real chance you will not get down alive.

Why do it then? One reason has to be days like the one of the butterflies and giant shadows cast across the glacier. A day such as that is indelibly impressed, a bouquet of flowers that forever brightens some recess of the mind. There are other reasons: meeting new, interesting people and having the chance, in the intimacy of a months-long expedition, to know them well; traveling to the earth's most remote corners—the Himalaya, the Karakoram, the Pamirs, the Hindu Kush. But perhaps the most salient reason is secreted away in that rare moment when a climber reaches the end of a long effort and stands on the summit of a high mountain. If the mountain is an Everest or a K2 or a Dhaulagiri, there will be the accolades and laurels that attend the achievement, which no doubt strengthens the motivation to do it in the first place.

But such rewards are transitory, emphemeral. There are few climbers, if any, who persevere in their quest for that reason alone. The reward is, instead, an inner, a personal, and often a necessarily secret satisfaction— one that perhaps can be shared with no one—from having made an un-compromised effort, from having risked life itself in an all-too-real way, to achieve the ultimate goal.

There is the key word: achievement. Climbers drawn to the Himalaya, climbers who are successful in reaching their goals, are compelled to *achieve*; yet on big expeditions there is often room for only a few to make that ultimate achievement, the summit.

There are other reasons for discontent, to be sure: stress from danger, stress from working hard, stress from having insufficient oxygen to breathe, stress from eating poorly. All these make people irritable, and all, no doubt, compounded the problems beginning to surface on the 1978 American K2 Expedition.

It was still too early for the bitter arguments that would erupt later in the climb when it became more clear who would get the chance to try for the summit and who would not. But already there was the subtle jockeying for position and already some subdued grumbling among the team. Some felt they were working harder than others, some felt they were being left out of the action, some felt they were being used so others could reach the summit. None of these feelings had surfaced to active de-bate, but the seeds of discontent were sown.

Inevitably, there was a growing difference in the performance of many members of the expedition. Some were tiring of the rigors of working in the increasingly thin air as we pushed the route to higher altitudes; some were growing homesick and losing the motivation to endure week after week on the mountain; some were becoming more and more intimidated by the difficulties of climbing the steepening rock and ice. Others were, if anything, getting stronger and more determined to push on: the more bad weather and the longer the delays, the more they mentally trenched-in and prepared for a long battle. It was fascinating to observe people's inner drives, their inner personalities emerging as the expedition continued into the month of August. There was something about this climb—its duration perhaps, stretching week after week to epic length; or perhaps its dif-ficulty, and the stresses to which it subjected us; or maybe our competition for the summit prize—but there was something that lay people naked. For better or for worse, all of us were exploring one another's secret places, as if each week that passed stripped each person of one more psychological garment, until, in the final days of the climb, we would stand completely bare of the protective little games we normally wore to cover our innermost selves.

6

Storms and Tempers

FROM JIM WICKWIRE'S JOURNAL

August 5. Except for John and me here at Camp III, and Jim and Dianne at Camp II, the expedition has withdrawn to Camp I to wait out the current storm. Heavier snowfall last night and today, and some wind this morning.

Couldn't sleep last night. Many long sequences of going to the summit and returning safely to Camp VI. I raked through my mind everything that has happened on the expedition so far. Then I thought how strong and healthy I am feeling at this stage, and I came to a very relaxed and settled notion of my own chances of reaching the summit. They are quite good. I am mentally and physically ready for the supreme effort of the past eighteen years of climbing to make a dream the reality of reaching the summit of K2.

Whether the team as a whole can make it happen is still open to speculation. To be successful we will have to work together for many more days before the attrition begins to take its toll and climbers start sloughing off. There are several who clearly do not have a chance for the summit, but I am sure they still dream of attaining the summit or they wouldn't continue to carry loads.

Although not expressly mentioned in discussion we had a few days back when Jim, Dianne, and Lou carried to III, it was clearly understood by all present that as things presently stand the four most likely to go for the summit are Lou, Rick, John, and I, based on performance to date. A number of

136

things could change this assessment, such as succumbing to altitude and the attendant problems that affect the human body, and ultimately I may have to eat the foregoing words, but that is how it appears as of now.

I had a good conversation with John today. Among other things, we talked about how willpower will be the key factor in going for the summit. Both of us are willing to make an all-out effort, including chancing a bivouac on the way down from the summit. We both realize the risks. John is prepared to incur further frostbite. I badly want to make it up there and return, and I too would be willing to make that kind of sacrifice. John and I are willing to lay everything on the line, except to pay the ultimate price—that would make reaching the summit meaningless.

Feel like I'm getting to know John a lot better now that I've spent a couple of days alone with him. He's a bit of a redneck, but basically an honest and straightforward guy. We share one passion: climbing to some high isolated summit such as K2. Both our wives also share similar positions, except that Mary Lou and I have more children. But combining the travels because of my legal work with my mountaineering expeditions, I am probably away from home and my family as much as John is on the basis of climbing alone. Both Mary Lou and Joyce accept these absences, and part of the reason for the successes of both John and me must in no small way be a result of that unfailing support. I know for me, at least, it is a continual source of inspiration, courage and energy.

So tired. Must get some sleep tonight. Thinking of you Mary Lou. Our separation is difficult, but we can easily withstand a few more weeks to enable me to fulfill my hopes and aspirations concerning a certain mountain upon whose slopes I sleep tonight.

August 7. The storm is over. John and I left before 7:00 A.M. to break trail down for the others coming up. We met Rick in the basin (above Camp II) on his way up. He had the letters with him. One from Mary Lou and one from Anne. Nothing too new except the cat got in the house and made short work of Jimbo the pet parakeet. The news was a month old, but it was so good to hear from my wife and my oldest child.

The three of us worked back to Camp III. Dianne and Jim followed later, then Craig and Skip. Doesn't appear Lou will make it up tonight; he has a sore throat, but nothing too serious.

Beautiful afternoon. The curious dust cloud that earlier filled the lower valleys seems to have dissipated. Should be a good day tomorrow; we all plan on making carries to Camp IV with the plan for Skip and Craig to move in the following day and begin pushing up to Camp V while everyone else continues the carries to the lower camps. Built a tent platform for Craig and Skip, then wrote a letter to Mary Lou and one to Anne.

Mary Lou, even though we are twelve thousand miles apart, I can still be with you. I can feel your presence. Mostly you are asleep when I am awake and vice versa, yet that doesn't matter. If we can climb this mountain and if I can be fortunate enough to make it to the summit, then soon afterwards we can be together again.

A LETTER FROM DIANNE ROBERTS TO SUSANNE AND JAKE PAGE

August 9
Camp II, 20,000 feet

Dear Susanne and Jake,

Can't begin to tell you all that's happened—that will have to wait for some wine-drenched evening when all this is over. Basically things are going very well. We have had some foul weather—typical K2 six- to eight-day storms—but have managed to carry loads on the mountain most days in spite of it. Most of the team is still healthy—Rob has had some problem with an old knee injury, and he is stuck in Camp I, and there have been minor sore throats and diarrhea—but nothing really incapacitating. There have been a few crabby times, but Jim is doing a masterful job of pulling people together and I think everyone is working pretty well considering the stresses involved. Jim and I are both feeling fine and strong. With any luck, by the time you read this, maybe August 20 or so, we will have reached the summit.

There have been so many times when, in my mind, I have wished I could sit down and write you a long letter. But we have really been working *very* hard, with very few rest days, and even during the storms there are tents to be dug out, snow to be melted for drinking, socks to be dried—all kinds of little mundane tasks that guarantee your survival in this incredibly alien environment.

Actually, when you think about it, it's amazing we can live up here at all. I can hardly think of any environment more alien to the human organism—the moon maybe? But even on the moon the astronauts had machines to help them gather the stuff they needed. All they had to do was walk around a bit, and with all those computers and people back in Houston to help them, how could they mess up?

Boy, there are plenty of ways to mess up around here. It is so very easy to lose motivation. This mountain is so big. It takes (depending on the conditions and the person and the weight of the pack) three to six hours to "walk" from here—Camp II, 20,000 feet, to Camp III, 22,275 feet. There were about fifty-five loads to be carried over that section of the route alone. Some of the climbers are up above pushing the route higher, so there are anywhere from five to ten people carrying those loads. Some have carried six of more times over that same route, every day if the weather is workable. It is a

"Keep your eye fixed on the path to the top, but don't forget to look in front of you." K2, orange in evening alpenglow, from Windy Gap; the NE Ridge—the route of ascent—rises on the right of the photograph. (Craig Anderson)

Right—Cherie Bech carrying her own load. (Dianne Roberts)
Below—Dianne Roberts and Jim Whittaker. (Craig Anderson)

Jim Whittaker
(Dianne Roberts)

Bill Sumner
(Dianne Roberts)

Diana Jagersky embraces Bill Sumner as he returns to Camp I from the higher camps. (Dianne Roberts)

Lou Reichardt
(Dianne Roberts)

Diana Jagersky
(Dianne Roberts)

Honar Baig, high-altitude porter
(Dianne Roberts)

Rob Schaller
(Dianne Roberts)

Cherie Bech
(Dianne Roberts)

Rick Ridgeway
(Dianne Roberts)

Nazeer Ahmed Sabir,
travel liaison
(Dianne Roberts)

Above—John Roskelley (*left*) and Rick
Ridgeway return to Camp III to wait out
yet another storm. (Dianne Roberts)

Left—Craig Anderson delivered many
valuable loads to the higher camps.
(Dianne Roberts)

Below—Craig and Skip Edmonds
practice spending long periods in small
tents. (Craig Anderson)

Jim Wickwire
(Dianne Roberts)

Skip Edmonds
(Dianne Roberts)

Terry Bech
(Dianne Roberts)

Above—The margin between success and defeat was but the thickness of a sheet of paper. "There was an unspoken feeling—more than camaraderie—more perhaps a feeling of fraternity—of sharing a common stress and hardship, a common danger, and a common victory." (Both Dianne Roberts)

Sanjerjan, high-altitude porter
(Dianne Roberts)

Tajiran Shah, high-altitude porter
(Dianne Roberts)

John Roskelley
(Dianne Roberts)

Chris Chandler
(Dianne Roberts)

Craig Anderson
(Dianne Roberts)

Gohar Shah, high-
altitude porter
(Dianne Roberts)

Dianne Roberts
(Lou Reichardt)

Below—Front row: Lou Reichardt, Tajiran Shah, John Roskelley, Jim Wickwire, Terry Bech, Dianne Roberts, Jim Whittaker, Mohammed Saleem Khan (liaison officer). Back row: Rob Schaller, Honar Baig, Cherie Bech, Chris Chandler, Diana Jagersky, Tajiran Shah, Skip Edmonds, Craig Anderson, Rick Ridgeway, Bill Sumner, Gohar Shah. (Dianne Roberts)

The Balti women were shy, and only the women of the expedition were able to easily approach and photograph them. (Dianne Roberts)

Above—350 porters gather to carry food and equipment 110 miles to Base Camp; the timeless feeling of caravans through the fastnesses of Central Asia. (Dianne Roberts)

Below—"There was another village below us, on the other side, bright green with early summer wheat . . . we planned our marches to end each afternoon in such a village." (Dianne Roberts)

The porters were paid $4.50 US a day—a fee determined by the Pakistani government and a good wage in a subsistence economy. (Dianne Roberts)

"There is no god but Allah, and Mohammed is his prophet." In Islam the world is a mosque, and prayer can take place anywhere.
(Dianne Roberts)

Top—The Koran says all men who die must cross a tenuous bridge before they may enter heaven. For many of the porters, the jury-rigged bridge over the River Panmah was the Muslim version of crossing the Styx.
(Dianne Roberts)

Above—The line of porters approaches the campsite at Lilliwa on the march in. (Dianne Roberts)

Top—Concordia: the magic confluence of three glaciers flowing from the heart of the Karakoram gives the team their first close view of their objective. (Dianne Roberts)

Above—The porters stay for one last carry to Advanced Base Camp—a magnanimous gesture that gained precious days and, in the final analysis, was an important ingredient in the ultimate victory. (Dianne Roberts)

Right—K2 Base Camp, 16,500 feet, the same location used by the Duke of Abruzzi, the early Americans, the Italians, and the rest of the team's forebears. (Dianne Roberts)

Top left—"It was clear from base to summit, a broad and heavy mass, four-faced and four-ridged like the Great Pyramid," wrote W.M. Conway in 1892—the first Westerner to view K2 from Concordia. (Dianne Roberts)

Left—"The trek into the inner sanctum of the Karakoram, into the icy upper reaches of the Baltoro, was a trek into the pages of the Book of Marvels." (Dianne Roberts)

Below—"The magnificence of the peaks on all points of the Baltoro Glacier evokes storybook fantasies." Paiju Peak, 21,654 feet. (Dianne Roberts)

Right—Avalanche, Broad Peak. (Rob Schaller)

Left—After two weeks of trekking through mostly desert, the beginning of the climb is welcome. The upper Godwin-Austin Glacier above Base Camp, en route to Camp I.
(Dianne Roberts)

Below left—Camp I with Broad Peak in the background
(Craig Anderson)

Below and right—The ascent of the ridge begins. Camp II (right) is established precariously between a cornice and an avalanche slope. Hundreds of pounds of food and equipment had to be stockpiled at Camp II to supply the later assault on the upper mountain. (Both Dianne Roberts)

K2 from Windy Gap, showing the entire route from Advanced Base Camp to the summit. (Craig Anderson)

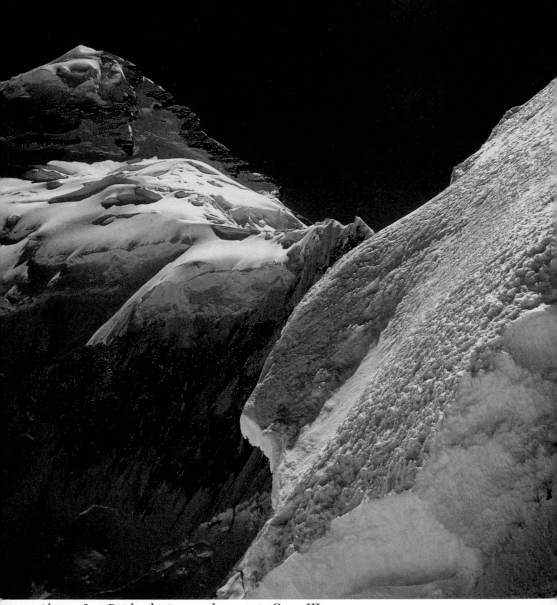

Above—Lou Reichardt pioneers the route to Camp III. (Jim Wickwire)

Above right—Camp III, 22,300 feet, is located under a serac on the crest of the ridge at the beginning of the knife-edge traverse. The team reached Camp III in only 12 days after arriving at the base of K2; their optimism that they could quickly reach the summit was soon dampened by the first of many storms. (Dianne Roberts)

Below right—Cherie Bech and Chris Chandler on the snow slope above Camp II. (Dianne Roberts)

Below—Rick Ridgeway leaves Camp III to begin the steep traverse to Camp IV—the most technically difficult section of the route. (John Roskelley)

Right—After the ropes were fixed, climbers could carry loads across the section in less than three hours; with bad weather, the same crossing could be an all-day ordeal, as Terry Bech learns. (Jim Wickwire)

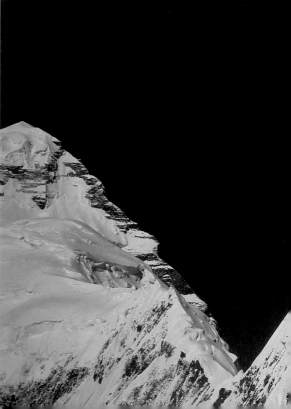

Left—The edge of a knife—the vertiginous ridge, the border of Pakistan and China—between Camp III and Camp IV. (John Roskelley)

Below—"The slope dropped away on both sides, steeply, dramatically, to glaciers thousands of feet below. Just out of Camp III we crossed the edge of the knife and, for the first time, we were in China." Camp IV would be placed in a low notch at the far end of the traverse, and Camp V, eventually, on the snow dome below the summit pyramid. (Craig Anderson)

Left—As the route pushed above Camp V, the climbers could look down on the entire length of the traverse. Camp IV is in the lower left, and in the upper right, Camp III. Two climbers are just visible leaving Camp III. (Dianne Roberts)

Below—August 26. Racing the setting sun, Dianne Roberts and Jim Whittaker fight against extreme wind to reach Camp IV. They made it just as night fell, avoiding bivouac and certain frostbite. (Jim Wickwire)

Above, below right—The struggle to push the route to Camp V, 25,300 feet, was the key to success—without it, there could be no summit attempt. Dianne Roberts (*above right*) carries her load toward Camp V. For 12 days the team fought storm, soft snow and avalanche conditions before finally gaining the elusive Camp V. (Photo below right John Roskelley; others Craig Anderson)

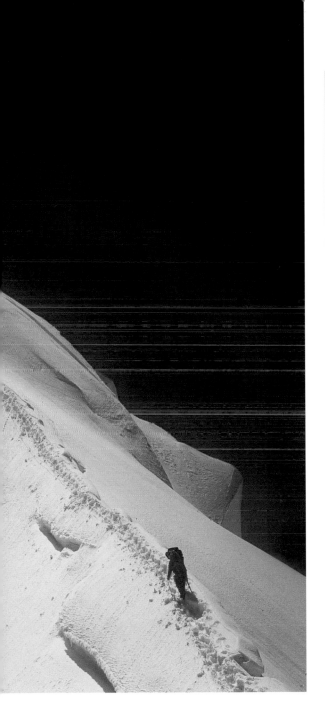

Below—Camp V was the springboard for the summit attempts. Before trying for the top, the team—low on food and fuel—had to wait out still more bad weather. (Jim Wickwire)

Right—Lou Reichardt pushes through soft snow to make the first carry of valuable food, fuel, and oxygen to the site of Camp VI on the Direct Finish, at the base of the summit headwall. (Jim Wickwire)

Below right—Unable to decide the best route to the top, the summit team divides, and Lou Reichardt and Jim Wickwire traverse under the summit headwall and establish another Camp VI, on the Abruzzi Ridge, at 26,200 feet (8000 metres). (Jim Wickwire)

Above—September 6. Despite soft snow, Lou Reichardt and Jim Wickwire push the final distance up the Abruzzi Ridge. With a 500-millimeter lens, the two climbers are photographed from Base Camp—10,000 feet below—as they make the last steps to the summit. (Rob Schaller)

Above right—27,000 feet. Lou Reichardt traverses under the ice cliffs high on the Abruzzi Ridge. The next day John Roskelley and Rick Ridgeway climbed this section unroped—an effort that demanded much concentration. (Jim Wickwire)

Right—The summit pyramid. The Abruzzi Ridge is defined by the left skyline; the ill-fated direct finish was to climb the snow and rock rib just right of center. (Dianne Roberts)

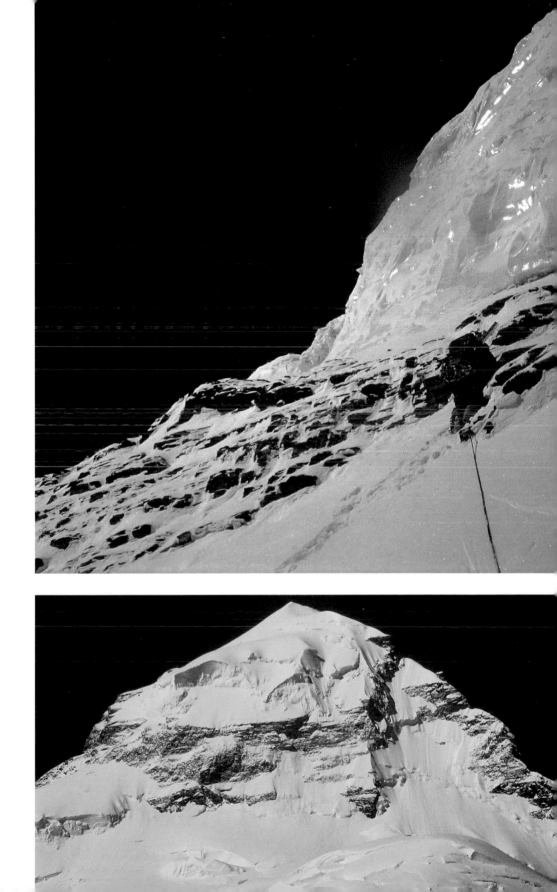

Right—63 days after arriving at the base of the mountain, Jim Wickwire and Lou Reichardt, right, make the last step to the summit as the sun sets behind the ridge. The 40-year quest was over; Americans had reached the second highest point on earth. (Jim Wickwire)

Below—The victory was even more substantial for Lou Reichardt, who was the first person to climb K2 without oxygen. (Jim Wickwire)

Below right—The next day, Rick Ridgeway gazes across the vast Karakoram as he and John Roskelley enjoy a perfect summit day. (John Roskelley)

Above—The ordeal begins: the summit team starts the long, five-day descent. From left, Reichardt, Ridgeway and Roskelley leave an abandoned Camp VI. (Jim Wickwire)

Below—Suffering pneumonia, pleurisy, paralyzed vocal cords and diaphragm, and frostbite, Jim Wickwire is assisted to Base Camp among cheering Baltis, who are delighted to see everyone down alive. (Dianne Roberts)

Right—The next day, too weak to walk, Wickwire was carried by the porters to Concordia. (John Roskelley)

Left—Fearing Jim Wickwire
might succumb to his illnesses,
the team called an evacuation
helicopter. Before leaving, Jim
(Rob Schaller behind) made
an emotional farewell
speech to the sympathetic Baltis,
who prayed to Allah for a safe
deliverance for their friend.
(Craig Anderson)

Below—Returning down the
Baltoro, the K2 expedition bids
farewell to the mightiest mountain
scenery on earth. By the slimmest
of margins they had achieved
success, and most important, they
had all returned. "There are no
conquerors—only survivors."
(Dianne Roberts)

K2, in building storm. "Don't think you're there just because you see the summit. Watch your footing, be sure of the step, but don't let that distract you from the highest goal . . ."
(Dianne Roberts)

beautiful route winding up along a corniced ridge separating China and Pakistan. Parts of it are steep, parts are nearly flat, but the snow is always deep, the packs always heavy, and there is never quite enough oxygen in the air. With each step you pause, take three or four breaths, then take another step. You get to Camp III and want desperately to stay there—it is *so* hard to go down again. But down you go—maybe one and a half hours down if the tracks haven't drifted in, more if you have to break trail. The next day you do it again. And the next . . .

That's the big difference between K2 and Everest. On Everest, twelve climbers might hire fifty Sherpas to help carry loads all the way to the top camps. But on this mountain—steeper and nearly as high as Everest—we have four "high-altitude porters"—Hunza guys who are friendly and strong, but who pooped out on their first carry to Camp III. We now have them back down working between Advance Base and Camp I, on the glacier. Up here we're on our own.

Today there are nine at Camp III making the carry across an extremely steep traverse to Camp IV. Two will stay at Camp IV and if the weather holds begin putting in the route to Camp V. It will not be as steep as the traverse, but it will be very long—nearly a 2500 foot-gain in altitude, and all above 23,000 feet. We are going to carry loads all the way to Camp VI, about 26,500 feet, without oxygen, because with so few of us it would be nearly impossible to carry enough oxygen bottles (which weigh fourteen pounds each and last for perhaps eight hours climbing) up there to use on anything but the final push above Camp VI to the summit. But we don't know how many of us will be able to carry loads that high without "O's" If we have to carry oxygen bottles up there to use below Camp VI, we will never have enough time and strength to go for the summit—we'll burn ourselves out on the lower carries.

Jim and I were talking the other day while we were holding down Camp II during a storm that the team has about enough collective strength to keep going until the end of August. If we get the weather and are lucky enough to stay healthy we should get to the summit before then. If we don't have it by then, it is doubtful we would have enough strength and determination left to continue. We reached Base Camp July 5. We have been on the mountain more than a month now, and by the end of August, two months. That is a long time.

Oh Susanne and Jake, I can't begin to tell you how hard this is. I can write and write and write and never convey what's going on here. Doing what we're doing makes less sense to me now than it did back in Seattle. Not that I ever claimed to understand then, but now nothing I say makes much sense at all. Yet I guess I am glad I am here. There are so many things I miss: the beach and the hot tubs and the red wine and the fresh fruit. But most of all my friends. Although the people on this trip will be friends, I suppose, in one way or another—we'll have reunions and get together and drink beer and tell lies to each other about what it was like—they're not the same sort of friends. It's funny how when you spend too much time with them even the nicest climbers start to drive you crazy. I guess being the "wife of the leader" doesn't help much.

I wish you two were here so I could talk to you. Can you read between the lines? When I'm plugging on up to Camp III, I think of you—this may sound corny, but that's what happens to you up here. You get very, very corny and sentimental—and it does make the going a lot easier. I'm not sure how, but somehow I'm ending up not doing this for myself at all. I came over here, I think, to take great photographs and do something dangerous and exciting and courageous so I could be famous, and somehow I'm ending up putting one foot in front of the other—sometimes it's so hard to put one foot in front of the other—just because I know you are back there at home, and a few other special people, hoping and praying that we make it. Sometimes, except for that, I think I would turn around right now. But I simply cannot abandon all that faith in us. I don't know why all of you want us to climb it, but somewhere there, there's a power and strength beyond comprehension. Sometimes I think it is diverted toward a useless goal. But I keep going, and so do the others. And I know I will keep going until I get as high as I can on this mountain, until some one of us, or two or three or more, gets to the top. Or until I can honestly look up and say, "Mountain, you got me." In either case, I could go home feeling O.K. As much as I want to turn around now, I could never go home and look you in the eye and tell you I quit, knowing I still had strength left to continue.

I miss you both so much.

Dianne

FROM THE DIARY OF RICK RIDGEWAY

August 9. We were up early again and made our second carry to Camp IV. Left at 6:30 and arrived in Camp IV at 8:30—two hours flat! We made good speed because much of the route was stamped in from yesterday's carry, and we were all more familiar with the ropes. It is really the most fun part of the climb so far. On the very steep knife-edge sections the rope loops like bunting from anchor to anchor. When you reach an anchor point you clip around, then let go and fly down the rope until you reach the bottom, then pull yourself up to the next anchor and do the same thing. Hanging over China, about seven thousand feet below, is quite exhilarating too.

John, Lou, Wick, Jim, Cherie, and I all carried loads across; Chris and Skip carried personal gear and will stay in Camp IV and tomorrow begin pushing up toward Camp V.

Craig was supposed to go but he is back in Camp III recovering from a bout of diarrhea. It's good to see Chris in the lead, and I have my fingers crossed he does a good job getting up to Camp V. That would do a lot to change the low esteem in which he's held by some of the team—especially Lou and John, and to a lesser extent Wick and Jim, who think he hasn't been doing his share of the work.

Cherie got across the traverse O.K. but she was the last one. She also left Camp III late—I don't know why she and Chris keep doing that. Anyway, after caching gear in Camp IV, cutting new tent platforms, and then inventorying the equipment and food (while Lou, as usual, feeling some inner drive to be out in front, fixed several hundred more feet of rope above Camp IV), we left to return to Camp III about ten. We passed Chris just coming into Camp IV, and he said the traverse was a piece of cake. That made John a little wild. He told Chris sure it was a piece of cake now that the ropes were in and the snow stomped to track like a sidewalk. Then we passed Cherie. I felt guilty. She would be coming back by herself, and it was her first time to cross the traverse. So I told the other guys to go ahead and waited for Cherie to come back. It took quite awhile, but we came back together. I'm glad I did it—little things like that can make us feel more like a team.

Back in Camp III we had a big discussion about whether or not to use oxygen all the way to the summit. Now that Messner and Habeler have climbed Everest without oxygen, there's no doubt it is humanly possible. But we've got harder climbing above Camp VI than they did on Everest. Also, my doubts and fears whether I can do it come back. I remember so well the trouble I had breathing—with oxygen—at twenty-six thousand feet on Everest. It's still a big concern of mine, but I haven't told anybody. I'm afraid if I show any doubts it might affect my chance of being chosen for the summit team. Still, I wonder if my body can handle that altitude. And without oxygen—I seriously doubt it.

John is strongly in favor of doing it without O's, and Lou is also. Wick is less certain, having never been to high altitude, but he too likes the idea. No final decisions have been made— we'll have to wait and see.

Someone said at the end of the discussion it's time to devise a strategy for supplying Camps IV, V, and VI, and someone else said you can't figure logistics for the upper mountain until you have a summit plan—and that includes choosing a summit team. We all know Whittaker is thinking about it. It's on everybody's mind. It's getting to be that time.

August 10. JIM WICKWIRE ROLLED OVER AND grabbed the Optimus kerosene stove, rolled toilet paper around the brass burner, and lit it. Once it was primed, he started the stove and balanced on top of it a billy loaded with snow. It was dawn; that day, Wick would make his sixth consecutive trip to Camp IV.

Wick did not have to worry about crawling out of his sleeping bag in the cold morning air: he did not have a sleeping bag. There were extra ones, to be sure, in our equipment reserve at Camp I, but Wick preferred to sleep in an "elephant's foot"—a half-size, waist-high bag. To protect his torso, he wore a regular parka.

"It's not as warm," he had once explained, "but it's very light. That will be important higher. By sleeping in it now, I won't get spoiled by a warmer bag."

With the stove purring, Jim Whittaker—the only other person sharing the tent with Wick that morning at Camp III—rolled over in his sleeping bag, looked at Wick, and spoke the first words:

"Without oxygen?"

"Huh?"

"You guys think you can do it without oxygen? I remember in '63 making those last difficult steps to the summit of Everest *with* oxygen, and it was hell."

"Might be able to," Wick replied. "Messner and Habeler did. It would sure be nice not to have the weight of those bottles. I don't know—it might be worth a try."

Wick finished preparing breakfast. John and I were in a neighboring tent, Craig and Cherie in another. All of us were getting ready for another carry to Camp IV; Craig and Cherie would remain there to help Chris and Skip push up to Camp V.

Whittaker yelled from his tent, "Before you guys leave this morning, why don't you come over here and we'll have a meeting."

Once we had assembled Jim said, "I think we're getting to the point in the expedition where we can start thinking about the summit attempt. As soon as the route is in to Camp Five, and a few loads carried up, we'll be ready to go for it. I have given a lot of thought to who should be on the first team. As I've said all along, I want to choose the people who have worked the hardest, shown the most strength, and who I think will have the most drive to make it all the way. Unfortunately, there isn't room for everyone who's capable—at least not on the first try. After talking with a few of you about our strategy for climbing the steep sections above Camp Six—about the probable need to fix some rope—it looks as if four should be picked for the first attempt."

We all sat quiet. I looked at my feet, then glanced up and caught John's eye. This was it: the moment we all had been waiting for.

"I think the first summit team should include Lou Reichardt, Jim Wickwire, Rick Ridgeway, and John Roskelley," Jim went on.

We all casually nodded approval. John and I glanced at each other again and exchanged barely perceptible winks. None of us were surprised, but it was thrilling to hear what we had been hoping for, officially sanctioned. Still, we wondered how the rest of the team would take it. Craig did not seem disappointed. None of us realized it, but he had been questioning whether he was capable of climbing to the top anyway. He had felt that, in many ways, he had reached the limit of his technical climbing ability just crossing to Camp IV, and had harbored considerable secret doubts about being able to push above Camp VI. Cherie, also—at least outwardly—seemed unmoved; later, we would find out she had been disappointed, not so much because her own chances were diminished, but because she felt Chris had been short-changed and deserved a place on the summit team.

"There is still the big question of whether you guys use oxygen," Jim said. "And your decision on that makes a difference to how we stock the next two camps."

John said, "I know I can do it without oxygen. Messner did it. I don't want to have to lead that steep section at twenty-seven thousand feet with a fourteen pound bottle on my back. I'll try it without."

"I'll try it without," Lou agreed.

"I've thought about it too," Wick said, "and I'll be willing to try without."

Everyone looked at me. The doubts raced through my mind.

"I don't know," I said. "I guess if I had to put number on it, I would say there's a forty-percent chance I could do it without, and a sixty-percent chance I couldn't."

As soon as I said it I wished I could take it back. I realized it immediately put me in a weak position. Would they drop me from the first summit team? But I had to be honest. And I knew what it was like up there as well as Lou and John did. I was not sure they could do it, either.

My mind raced through the past. I was back on Everest, Camp II, October 4, 1976. We were having a meeting just like this one, and everything got shuffled around. I got put on the second summit team, and we never made it. Winds picked up, Sherpas refused to carry again. In truth, I knew that—even had I been on the first attempt—I never would have made Everest. At twenty-six thousand feet, in spite of using oxygen, my lungs had filled with mucous. Had I been on the first team, I would not have been able to go any higher. I never had known whether it was a bronchial infection or a psychological limitation that had prevented my respiratory system from functioning at those altitudes. Yet here I was, trying to decide whether I could climb that high *without* oxygen, when I was not even certain I could do it *with* oxygen. You have to be honest, I had just told myself. Still, if you reveal all your doubts, you will be excluded for sure. Maybe it had just been a bronchial infection...

"I want to stay on the first team," I said firmly. "I'll go without oxygen."

Everyone nodded approval. I was relieved that, at least, a decision had been made. Then, almost as an afterthought, Lou added a point that gave me another option.

"We're overlooking the fact," he said, "that we'll need one, preferably two, bottles of O's at Six for emergency medical use. It might not be too hard to haul two more up, and then if we decide to use it above Camp Six, we can. We'll at least have the choice."

The wisdom of Lou's words was obvious. The ultimate decision on oxygen would be made at Camp VI. We would see how we felt at that point. And if possible, we would climb K2 without it.

The trip to Camp IV became easier each time. With a six-inch- to one-foot-wide ledge stamped in the snow beneath the ropes, it was easy to lean back on the taut lines for balance, then simply walk across the narrow pathway. The whole section was now familiar, and it was possible to make the crossing in just under two hours. For John and me, it was the eighth trip across the traverse; before the end of the expedition I would make eleven round trips—twenty-two crossings in all—and there would be several others with the same record.

John, Wick, Lou, Jim, and I got to Camp IV about the same time as the day before: ten-thirty. Occasionally, we had been able to see Chris and Skip en route to Camp V. But they had not left IV until late—about seven-thirty—and it had been after eight when they reached the top of the rope Lou had fixed a few days earlier. Now they moved slowly across a widened section of ridge broken by ice blocks and crevasses.

We found a note Chris had attached to the one tent in camp:

> *Cherie and Craig: There is no space here to pitch*
> *another tent. Those guys should have put the camp in*
> *higher up where there is a better platform. We have*
> *two choices: we can crowd into this one tent, or later*
> *move the camp up. Later—Chris.*

"That's ridiculous," Wick countered. "All we have to do is dig another tent platform out of the ridge."

John was furious. The note was an obvious barb, criticizing our choice of campsite. The rest of us were both perplexed and offended. That Chris was making such slow progress above only added to the insult. Venting our anger, the five of us set to the task of digging another tent platform.

Camp IV was located on what was still very much a narrow ridge; it was necessary to move considerable amounts of snow to widen it enough for a tent platform. Even then, both sides of the tent were exposed to the steep dropoff—one side falling away to China, the other to Pakistan.

Chris had been right; there was a flatter place four hundred feet higher. But when we had first fixed the ropes across the traverse, we had not realized it would be possible to cross in such a short time; we had not wanted to increase the distance between Camps III and IV. Also, we knew that if a storm came, burying our little footpath in fresh snow, the crossing would take much more time. Chris, on the other hand, had not realized it was a relatively easy job to dig another platform; in less than an hour, we had excavated sites for two more tents.

Craig soon arrived, followed by Cherie. She hurried into camp, obviously upset.

"I think Chris and Skip are in trouble," she said. I saw one of them disappear a few minutes ago, and he hasn't come back into view."

We had also seen what appeared to be Chris drop over an edge but we thought it was likely a crevasse he was working to cross. That Skip was still visible, and obviously not panicked, seemed to indicated nothing had gone wrong.

No one responded to Cherie. We kept working, widening the tent platform and rudely ignoring her.

"Maybe we should go up and see if they're O.K.," she persisted.

"Don't worry about it. If anything was wrong they would yell down," Jim said.

Cherie was silent fuming. Finally, she burst into a tirade directed at Jim.

"I'm getting sick of the way you're making decisions on this thing," she said bitterly. "It's like you and these others are the only ones here—the super-machos out forging the trail—while the rest of the peasants carry your loads. You haven't given Chris an even chance on the climb yet."

Jim was stung badly. He was not the sort of person who listened easily to such sharp language.

"Look, Cherie," he shot back. "I'm also getting a little short with *your* attitude. I don't mind you criticizing when it's needed, but I'm a little fed up with the way you carp about everything. Anybody who earns it is going to have a chance to do well on this climb. But so far you haven't shown me much, and neither has Chris. Why should I give the summit to a guy who can't even dig a tent platform?"

They argued until Cherie broke down, crying. Perhaps Jim had been too vehement in his counter. The rest of us failed to realize how Cherie had been injured by recent decisions of who should lead to Camp V. Originally Skip and Craig had been earmarked for the job, but Craig had declined, saying he needed a rest day. Chris was then offered Craig's position, but he said he wanted to climb with Cherie. Skip then countered by saying he didn't care for that arrangement, which consequently hurt Cherie. Finally it had been decided that all four—including Craig—would push the route above Camp IV, with Skip and Chris on the job that first day. The whole thing had been messy.

We were all a little embarrassed and quietly finished the platform. In the silence I thought how our expedition—despite our attempts to communicate and despite the days when things went well and we all worked closely as a team—was, as often as not, turning to petty argument. We were still at least ten days—probably more, even if the weather held—from the summit. One more week and one more argument, I thought. We all stand just a little more naked.

We headed back to III, leaving Chris, Cherie, Skip, and Craig in Camp IV.

That evening, Jim announced on the radio his selection of the first summit team. He asked everyone for comments and opinions.

Bill Sumner, from Camp II, in his usual, easygoing voice, said it sounded like the strongest summit team, and supported the idea; Rob Schaller, convalescing in Camp I from a twisted knee suffered while climbing to Camp II, thought it was a bold move to attempt the summit without oxygen, and he was concerned we would be increasing the risk of severe frostbite, with the greater hypoxia. Rob added that if the first attempt should fail, the team would likely have to descend to Camp I to recover. Jim agreed, and added that it would then be up to a second team to make another attempt. The only reaction from Camp IV was a laconic reply from Skip, their radio spokesman, who said, "Sounds O.K." At Camp III, we wondered what conversation had really taken place at Camp IV.

The next day was, in most ways, a repeat of the previous one: more carries to Camp IV, leaving it fully stocked and ready to stage the upper-mountain assault. But there was little rejoicing. Again, the team pushing to Camp V had made almost no progress, this time with good reason. Unbelievably, it looked like another storm was moving in: there was zero visibility above Camp IV, and it was snowing lightly. A pattern seemed to be developing, with just three or four days of reasonable weather separating storms lasting five to eight days. But this was the first of these short periods of good weather during which we had failed to establish a new camp, and it had a grave effect on our spirits. Other than the few loads transported to higher camps, there had been no progress on the mountain. For the first time, several of us speculated on whether we would reach even Camp V, much less the summit.

In one important way, this storm was different from the previous ones: this time, part of the team was trapped on the far side of the traverse. All of us knew it would be, as the Brits would say, "a nasty business" crossing those ropes into the teeth of a gale.

It snowed heavily through the night, and on the morning of August 12 increasingly strong gusts drove snow against the thin nylon tent walls. It was cold. Over the radio we discussed our options. It was clear we should again bail out for Camp I, leaving only a skeleton crew to break down when the storm cleared. It was generally thought all in Camp IV should cross to III immediately, before the storm worsened and forced them to stay. If they were to remain at IV they would consume supplies that, at this point, represented weeks of struggle and carrying, and in addition, it was dangerous to have people stranded that high in a bad storm. The problem was that those at Camp IV did not agree: they thought it already too late to descend safely.

Jim argued by radio that they should come down immediately; they argued otherwise. Finally, they said it was too late to move at all that day, one way or the other.

"No, I think there's enough time," Jim said, talking from his tent at Camp III. "You guys should get under way right now."

There was silence while Camp IV discussed the request. Skip came back on the air:

"Then have somebody break across from Camp Three to clear the trail."

John Roskelley, listening to the conversation from a tent near Jim's, lost patience and picked up an extra radio.

"For Chrissake," he yelled into the walkie-talkie, "It's *uphill* from here." (While most of the distance to Camp IV was a horizontal traverse, there was a steep uphill section just out of Camp III.) "You want us to stomp uphill for you?"

"O.K., calm down, John," Jim called over from his tent.

"I'll break the trail as far as the col" (a point about one-quarter of the way across), Wick volunteered. "Just tell them to get their asses down here."

"I can't believe it," John fumed to me. "Incompetents. Why in the hell do I always end up with incompetents on these trips. There are so many good climbers who wanted to come on this expedition. Where are the Henneks and Schmitzes when I need them?" Both were well-known climbers, friends with whom John had shared previous climbs.

While it was easy for us, in the comfort of Camp III, to say those in Camp IV should descend immediately, the picture on the far side of the traverse was quite different. At Camp III, a large serac under which our tents were nestled protected us from the stronger gusts. But at Camp IV, the tents clung to the narrow ridge, exposed to the full fury of the gale. Periodic gusts would knock them flat, forcing the walls down over those inside; peering out the door, the last thing they wanted to do was go into the maelstrom to negotiate the steep traverse, along ropes now covered with rime.

Nevertheless, they bent to the pressure from those in Camp III and at midmorning started out. Craig and Skip left first while Chris and Cherie broke down the tents and weighted them with snow blocks. That task finished, they waited for nearly an hour while the other two struggled to reach the top of the pinnacle, the first gendarme, such a short distance from the collapsed tents. They failed to do it and returned to the campsite. Skip was having trouble balancing in the vicious wind; he came back on his knees. There was no choice but to repitch the tents and radio their failure to cross.

Meanwhile, the rest of us—except for Terry and Wick—had left Camp

III and rappelled to Camp I, there to wait out this latest storm. It was becoming so habitual to yo-yo up and down the mountain that most of us just shrugged at the prospect of yet another long climb back to the high point once this latest storm cleared; by now, we were anesthetized to the drudgery of jumaring fixed rope at high altitude.

Wick and Terry had set out from Camp III to tackle the strenuous job of tramping snow and pulling out ropes for several hundred yards above Camp III, to lessen the difficulty for those coming down from IV. They had no way of knowing the Camp IV crew had turned back without really starting. Wick and Terry's effort was especially laudable since much of the distance was uphill. They waited and waited, but when no one came, they were forced to return to Camp III where, by radio, they had finally learned the others had turned back. Wick noted in his journal:

> When we learned on the radio they turned back my initial reaction was anger and frustration, but that passed quickly as there was nothing to be done about the situation. Skip was apologetic and said they would try again the following morning. Since Terry and I made it to the col, even though I did most of the trail breaking, their excuse of deep snow doesn't seem enough reason for not making it. This occurrence merely underscores the judgment many of us have that it is a weak group that is attempting to establish the route to Camp V.

The view from Camp IV was quite different. There was no denying conditions on the ridge were hostile. But perhaps one reason for their trouble getting across was that they really had not wanted to; without a driving reason to keep you going, it is easier to be stopped by gale-force winds. In any case, Jim had more or less ordered them down, against their own judgment; that had raised their ire. In a later conversation Chris observed:

> When the "order" to come down came through we were all mad. We had given the radio to Skip because, of the four of us, he had the most tact with words. We understood the reasoning behind it—to minimize food consumption—but the question in our minds was whether it was safe to go down. I was opposed to it. There was a lot of fresh snow, it was windy and cold, not the kind of day to go down. It wasn't clear if the food saved was worth the risk. Later in the trip, during other storms, people did stay in Camp Four and consume food. It was like people were playing with my life for a few sacks of food. The night of the twelfth I didn't sleep well at all. I lay in my bag with various scenarios going through my mind. We got up early the next morning and started down. Craig and Skip broke first. It was a total whiteout with a strong wind. A lot of fresh, drifted snow. There was a real balance problem going along the knife-edge out of Camp Four. The whole way across, slabs kept breaking off as we pulled the rope out. Just

past the rappel, an avalanche came down and buried me. I was third on the rope. At the moment it covered me I was standing midway between two anchors. I sunk my axe and held tight. I was clipped into the fixed rope. I felt the weight come down; I hugged the slope as close as I could; I felt the weight increase and I pulled out and came down on the rope. My mind flashed, "Jesus, this is it." Then it let up, but I couldn't stop shaking for half an hour.

August 13. IT TOOK EIGHT AND A HALF HOURS for the four to make it across to Camp III. When they got there the camp was deserted—Wick and Terry had left the previous day, after learning the others had failed in their first attempt to cross back. Their morale was low. Skip had lost feeling in his toes, and inside the tent he removed his boots and socks and placed his cold toes on Cherie's belly—the best treatment for suspected frostbite. Feeling came back, along with pain that, while unpleasant, at least meant there had been no serious tissue damage. All our suspicions had been confirmed regarding the chameleon nature of the traverse: in good weather it was a piece of cake; in bad it was the most miserable of survival tests.

In contrast, the scene at Camp I could not have been more pleasant. We slept late that morning, not getting out of our bags until nearly nine. Then we lazily sauntered to the cook tent, where Diana had laid on pancakes with rehydrated peaches and boysenberry syrup. There was hot eggnog sprinkled with nutmeg, canned Danish bacon, and Gold Label coffee with powdered full-cream milk rifled from Bonington's deserted base camp over on the west ridge. A lyrical Judy Collins tape played on the stereo. That evening, to celebrate my birthday, Diana prepared jumbo shrimp sauteed in garlic butter, with pea soup and nuggets of ham. Featured music for the evening meal was a Beethoven violin concerto. We were in heaven.

The following morning, the group at Camp III decided to remain there rather than descend because a radio report—relayed to us by Saleem from Base Camp—indicated the weather in Skardu was improving. If previous patterns held, this was a harbinger of better conditions in our area; it was thought that if the four stayed up, two could, when the weather improved, break trail down, clearing the way for those coming back up, while the other two—the strongest—would open up the way to Camp IV. The next day, however, the weather remained foul.

For two more days we patiently marked time while snow continued to fall. There was little to do but read, chat, and think. John spent two days trying to trap a gorak—large ravens that are seen at high altitudes in the Himalaya. When we first came to the mountain there were only a couple of them, but apparently word had spread through the gorak grapevine that there was plenty of garbage at the base of K2; now we had a healthy flock of ten or twelve birds permanently hanging out at Camp I. Like all crows, goraks are highly intelligent. Jim told John they had caught one on Everest in 1963, using the old propped-up-box trick, but these goraks were well beyond that. John constructed an elaborate snare made from a bent sapling (brought up from Askole for a marker wand on the glacier) and baited with Corn Nuts. Several times he nearly caught one, but he refused to answer when asked what he intended to do with the bird if he did catch it. He merely smiled inscrutably, mumbling something about a team mascot.

The talk about a second summit team continued. Several of the climbers —Bill Sumner, Skip Edmonds, and to some extent, Terry Bech and Craig Anderson—said they would be content playing a supportive role from then on, as they recognized their chances of reaching the top were small. But Chris and Cherie both wanted, and felt they deserved, a chance to go for the summit. Jim agreed, saying they should form the core of the second assault effort. Jim also agreed to let them have another try at reaching Camp V. Some of the team however—especially those of us already on the summit team—believed they did not have the spunk necessary to push through the deep snow at twenty-five thousand feet to Camp V. Unless that camp could be established quickly after the next break in the weather, our chances of a successful climb would be small indeed.

For me, the two days in Camp I were a time for continued reflection on my own ability to meet the task. I was still preoccupied with the lung problem I had had on Everest. I confidentially voiced my concerns to Rob Schaller, who offered to give me a physical. He listened carefully to my lungs, reporting that they were clear and strong-sounding. I had some minor congestion in my throat, and a cough, which are more or less normal when you have been working high for any length of time. I was losing a little weight, especially in my torso, but this too is common at high altitude. Rob recommended I take with me a packet of time-release decongestant capsules, and if I had any problems above, use them. He thought simple congestion could have been my problem on Everest.

A big fear at high altitudes is of sudden pulmonary edema—a bursting of the alveolar sacks and consequent filling of the lungs with fluid. In effect, you die drowning in your own blood. It is a not uncommon problem at high altitudes, especially the altitudes at which we would be working, and we had all learned to listen for the telltale gurgling in the lungs that indicates the beginning of P.E. Having had trouble before, even if Rob thought it had been only congestion, did not increase my confidence that I could climb without trouble at twenty-eight thousand feet, without bottled oxygen. That evening I wrote in my journal:

> Am I mentally prepared? I have self doubts. I don't know if I can function at twenty-eight thousand feet without oxygen. But sitting here at Camp I, I am girding my loins for the

hardest task in my life. I meditate on the formidable job ahead, and the more I concentrate on it, the more I clear the doubts.

What motivates me to such a task? The risks are so great. I could push myself enough to risk P.E. and die. The risk of frostbite is not only very real but in fact probable. I know at that altitude an hypoxic body will sacrifice its outer limbs to heat the more vital inner core. A bivouac is almost certain, and at that altitude it will almost certainly end in frostbite, with the possibility it will be fatal.

Yet I know if we manage to climb K2 by this new route without oxygen it will be perhaps the most significant achievement in American mountaineering. Is that what motivates me? Doesn't everybody wish to leave some mark in their life? To tread across unknown territory? Cross new thresholds and frontiers? Perhaps this drive is only the result of some large ego. I'm not sure, but there has got to be more to it that that. I do know this: I have a burning desire to do this thing that has never been done. God only knows, though, I hope I can do it.

August 16. WHITE ICE AGAINST COBALT SKY. Early morning with a slight wind that carries a sharp, biting cold. The feel of late fall, Indian summer heralding an icy winter.

I thought, The clearest day we've had since July 31. Kind of feels like winter, though. Cold. But for sure we will move today. It's back up the mountain.

It was 5:15 A.M., and there was a scheduled 5:30 radio call with those in Camp III. The walkie-talkie was in John's and Wick's tent. So, half-dressed, I carefully walked the icy path over there.

"Hello Camp Three. Hello Camp Three. Camp One calling. Over," Wick transmitted.

"This is Camp Three. Come in." It was Skip's laconic monotone.

"Looks like a good day," Wick continued. "The storm's broken—this is the best day in weeks. Looks like we move."

"Yeah, it's beautiful up here," Skip answered. "We've been talking about what to do. Seems like there is a lot of new snow up here. Might not be safe."

"Well, it's not like you've got to climb up," Wick said. "You're breaking down. That's safer—you can break the slabs off as you come down. But you need to clear the way before we can go up."

John looked at Wick and me and said, "Even if they come down we still don't get anywhere unless Chris and Cherie break over to Camp Four. We'll just logjam at Three otherwise."

"One thing at a time," Wick said.

Skip resumed his transmission. "We'll have to have a closer look at the snow conditions. Why don't we call back at eight-thirty."

"O.K.—eight-thirty. Camp One over and out."

*...The last step
depends on the first...*

*. . . The first step
depends on the last.*

I walked back to my tent feeling an impalpable uneasiness. If those in Camp III did not move today.... I did not want to think about it. But soon my fears were borne out. A couple of hours later, Wick wrote in his journal:

> It has started out as one of those days when the personality problems have risen to the fore and dominate everything— including the awesome grandeur of K2 rising ten thousand feet above this camp.

Before the 8:30 call we gathered in the cook tent for breakfast. Despite the brilliant day, our enthusiasm had palled with the hesitation of those above. The breakfast gathering became a purgative for pent-up emotions. Jim and Dianne had gone down to Base the day before to pick up mail, and their absence gave air to many criticisms of Jim's leadership—or lack thereof.

"I guess what irks me most," Bill said, "was the decision to risk all on one oxygenless ascent with only some fuzzy plan for a second attempt with oxygen. At least he could have asked our opinion before simply announcing his decision on the radio."

Several others also felt Jim had not sufficiently planned for a second assault team, but it was surprising that it bothered Bill—the implication was he still considered himself a candidate for a backup team.

"And it is one of the few times he has made a definitive decision," I added. There had been criticism of Jim's equivocation on several issues, especially that Chris-and-Cherie question. Some felt that, had Jim ordered Chris and Cherie to descend from Camp II during that first storm, the issue would have been discussed openly and later innuendoes and backbiting avoided. Some also felt Jim should have been more exact in planning logistics for the upper mountain assault. Many times people had simply carried what they wanted to, and however much they wanted to; although this had never resulted in any major supply problem, there was a feeling that we lacked a tight strategy for the assault. During this last storm, however, Jim had designed a very specific plan that called for fifteen loads to be carried to Camp V—enough gear, he estimated, to supply two summit attempts.

In Jim's defense, it should be pointed out he was in a damned-if-you-do, damned-if-you-don't dilemma. While Bill criticized him for not consulting the team before making a major decision, many of the rest of us complained he listened to too many opinions and consequently waffled on decisions. Jim was still sensitive to the mistakes of the '75 expedition and was committed this time to running the expedition more democratically. The problem, however, was that we were such a disparate group, there were times we would have been better governed by a benevolent dictator.

"Jim has too often let things happen, when he should have more affirmatively directed events," Rob asserted. "In the next few weeks we need strong leadership. We're running out of time. It was noticeably colder this morning, and I'm afraid winter might arrive before we get our chance. The HAPS say we can expect the winter storms to arrive anytime after late August. By the way they describe it, the storms we've been having are nothing."

It was 8:30, time for the radio call. In a few minutes Skip's voice came on. "Chris thinks the slope above camp is unstable. Craig and I went below camp two rope lengths, and we tend to agree with Chris."

We looked at each other, our fears realized. Another day of good weather lost. We considered the implications. It would be very difficult, and probably too dangerous, to work back to Camp III until Craig and Skip cleared the way from above. The larger problem, however, was that even if we did get to Camp III, there would be little useful work to do until Camp V was established. All camps through IV were more or less stocked, and all progress on the climb hinged on how quickly Chris and Cherie could get back to IV and push the route on to Camp V.

"If those guys could just break down to Camp Two," Terry said, "I would be willing to double-stage to Camp Three today. It might be fruitful if I had a talk with Chris and Cherie. It might help impress upon them the importance of getting to Five, and I could also explain the details of Jim's plan for a second assault—how they are the core of the plan. That would perhaps encourage them to push harder."

We agreed that, of anyone on the team, Terry would be the best to encourage Chris and Cherie. If he personally could talk with them, it would be much better than the frustrating communications by radio.

"I'll go with you," Bill volunteered.

Terry and Bill left camp; Skip and Craig would break down if, after further surveying the snow, they thought it would be safe. At nine they called, however, and said they felt they should not descend. They, along with Chris and Cherie, were going to stay in Camp III. It became obvious Terry and Bill would be able to climb no higher than Camp II. In my journal I noted:

> Another day wasted, and it appears that Terry and Bill won't even make it to Camp III to try and dangle a carrot in front of Chris and Cherie. The problem is we are not in a position to judge their assessment of avalanche conditions, but we have broken down to II after storms twice now. We can't help but wonder if they are running out of gas up there, and no doubt our skepticism comes across in our radio communications. They are probably getting a bit upset with us, first for pressuring them to cross the traverse in the storm, and now for questioning their judgment on avalanche conditions.
>
> Whittaker has been at Base Camp, but we told him this morning he is needed up here badly. We must get Chris and Cherie to move up—we've got to get V. We're at a crucial stage in the expedition; leadership and decisions are sorely needed.

Jim returned that evening. We had a meeting, and although Jim felt many of our grievances exaggerated, he left no doubt Chris and Cherie had only one try to get Camp V. He promised to keep tighter reins on the expedition—we all came away feeling much better. That evening, in the privacy of their tent, Jim told Wick, "Don't worry, if Chris and Cherie don't charge up to Camp Five, you tigers get the green light to go right up their tailpipes."

7

The Snow Dome

August 17. CAMP III, IT WAS HOT. THE STILL, thin atmosphere allowed the noon sun to cook the tents to oven temperatures. The camp had the refuse-strewn ambience of a tropical fishing village in some backwater country: garbage decorated the slope below the tents; urine-stained snow created abstract yellow designs on the camp's periphery. Three goraks, looking evermore like vultures, lazily scavenged through the empty beef stroganoff and turkey tetrazzini packages, squawking and occasionally pecking each other. In all, there were three tents. Chris and Cherie were in one, Lou in a second, and John and I shared the other.

Lou, John, and I had come up from Camp I that morning, climbing the ropes cleared by Skip and Craig as they descended. We had passed them just below Camp II. Wick, Jim, and Dianne were also climbing up, Wick making slow progress; he had awakened with severe diarrhea and consequently was suffering from dehydration in the strong sun.

The departure from Camp I had been emotional. If everything went as planned we would be leaving for the summit in five or six days. We left camp like soldiers into the last battle, with many wishes of good luck. Diana gave everyone a farewell hug, and with restrained emotion wished us a safe return. It would be the most dangerous part of the climb, and she had been thinking of Dusan. When she hugged Wick, he sensed her thoughts and whispered to her, "When I get to the top, Dusan will be there with me." Diana wiped a tear from her eye.

With the weather clear at last, the plan had called for Chris and Cherie to clear the route to Camp IV that day and begin pushing to Camp V. So we were astonished, when we trudged into Camp III, to find them still there.

No one said anything and I followed John as he crawled back into the tent we had deserted days before. Lou arrived a few minutes later, and sensing any comment would be a mistake, crawled inside his old tent and waited for Wick. Feeling I should at least say hello to Chris, I went over and sat in his tent.

"We started across," Chris explained, "but at the col there had been an enormous slab breakoff on the Chinese side, and the snow just didn't feel safe. It was real spooky, and I didn't want to risk it."

"I understand," I answered laconically. I went back to the tent I shared with John, and in a few minutes we spotted Wick making the last steps into camp. He stopped in front of our tent, unshouldering his pack. As he started to greet us, he noticed Chris and Cherie in their tent.

"Do my eyes deceive me, or is that who I think it is?" he groaned.

"That's them," John said. "On extended honeymoon. Nice place here, Camp Three. Warm, plenty of food. No reason to go anywhere else."

I knew Chris and Cherie could hear the conversation and I felt the rancor spread through the air like vaporized gasoline waiting for the next small spark. But nothing happened. We all sat in our respective tents and whispered. Jim and Dianne soon arrived, and once again I was surprised that Jim seemed to accept with equanimity that Chris and Cherie were still in camp. I had the impression he was disappointed but realized anger would get us no sooner to the top of the mountain. Instead, he set to work designing a new strategy that would put us quickly to Camp V, yet still preserve as much team solidarity as possible. He called a meeting in his tent later that evening.

"I've been thinking how best to use our strength from here on," Jim opened. "And I think John and Rick should break trail tomorrow to Camp Four. They know the route better than anyone, and they should be able to get across fast."

Everybody nodded silent agreement except Cherie, who sat stone-faced, anticipating the worst.

"Then I think Chris and Cherie should follow right behind," Jim continued, "get to Camp Four, and start pushing the route. They're the only ones who can do it because they know where the ropes are buried." Unlike the lower sections, above Camp IV we had fixed only the steepest slopes with rope, and with new snow covering them it would be necessary to know where to locate each segment. "Terry and Bill can follow to help carry extra rope and take over leading if the other two need relief. We won't reach Camp Five in one day, but we should get far enough to finish it the following day."

John's and Lou's disappointment was obvious. Wick sat in a corner, still suffering badly from the dehydration caused by his diarrhea, too drained to enter the discussion.

"It sounds like a weak plan," Lou countered. "Chris knows where the ropes are. I think Cherie simply isn't strong enough to lead to Camp Five. It will be the longest distance, the greatest altitude gain, between any of our camps; we will have to climb above twenty-five thousand feet with heavy loads without oxygen. Furthermore, if there is any delay getting to Five, that means there will be a logjam in Camp Four, and seven climbers eating food is crazy. I think they have had a fair chance to put in the route, and you—Jim—have lived up to your obligation to give everyone a fair chance at leading. But it's time to give the job to somebody else."

In a constrained voice, trying to sound imperturbable, Chris replied, "Lou, you have had a low opinion of Cherie and me from the beginning, and I think your prejudice is blinding you to even considering that our concern with the avalanche potential on those slopes just might be justified. You haven't been out there to see the slabs that have recently broken off. If it had looked safe, Cherie and I would have worked as hard as anyone to reach Camp Five, and we still will. But only if it's safe."

Cherie sat near the tent's vestibule entrance. She wore her jumpsuit and had her hair tied in two ponytails falling over the front of her shoulders. Her nose was still clown-white with sunscreen; the taut and lined skin of her face betrayed the stress of living and working at high altitude. Like everyone else's, the veins on her temples, the backs of her hands, and her forearms were raised in a growing bas-relief, as her blood thickened to acclimatize to the increasingly thin air. Her lips were pressed thin and serious.

"I'm getting sick of hearing how I'm not as strong as the rest of you," she snapped. "Everybody's always saying, 'Get rid of Cherie and have Craig or somebody take her place!' Hell, man, I can carry as much as him or most of you guys, and I'm getting tired of not being treated the same."

Cherie rolled up her sleeve, flexing her biceps in a mockery intended to carry no humor.

"Cherie," Jim said sharply, "sometimes I lose patience with you, and I think you could be a little more polite..."

"Oh, look who's talking now! Mr. Universe. Big Jim. It all makes me sick. All you bloody machos."

Jim's patience dissolved. "It's too bad you *aren't* a man," he shouted, "because then I could punch you right in your frigging nose."

Terry finally broke up the argument. "O.K., both of you, I don't think this is getting us anywhere. We've got to calm our tempers and think rationally."

Jim and Cherie apologized, but the truce seemed shaky. Lou remained disappointed with Jim's decision, and as the meeting adjourned he said he would sooner go down and carry loads between II and III than face the frustration of climbing behind a weak lead team. We went back to our tents, where each group prepared its own dinner. (It was the way meals were usually cooked; since all our food was packed in separate sacks, each containing two man-days of food, and since each tent had a separate stove, it was easier than shuffling food between tents.) The moon was full that night, the sky cloudless and the air clear. The high peaks cast great moon-shadows across the glacial valleys thousands of feet below. Although no one stayed out too long in the cold night air to enjoy the panorama, the grandeur of the scene beneath our aerie ameliorated much of the animosity in camp.

In the morning, John started our stove at 4:00 A.M.; at exactly 6:00 we shouldered our packs and left Camp III. Lou, after a good night's sleep, had decided to follow us across the traverse to pull out the first 400 feet of rope above Camp IV. Chris and Cherie would be right behind, then take over, navigating to where they knew the next section of fixed rope lay buried. Bill and Terry would also cross to Camp IV to help in the following day's push toward Camp V. The others, including Wick—who was still recovering from diarrhea—stayed in Camp III.

Digging out fixed rope buried by new snow is very hard work. It was better when we were able to keep a skeleton crew at a high camp during a storm; after the storm, it was much easier going down while pulling ropes than doing the same job going up. But on the traverse it would not have made much difference anyway, since most of the distance was sideways with only occasional uphill sections. The technique was to slide the jumar clamps up the buried rope, then lean back with all your strength, pulling up; with luck, four or five feet of rope would pop out. Then you'd slide the clamp up again, and again pull. A 150-foot section, especially if it was uphill, consumed all your energy, then another climber would have to take over. Fortunately, much of the traverse was so steep that little snow had accumulated on most sections.

We reached the col—the point where Chris said he had spotted the fracture edge of a big slab avalanche, the one that had made him question the slope's stability and turn back. We looked down the Chinese side of the ridge. There it was: a sharp step in the snow slope, at least a hundred feet long, where the slab had separated and avalanched to an icefall feeding K2's north glacier. There was no question the nonavalanched part of the slope was unstable. Fortunately, we would cross high above the most dangerous part, but it boded ill for other slopes farther along that we would soon have to cross.

"It doesn't look safe," I said to John.

"I know," he agreed. "Chances are, the snow hasn't accumulated as much on the steeper sections ahead. Still, it's not stable. But if we don't go across we might as well go home. We've got to get Camp Five now. Time's short, winter is coming."

I knew he was right: I knew we had to do it. We paused for a few minutes to rest and sip lemonade before carrying on. I looked over the hills of China and thought, as I sometimes had on dangerous days: I wonder if this is the last one. Is this the date on your calendar when all past events focus, to be carried together in one big avalanche of snow and buried in an icy crypt in some remote corner of western China? It was morbid, but I could not push the thought away. It kept recurring: Is today the day?

Our decision to carry on, despite dangers, crystalized before me a picture of the problems and factions on the expedition. Suddenly, it was so easy to understand; suddenly it was possible to look at the climb through the eyes of the others. To Lou and Wick, John and me—the four going to the summit—crossing this slope after a storm was worth the risk simply because we had so much to gain. But why should Chris and Cherie, with only a fuzzy plan for some second attempt, risk their necks? And for four people who they felt had wronged them. I, too, would have been bitter being ordered, against my own judgment, to descend from a high camp in a storm. And how would I have felt with rumors circulating behind my back about a friendship with a woman, when the hubbub over a supposedly irate, cuckolded husband was unfounded? Chris had come on this expedition leaving behind a hornets' nest of problems resulting from a bitter divorce. Was it so surprising he would seek the company of someone in whom he could confide his problems?

At the same time, I could imagine things from the others' points of view; they, too, would have understandable qualms over risking their necks for the glory of the summit team and Jim Whittaker. Terry would continue to work hard, especially to support the outside chance Chris and Cherie would have a shot at the top should the first attempt fail—or perhaps even if it were successful, and the weather held. Bill said he would work to support our attempt, but he seemed to be losing interest and did not appear strongly motivated. Skip was homesick for his wife, and Craig the same. Who could blame them? It had been fifty-eight days since we started walking, so long ago, across the deserts of Baltistan, forty-four days since we set camp at the base of K2. Forty-four long days above sixteen thousand feet, spending most of that time hauling heavy loads or installing ropes. There was so much work, so much stress from the altitude and the danger, so much to ask of people who now had so little to gain.

The team was dividing into two groups—three, if you thought of Jim and Dianne as a neutral, mediating party. Somehow, we started referring to the groups as the A Team—the first summit group of Wick, Lou, John, and me—and the B Team—centered around Chris and Cherie, the core of a second summit effort, supported strongly by Terry. Bill, Skip, Craig, Rob, and Diana were not really associated with either group, at least not at that point. I first heard the designations used by Terry, and I asked him their significance.

"B," he replied, "is for Best."

"And A?" I asked.

"A," he said, "is for Assholes."

We still had so far to go. We could only hope to stay together long enough, and get a long enough break in the weather, to make the summit. It would be so disappointing—more than that, so tragic—to head home after so many weeks and months of effort, without that summit.

"Let's go," John said. "We've got to get over there early so the others can start pushing. They'll be on our heels soon."

ALL PREOCCUPATION WITH SPLITS IN THE team, personality problems, petty quarrels—even most of the concern about slab avalanches—was lost in the work of clearing the ropes to Camp IV. I had not felt so good since John and I had led this traverse twenty days earlier. The weather was superb. There were just the two of us and the surrounding mountains, and it was easy to forget the rest of the expedition even existed. We climbed as fast as possible, methodically kicking a new trail in the snow and pulling out the ropes.

Jim Wickwire, resting in his tent at Camp III, wrote religiously in his journal:

> Incredibly, at 9:00 A.M. we could pick out two climbers on the snow pyramid just in front of Camp IV, a scant three hours after John and Rick left, and a virtual refutation of Chris's judgment of yesterday that snow conditions on the Chinese side of the ridge were too risky. So we were back in Camp IV ready to resume the long-awaited push to Camp V.

John and I unshouldered our packs and set to work excavating the tents that Chris and Cherie had collapsed to prevent their ripping in the wind the week before. It was a slow job. Care was needed to avoid tearing the light tent fabric with the snow shovel. In a half hour Lou arrived.

"Are Chris and Cherie behind you?" we asked.

"They hadn't left camp when I took off," Lou said with obvious displeasure. "And there was no indication they would be ready soon."

John and I were disappointed. We had worked as hard as we could to open the way to Camp IV quickly so Chris and Cherie could follow right behind us and start toward Camp V.

"I'm going up to clear the ropes as far as they extend," Lou said, indicating the slope above Camp IV.

"I'll go too," John said, "and help you out."

The two left as I continued to excavate the tents. By ten-thirty Chris and Cherie still had not arrived; by eleven I realized our plan was going sour. There was too little time left that day for any substantial effort toward Camp V.

Lou and John reached the end of the first fixed rope and, not knowing where the next section was buried, came back down. Finally, at noon,

Chris and Cherie hauled into camp. The tents had been repitched, and everyone was inside seeking protection from the sun. Chris and Cherie crawled into a deserted tent without a greeting. Again, there was the awkward, deadly silence I so loathed. Even John, atypically, said nothing.

At one, Chris announced he and Cherie were going up to start pushing the route. Relieved that at least some effort would be made, I allowed myself the thought that, if they worked to sunset, they might move a worthwhile distance toward our goal. Neither John nor Lou, however, seemed to care whether the two went up or not.

About two-thirty we saw Chris and Cherie coming back down. Back in camp, Chris said, "We started across the flat section above the first ropes and there was a big crack—a really loud pop—in the snow. It sounded like a slab cracking. I think it is still unsafe and I'm not going to climb higher until it looks better."

"Maybe it was just a crevasse cracking," Lou said.

"No, it wasn't a crevasse."

Chris went back to his tent. Terry and Bill had earlier come in from Camp III. Again, other than the occasional whisper, there was silence.

Lou, John, and I quietly began to formulate a new plan. It was obvious we would have to put in Camp V ourselves; we felt there was a chance we could do it in one day.

"The three of us can share the leading, but we still need Chris to show us where the ropes are buried," Lou observed.

Chris called from the neighboring tent, "I'll go with you."

"Terrific," Lou said. "You can share in the leading if you want." Lou's voice had a conciliatory tone.

"O.K.," Chris said.

"And if everyone else carries loads behind us tomorrow, we can not only reach Camp Five, but stock it with half the supplies we'll need up there."

Terry responded enthusiastically; Bill and Cherie also agreed to carry loads. Rising from the mood of despair was a kindling optimism, and we started to talk about the possibility of a summit assault in four days. All mention of the dangerous snow conditions Chris had suspected was dropped. Later that evening we radioed the plan, with enthusiastic response, to Camp III. Jim had independently devised a similar plan; he was pleased Chris was included. He had his fingers crossed this would end the widening schisms; little did he—or any of us—know it would only make them worse.

4:45 A.M. FIRST DAWN. A CLOUD RISING BE-hind the Abruzzi Ridge, billowing on the morning convection. Pastel colors backlight the roiling cumulus; a phantasmagoria of dervish sworls.

"Hold your boot over the stove," I told John. "It's worth the fuel to start with warm toes."

We defrosted our boots over two butane cartridge stoves. Steam rose from a cup of cocoa in a vapor like the cloud rising over the Abruzzi Ridge.

"Hope the weather holds. I would prefer a clear sky this morning."

"It's got to hold. We only need four more days to top out. Just four."

"We'll get Camp Five today, at least."

"Even if we reach Camp Five, it won't do much good if another storm comes. We're not fixing much rope. The snow would cover our tracks and we'd be back where we started."

"Maybe we can get some loads up, then. That would accomplish something. Anyway, the weather has to hold."

I set down my boot and picked up the cocoa to finish it before its warmth was wasted to the cold morning air. I wrapped my fingers around the cup, luxuriating in its warmth; I knew they would soon be numb when, outside, I fastened the metal crampons on my boots.

We left Camp IV a few minutes before six—a good, early start. John, Lou, and I were first on the trail, and Chris followed a few minutes behind. The others would follow, but as usual they were late getting started. By seven-thirty we were at the end of the ropes Chris, Cherie, and Skip had fixed in their previous efforts. Above us, a steep snow slope rose about four hundred feet to the top of a large pinnacle. Having studied the route from below through binoculars, we knew it would be an easy walk from the top of the pinnacle several hundred yards to the base of a large snow dome about fifteen hundred feet high, which formed the terminus of the northeast ridge. The dome sat directly under the immense summit pyramid. At the top of this dome we would place Camp V.

I took the first lead, stretching out a hundred fifty feet of rope. The slope steepened dramatically near its top, and this lead would be the toughest, especially with the heavy packs we were carrying. Not only did we hope to establish Camp V, but we also carried full loads. We were determined to make progress that day. I finished my lead; it looked like one more section to the top of the pinnacle.

"I'll take this pitch," John said.

Chris came up last and for a few minutes stood with Lou and me on a small platform stomped in the slope while John worked toward the top of the pinnacle, struggling in the soft snow on the steep slope with his heavy load. It was an impressive performance.

"I'm going down," Chris said.

"Huh?"

"I'm going to rappel down and wait under that serac." Chris pointed to a large ice block about a hundred fifty feet below.

"What for?" I asked. "Why not stay here, instead of going down and having to come back up?"

"It's safer down there."

Lou said nothing. We had hoped Chris might share in the leading, but he would not be able to take over if he was down below. There would be the snow dome, though, and plenty of opportunity to lead up the fifteen-hundred-foot gain to the dome's top.

The slope on which we were climbing was covered with at least a foot of new snow, and while it was not the safest place to be, there was no better choice, other than turning around. I watched Chris rappel to the serac. The space between us seemed to represent our continually increasing psychological separation. I knew Lou was disappointed but not surprised. Even if the slope was dangerous, I wished Chris had stayed. Just so we could be standing together in the same place, I thought.

John reached the top of the pinnacle and secured the rope to an aluminum deadman anchor. Lou climbed up next, and while I followed Lou began plowing through soft snow toward the base of the dome. The three of us alternated leads. The wind picked up, sending spindrift sweeping across the surface snow, stinging the exposed skin of our faces. Ground-hugging clouds scudded up the snow dome—and the cumulus that earlier in the morning had rolled up the far side of the Abruzzi had increased, covering part of the mountain in front of us. The building clouds would soon cover us, too.

We were at twenty-four thousand feet. We each carried a thirty-pound load; with each step we broke through hard crust and sank to our knees. Progress demanded a slow, even pace. It helped to drift into a meditative trance as I lifted one leg, stepped up, broke through the crust, breathed a few times, then lifted the other leg—again, and again, and again. Chris was some distance behind, by himself, keeping the same pace, not catching up with us.

The slope gradually inclined as we approached the snow dome. Crevasses were visible on its slope, and we hoped these would not cause problems in navigation. We picked what looked to be the best route, hoping we would not find soft snow on the slopes of the dome. With heavy loads at high altitude, that could thwart all efforts.

We started up the base of the dome. Luckily, the surface was wind-packed, with a crust thick enough to support our weight, and we only occasionally broke through. Taking turns in the lead, progress was steady.

We reached the crevassed section but before crossing it uncoiled our climbing rope and tied together. I could see Chris below, slowly climbing up the slope.

"Maybe we should wait for him so he can tie in," I said.

"We can't delay," Lou argued. "We've got to get to the top of the dome."

"It's not our fault he's slow," John added. "If we waited for everybody on this climb we wouldn't get to the top of the thing until Christmas."

I glanced back at Chris, then at the crevasses. They were not so bad; it would not be too dangerous crossing them after we had scouted a route. Still, I would have felt more comfortable waiting for Chris to tie in with us. And I would have felt less guilty. "He should have stayed with us in the first place," I said as we continued on, every now and again glancing back.

I thought, Chris should be able to move faster. We are breaking the trail, kicking the steps, and he's just following them. But the distance between us was closing only very slowly.

It was my lead. I climbed up to John and tied in to the end of the rope while he took my place in the middle. I rested, then started up. The wind had lightened, but there was more cloud—it had the feel of storm. Chris was still behind, and I kept checking back.

I should say something to Lou and John, I thought. I should insist that we wait for Chris to catch up. But John and Lou won't like the idea of waiting; we have to reach the snow dome, and there isn't much time.

"Maybe we should wait for Chris," I said. There was no answer from Lou or John. I went on climbing.

My mind drifted into a trance: *Lift your foot and plant your crampon and pull your other foot up, but casually so as not to waste effort, breathe a few times. Keep a steady pace. Got to get to the top of the dome. We should tie in with Chris. We should wait for him. It's more than just the safety of being on a rope, you know: it symbolizes everything. That's it, it's a metaphor for all the problems and everything that has gone wrong and the distance that's grown between us and the loss of our friendship. We're not roped up and you know he's thinking the same thing, how his pal is ahead of him now, gone over to the other side, gone over to the A Team, (remember, A is for Assholes) and won't even bother to wait so he can catch up and tie in to the rope. Yes, it's everything. The feeling at the beginning of the climb when you wanted to team up with Roskelley because you knew that was the best way to get to the top even though it meant deserting your friend. Lift your foot and place your crampon and pull up and drag your other foot and place your axe and breathe a few times. Keep the steady pace. Got to move as fast and as far as Lou and John, and Chris is still back there catching up but not fast enough and it's over 24,000 feet here and it's hard to breathe and think right . . .*

"Let's stop and have lunch," Lou suggested.

I had been leading for what seemed like forever. The watch showed it had been only fifteen minutes. The three of us took off our packs to use them as seats on the snow. We had each brought a few lunch items: crackers, cheese spread, a can of tuna, two candy bars, and a few pepperoni sticks.

Chris slogged on toward us. At least he could now tie in to our rope, but I wondered if he felt the same estrangement. He would know we stopped, not to wait for him, but only to have lunch. Later, weeks after the expedition, I would talk to him about the incident:

> I remember that day well, climbing alone behind the rest of
> you, feeling completely separate and cut off. I even felt
> separated from the others below, and I wondered why you
> didn't stop so I could rope up with you. But I knew why,
> really, in the back of my mind.

The clouds swept by us, obscuring the view of the glaciers below, giving us only peeps through momentary windows of the mountains across the valley: Broad Peak and the Gasherbrums. There were all the signs of more bad weather.

"All our efforts are going to be wasted," John said. "The main reason for coming up here is to kick a trail so we can haul the rest of the loads tomorrow and the next day. If the trail gets covered with snow, all this work will be for just about nothing."

"We've got a few loads with us," Lou said. "If we get this stuff to Camp Five it will count for something."

"Not much," John said. "We can cache it here."

"Yeah," I agreed. "I'm not sure it warrants the effort to carry it higher." I was feeling enervated, drained; it had been very hard work to get this high, and we still had a thousand feet to go. The snow was softer in places, too. At that altitude, it took every effort I could muster to kick steps with the heavy pack and keep a good pace. Camp V would be over twenty-five thousand feet. The thin air was a soporific that sponged from my psyche all its willpower.

"We've got to get to Five," Lou reiterated. "*Especially* if there is another storm coming. It's more than delivering a few loads. If we don't get to Camp Five now, and we're delayed again, a lot of people will lose the motivation to keep going. It will be a great psychological boost to tell ourselves that we've got to Camp Five."

John and I knew he was right, but it was such an intangible reward to justify the work ahead of us. It was painful to accept the reality that our efforts kicking the trail would only have to be repeated after another storm.

"I'll lead the rest of the way," Lou said tenaciously. We knew he would, too, if we let him.

"Oh, hell," John sighed. "We're going all the way, and we'll switch leads."

All of us smiled. I watched Lou finish lunch and thought of the time, weeks before, when we first reached the Camp II site, when Lou and I sat together eating lunch. He looked just the same now: the torn red parka he had used for years on all his climbs (he had been given a beautiful Gore-Tex jumpsuit, as we all had, but he had left it behind in Skardu, saying,

"My red parka still has lots of use left."), the beard matted with sunscreen, the tufts of hair sprung out between his ski-goggle straps. The only thing different was that now I knew him a little better. Not a great deal better— I still thought him the most enigmatic person on the expedition—but a little better. While I was still puzzled by what inner drives could be responsible for his almost unbelievable motivation, I at least had had several weeks to observe the empirical results of those drives—such as forging on, when the rest of us were so close to turning back, to Camp V. It was as if his mind thought an idea through to its logical conclusion, then if that conclusion demanded of his body some phenomenal physical effort, the body simply obeyed orders. It was as if he lacked what, to the rest of us, was the main limiter of our efforts: feedback from the body to the mind. Lou's body just carried out the mind's orders, and from observing him there was no indication any signals got through the other direction.

"How you doing?" John asked Chris when he caught up with us.

"O.K.," Chris replied laconically. "My load is heavy."

"Yeah, so's ours," John said, with the clear suggestion we were not only carrying loads, but breaking trail as well.

"Have some lunch," Lou offered.

Chris sat down. We glanced at each other, not speaking. I felt the distance between us was now a gap too wide to span; I was on the A Team, Chris was on the B Team, and our courses were inexorably destined to part.

We finished lunch in silence.

"Care to take a lead?" John asked Chris.

"My pack is too heavy. I've got a big load," Chris answered. "It's all I can do to keep up."

"O.K.," John said. He prepared to lead the next section. We fell into a mindless routine. John, Lou, and I switched leads, with Lou pushing farther than John or me each time. We were soon more than halfway up the dome and knew we would reach our goal in time to return to camp before dark. Behind we could see the other three: Bill had turned back, apparently caching his load partway; Terry and Cherie were also a long distance behind, moving very slowly, and it seemed unlikely they would reach Camp V in time to get back down. We were discouraged—it minimized further the value of our efforts stomping the trail all the way to the top of the dome. It looked as though the only major benefit from our effort would be, as Lou had said, the psychological boost to the expedition's morale.

For most of the way up the dome we climbed simultaneously, the four of us tied together on one rope. At a crevassed section, however, we would stop to belay the first man across before the others followed. Lou was leading and called for a belay before exploring a bridge over a crevasse partially buried by snow. Chris braced himself and fed the rope from around his waist to Lou. John and I stood by, resting. Lou probed the crevasse with his ice axe, searching for a secure crossing. For a minute no one said anything; we just stared at the clouds sweeping up the east side of K2. Then John suddenly piped up:

"I've got nothing against you personally, Chris, and even though I don't imagine we could ever be good friends, I think we can clear this up enough so we can get along for the rest of the trip."

I glanced at John. In his usual style he was saying exactly what was on his mind, and for a moment I admired his ability to bring things into the open. I thought perhaps we could air our grievances and mend them. Chris nodded his agreement. My sanguinity vaporized with John's next comment:

"But there's one thing I've got to get clear. I don't like you and Cherie blaming Rick and me for what has been going on between you and her. It's clear to everyone what's been going on."

Oh, no, I thought. Here we go again.

Lou, fifty feet above us and oblivious to the conversation, went on exploring the crevasse. Chris shot back in defense:

"That's not the way I understand it. According to a lot of people on this expedition, you and Rick are responsible for the rumors and most of the mess."

"Who said we were responsible?" John shot back, his voice rising.

"Whittaker for one. And most of the others."

"That's bull. It's been obvious to everyone what's been going on—all you need is two eyes. Rick and I were no more responsible for it than anyone."

My mind quickly thumbed through the scenario. Things had been going on of which John and I were not aware. It sounded as if others, not just Chris and Cherie, had blamed us for raising the issue. We both felt wronged, taking all the blame.

Chris belayed the rope out to Lou while arguing with John. I stood watching as they bitterly accused and counter-accused one another of being responsible for the divisions in the team; occasionally, I glanced up to see how Lou was doing. Lou still seemed unaware of the argument; he was engrossed in the job of reaching the other side of the crevasse.

Suddenly the rope went taut and I looked up. Lou was gone, disappeared down the crevasse. The sharp pull momentarily threw Chris off balance, but he quickly recovered and held the rope. Both he and John saw Lou had broken through the bridge and was in the crevasse. But they turned back, face to reddened face, and resumed their argument.

"Hold the belay and I'll climb up to see if he's O.K.," I hollered.

Chris did not so much as nod, but held the rope tight as if by instinct. He was so absorbed in the argument it was as if he were not aware of the problem.

"I don't see what my personal life or my personal business has to do with the expedition anyway," Chris yelled at John. "It has nothing to do with whether we get up this mountain or not."

"That's just more bull," John yelled back, eyes flaring. "We're in this thing together, and it affects us all."

I climbed as quickly as I could toward Lou, but at twenty-five thousand feet I was necessarily moving slowly. I shouted to Lou, but there was no response and no sign of him. I stopped for a few seconds to catch my breath, looked up to see the rope disappearing bar-taut down a hole in the snow, then looked the other way to Chris and John wildly yelling at each other. Chris still had the rope tightly belayed around his waist. Both of them ignored Lou's predicament.

"And what about you and Diana?" Chris yelled. "You've been sleeping in the same tent most of the trip. Tell me about that."

John and Diana had developed a close friendship and had often bunked in the same tent. But everyone knew their camaraderie went no further. Quite apart from John's fidelity and conservatism, we all knew how much Diana still loved Dusan, and how strongly she felt Dusan's presence on the expedition. That she would be with anyone else was simply unimaginable.

"At least I can deny that," John shot back. "Go ahead and deny that there's been something between you and Cherie."

"I don't have to deny anything to you," Chris yelled.

I was nearly at the hole into which Lou's rope disappeared, with John and Chris still arguing heatedly. Just before I peeked over the lip, out popped Lou's head, like a seal surfacing, disoriented, through a hole in pack ice. His goggles were pushed down over his nose, his glasses under the goggles packed with snow. He could not see. Snow clung to his hair and beard. I stared at Lou, then down at Chris and John still yelling at each other, not even noticing that Lou had surfaced. It was like a Jerry Lewis comedy act. I started to laugh at the absurdity, which seemed to confuse Lou all the more.

"You O.K.?" I asked him.

"Yeah, I guess so. I didn't expect the bridge to break. Guess I better move over to the right." Still half hanging in the crevasse, he removed his glasses and cleaned them. Then he said, "What's going on down there, anyway?"

"A little argument," I said, and turned to climb back to Chris and John, still blustering at each other. Lou crawled out of his hole, dusted the snow off his hair, and headed on up, crossing the bridge at a more secure spot farther right. The rope went tight, forcing Chris to start climbing. He yelled at John as he climbed, turning back now and then to make his points.

"I'm just sick of your applying your redneck values to everyone on the expedition," Chris shouted back.

"At least I have values," John screamed.

Losing patience, I yelled, "God, I'm getting sick of this. I wonder if we're ever going to learn to act our ages on this climb."

Chris turned back to climbing; the exertion of climbing and arguing simultaneously at nearly twenty-five thousand feet was too much, and he continued in silence. There were still fifteen more feet of slack rope before John would have to start up.

"You know," I said to John, "sometimes you ought to watch your temper and think a little before you start saying stuff."

"Yeah, but I've got to say what's on my mind."

"I noticed the habit."

The rope paid out and John started climbing. In a few minutes our minds were again lost in the drudgery of placing one boot in front of the other and slowly, slowly climbing. At the end of another hour we made the last steps to the top of the snow dome. It was Camp V.

WE WERE FORTUNATE TO HAVE ON THE EX-pedition a person with the unwavering drive of Lou Reichardt. Without him we probably would have turned back low on the snow dome. As Lou had predicted, another delay from the new storm brewing, coupled with another failure to reach camp, would have so disillusioned us that it is conceivable we might not have mustered the spirit to go on. Reaching Camp V that day was a small success that nourished the stamina we would need to weather the extremely difficult trials that still lay ahead.

As we descended from the top of the snow dome, where we had located the cache that would eventually become Camp V, it looked more and more like another storm was on its way in. Clouds moved swiftly up the east side of K2, sweeping over our ridge and off into China. Flurries of snow danced on the wind. The arrival of this latest round of bad weather seemed to fit the pattern: there had been four days of good weather, and if the usual cycle we had observed since our arrival on K2 was repeated, there would follow five to seven days of bad weather. I began to prepare myself mentally to spend more days inside the tent, perhaps even to go all the way down to Camp I.

Through breaks in the clouds we could catch the occasional glimpse of Terry and Cherie still climbing up the lower part of the dome. There was no way they could make the top. They had been moving too slowly; they would have to cache their loads, come back, and finish carrying them up another time. We were descending rapidly and in a few minutes crossed paths.

Cherie was defensive about not getting the loads up.

"We didn't get started until nine," she said, "because we were watching you guys lead to the pinnacle, and it didn't seem like you were going to make it. Then Bill turned around and I wasn't tied to anyone so I had to wait two hours at the base of the dome for Terry to come so I could have somebody to rope with. And, you know, we had very heavy loads and we had to leave some of it back there."

She pointed down the route to a cache some distance away. I was losing my temper. John was also upset. Lou had not even stopped to talk—he was already a hundred yards farther down the trail. I was angry that not only would the loads not be delivered to Camp V, but equipment was strewn all over the mountain; if this next storm was a big one, the gear might be lost under new snow.

"Why didn't you just carry light—thirty pounds or so—to begin with?" I asked. "It would have been much better to get a smaller amount to Camp Five than to have stuff littered all over the hill where it will probably get lost."

"Well, if there had been more time I could have made it," Cherie protested. "I feel good right now, and it's only another hour up there, huh?"

"Try three and a half," I said caustically.

"Well, with more time we could have done it," she said in a voice so confident it betrayed an underlying uncertainty. "We'll just have to come back tomorrow and carry up there."

In my anger I failed to understand their point of view. We had all agreed that they should not leave Camp IV until we had made some progress, to avoid a logjam—so it was understandable they had a late start. But I was not thinking rationally.

"Better mark your cache with careful coordinates," I said. "And I wouldn't count on getting it to Camp Five in the near future."

By then it was snowing steadily. John had already put on his pack and left. I grabbed my empty sack and took off, soon losing sight of everyone in the diminishing visibility and finding my way by following our tracks, which were slowly filling with new snow. The wind ceased. Descending alone with only the silence of big snowflakes floating down put me in a better mood.

When we got back to Camp IV we radioed the day's success to the others at various positions lower on the mountain. As expected, the news was enthusiastically received and seemed, at least temporarily, to buoy spirits despite the building snowstorm. Rob Schaller, still in Camp I with his knee injury, radioed back his impression of this latest storm:

"We haven't had one like this before. It's warmer than ever—sort of mixed rain and snow—and it's coming down very hard. But the sky is bright and the air temp is up twenty degrees. It's remarkably warm down here."

Perhaps that meant the storm would be shorter. There was no real evidence on which to base such a hope except that this storm seemed different. Which could also mean it would be longer. All we could do was cross our fingers.

Our discussion about how best to deal with the worsening weather started that evening and continued into the next morning. It snowed through the night, and since there were all the signs the storm would last at least a couple of days, the next morning we decided everyone should go down and wait in Camp III, or lower, except for two who should stay in Camp IV to open the trail back up the snow dome the minute the weather broke. An argument ensued—partly over the radio—over who should stay high and who should descend.

"I don't mean anything personal," Jim offered, speaking over the walkie-talkie, "but if people can't earn their keep up here and deliver loads to Camp Five, they should go down. That's my completely objective opinion of how we can best get to the top of this mountain."

Jim knew, however, it would not be taken that way. He was now particularly sensitive to hurting the feelings of Bill Sumner, who had made less distance than anyone the day before. Jim had earlier chewed him out over the radio and ordered him to descend, in language that allowed little doubt of its meaning and left everyone feeling glum. Jim later apologized for his outburst, but the damage was done.

Bill told us he had turned around so soon because he thought the weather was rapidly deteriorating and we would not make it to Camp V; since he wanted to cache his load where it could be easily found, even after heavy snowfall, he had left it at the top of the last fixed rope. IIe also candidly admitted, however, that he was exhausted and not certain he could have made it to the top of the snow dome at any rate. It was sad to see Bill running out of gas, and it seemed his spirit and enthusiasm were also flagging. For some reason I felt the cause was not merely the difficulty he had climbing at high altitude, but also the distaste he felt for what he considered petty squabbling and bickering. Most of the time Bill stayed apart from the arguments, the philosophical observer watching and taking notes, but not participating.

Until the push to Camp V, I suspected Bill had harbored hopes of getting a chance to try for the summit. He had voiced as much the week before in Camp I when he told Rob Schaller he felt he had not been fairly considered for the first summit team, or even the second. Now, however, he seemed to be realizing his own limitations, which no doubt added to his disillusionment.

A few days earlier, Wick had written:

> Bill seems extremely lethargic lately. He was a fine companion on McKinley, and there have been many good moments with him on this expedition. Yet he now seems preoccupied much of the time—he doesn't seem happy here. Maybe, like most of us, he is better in smaller groups—on smaller expeditions. All the personality clashes, the stresses, the intrigues, may have gotten him down. He seems to be merely going through the motions, exerting a miminum effort to get someone to the top so it will be over and he can go home.

Bill Sumner refused to go home, however, taking no valuable experiences with him. Early in the expedition he told Wick that, even more important to him than reaching the summit, was his friendship with the HAPS and Saleem, the knowledge he had gained of their culture and religion, the personal closeness with these affable people from the remote valleys of Hunza. Bill had achieved that friendship more than any of us. For Bill, though, active participation in the front lines of the climb was over.

Chris did not agree with my opinion that those not able to carry to Camp V should immediately go down:

"You're judging people on their performance for one day only," he said. "You might want to consider giving people more of a break than that."

"Yeah," Cherie added. "I'm getting sick of hearing about this muscle business all the time. Anybody can make it to Camp Five when they're only carrying twenty-five pounds."

"Twenty-five pounds?" I roared back, incredulous.

John sat up in his sleeping bag with a scowl on his face, and I saw Lou also turn his head. We were talking through tent walls: Lou, John, and I in one tent; Cherie, Chris, Terry, and Bill in the other. Cherie had hit an exposed nerve, and she knew it. She did it on purpose just to tease; she knew we had carried more than twenty-five pounds the previous day to Camp V. She knew it was an even more sensitive subject because when we arrived at Camp V Chris unloaded his pack, and we saw only five food bags—about forty pounds. That was little more than the weight of our own loads, and we had done all the exhausting step-kicking, exempting Chris because we thought he had much more weight. Although no complaints had been spoken, Cherie was well aware of our disparaging opinion of Chris's performance.

"Listen, Cherie," I went on. "John had two bottles of oxygen and a sleeping bag [about thirty-five pounds], Lou had a tent and a bunch of sleeping bags [certainly over thirty-five pounds], and I had a rope and a bunch of hardware [about thirty-five pounds]."

"You know that's a bunch of bull," John swore through the tent wall. "Twenty-five pounds!"

Lou was piqued as well. He was ready to fire his own salvo through the nylon barrier. Then we heard Cherie laughing—at our expense.

"I thought that would get a rise out of you," she said.

There was silence between the tents, then John's lip curled in a sly smile.

"Don't worry, Cherie," John called over, "one thing you'll never get out of me is a rise."

John's humor helped to relieve tension between the tents. Everyone laughed, if a bit cautiously. It was more than a laugh just at the witticism, it was also a laugh at ourselves: for a moment, we had exposed the human foibles—the desires, ambitions, frustrations, fears—that lay in the origin of our quarreling, and, for the moment at least, we forgot the storm and the mountain against which those foibles were pitted. A white flag waved a truce, welcomed by all.

It was eventually decided that John and I should hold down Camp IV while the others bailed out. Lou would stay in Camp III with Jim, Wick, and Craig; the others would go all the way down to Camp I. When the storm was over John and I would break trail to Camp V while the Camp III crew crossed the traverse to IV then, if possible, made the final carry to Camp V that same day. This would leave us positioned for a summit push two or three days later.

The others left, and John and I lay in our sleeping bags with only the soft sound of snowflakes sliding down the tent fly. I closed my eyes, visualizing where I was, as if I were a giant zoom lens on a satellite, pulling back to expose the whole scene: a sleeping bag in a tiny tent on a knife-ridge snaking down from the summit of the second highest mountain in the world, on the border between China and Pakistan in the remote vastness of central Asia. Waiting. Waiting out yet another storm, and hoping—on this forty-eighth day that we had been on the mountain—that we would get the four days of clear skies we needed to reach the top. Jim Wickwire, at that moment a mile away in another tent in another camp, wrote:

> The storm frustrates us all. It is a big factor in causing the disputes and squabbles we suffer from. We are all becoming increasingly impatient to wind up this expedition—on a successful note. For nearly a month now, we have had storms and only a few days of clear skies. And we are back in the soup again. Three, four, five days, we aren't sure how long it will last. But one thing *is* for sure: if we cannot take maximum advantage of the next clear spell, our chances for the summit will be virtually nil.

8

Problemas Grandes

August 23. CLOUDS STREAMING UP THE RIDGE from both directions, from Pakistan, from China. Meeting on the crest, roiling, jetting upward, curling, arching downward. A maddening vortex, Dantian Hell, fierce and awesomely beautiful. Day forty-nine on the mountain. Day sixty-three including the approach march.

It was the most severe storm of the expedition. At Camp III, Jim Wickwire's altimeter registered a 250-foot gain as the barometric pressure dropped. Gusts hit our tent and pressed the walls down, bending the fiberglass poles to near-breaking, and we held the fabric off our faces with our hands.

"If the tent goes we're in big trouble," John said.

"*Problemas grandes,*" I said in my best Spanish, talking loudly above the noise of the storm.

"Might have to dig a snow cave to survive."

"That would ruin my day."

We lay in the tent staring at the walls. We could hear the stronger gusts before they hit, and we wondered which would be the one that snapped the tent. The other climbers had descended four days ago. Now they had abandoned Camp III and everyone was in Camp I—everyone except John and me, still holding out at Camp IV.

We had finished breakfast and there was nothing to do. The nylon walls hummed like a tuning fork, vibrating the air inside so our condensed breath and the steam from the stove oscillated at the same high fre-

178

quency. There was little to talk about, other than the continuing arguments at Camp I, about which we were updated in daily radio calls from Rob Schaller. We were bored with that subject as well.

"Could be trouble coming," I said.

"You see a tear in the tent?" John perked up.

"No, I feel the urge coming. Think I will have to go outside."

"Well I'm sure as hell not going to let you do it in here."

I held off as long as possible, but finally there could be no more procrastinating. I laced my boots, pulled on my jumpsuit, and snapped my parka. Unzipping the door, I exited quickly to minimize spindrift blowing in.

Relieving oneself in bad weather is one of the most disagreeable aspects of high-altitude climbing. It also provokes the most frequent questions in discussions with nonclimbers—everyone wants to know how you do it. The answer is simple: you unzip and take care of business as fast as you can before you freeze up. That danger—freezing up—is a real one, too. Two weeks earlier, Craig Anderson had suffered frost nip* at Camp III and the feeling still had not returned. The most innovative solution to the problem that I had witnessed was on the Everest climb. One of the climbers—who shall remain nameless—had eaten large quantities of Lomotil above a certain altitude and was never faced with the horror of dropping his drawers in a blizzard. When Jim Whittaker climbed Everest, however, he was less fortunate. On the summit in a howling gale, he faced the decision of baring himself or somehow mustering willpower to wait. "No sense carrying it all the way down," he thought, and finished the task in the lee of the south summit, 28,750 feet. Three weeks later, when Barry Bishop reached the summit, he unknowingly skewered the frozen result with his crampon, and carried it partway back to the summit. Jim not only is the first American to climb Everest, but in all probability holds another record as well.

I finished the job and crawled back into the tent. We had read the only two paperbacks in camp—the second book of the *Lord of the Rings* trilogy (no one had any idea where the other two books were) and a dog-eared, underlined copy of *Zen and the Art of Motorcycle Maintenance*. Anyway, it was almost time for the midmorning radio call, so John and I discussed the latest disputes. As the storm had continued, so had the controversies. For the past two days—before the final hangers-on at Camp III had descended—the arguments had focused on a revised summit strategy developed by Lou Reichardt and approved by Wickwire and Whittaker.

Lou's plan was designed around an immediate summit push the minute the storm let up, using only the people already high on the mountain. Not surprisingly, the people at Camp I were opposed, claiming—with justification—that the plan excluded any contingency for a second assault. John

---

*Fortunately, only on his fingers.

and I also were opposed, thinking there would not be enough people to carry the necessary loads to Camp V. The plan depended on Dianne Roberts, who had stayed at Camp III, to deliver an oxygen bottle and some valuable food bags to Camp V, and neither of us were certain she could do it. Lou bristled at our criticism, telling us he felt "betrayed." John and I fumed back; for the first time there were splits in the A Team.

But as the weather further deteriorated, those at Camp III had decided to descend; Whittaker had ordered John and me down also, saying there was no longer reason to justify our staying high. We would be better, he had said, waiting at Camp III, so we could break down from there after the storm.

"O.K.," I had told Jim. "We have to brew up, collapse the tents, and then we'll be down."

With the radio call over, John had grumbled, "That's the dumbest thing I've ever heard of. There will never be enough time to make the top after the storm clears."

Not thinking too clearly myself, I had replied, "This time, I'm going to take my personal gear down. I have a feeling we might not ever get up here again—you know, this might be the end of the expedition."

That was when John and I had devised our own, even more haphazard and foolish, summit strategy. The controversy fired by that plan was now raging. John had initiated the idea:

"I'll tell you one thing," he said. "Messner would never put up with this. That's why he's the best. He would just go for it. He's been screwed on too many of these big expeditions. That's why now he only climbs with one other guy."

There was a silence, then John said, "Well, what about it?"

"What about what?"

"Just you and me. As soon as the weather clears, we'll go for it. We don't need the rest of them. We'll alpine-style it from here."

I considered the plan, vacillating. On the one hand, it seemed our best chance of reaching the top. I was beginning to despair, thinking if we did not give it one bold effort in the next clear spell (assuming there was another clear spell) there would be no chance of success. And with everyone descending, it seemed there was no other way to take advantage of a clear spell that—if past experience held—would probably last only three days. On the other hand, I knew it would outrage everybody, whether we made it or not.

"It's worth considering," I told John. "We'd be hanging it out, though. On our own completely. Absolutely no support."

"It's our only chance," he said. "I want to climb K2."

On an earlier radio call, we had revealed our bold plan. As expected, the idea had been received with incredulity. Wick had observed:

> Rick and John are talking of attempting the summit themselves. What in the hell are those two thinking about? First,

they reject our plan saying we need two or three others from
below to come up and carry loads. Now, they go the opposite
direction and think they can do it themselves.

That morning, while John and I listened to the storm buffet our tent,
the clashes in Camp I continued. Reichardt, backed by Wickwire, still ad-
vocated his spartan attempt, and he had lobbied the tentative support of
two others: Craig Anderson and Diana Jagersky. The rest—principally
Chris, Cherie and Terry—contended Lou's plan excluded carrying
adequate supplies to Camp V for a second attempt, and they were ada-
mantly opposed to it. They insisted enough supplies must be carried to
Camp V for two assaults:

"If the supplies aren't carried to Camp Five," they threatened, "we will
quit the expedition and leave." Whittaker resisted their idea, saying there
was not enough time or strength left. Meanwhile, Roskelley and I were at
Camp IV, proposing the zaniest idea of all: to ignore everyone and climb
the mountain by ourselves. Clearly, the expedition was in crisis.

At Camp IV, we turned on the radio for the midmorning call. We knew
we would be talking to Rob Schaller; the radio was kept in his tent. Rob
had spend most of the expedition housed in that tent. Early on the
approach march he had contracted a flulike virus that kept him ill during
the beginning of the climb, and only a short time after recovering he had
broken a piece of cartilage inside his kneecap on the steep face below
Camp II, forcing him to stay at Camp I.

It had been bitterly frustrating. Rob was among the core of people who
first dreamed of applying for a permit to climb K2 in 1972, before Jim
Whittaker had joined as the group's leader. He had suffered the defeat in
1975, and then had joined Jim, Dianne, and Wick to organize the 1978
attempt. It was heartrending to watch Rob sidelined in that tent at Camp
I, knowing so many of his years were invested in the dream.

Despite his incapacitation, however, Rob had been far from unproduc-
tive. Although no one had been seriously ill or injured, he continued as our
chief physician. He had nursed Diana Jagersky to recovery from a painful
gastrointestinal ailment, and since any abdominal pain could telegraph a
serious ailment, it had been important, especially considering our remote-
ness, to quickly and accurately diagnose her problem.

There had been another important duty: During the heated arguments
Rob had played the role of the team arbitrator, either directly intervening
or as go-between over the radio, mediating between factions, calming
tempers, and often restoring harmony. Sitting in Camp I, he perhaps
better than anyone was able to watch the progress of the expedition with
the most objective understanding, and he more than anyone was able to
empathize with all sides during the arguments that came so close to ending
our expedition. In that role Rob was cast as one of the team members
ultimately responsible for our success.

Rob's voice came on the air:"I'm in agreement with your desire to get to the top," he said, in the most diplomatic of voices, "but you don't realize why everyone had to come down. There are no supplies left up there. There are only seven food bags and ten fuel cartridges in Camp Three, and no fuel and very little food in Camp Two. Here at Camp One, we have no Base Camp supplies left, and we have only one day of upper mountain provisions in the stockpile. Several people went down to Advance Base today to bring up more supplies, but clearly we are short."

"That's all the more reason we have to move fast when the weather breaks," I replied.

"But you can't do it by yourselves," Rob continued, appeasingly. "Look, there's still a lot of people down here capable of carrying high. Things are pretty bad right now—in fact, we're near revolt—but we're having a meeting soon and I hope we can work things out. I admit it's anarchy right now—everybody making their own plans and decisions. Whittaker's going to have to do something fast. But you guys saying you're going to climb the mountain alone doesn't help much."

John and I finally capitulated, agreeing to scrap our plan, but we stressed the importance of people returning high as soon as possible to take maximum advantage of any good weather. Rob said he would call back at 5:30 to update us on the big meeting.

"This is a crisis," he said. "I hope this meeting pulls people together. Otherwise, I fear the worst."

THE CORE OF THE B TEAM—CHERIE, CHRIS, and Terry—and a few of those peripherally attached—Craig, Bill, and Skip—had descended that morning to Advance Base to pick up more supplies. On the way back to Camp I, they discussed their complaints and grievances: Whittaker's supposed overall lack of leadership, his premature selection of the summit team, his exclusion of a strong second attempt from his summit plan, his ordering Bill Sumner to descend. Of all their grievances, the last was perhaps the most emotion-packed. Affable, quiet, highly regarded by most of the team members, Bill Sumner crossed between the warring factions better than anyone, and when Jim had ordered him down for not completing his carry to Camp V, it had raised the ire of many, especially those in the lower camps.

By the time they got back to Camp I, their tempers had reached a blow-valve pressure. The group from Camp III—Lou, Wick, Jim, and Dianne—had themselves just made an arduous descent in whiteout, blizzard conditions. But despite his own exhaustion (Jim had described the descent as the hardest day he had had on the expedition to that point), Jim went out to greet the others with a big handshake and a hearty backslap when they came into the camp with their loads. "It was such a warm welcome," Craig said later. "It was difficult to still be mad at the guy." Jim, a politician at heart, had masterfully defused their tempers—not through calculated subterfuge, but through genuine goodwill. He announced there would be a meeting that evening in the cook tent.

At the appointed time everyone—except John and me—gathered. The cook tent was about ten by ten feet, rising four-sided, Lawrence-of-Arabia-style, to a pyramid roof. There was a canopied entrance, and inside, seats arranged on food boxes and sacks of atta and dahl. In one corner sputtered two large Primus stoves, heating brew water; behind them were stored the meager remaining provisions.

Jim opened the meeting. "The first thing I want to do," he said in a low, mild voice, "is apologize to all of you for being so heavy-handed, for acting so excessively in the past. If I've been unfair to some of you, I'm sorry."

He paused. The only sound was the sputtering of the Primus. It was nearly dark in the tent, and cold.

"It's been a forty-year dream of Americans to climb this mountain, and many of us in this tent have been involved in that struggle for more than five years. The history of American climbing in the Himalaya is centered around this mountain—the British had their Everest, the French their Annapurna, and the Americans have K2. I think we owe something to all the climbers who worked so hard before us to realize this dream; I think we owe it to ourselves, who have already put in so much effort, to work together with everything we have to get one of us—any one of us—to the top of this mountain. But no one or two or even four of us can do it alone. It will have to be a team effort."

Another silence. Everyone was much moved, both by Jim's appeal for unity and by his contrition, and although the discontent was too deep to be erased by apology or appeal alone, it nevertheless set a tone of conciliation for the rest of the meeting.

In a mild, diplomatic voice Terry spelled out the B Team's grievances:

"I suppose the main complaints are that many of us have been treated as just load carriers—as Sherpas—for those already chosen to go to the summit, and that we've not been fairly considered or given an opportunity to devise a summit strategy ourselves. We feel we have as much right to go to the top of this mountain as anybody."

Chris added his opinion: "I think the criteria used to choose the summit team were wrong. You judged people on how much leading they did on the route, and how fast they carried loads between camps. I just don't think that has anything to do with how well people are going to climb above twenty-six thousand feet."

Chris had made a valid point, a point based on his earlier experience on Everest. There, he had discovered that the Sherpas—who had been exceptionally strong load carriers at lower altitudes, stronger, in fact, than any of the sahibs—had seemed to hit a barrier at about 8000 meters (26,240 feet). Above that, both sahibs and Sherpas had been slowed to the same lethargic pace; the altitude had been so debilitating it seemed to matter less how strong a climber had been at lower altitudes than how strong his desire was to continue pushing his body up through increasingly thin air.

Jim had also climbed Everest and knew those problems as well as Chris, but if he should not have based his summit team decision on the criteria he had chosen, what other criteria were there? The distillation of the B Team's argument was, then, that if it could not be accurately determined at lower altitudes who would be best to go to the summit, Jim should wait until much later to choose the team, thus giving more people a chance to prove their mettle at extreme altitudes.

There was criticism that Jim had been premature in choosing the summit team, that he should have waited until later in the expedition. In retrospect, Jim no doubt agreed with this, since it could have helped prevent the estrangement of nearly half the team, but when he had made the selection—weeks earlier—we had been potentially only a few days away from a summit attempt. No one could have predicted the storms that had so wreaked havoc on that original schedule.

Jim considered what Terry and Chris said, uncertain what to do about it, until a suggestion from Wick broke the stalemate.

"If you feel strongly that the summit team was chosen too early, and with the wrong qualifications, why don't we simply rescind the choice," he said. "From now on there won't be a summit team, and we will wait and choose one after Camp Five is stocked and we're ready for the top. I don't mind. I still feel strong and have the confidence I can make the team later as well."

Everyone looked surprised but nodded their approval of the idea. Terry was the first to ask the obvious question: "Who, then, should choose the summit team?"

After discussing different possibilities, everyone finally agreed it should be Jim, but that he should consult everyone on the team before making the final choice.

"That still leaves one problem unresolved," Terry resumed. "We think we need a plan that allows room for more people to go to the summit. Over the last several days, some of us have worked out such a plan, and that's what I want to discuss now. I should also add that if this plan hadn't been developed, and if several of the team hadn't thought it would be approved, they would have quit the expedition by now. I don't know if all of you here realize how serious this is."

Everyone listened quietly while Terry outlined the plan. Lou sat in a corner, taking notes.

"Basically, we propose two simultaneous assaults," Terry said. "One by the direct finish up the northeast ridge—the Polish route—and another by the Abruzzi finish. The Abruzzi assault would most likely consist of the B Team. We think the advantage of this is that it not only gives more people a chance to go to the summit, it also increases support for the direct finish team. We still have doubts it will be possible to complete the direct finish, but if some people do get up it, it would be much easier for them to descend the Abruzzi, especially if another team has marked a route and established a second Camp Six for refuge on the way down.

"We have figured a detailed list of equipment needed for the simultaneous assault, and we think if we make a coordinated carry to Camp Five as soon as the weather breaks, we can stockpile enough stuff for both assaults."

Terry outlined the details of the proposal. Whittaker listened carefully. It would be logistically more complicated: the need for two Camp VI's meant more supplies would have to be carried to Camp V. Jim's original fear that the heavier stocking of Camp V for two assaults would delay the summit attempt by at least a day—time that could make all the difference if another storm threatened—was offset by the larger number of people willing to carry to Camp V for a double assault. He realized that was the real value of the plan: it would unite the team, and once again we would work together to a common goal.

"Also, the plan better guarantees success," Terry concluded, "because if the direct finish isn't possible, we'll have an alternative, backup strategy for getting to the top."

"It's at least consistent with my main goal on this expedition," Jim concurred, "to get somebody to the top of K2."

Everyone nodded agreement. Jim concluded the meeting:

"We can never forget the thousands of people whose prayers are supporting us in our attempt to climb this mountain," he said. "We can never forget those thousands of postcards each of us signed.* In the last mail, there were dozens of letters from all over the country, from people saying they were praying for our success. Saleem just received a radio call from General Butt in Gilgit and he says they are all praying to Allah we will be successful and all come back uninjured.

"And we can't forget Al and Dusan and Leif. I know they're all here, right now, encouraging us on. I think we owe it to them, most of all, to climb K2."

There was a quiet inside the cook tent: thoughts were with lost comrades. That evening there was camaraderie the team had not had since arriving at the foot of K2. Complaints about Jim's lack of leadership had been scattered before the diplomacy he had shown in chairing the meeting.

"*Inshallah* [God willing]," Jim had said, "we'll make the summit together."

---

*Every person who contributed $20 or more to the expedition received a postcard signed by all team members, carried by runner from Base Camp and mailed from Skardu.

A LETTER FROM DIANNE ROBERTS TO SUSANNE AND JAKE PAGE:

August 23, 1978

Dear Susanne and Jake,

Well, the weather has stopped us—really stopped us. I fear that summer has turned to winter, and our supplies might run out before we get the four to five days of clear weather that we need to complete the climb. The team is still in good shape in most respects, but there is no question we are getting gradually weaker from such a long time at high altitude. I *know* I can go back to Camp III, carry loads to Camp IV and V, and maybe even to Camp VI, but if you ask me to do it twice, I'm not sure. Can we last into September if we have to? There is an old rule of thumb on Himalayan climbs: if you don't get the mountain in forty-five days, you don't get it at all. We arrived in Base Camp July 5: fifty days ago today. Psychologically I think we have some problems. A few people are home-sick—not enough to keep them off the mountain, but it shows in their motivation. I think most everyone still wants the summit, and will work to get someone there, but there are a few who would be just as happy to go home now without it. We have also split, perhaps inevitably, into two groups. I'm not sure how or why this happened, but it has to do with styles, personalities, and moralities. Jim is doing his best to keep the group together—doing a good job, I think—but he is taking a lot of flak from a lot of people. Perhaps that's the lot of a leader.

Right now we're trying to work out logistics for two simultaneous summit attempts with slightly different routes from Camp VI to the summit. Personally, I lean towards throwing all our eggs in one basket and heavily backing one summit team with a support party in position to move up the following day. But we have so many prima-donnas who think they can walk to the top of this thing. No one could agree on a summit team and when Jim tried to name one the others called "foul" and more or less refused to carry loads for the first team. Mo Antoine, a British climber (one of the best) whom we met on the approach march, commented (rather prophetically, as it turned out), "The reason not many of you Americans get to the top of your mountains is that you're too damn democratic."

We had a good meeting this evening. A lot of mudslinging, but feelings had to come out. Jim (bless his heart) took a lot of mud in the face, and tried to pull people together. Maybe it worked—we'll have to wait and see. All we really need is the weather. With a few clear days we would have had the summit long ago, I know it. When a bunch of independent s.o.b.'s (i.e., mountain climbers) get stuck in their tents for days on end, something wierd happens to their rationality. Rather than blaming situations on fate, or the luck of the draw, or simply accepting them, people start feeling victimized. All the fine qualities that emerge when people are working hard towards a single goal somehow disappear, replaced by suspicion and vindictiveness. Sigh. I think we still have the strength and desire to climb the mountain (God knows, those of us who have worked on this thing for five years surely don't want to go home without it, unless we're truly beaten—which we're not yet), but it is going to be a delicate operation for Jim to keep people together. We are all still talking to each other, which is a good sign.

No one has openly threatened to leave, though I heard rumors a couple of people wanted to a few days ago. If only we could have five clear days, five days of clear, or even mostly clear, weather, five days to make a mad rush from Camp I to the summit, in whatever combinations of people, by whatever route, I would be delighted, even if someone I hated (which is, fortunately, no one on the team—yet) got to the top. In the long run we would all share in the achievement, and eventually everyone would forget the petty squabbles anyway.

I hope by the time you get this letter you have read in the newspaper we made the top and we are on our way home. I guess we will settle, though, for whatever the fates dish out. And whatever happens, I have learned a lot about myself (probably even more before it's over), and I had some good times. But, by God, I need a bath and a manicure and a pedicure and a haircut, and I'm dying to put on a beautiful, expensive dress and leaf through *Vogue* magazine. I need to listen to a real symphony instead of the eighty-ninth rerun of Bob Dylan's *Nashville Skyline*, not to mention the soundtrack from *Saturday Night Fever*—AARGH!—on our tape machine here in camp. I need to drink some good wine, eat a salad, I want to lie in the grass someplace where it's warm enough to stay out in the rain with no clothes on. I need to have ten bouquets of fresh flowers in the house at the same time. I want to sleep for twenty-four hours in a bed with a mattress and cool cotton sheets. I'll be home soon, but not soon enough.

Dianne

FOR TWO DAYS AFTER THE BIG MEETING THE storm continued. From the twenty-one-thousand-foot level up, K2 remained shrouded in clouds. Away from the peak, occasional holes opened to blue sky, but toward Concordia the clouds, if anything, thickened. The spirit in camp, at least for the first day after the meeting, remained affable, and there was laughing and joking in the cook tent at meal times. "For the first time in weeks everyone is talking to everyone else in the most amiable terms," Wick wrote in his journal.

Still, the truce was shaky at best. With nothing else to do while the storm raged on, each faction, the A Team and the B Team, scurried around lobbying support, as if at a political convention, for their summit effort. It appeared Bill Sumner was finally entrenched with the B Team, but Lou managed to persuade Craig Anderson to carry for the A Team. Skip Edmonds, who did not envision himself in any frontline summit effort, leaned more toward the B Team.

Two nights after the big meeting, there was another gathering in the cook tent to discuss further logistic details; it ended with both Lou and Chris stomping out in protest. Chris left first because Lou had persisted in objecting to the concept of a dual summit assault, arguing that the upper mountain would be so difficult, and the anticipated window of good weather so short, that everyone's efforts would be needed to get just one party to the top. Lou pushed for a decision there and then on one route only: either the Abruzzi or the direct finish. Terry held out for his dual-assault plan; both he and Chris had begun to refer to part of the provisions in Camp IV, and the equipment cached halfway to Camp V that Terry, Cherie, and Bill had carried before the storm, as "our" food and "our" oxygen. Wick took exception to this language, saying the supplies did not belong to anybody or any group. He felt the major weakness in Terry's plan was that it assumed ten people, whether summit climbers or support climbers, would go all the way to Camp VI.

"It's just preposterous to believe that ten of us can go to twenty-six thousand, three hundred feet," Wick said. "It's sheer fantasy."

"But if we don't try," Terry replied, "if we opt for only one push now, several people will be severely demoralized. We've got to keep the dual assault idea open."

"Well," Wick concluded, "the mountain is going to sort out how many can get to Camp Six. And I don't think we'll see anywhere close to ten make it."

Lou saw no compromise in sight and left the tent. Lou was pressured by more than just his own conviction that limited weather and limited team strength allowed for only a single assault: he also felt pressure from John and me to head back up the mountain as quickly as possible to organize one last push for the summit. He was still offended by the manner in which we had flatly dismissed his own summit plan, and he felt there were schisms in the A Team as deep and as serious as splits in the expedition as a whole. He particularly felt a growing distance between John and himself. With so many previous common experiences, they had started the K2 expedition as close pals, anticipating yet another shared adventure. More important, their friendship had been based on a mutual respect: Lou looked to John as America's foremost mountaineer, and John saw Lou as a man who—in combining a distinguished climbing record with a brilliant career in neurobiology—had impressed him as the most versatile, brilliant, and accomplished person he had ever known. Now, the potential damage to this mutual respect bothered Lou more than any of the other strifes.

After giving up our impractical plan to climb K2 by ourselves, John and I had, in the frequent radio calls, repeatedly emphasized the necessity of moving people back into position as quickly as possible at the first sign of good weather. We had reluctantly descended to Camp III so we could break trail down to Camp II as soon as the weather permitted; with the trail opened for the others, our plan was to go back up that same day, moving straight through to Camp IV. Everything to save time. That way, we believed we could break to Camp V the following day, with the others moving in behind us a day later. But Lou had something else in mind. If he and a few others who—in his opinion—would have the strength to push in one day from Camp I to Camp IV would rendezvous there with John and me, we could all go together the next day to Camp V. That would save one whole day, which could make the critical difference if, as in the past, the next period of good weather was short.

Lou's next decision was what he would later call a "terrible mistake." He had queried Wick to see if Wick considered himself strong enough for such a demanding one-day push; Wick thought he could do it, and agreed with the value of saving precious time. Lou had then asked Craig, whom Lou considered the strongest climber outside the A Team. It would be a climb from eighteen thousand feet to twenty-three thousand feet carrying a load—an extremely demanding goal. Craig agreed; he also saw the advantage of the extra day gained. Wick mentioned the plan to Jim, who supported the idea. But Lou decided, and the others agreed, not to let the rest of the team know of their plan.

Lou's main reason for keeping the plan quiet was to postpone the furor he suspected would be sparked by any departure from the agreed-upon dual assault strategy; he had the notion that once everyone arrived in Camp V, criticisms—and ambitions—would be mollified by the realities of climbing at extreme altitude. He was also influenced by the more or less prevalent attitude that each group was making its own decisions, soliciting its own support, recruiting its own load carriers; if his group wanted to speed its own design by one day, he thought, that was their business and no one else's. Lou arranged to radio John and me that evening at a time when no one else would be monitoring: we agreed it was a good plan, if it could be pulled off. Lou mentioned it would be done without lengthy debates and discussions with the rest of the team. After turning off the radio, I turned to John: "I've got my doubts they can make it all the way in one day, though."

"Talk's cheap," John agreed. "I'll believe it when I see them in Four."

Lou organized loads and listed the gear that would have to be packed up from Camps II and III and ferried to Camp IV. One crucial item, in the possession of Chris Chandler, was the wrench to tighten oxygen regulators. Lou went to Chris and asked for it.

"Don't worry," Chris said. "I've got it packed and I'll make sure it comes up with me."

Lou gave Chris some explanation about testing regulators for leaks, and Chris handed it over. Later, Chris related the incident to Cherie, who began to suspect something was up. She knew there had been a clandestine radio call, and also, Lou had flatly declined their offer to break trail to Camp III. In the past Lou frequently had assumed that job; he told them he would be leaving at 4:30 A.M. and he would break the trail himself. Cherie's suspicions increased when she learned Wick and Craig were also planning to leave at 4:30, but she did not go so far as to suspect any new design on the part of the A Team. Regrettably, Lou and the others involved failed to realize just how serious were to be the repercussions—the feelings of betrayal and of being duped—when the B Team learned Lou and the others had climbed through Camp III and were on their way to Camp IV.

No one, however, was going anywhere until the storm ended or at least lessened in severity. Not surprisingly, our continued imprisonment in small tents was affecting morale. Even Jim Wickwire's optimism flagged. Early on the morning of August 25 he wrote:

> We are at the mercy of the weather. The continuation of the storm has forced a realization that I may walk out of here in three weeks without having climbed the mountain. We have only about that much food left, and several of the team members are so homesick that three more weeks is about all they can withstand. Tonight at dinner it was agreed to order the return porters to arrive by September 10.
>
> I remember the gradual realization in 1975 that we would not climb the mountain. It was painful after all the dreaming, hoping, and planning. That time is again approaching. In the past thirty-three days we have had seven days of clear weather. If September 10 is the cutoff, we have seventeen days to climb the mountain. Of that seventeen, we need seven good days. The odds are heavily against us. We are not defeated yet, but our backs are to the wall.

Later that evening the storm clouds rapidly—miraculously—cleared. Stars glistened, brilliant in a sky as clear as space. Wick made another entry in his journal just before turning in:

> A sudden 180-degree turn in the weather. We are going for it in the A.M. Lou and I, along with Craig, are leaving at first light—4:30. Jim and Dianne will follow. The rest will come later. Our plan is to go from here to Camp IV tomorrow in one long day. The HAPS believe the good weather will be short. We've got to make maximum use of it. Jim gave me the microfilm list of names to leave on the summit. God give me the strength to meet the rigorous demands of the next few days.

Wick had no idea just how rigorous those demands were going to be. With the sudden clearing of the weather his depression also cleared. That evening, he concluded his long journal entry with his customary words to his wife, the woman from whom—in the weeks ahead—he would derive the strength to survive:

> It is fitting, Mary Lou, that this reversal in fortunes, this clearing of weather in the last hour, has occurred today, our anniversary. I promise to be careful and come back to you.

August 26. SPINDRIFT SCUDDING UP STEEP ICE walls. Ice crystals airborne with cutting velocity, burning and freezing exposed skin. A figure close, inching across the ropes, just visible through wind-driven snow. The feel of fingers beginning to freeze, and the fear of a nose already frozen. Memories: that photograph of Scott and his team in Antarctica, taken by themselves, noses black with frostbite. The last photo, just before they died; the scene in the film classic, *Nanook of the North*—an Eskimo struggling against blasting spindrift to build an igloo in a race with death. A return to the here and now, climbing against very strong winds, and bitter cold.

"This is crazy," John yelled above the wind. "I'm worried about frostbite. Can't feel my toes—they're going."

"Nose is gone," I yelled back. I held my mitten over my nose, directing my breath up around my face. That, however, further fogged my goggles, which were already glazed with ice. I tried to clean them: I rubbed my mittens over the lenses, but though I had removed the ice crust and cleared the fog, the wool had left hairs and water streaks on the lenses, still obscuring my vision. It was no good to try to climb without goggles. The ice particles jetting up the face drove into my eyes, blinding me. I replaced the goggles, forced to make do with partial vision.

My nose was of greater concern. I could not get feeling in it, and I cursed myself for leaving behind my thermal-foil face shield, designed to protect against wind and sun. My fingers were also starting to freeze, but I could more easily regain circulation in them by occasionally breathing into my mittens. The nose worried me, though.

"The others will never make it across in this wind," John screamed. He was about ten feet from me. "Maybe we should go back to Camp Three. Even if we get across with no frostbite, there might be no point if the others don't follow."

"Give me a second," I yelled. "Need to think." Again I covered my nose, not caring that my goggles fogged. Spindrift drove up the ice wall and left the crest of the ridge: white fingers of snow streamed above the crest in a trajectory that reflected the steep angle of the ice face. Ice-white fingers, wisps, against deep blue sky. A few more breaths and my nose began to regain some feeling. Relieved, I tried to sort out the options.

John and I had left Camp III early that morning, descending halfway to Camp II to break trail for those coming up. Three of them were going to try to make it all the way to Camp IV that day, and John and I wanted to give them every assistance. We had returned to Camp III, stomping good footholds in the new snow. We rested for an hour, brewed a cup of hot cocoa, then left to break trail to Camp IV. As soon as we crossed from the Pakistan to the Chinese side of the ridge, however, we were hit by strong winds gusting off the Sinkiang steppes. Since there was some doubt whether the others could climb from Camp I to Camp IV in one day with good weather, it was even less likely they could do it in such severe winds.

"We've got to decide," John yelled. "Can't stand here waiting. Toes freezing fast."

"Can you make four without frostbite?"

"Maybe if I move fast. But I don't think the others will follow."

"Let's try it anyway. No more room for setbacks. We've got to push—now or never. Maybe they'll make it."

"O.K.," John yelled. Without further words or hesitation he turned and climbed into the spindrift, anxious to keep moving, to keep his toes working in his boots. I uncovered my nose and followed. My goggles remained frosted and I climbed partly by feel. We moved slowly but persistently, not stopping for fear our digits would freeze. I tried to pull the collar of my jumpsuit high on my face to protect my nose, and although it only partially covered, it was enough to prevent freezing. With every opportunity to free my hands, even momentarily, from clinging to the rope, I curled my fingers back into my mitten and held them until they started to ache. That was a good sign: If I could bring the pain I knew they had not yet frozen.

Three hours passed. We crested the gendarme and through the spindrift we could just make out the bright red tents at Camp IV. The wind was gusting stronger, and it was difficult to balance upright on the narrow ridge crest. We covered the last distance stooped against the wind. Inside the tent we removed our boots and mittens, and John placed his bare toes inside my parka, against the bare skin of my belly. He grimaced with pain.

"They'll be O.K. as soon as they warm a little more," he said. "I don't think there's any damage. How is your nose?"

"It's okay," I replied.

The warmth of the tent had restored feeling, and although my nose was too tender to touch with pressure, I had suffered no frostbite. My fingers were numb and white, but I felt they, too, were O.K.

"That was a wild crossing, though," I said. "Kind of exciting on that last section. In the stronger gusts I thought I was going to be air-mailed to Base Camp."

We started the stove and began melting snow. It was 4:15. We had left

Camp III at 11:30. In good weather, we would have traversed in less than two hours.

"It took over four hours," I said.

"Yeah, and you know we're going to be faster than the others if they try and make it here in one day. I doubt seriously they'll try it. We'll find out at the five o'clock radio call."

Meanwhile, lower on the mountain, there was another crisis evolving. As usual, Lou had been in the lead all morning, and he reached Camp III about 1:30. Even though John and I had dropped down earlier and stomped a good trail, spindrift had filled most of our steps and Lou had had to struggle to punch new ones. He had moved more slowly than usual, but he knew he had to pace himself to reach Camp IV. Craig, Wick, Jim, and Dianne reached Camp III just behind Lou; the others, the B Team, were still some distance below.

The five discussed the wisdom of proceeding to Camp IV; none of them had been exposed to the gale on the traverse and had they known what was ahead they might not have been so eager to push on. Lou was anxious to move ahead, however—he felt strong, and he knew he could lead the entire distance. He wanted to start before the tracks made by John and me filled any more. Wick and Craig agreed to follow: Jim and Dianne, both of whom had so far kept up with the others, were also considering crossing.

"I think I can make it," Dianne said. "I feel strong. And maybe tomorrow I can take a load to Camp Five."

Lou left camp at 2:15. The others lost time fidgeting with a malfunctioning stove so they could brew hot chocolate, but finally got underway at 3:00. When they left, the B Team still had not arrived.

As they left camp, Wick turned to Dianne and warned her of the need to climb quickly.

"It's late and you'll have to keep a steady pace to reach camp before dark. If you get stuck out here it will be serious."

"Don't worry, I'll make it," Dianne yelled back. They were feeling the full force of the wind as they crossed to the Chinese side of the ridge. Dianne realized the implications of not reaching camp before dark, and she was prepared for her hardest physical effort of the expedition.

At the base of the first steep pinnacle, Wick waited for Jim and Dianne so he could be near them on the traverse in case Dianne needed assistance. He let Craig Anderson pass. Craig had, so far, met the physical rigors of the triple stage, but when he left the protection of the lee side of the ridge and was hit by the full force of the gale, he sensed the danger of the task ahead. Had he known that to survive the next few hours would demand more stamina than he had ever mustered on any previous experience in the mountains, he might have turned back. Craig pushed on; Jim and Dianne caught up with Wick, and the three of them followed. Already, twenty-four-thousand-foot Skyang Kangri, rising on the far side of the glacier that descended off the Chinese side of the ridge, was beginning to glow golden in the light of later afternoon sun.

None of the five fighting the gale, racing the setting sun, had a clear notion how the B Team would react when they arrived to find Camp III deserted. Craig had an inkling of their possible response just as he left Camp III. He thought: The others are going to take this all wrong. It's just a plan to gain a day, to get to Camp V earlier. But they won't see it that way. Craig was concerned that his good friends, Skip and Bill (especially Bill, who was then so committed to the B Team effort) would misinterpret his intentions. But by the time the B Team trudged into a deserted Camp III, Craig and the others were too absorbed to consider anything but their own struggle to survive.

Bill Sumner and Diana Jagersky were first to Camp III. Diana later recorded her impressions:

> A few feet out of Camp III, I had a sick feeling when I noticed an emptiness. Then I glanced up and saw Lou disappear behind the first gendarme on the ridge, and then I saw Jim and Dianne further behind. I sensed trouble ahead. Already Bill was very upset and fuming.

One by one the others arrived: Chris, then Cherie, Terry, and Skip. Their reactions were the same: anger. Especially from Chris, Cherie, and Terry, who felt they had been deceived not only by the A Team, but by Whittaker as well. Their resentment, however, was for the moment checked by the demands of pitching another tent in strong winds, and also by the growing realization the others might be in serious trouble.

It was bitterly cold, and those at Camp III were exhausted. Bill, Skip, and Diana huddled in a small, two-person tent pitched on an uneven platform that Diana said was like "lying on a bunch of old saddles." Chris, Cherie, and Terry were in a larger four-person tent. Terry assumed the task of camp spokesman, making the five o'clock radio transmission to alert John and me, as well as Rob in Camp I, that the others had continued across the traverse and might be in trouble.

"There's no sign of any of them yet," John radioed back to Terry. "Keep monitoring, and we'll call as soon as we learn anything."

John looked at me and said, "That's the dumbest thing yet. I can see Lou and Wick, and maybe Craig and Jim, trying to get across, but bringing Dianne over those ropes in wind like this with only a couple of hours of daylight left—that's lunacy."

We waited. Every few minutes we poked our head out the window flap to search for any sign of our teammates. An hour passed, then an hour and a half. There were only a few minutes of daylight remaining. I wrote in my diary:

It is 6:30 and there is still no sign of them. Lou, who is always faster than anyone, hasn't even arrived. If they're not already in trouble there is a good chance they will be. It seems unlikely they will arrive before dark. John is increasingly irate at what he thinks is Jim's bad judgment to allow Dianne to cross the ropes. A few minutes ago we talked to Camp I, and John asked Rob if Shelby Scates [a newspaper correspondent who had come up to Camp I with a trekking party] was listening. Rob acknowledged that he was, and John said, "Good, I just want him to know that Whittaker is jeopardizing the entire success of this expedition, and possibly the lives of others, by dragging his wife across that traverse."

I took the radio from John.

"I agree with John that Jim made a mistake," I said. "But I just hope it's not a serious one. They must be very cold right now—it's blowing like hell out there—and I doubt they make it in without some frostbite. I just hope they make it in any condition."

Even Jim Wickwire was finding it difficult to muster the necessary drive to keep pushing through the spindrift that stung his face and made it difficult to breathe. Several times he caught himself resting on the ropes for no apparent reason, just hanging, his mind going blank. He had to snap back to the reality of making headway, and force himself to keep going. He continued to open distance between himself and Jim and Dianne, who were moving slower. But he could not wait; if he stopped too long he knew it would be too difficult to start again.

Craig was also having trouble. The route gained the crest of the knife-blade ridge, and Craig found it necessary to half crawl to keep balance. The spindrift was blasting with full gale strength, and he had to remove his dark goggles to see at all. The ice crystals cut into his eyes and accumulated on his brows and eyelids. He realized he was in danger—he had only two hundred feet more, but each step was becoming increasingly difficult. The wind gusted stronger, forcing him down on all fours. Crouching, he thought about the danger of his position, then the danger of the entire enterprise, the whole expedition. This is definitely not worth it, he thought. This is craziness, absurdity. It's too easy to die here. He needed motivation to keep going, and he found it. He thought of his wife and his kids, of the stacks of letters he received at each mail call, of their need for him to come home to them. He got up and staggered toward Camp IV.

LOU WAS THE FIRST to arrive, at about six-forty-five. John and I spotted him about fifty feet from the tent, moving steadily against the wind. He wore his faithful patched and mended red parka, and his beard and mustache were coated with ice. He crawled shivering into our tent.

"It's a little nasty out there," he said.

"Any sign of the others?" I asked.

"Craig is just behind me, and Wick not too far behind him. I don't know about Jim and Dianne. I think they're still a ways back."

It was dark, and John and I looked at each other, knowing our thought was the same: What a night to have to rescue someone. John called the lower camps to report Lou's arrival, telling them he would keep them posted on the others.

We gave Lou a cup of tea. In a few more minutes Craig arrived, then Wick. They crawled into the other tent and began melting snow for a brew. We called over: "Any frostbite?"

"Just tired, otherwise O.K. Jim and Dianne are a ways back, moving slow," Wick answered.

We waited, agonizing, wondering if we had the strength left to suit up and leave to help them. About eight o'clock we heard their voices. Dianne stumbled up to our tent, visibly shaking from exposure.

"I'm O.K.," she murmered. "No frostbite, I don't think. Only a little cold." She had trouble pronouncing the words, and her lips were quivering.

Awkwardly, she made the last few steps to Wick's and Craig's tent. Jim was a few feet behind her, exhausted, but apparently in better shape. Wick opened the tent door and Dianne fell through. He wrapped her in his down parka and half bag, and even though both he and Craig were very thirsty, they poured most of their kettle of steaming brew water into Jim's and Dianne's cups. Still shivering, Dianne managed a "Thank You" and tried to smile. From our tent, John radioed the news that everyone was safe to a much-relieved audience at Camps III and I.

"You've got to admit," Lou said quietly, "Dianne made a very impressive performance. Believe me, it was rough out there. And she's not a very experienced climber."

"She should never have tried to come across, but I'll agree," John said, grudgingly. "She did a hell of a job getting through that wind. She's got a lot of drive."

August 27. BILL SUMNER AWOKE IN CAMP III groggy and queasy—the evening before he had taken a Dalmane sleeping pill after battling several wakeful nights. He seldom used drugs of any kind, and he now felt miserable.

"I don't think I'll be able to go up today," he said. "Just don't feel good."

"That's too bad," Diana replied. "It's an incredible morning. No clouds, and the wind is not bad at all."

The three of them—Diana, Bill, and Skip—had passed an uncomfortable night crammed into their small tent. The other three in the tent next door—Chris, Cherie, and Terry—were preparing to leave.

Diana Jagersky felt excitement at finally getting a chance to go to Camp IV, to cross the traverse. She was as good a climber as Cherie or Dianne, but because her duty to the expedition was to manage Camp I and organize loads lower on the mountain, she had not had the chance to climb high. However, if Diana had suffered any frustrated ambitions, or consequently held any grudges, it was not at all obvious; she had continued to meet her duties with few, if any, complaints. Since everyone except Rob was moving high on the mountain for the final summit push, she had seen her chance to follow to higher camps and realize her climbing ambition on the expedition—to cross to Camp IV.

Those in Camp III had had a night to meditate on what they considered a subterfuge by the A Team, supported by Whittaker, to get a one-day jump on them, thereby scuttling the plan for a simultaneous assault. Now —the following morning—still disappointed, they nevertheless decided to continue their effort and follow as close behind as they could. They intended to head to Camp IV, then the next day climb to V.

But about ten minutes before their planned departure time there was a radio call from Camp IV. John's voice came over the air; Terry monitored.

"You can't come over today," John said. "You'll have to stay in Three. Everybody is too wiped out here to move up to Five today. We had a hell of a time getting across the traverse last night. Dianne was hypothermic. Nobody was able to melt enough water and rehydrate. This morning everybody is lying around hardly able to cook breakfast. Looks like a rest day, so there's no room for you guys over here. No tent space."

"Those bastards," Cherie spat.

Terry grimaced. Chris sat Indian-style on the tent floor, staring passively, no longer surprised by anything. "And those are the guys always complaining about us not moving fast enough," he said.

John's voice continued, "It's also still windy here this morning, and cold. Unless the weather changes it's too rough to cross."

Although the weather seemed near-perfect from the perch at Camp III, protected as it was in the lee of the serac, strong gusts still buffeted the tents at the exposed Camp IV. Despite the sunshine, crossing the traverse would have been rigorous.

"What's up?" Diana called from the next tent.

"That son-of-a-bitch doesn't want us to come across," Terry called back. Diana accepted the delay with equanimity, and Skip did not mind a rest day. But the other three saw it as yet another scheme to keep them a day behind. Terry raged, saying if another day was lost the weather might deteriorate and nobody would get to the top.

Terry called John back: "Listen, you son-of-a-bitch, you're not going to tell me or anybody where we can go or what we can do."

At Camp IV John was also fuming. As Terry's voice came over the air, he looked at the radio as if he might throw it all the way to Camp III. Lou and I shook our heads, anticipating another heated exchange. Next door, Wick, Craig, Dianne, and Jim lay in their tent brewing tea and cocoa, too exhausted from the previous day's effort and a very crowded, uncomfortable night to care what was going on.

John radioed back to Camp III: "Put Diana on the radio."

At Camp III, Diana had already left her tent and was standing near the entrance to Terry's tent. Terry looked at her, then reluctantly handed her the radio, saying he could not talk any more to John anyway.

"Hello, John? This is Diana."

"Good. You're the only one down there I want to talk to. Look, explain to those people we're not trying to keep them off the mountain—it's just that there's no room for them here. The others came in late last night and they're wasted. The winds are high, and we don't think people should cross."

There was a pause, then John continued, "We're trying to get people to the summit, and we don't care who they are. But goddamn it, if they don't want to work together, let them get the hell off the mountain."

Terry exploded and shouted at Diana, "Get that goddamn son-of-a-bitch off the radio. _He's_ the one who shouldn't be allowed on the mountain!"

Diana was in the middle, still standing outside Terry's tent. She had been trying to transmit to John with Terry shouting in the background, and we had heard him in Camp IV.

"Who was that calling me a son-of-a-bitch?" John called to Diana.

"Give me that goddamn radio," Terry ordered Diana from the other direction.

"Tell that son-of-a-bitch he'd better be careful who he calls a son-of-a-bitch," John called back.

Diana turned the radio on and off to prevent Terry from hearing John's tirade. The broadcast was also being monitored at Camp I, where Rob Schaller feared that another blowup of tempers at this late stage might be fatal to the summit effort. Newspaper correspondent Shelby Scates was taking notes furiously. And down in Base Camp, our Liaison Officer Mohammed Saleem Khan—who for weeks, with only the company of a cook boy, had manned the sideband radio linking us with Skardu—had just finished his midmorning prayers to Allah. He listened perplexedly to the heated harangues.

Chris still sat cross-legged, listening, and watching Terry bellow at Diana to give him the walkie-talkie. He did not say anything. Cherie, however, entered the debate and also demanded the radio. John persisted in transmitting insults while Diana turned the radio off and on. Finally, she interrupted John and said, "Look, shut up for a minute, will you. We've got a problem down here."

Diana walked away from the tents to where the others were out of ear-shot; she hoped their tempers would calm.

"Look, John," she resumed. "There are some hot tempers down here, and a few people who feel like they're being screwed. You've got to calm down and hold your tongue."

"I'll say what I'm thinking," John replied.

Meanwhile, back in Terry's tent, things were hardly cooling: Terry was still boiling mad.

"I'll show them," he blazed. "Let's leave this mountain right now. We'll go down and cut all the ropes behind us, and burn all the tents. That will fix those sons-of-bitches." His eyes bulged madly.

That finally provoked a response from Chris, who said calmly, "You can't do that Terry. That would be murder, or at least manslaughter. People would die."

"Yeah," Cherie agreed. "You've got to calm down."

Terry regained composure. Diana returned to her tent and for a while there was peace. Terry was getting used to the idea of losing a day. Chris was still pensive, melting snow for tea. In the other tent, Diana, Skip, and Bill napped.

Suddenly they were jerked awake.

Whomfff!

"Avalanche!"

Skip and Diana bolted for the tent door. Bill was a second slower. Diana got her head out the door expecting to see the serac above the camp tumbling down. Instead she saw the other tent on fire. It was not an avalanche at all; a stove had blown up. Diana ran over—Terry and Cherie were throwing gear out the tent door. They put out the fire. Inside, Diana could see Chris. He had been changing cartridges on the butane stove; what he had thought was an empty canister had held residual gas, which had escaped and ignited on the other stove. His face had been directly above the explosion, and although he was uninjured, he looked a mess. His eyebrows were burnt, his mustache was partially gone, a section of beard was missing. There was the pungent smell of singed hair and a gaping hole in the tent.

"Whew, what a relief," Diana said. "It was only the tent blowing up."

Diana helped move the scattered gear back into the tent. When things quieted down, she noticed that Cherie was crying softly. "Chris is quitting the expedition," Cherie said. "He's going down."

Diana looked at Chris, now a frightful sight with half his hair missing. She managed to get Chris aside to try to talk him out of it.

"Chris, you're making a mistake. I know things are bad, but you're too close to all the problems to get a clear view. You should wait a couple of days. You still are strong; you still have a chance to go to the summit. And even if you don't get to the summit you still need to feel like you've done everything you can, because a couple of months from now this won't seem like such a big deal. You'll forget all these arguments."

"No," Chris replied, "my mind is made up. I'm going down."

"You'll regret it."

"My mind is made up."

All morning, while Terry and John had been arguing over the radio, Chris had been thinking through the possibilities, and they all led to the same final scene: physical violence with Roskelley. Chris had envisioned a fight, maybe even resulting in one of them pitching the other off the knife-edge ridge. Chris told himself that was not why he had come to the mountain. Somehow things had gone wrong. The only solution he saw was to withdraw quietly.

THINGS CERTAINLY HAD GONE WRONG. BUT why? Were we not mature adults who had all been on previous expeditions, who had all climbed before in the Himalaya and who were all, therefore, accustomed to working together under difficult conditions? Had we not all made a vow to work together to get any one of us to the top of this mountain, K2? With the passage of each day, those words seemed buried deeper and deeper in a halcyon past.

What was it, then? Was it that we were achievement-oriented personalities in a situation where there was only a small amount of the ultimate achievement—standing on the summit—to go around? That fact alone could have explained much of our dissension. Perhaps it was the prolonged stress from lack of oxygen, the constant exposure to danger. We had all been climbing at altitudes varying between sixteen thousand and twenty-five thousand feet for fifty-three days—almost two full months. That is long enough to strain the camaraderie of even the most affable of personalities.

Bad weather has to share some of the blame. Rob Schaller, sitting at Camp I, often with only the HAPS for company, had time and was in a position to view the expedition overall. He later said:

> I think the weather was the culprit: it caused our problems. If we had had better weather, which we would have had if we could have arrived at the mountain a month earlier (remember, our itinerary had been delayed a month by the Pakistan government to avoid overlapping Bonington's climb), we would have had superb weather. Our crises occurred because there were only supplies for a limited number of people at higher camps. It caused people who had summit aspirations to subjugate their desires, to supply and support others who did try for the summit. The weather forced conflict because it forced people's roles to change on the mountain.

Storms also caused physical separation of people stranded at different camps. Many of the rows had taken place over the radio; had we more often been all in the same camp at the same time, where we could have worked out our differences face to face, no doubt there would have been fewer conflicts. Feelings and opinions are easy to misinterpret over the radio.

As with most breakdowns in human relations, the struggle to communicate with one another—that is, understand and empathize with one another's attitudes, beliefs, and opinions, with one another's desires and goals—was at the root of our problems. It was not the physical separation alone; even when we could talk face to face, we often misunderstood one another. Had Chris, Terry, and Cherie been able to understand John's background—if they could have looked through his eyes to when Devi had died on Nanda Devi, to when the eight Russian women had frozen to death in the Pamirs—perhaps they might also have understood why he objected so strongly to women going on expeditions. Or had John and I, on the other hand, been able to see Chris as a man facing a labryinth of problems from a bitter divorce, a man who needed to confide in and talk with someone, we could better have understood his actions. We could have tried to learn more about Terry and Cherie. Had we known that, before the expedition, Terry and Cherie had agreed between themselves to try, whenever possible, to climb on separate ropes with different people, because that way if something happened if there was an avalanche or an accident—chances would be better that one would survive to look after their children; had John and I known that simple, stark fact— perhaps we could better have understood Terry and Cherie.

But the fact remained: Chris had quit the expedition. I was saddened when Terry announced, over the radio that night, that Chris had descended to wait out the expedition at Base Camp. The memories came flooding back, and the guilty feeling that somehow we had not worked things out as we should have, that we had failed to understand each other. I recalled that poignant scene the day we had established Camp V, when Chris had been climbing behind us, and we had not waited for him. The rope had symbolized everything: the distance that had broken our friendship.

I wondered if we could ever repair it.

On the positive side, Terry announced that, after much soul-searching, he and Cherie were committed to offering whatever support and assistance they could to get someone to the top. At that point, the A Team was again the de facto first summit party, and it was encouraging to hear Terry's reversal of temperament.

The wind had ceased, and the weather remained clear. That afternoon at Camp IV had been superb—windless and warm. Those who had made the previous day's debilitating push across the traverse were recovering, and everyone at IV was eager for an early start to Camp V the next day.

We felt the summit was near; Camp V tomorrow, then Camp VI, then the summit, then home.

August 28. 4:30 A.M. NO WIND. NO MOTION OF nylon tent walls. Quiet darkness. Zip open the tent window: a clear, black sky: cold, cold air and starlit snow and ice; black shadows like fathomless holes—passageways to the center of the earth. A memory: the first astronauts to walk on the moon saying the surface shadows were absolutely black, with no atmosphere to scatter light, and they had stepped in shadows only with a primordial fear of falling. The summit pyramid through thin, cold, predawn atmosphere. Moonscape.

I zipped shut the tent window and lay back in my sleeping bag. John would be awakening soon and starting the stove to bring meltwater to boil for the morning's brew. I stared at the tent wall, lit sufficiently by starlight to outline the checkerboard pattern of the rip-stop and thought, It will be a long, long day, and we need an early start. A long carry to Camp V, but our last carry. The weather looks right. In three days we will be on the summit of the second highest mountain on earth.

It was a luxury to have a few minutes to gather thoughts before starting on the morning chores. The cold predawn had a meditative quality, ideal for reflection. My mind flipped over the previous day's events: the heated arguments with Camp III; Terry and Cherie deciding in the end to support the first summit effort; Chris quitting the expedition. I thought of the conversations we had had all that afternoon, trying to decide on a summit route, and that gave me a slightly uneasy feeling.

For several days, Lou had been suggesting that the first summit group also try the Abruzzi finish. He was not absolutely committed to that route, but he had pointed out it did offer advantages: It would be an easier and therefore a more certain access to the summit; it would probably be safer; it would be a better route of descent. He had also noted it would require no fixed ropes. The direct finish, on the other hand, had a very steep —perhaps completely vertical—section halfway up, and it would most likely be necessary to climb above Camp VI, work to fix ropes over the steepest sections, go back to Camp VI, then the following day go to the summit. That would mean an extra day—an extra day to depend on good weather holding.

John and I had been adamant, nevertheless, in our desire to finish by the direct route. In fact, we were intractably committed to it, arguing it would be the most aesthetic finish to the northeast ridge. John also argued we could do it in one push, not feeling, as Lou did, the need to fix ropes. We knew it would be difficult: the Poles had climbed all the hard sections in 1976, and from their accounts we knew what to expect. They had found it so difficult, so exhausting, they had been unable to finish the last five hundred feet to the summit, even though they had climbed above the steepest and hardest sections. Nevertheless, John and I felt we had a good chance of completing the route.

Lou and Wick had been frustrated by our recalcitrance, and the ultimate result of our debates was the uneasy decision to split the summit attempt: John and I would go it alone on the direct finish; Lou and Wick, possibly supported by Craig, would traverse to the Abruzzi Ridge. Jim, and perhaps Dianne if she was strong enough, would carry loads to support John and me on the direct finish.

We had been careful not to divulge this plan to those at Camp III, realizing it would feed their feelings of being victimized by our machinations to get to the summit. Since they themselves had planned and hoped for a dual assault using B Team personnel, to hear that we now planned a similar strategy, but with a split A Team, could only be taken by them as yet another example of our skullduggery. I had to sympathize with them, too: I would have felt the same. But at the bottom of our plan, with its element of deceit, was our belief that without Chris, the B Team simply did not have the power to make a serious summit bid. Obviously, we could not tell them that. We could not risk losing any more of the team.

I was feeling uneasy about our plan because I realized John and I would be sticking our necks out—way out. Alone on the direct finish up the summit pyramid. I closed my eyes and imagined what it would be like: at 27,500 feet, climbing up ice nearly vertical. To the right I would see the great north glacier and beyond, 18,000 feet below, the burnt hills of Shaksgam and Sinkiang. Above, blue, vertical smoothness. Would we have oxygen? If so, the bottle would be pulling on my back, pulling me off balance, and I would have to fight to hold on to the ice pick stuck in the frozen blue. My feet—only the crampon front points would be stuck in the ice, a mere half inch. If my axe popped I would fall backwards. In my imagination, I looked and saw John below, belaying the rope, and under him the wall of the pyramid sweeping down, down, thousands of feet to the Godwin-Austen Glacier. If we did not use oxygen? No oxygen, 27,500 feet, very steep, hard climbing. I would have to economize every movement, breathe as evenly as possible to avoid blackout. The glacier so far below. Could I do it? To 27,000 feet—27,500—28,250—without oxygen?

Some of the reservations I had felt weeks earlier returned. Once again I remembered how, on Everest, my lungs had filled with mucous at 26,000 feet. Would that happen again? Would it be more serious this time? At least I had already climbed to 25,000 feet several days before to Camp V, carrying a heavy load, and I had felt strong. Perhaps I could handle the additional three thousand feet. I knew, however, those three thousand feet would be critical: there is an enormous difference between 25,000 feet and 28,250 feet. At that latter elevation—the summit of K2—only thirty-three percent of the normal sea-level oxygen remains in the atmosphere.

One other fear surfaced there in the quiet predawn: bivouacking. On the direct finish, an emergency bivouac on the descent seemed almost certain. If it was a windy night, if the weather went bad, it could mean dubious chances of survival, almost certain frostbite. Was I willing to risk toes and fingers? I thought about it: the answer was yes. Weighing all things, I felt ready for the effort of my life.

I heard John roll over and fumble with the stove. I was in a good mood.

"I say old chap, how about coffee?" I chirped.

"Shall I serve it with beef jerky, or do you care for Corn Nuts?" John answered. " We also have shrimp creole left from last night, if you prefer."

"I'll pass on the creole. Just ran out of Rolaids. Coffee's fine, thank you."

Lou was also awake. "How's the weather?" he asked.

"Bright and clear."

"I think we've got it this time. Three days to the top."

Presently, the first light colored our tent soft yellow, and everyone was busy thawing boots over stoves and drinking as much as possible. We all knew the key to acclimatization, and to minimizing the chances of hypothermia, frostbite, and pulmonary problems, was maximum hydration.

All of a sudden there was a frantic movement in the next tent. Another stove explosion, quickly extinguished. Wickwire beat out flames from his beard, then tore pieces from his nylon wind shirt to patch the hole in the tent. Wick stayed behind an extra half hour to sew up the hole while the rest of us got under way with full loads; with the route already stomped down, he was able to catch up with us.

It was a magnificent day, and when we rested between kicking steps up the snow dome, we were high enough at nearly twenty-five thousand feet to see over most of the mountains to the east: not Broad Peak or the Gasherbrums, but over smaller Karakoram mountains in the distance. We were mesmerized by the brown hills of China stretching hundreds of miles to the north, to the gently curving horizon. Wick, Lou, John, and I were in the lead; Craig, Jim, and Dianne followed a distance behind.

Only one thing marred our pleasure: To the north and west, floating at extreme altitude far above the summit of K2—at perhaps forty thousand feet—was an enormously wide but thin, saucer-shaped cloud. It did not look like a normal lenticular. It was tinted light brown, with an ethereal, other-worldly look, and while on the one hand it had a benign, angelic quality—like a halo over the summit—that quality seemed somehow guileful, somehow sinister. We could only hope it was not a harbinger of more bad weather, for that would be the end of all hope of reaching the summit.

We all reached Camp V and held each other in bear hugs. For Dianne, it was an especially satisfying accomplishment. At 25,300 feet, she was higher than any North American woman had ever climbed, and she had also delivered two oxygen bottles—not bad for someone who only a few years earlier had made her first climb.*

The cache of equipment we had buried under a tent fly nine days before was in good shape, and we set to the task of shoveling tent platforms. We pitched three tents, and with seven people in camp that night, we felt we had mustered the supplies and strength necessary for a serious summit bid.

Spirits were high as we cooked dinner and melted water for the next day's efforts. Terry, Cherie, Skip, and Diana had moved to Camp IV, and by radio we learned they planned to climb to V in the morning. Our own plans changed when we reconsidered our logistics. There was not enough equipment to support a dual assault, and Craig made the valid point that if he carried for Wick and Lou to their Camp VI on the Abruzzi, he would have to return by himself, unroped. He was reluctant to do that. John and I remained committed to the direct finish, so in the end, Lou and Wick decided once again to join forces with John and me. I went to sleep that night feeling better then ever. I had felt very strong climbing to Camp V that day. Fear that my lungs would not hold out was beginning to disappear. Maybe the problems I had suffered on Everest had indeed been simple congestion. I was more confident of my ability than ever.

The thought of having Lou and Wick with us, and the others in support, cleared my remaining doubts. I was sure we could make it now, and everyone in camp felt the same. The strange saucer cloud had disappeared. As we fell asleep the night sky was clear and cold.

Dreams came easily, pleasant dreams of pleasant places. I was tucked cozily in my sleeping bag, relaxed, and my dreams took me to tropical islands, warm and sunny, to white sand and trade winds. Sometime in the early morning I awoke. I had consumed so much liquid I had to relieve myself. That was good: it meant I was rehydrated, and that would give me an edge on making the push to Camp VI, just a few hours later. Still feeling the warmth of the dream, I zipped open the window and squirmed to get half my body outside. It was very dark. It took me several seconds to realize what was wrong. I looked up. Blackness. No stars. Then I felt them, big and soft, delicately cold, floating, drifting, silently landing on my hair, melting. Another storm.

*Dianne's record was passed a few weeks later when two climbers from the American Women's Annapurna I Expedition reached its 26,545-foot summit.

9

Into the Death Zone

August 29. "IT'S POSSIBLE WE COULD PUSH through the bad weather and make Camp Six," Jim Whittaker said. "And you four summit guys could stay there and hope the next day the weather clears. But if it doesn't you'll have to come down. There aren't enough supplies to wait." He paused, then added, "I'm not sure you would have it in you to push all the way back up again."

"We can't stay here, either," Lou said. "There's only enough food for one more day, maybe two if we stretch. Our only option is to go back to Camp Four and wait there."

"That probably makes the most sense," Jim agreed. "At least there you can conserve your strength for another push."

"Terry, Cherie and the others now in Four will have to drop back to Camp Three," Wick said. "Otherwise there won't be enough room—or supplies."

John added his opinion. "Even if we are short of supplies here at Five, I think we need to hold out as long as we possibly can. I just have a feeling if we go down again now, that will be it."

We had awakened that morning to wind and snow. Now, at midmorning, we gathered in the largest tent to decide our best strategy. Through the morning the clouds had periodically opened, revealing a few clear areas over China, but from the opposite direction—from Pakistan— the clouds rose thick and covered the mountain. We decided to wait until

208

noon. Despite John's reservations (and I agreed with John), it looked as if we would be forced, once again, to descend.

We returned to our tents and passed another two hours napping, writing in our journals, or staring at the walls. There was little conversation. It seemed so much of the climb had been spent waiting, sitting in tents, patiently lying on sleeping bags, holding out for weather to improve. I wondered how much longer our patience could last. Fifty-five days on the mountain. We would be without doubt climbing into September. I recalled the Polish account of their attempt on the same route in 1976. They had made two assaults on the summit from their Camp VI—one on August 14, another on August 15. When both failed they pulled back to rally for another try. But a major storm hit, and did not end. Finally, on September 4, fighting snow up to their waists, they abandoned the mountain. Winter had come to K2.

I wondered if winter had come for us as well. It was much colder than it had been in the previous weeks, and this time the interval of good weather had lasted only one day. I remembered that the HAPS had said, several weeks earlier, that we had to reach the summit by the end of August, at the latest, to beat the winter storms. That morning, I noted in my journal:

> We only need two or three more days of reasonable weather to top out, yet I'm not certain even that small request will be granted. I can't help but fear that this may very well be the high point of the expedition. After so many weeks and weeks of struggle, it seems tragic.

I lay back on my bag, between John and Lou, and stared at the walls. We could hear snowflakes falling on the tent, and an occasional gust of wind.

"How about carrying a load to Camp Six?" Lou said.

"Cabin fever?" I asked.

"Have you looked out?" John said. "It's a whiteout—you won't even find Camp Six."

"There's an occasional hole in the clouds, enough to get to the campsite. It's well marked under that prominent rock buttress," Lou persisted.

"No thanks," John said.

I also declined, and Lou left the tent and crossed to Wick's. There he had better luck: although Wick had been napping, he reluctantly agreed to go. About ten-thirty the two left camp and only a short distance from the tents disappeared in the shrouding clouds. John and I zipped shut the tent window and lay back down on our bags.

"I wonder what drives Lou?" I said. "I don't think I've ever met anyone who pushed as hard as Lou does."

"I think he just wants to get to Camp Six—to eight thousand meters. That will likely be the high point of the expedition."

"Maybe we should have gone with them."

"We could have hauled all the gear up there in one carry. They don't need to go up there in this weather. It's wasting time."

"Well, maybe. But having any gear up there is a help. I just feel like maybe we're not doing our share."

"The hell with it," John said, and rolled over on his side, facing the tent wall. "We'll need all our strength when the time comes. No sense burning out on useless carries."

"When the time comes. The time," I sighed, staring at the ceiling, then adding, "Just three days. That's all. Three short days. . ."

There was silence and we drifted in sleep. It was still uncertain when we would descend to Camp IV. With Lou and Wick going to Camp VI, it was possible they would want to rest at V for another night before dropping lower. It was a long, slow descent down the snow dome back to Camp IV; in bad weather it would take several hours.

Jim called from his tent. "Maybe we should get ready to go so we have time to get down."

John and I looked at each other. Neither of us wanted to descend; we shared the conviction that if we left camp, if we went down at this late time, we would never be back up.

"What if you guys went down," John yelled back, "and Rick and I stayed and waited for Lou and Wick? We wouldn't be using much more food, and if the weather broke, the four of us could go it alone in the morning."

There was a pause, then Jim said, "O.K. Dianne, Craig, and I will go down."

In half an hour we heard them leave camp. They wished us good luck, but I knew—short of a miracle—we would soon be down ourselves. It *would* be a miracle, I thought, if the weather broke. The longer I lay thinking the more I became convinced the climb was coming to an end. Another American defeat on K2. The sixth in a row. Forty years, and we had not reached the top.

Lou and Wick returned from Camp VI later. At higher elevations they had climbed above the clouds and it had been a gorgeous afternoon. Other than deep snow the final three hundred feet, they had no trouble locating Camp VI under the prominent rock buttress.

"No chance of putting the camp higher?" I queried. During our planning, we had always hoped to locate the tent platform as high as possible on the summit pyramid. We regarded the low altitude at which the Poles had placed their Camp VI as a major factor in their defeat; now it appeared we had established our camp at the same site.

"I don't think so," Lou said, removing his old parka and dusting snow from his hair. We had cups of hot cocoa ready, and they both drank eagerly.

"Not only is there probably no platform higher," Lou continued, "but it wouldn't be worth the effort to try to carry supplies any higher through the deep snow."

We had to accept that our high camp would be more than two thousand feet below the summit, and we all knew what that meant: There would be little chance, after a long climb to the summit, that we could make it all the way back to camp the same day. We would have to bivouac. We spent the afternoon discussing the summit push: Should we spend time fixing ropes, should we use oxygen? We had managed to deliver five bottles of oxygen to Camp V, which gave us the option of using it. Several days before, we had reversed our previous decision and concluded it could increase our chance of reaching the summit if we did use it. But now, the subject was again under debate.

"You can use my oxygen if you want it," John said. "I'm going without it."

Lou recoiled. "We agreed we would all use it, or all not use it," he snapped.

"I don't want to lead those steep ice pitches with seventeen pounds pulling me backwards," John retorted. "I've been high without oxygen before, and I know I can make the summit of K2 without it. Besides, I only agreed to use it if both Wick and Rick insisted."

Caught in the middle, I told Lou it did not make any difference to me whether John used oxygen or not. Lou felt, however, that if only one of us went to the summit without oxygen, it would "cheapen the ascent" for those who did use it; presumably he thought those using oxygen would end up doing all the trail kicking, but those without would get all the credit.

"Who cares," I said to Lou, "if John does get more attention? Besides, there's a good chance he won't even make it."

All that mattered to me was getting myself to the top of K2—with or without oxygen—and I would not have cared if John climbed the thing nude. Lou, however, did care.

"If John is going without oxygen," he said, "then I will drop out of the summit team. I'll go ahead and support you guys, but that's all."

"What the hell's wrong with you?" John shot back. "Don't use any yourself, then."

"We agreed either to *all* use it, or none of us. I think you should feel obliged at least to honor your agreement."

The split between John and Lou was serious, and our prolonged stay at altitude, along with the continued bad weather, only exacerbated the schism. All along Lou had thought—with considerable logic—that John's and my summit plan was unsafe, if not stupid. A few days earlier, John—knowing he was the fastest of us on the technical pitches—had questioned whether Lou should lead any of the extremely difficult ice at the twenty-seven-thousand-foot level of the headwall. Lou had been indignant. The oxygen incident was the last straw.

"Lou, we've got to have you up there," I said. "You're still the one of us with the most drive, and God knows, we'll need all that we can get."

Tempers calmed, and Lou grudgingly agreed to rejoin the summit team, but only after John grudgingly agreed to use oxygen. It was snowing heavily as we finished dinner and crawled into our bags. Early the next morning I awoke and zipped open the window. I hoped we might have our miracle: the sky clear, that day to Camp VI, next day to the summit. I worked my torso out the small opening and looked around. Blackness, no stars, big snowflakes. We would have to desert Camp V and once again descend. I thought, You should have gone with Lou and Wick, and at least made eight thousand meters. Now, after all this work, you won't even get that high.

I zipped shut the window and crawled into my bag, waiting for the dawn, brooding, a hollow feeling spreading over me.

GAZING AT THE TABLE BEFORE ME, I HESI-tated, undecided. I dipped in my hand and scooped a mouthful of Waldorf salad festooned with fresh fruit, then ripped a drumstick from a golden-baked turkey. Best of all was a huge garden salad with red, firm tomatoes that, when I chomped into them, squirted juice and seeds. Baskets of fruit—apples, pears, bananas, pineapples. Wine and bread, vegetables marinated in oil and vinegar. Then ice cream, huge mounds of it, pistachio-almond, peach, chocolate chip mint . . .

I awoke to a scraping, scooping sound. I opened one eye and saw John still sacked out across from me—must be Lou or Wick shoveling snow. The storm was still with us.

I had never had a more realistic food dream. I could still taste the fruit and salad. For some reason, however, I had no desire for Slim Jim pepperoni sticks, or freeze-dried anything. But what would I give, I thought, for a tomato or an avocado? Or fresh meat—anything but that freeze-dried leather that always reminded me of Charlie Chaplin eating his shoe. Food dreams had been recurring frequently, almost nightly. At the beginning of the trip, my dreams had been the normal sort, but now I no longer dreamed even of women. The only desire left was fresh food. Continued endurance at high altitude was reducing my weight; already I had lost probably fifteen pounds. At extreme altitude the body has trouble digesting proteins and other complex molecules and consequently begins to lose muscle tissue. (Within ten days, I would drop another fifteen pounds and end up looking like a prison camp survivor.)

My attention shifted back to the scraping sound of the snow shovel, then I noticed John was awake.

"Is that you, Lou?" John called.

"Yeah."

"Still snowing hard?"

"We had a foot or two last night. You'd better come out and excavate your tent before it collapses."

John sat up and tugged on his jumpsuit, then his boots and mittens. I lay still; I had no motivation to move. John zipped open the door and crawled out. The bright, opaque-white glare hurt my eyes. He quickly closed the door to keep out blowing spindrift, then began shoveling. I propped on an elbow and started the stove to make breakfast.

I thought over yesterday's depressing events: Lou, Wick, John, and I had descended from Camp V in a blizzard; Cherie and Terry had greeted us at Camp IV. Because of crowded conditions and short supplies, Jim, Dianne, and Craig, along with Diana and Skip, had descended to Camp III and would wait out the storm there. We had talked to Jim that evening by radio, but it was a frustrating conversation. All Jim could talk about was the problems at Camp III. Most of the stoves had been carried to the higher camps, leaving only one clogged, sputtering relic at III, and Jim was barely able to melt enough snow for all of them to drink. Dianne's goggles had iced up in the whiteout crossing the traverse; she had removed them to see enough to get across and was now snowblind. Jim had twisted his knee and doubted he would be able to climb back up when the weather cleared, and Skip's toes were again numb from frostbite.

Now, the next morning, matters were worse. Jim's radio batteries were weak and he could only transmit three or four words before his message became gobbledegook. At Camp IV the only radio was in Lou's and Wick's tent, and listening through the tent walls, I was not certain if any of our messages had been successfully transmitted. John came back in; we finished breakfast and decided to crawl over and discuss our options with Lou and Wick. Before leaving, I zipped open the window and looked out. The wind was blowing very hard.

"You're not going to believe this," I yelled back to John, "but the wind is so strong it has blown all the new snow off the ridge and I can see the tracks going back to Camp Three. Unbelievable."

From the next tent Wick called over. "You can see those tracks because they're not old ones—they're new ones."

"What?"

"They're Lou's. He just left for Camp Three. By himself."

"In this storm? What for?"

"Wants to talk to Whittaker. He couldn't get anything across the radio, so he's going to talk to him face to face."

John and I looked at each other, astonished.

"Man, that guy must have some mighty big ants in his pants," I said, "and they're all biting at once."

John and I dressed and went over to Wick's tent to get the details.

"He was afraid Jim might be losing motivation to see this thing through," Wick said, "so he wanted to make sure Jim understood our commitment to stay as long as it takes."

"He asked me if I wanted to go, but I declined," Wick added.

"He didn't even tell us he was going," John said, "much less ask us."

"He figured you guys wouldn't want to go, anyway," Wick said drily.

"That's sure as hell true," I said.

John and I were unaware that Lou, as unofficial logistics manager, was seriously concerned about the developing food shortage—more would be needed from Camp III if we were to make the summit. But in spite of the need for an extra load carrier, he had hesitated to approach either of us for fear of reopening the Camp VI argument.

After a pause, Wick added, "He's going to talk to Whittaker about the Abruzzi finish also. Lou's still interested in drumming up support for it. He's still upset at you guys—especially you, John— and he wants to talk me into going up the Abruzzi, and to try and get Terry and Cherie to support him."

"What do Terry and Cherie think?" I asked.

"They're still committed to helping us get to the top, regardless of the route, but Terry admitted he would prefer the Abruzzi since that would give Cherie the best chance of going with us. I guess they're still entertaining the possibility of Cherie joining the summit team."

"What about you?" I said.

"I don't know," Wick replied. "I've still got to think about it."

"You're welcome to come with Rick and me on the direct finish," John said. "Three on a rope would work. Lou could go with the Bechs on the Abruzzi."

"Thanks, I appreciate it. But I still have to consider everything."

"We'll support whatever choice you make," I added.

We decided to meet when Lou returned. Meanwhile, since Wick obviously had much to think about, John and I decided to head back to our own tent. Just then, Jim's voice crackled over the radio. Apparently, Jim had jury-rigged his headlamp batteries to power the walkie-talkie, and his transmissions were now intelligible.

We informed Jim that Lou was on his way across, and Jim gave us news from Camp III: Dianne was still snowblind, but expected to improve in a day or two; Jim felt his knee was good enough to break trail partway down, should the weather improve, so those below could ferry up badly needed supplies. Food and fuel were critically short at Camp III, and Lou was going to completely drain them. But even if the camps could be re-supplied, Jim was pessimistic we could hold out much longer.

"We might last ten more days at most," he said. "By then, the porters will be here anyway, and I'm afraid we'll have to go off the mountain and call it quits."

There was fatigue, dejection, in his voice.

"I think it would be too much strain on everyone, too much of a risk to everyone's lives, to stay after September tenth. I still want as much as anyone to get this mountain—and we still might have one more assault left in us—but I just don't want to risk lives doing it. The storms are getting colder and longer and we can't stay up here forever."

Jim finished his transmission, then Wick said, "I hope Lou has some success buoying Jim's spirits. Still, there is some truth in what he says. We do only have one more chance."

John and I crawled back to our tent. It was not until late afternoon that Lou got back, and since it was still snowing heavily, allowing little chance that we would move the next day, we postponed our meeting. Through the tent walls Lou informed us, however, that he had had a good meeting with Jim and had convinced him we still had a chance of making the mountain.

"He's also very much in favor of us doing the Abruzzi finish," Lou yelled. "Jim feels it would be fitting, since that's the route Wiessner came so close to completing in 1939."*

John and I passed the rest of the afternoon eating and sleeping, and the next morning we were ready for the meeting. We fully expected Wick to go for the Abruzzi. Before we could gather, however, Wick called from the neighboring tent:

"The direct finish is on."

John and I looked at each other, wondering what would be Lou's decision.

"I'm with you guys, too," Lou yelled. "The four of us together on the direct finish."

Wick and Lou had spent much of the previous night discussing the choice of routes. Wick had been leaning toward the direct finish, and further considering the advantages of pooling our strength into one attempt, had talked Lou into joining forces with us. John and I, of course, were very pleased with the decision; it would put maximum strength on our choice of summit route. We decided to meet at noon, in Wick's and Lou's tent, to discuss details.

Cherie and Terry joined the conference, and although obviously disappointed with the choice of the direct finish, they still made a pitch for Cherie's being included in the summit attempt.

"I think five on the summit team would slow things," John said, "especially on the descent. It would just be too dangerous."

"To be candid and honest," Wick added, "I will have to say I would be unwilling to rope with Cherie on the summit push, especially up the direct finish."

*On the 1939 American K2 Expedition, the group's leader and strongest climber, Fritz Wiessner, along with a Sherpa from Nepal, climbed to within seven hundred feet of the summit via the Abruzzi route. Except for a mistake in routefinding on the final section, which left them in a cul-de-sac at a rock cliff, Fritz would, in all likelihood, have reached the summit—without oxygen. Had it been completed, the ascent would have gone down as the greatest achievement in the history of mountaineering. Today, Fritz lives quietly in his Vermont farmhouse; very few people know of him. Such are the whims of immortality.

Looking at Cherie, he explained, "It's just that I haven't climbed with you before."

"You've got to climb with someone you can trust and depend on," John agreed. "I'd have complete confidence going with Rick, for example, and I'm not going to rope up with anyone else."

"It's something you've got to be adamant about," I added, hoping to assuage Cherie. "I've been on other expeditions when I've been asked to rope with someone I didn't have experience with, and I've always refused."

"I understand," Cherie said, quietly and cordially. Both she and Terry, despite their disappointment, agreed to support the attempt and do what they could to carry gear to Camp VI. It was a magnanimous gesture, made more generous considering the strife the team had suffered over the last weeks. At the eleventh hour, it seemed we were again pulling together as a team; we shared the knowledge that only a collaborative effort would allow us to climb K2. Sitting together at 22,800 feet, during this final storm, I felt a camaraderie with my companions, more complete than at any previous time.

At the moment, though, Wick did not fully share my feelings. He had been as moved as the rest of us by Terry's and Cherie's unqualified offer of support. But he was stung by John's and my revelation that we would rope with no one else, that we were an inseparable pair. To Wick, that smacked of hypocrisy, especially in view of our earlier remark that we would be happy to have him join us on the direct route, forming a rope of three. Although John and I had intended our comment more for Cherie (Wick being a person in whose climbing ability we had confidence), he nevertheless saw it as reason to reconsider his decision to throw in his lot with us on the direct finish.

The meeting broke and we returned to our own tents, believing everything settled. For Wick, however, everything was not settled: He spent the afternoon pondering what to do.

There was a factor in Wick's decision that the rest of us were not fully aware of. Wick knew the direct finish would be more dangerous: Not only would the climbing be more dangerous and more difficult, the descent would be much harder and consequently slower. We would almost certainly have to bivouac, and if at the same time we suffered bad weather, it would seriously diminish our chances of surviving. It was something we all thought about. I myself had few responsibilities at home and could more easily live with my decision. John and Lou had wives and children. And Wick had a wife and five children; he, more than any of us, felt the weight of his responsibility. He spent the afternoon wrestling with his decision, then at four o'clock, he crawled through the door of our tent.

"I know you guys will be upset," he began, "and I know how crazy it is this late in the expedition to waffle over such important decisions, but I've changed my mind again. After considerable thought, I'm going to have to go back to the Abruzzi. There're several reasons. I still feel odd man out—both of you are such a tight pair, I don't see how I, or Lou for that matter, can fit in. There's more to it than that— it's also the responsiblity to Mary Lou and our kids. I don't know if I can explain it . . ."

There was a pause. John and I were moved by Wick's candidness.

"Wick, I told you earlier I would respect whatever decision you made," I said, "and I still mean it—more than ever. You'll leave this tent with two good pals, and we'll climb K2 by two solid routes."

"Thanks. That means a lot."

We embraced, and Wick crawled out of the tent. So the die was cast: John and I would now without doubt be alone on the direct finish. The Bechs, of course, would be elated, since it might give Cherie an opportunity of joining the summit team, or perhaps both of them a chance to go along with Lou and Wick.

But for me, the uneasy feeling, the trepidation, the fear of being only with John on such a difficult route, returned. We would be far out on a limb, or, as climbers put it, we would be very extended. If even the tiniest thing went wrong. . . . But if we pulled it off, it would be the ultimate achievement of my life. That alone seemed worth the risk.

Lying in the tent that evening, the vision of standing on the lonely summit of K2, gazing through rarefied air to an earth falling away in all directions, perched on the edge of space where the stars shine faintly in the daylight—that vision had a religious purity.

There was still hope of climbing the mountain. At Camp IV, on September 1, 1978, six climbers perched on a knife-edge ridge below the enormous summit pyramid of K2, bedded down in their sleeping bags, and along with their eight companions in lower camps, prayed for two or three days of good weather. We had no way of knowing, but at that moment the meteorology of the great Karakoram was slowly changing, as a high pressure cell formed over Central Asia; the prayers of those fourteen climbers—so insignificantly small against the vastness of this largest of mountain ranges on our planet—were being answered.

September 2. A STEEP WALL OF ICE AND A PINK-and-black rope going straight up. Above, a climber ascending the rope, below, four tents, barnacles on a knife ridge. Two climbers leaving the camp, moving slowly. On the horizon, to the east, a long, low, dark cloud, singular, backlighted in dawn. A feeling, a hope: Is the cloud moving away? Is it friendly? Otherwise, clear, cobalt sky. This is it. The test begins. The effort starts.

The two climbers leaving Camp IV were Terry and Cherie. I wondered why they had, once again, made a late start. It was past seven, and John, Lou, and I had already made good progress toward Camp V. Just below me, coming into view from behind a serac, I spotted Wick.

For Wick, the departure that morning was an emotional one. He left a short distance behind the three of us. Climbing by himself, he found he had tears in his eyes. They were not tears of sadness, or of mourning, but of thanksgiving. He was going for the summit. It was the culmination of six years of dreaming and planning and working, and as he made each step up the ridge, sliding his jumar up the rope, he gave thanks for the people who had allowed him that moment: his wife, his children, his mother, his father. For nineteen years—the length of his career as a mountain climber —they had given their unfailing encouragement to his dreams, their support through his defeats and tragedies.

John and I took turns breaking trail to the end of the fixed rope. We unstrapped our packs and, sitting on them, snacked on candy bars and lemonade until Lou and Wick caught up. Because of the crevassed section on the lower part of the snow dome, we roped together before moving on. There was excitement in climbing beyond that last fixed rope. From there on, it was "alpine-style" climbing—no fixed ropes, no yo-yoing between camps carrying loads—just daily progress upward. We were on our own.

The route was over familiar ground. For John, Lou and me, it was the third trip to Camp V at 25,300 feet, and I quickly was hypnotized by the monotony of placing one foot in front of the other. Despite the heavy snowfall, there had been enough wind that the surface was firm, and only occasionally did our boots break through and sink into the softer subsurface. When we did break through, the harder surface crust knocked sharply against our shins. At the end of a day of such postholing, you are not only exhausted, but your shins are badly bruised. The wind crust also increased the avalanche danger, and we had to be careful to choose a route that avoided open areas prone to slabbing.

We reached the site where, weeks earlier, Cherie and Terry had cached their loads on the way to Camp V. It was part of our current plan to retrieve that gear and, dividing it, carry it on up to Camp V. But heavy snowfall had buried it; it took a half hour of digging to locate it.

Meanwhile, we had spotted Cherie approaching the base of the snow dome, but Terry was nowhere in sight. We speculated that he had, perhaps, turned back.

"She shouldn't come up here unroped," Lou said.

Only a few minutes earlier, John had nearly gone into a crevasse. We sat and waited for Terry to appear, hollering to Cherie not to come farther without a rope. She was several hundred yards away, and because we were all hoarse from breathing cold air for so many weeks, it was hard to shout. But she understood the message and stopped to wait.

Another half hour passed, and we began to chill. It was surprising how much the temperature had dropped over the past week. There could be little doubt winter was close. That morning, Saleem had relayed from Base Camp the Radio Pakistan weather report for the Karakoram: "For the twenty-five-thousand-foot level, wind twenty knots and temperature minus thirty Fahrenheit." We could not wait much longer; our toes and fingers were starting to freeze. Finally we saw Terry, moving slowly.

"They'll rope up when he catches up with her," I said. "Let's get moving."

The four of us traded equal time kicking steps up the long snowfields to the top of the dome, resting only occasionally. The effort took five hours.

At 3:15, we made the last steps to the deserted campsite, a camp now in ruin. Two of the tents were still standing, although partly buried by drifted snow, but the poles of the larger four-person tent had snapped in the strong winds of the storm, and we found pieces scattered down the slope. We excavated the two undamaged tents, and gathering as many pieces as we could find, jury-rigged the other one. It was slow work, and by the time we crawled in, John and I had lost feeling in our toes. Inside we spread our sleeping pads and bags, started the stove for brew water, then put our feet against each other's stomach. It took over an hour before feeling returned, and by that time, 7:00, it was dark, and Terry and Cherie had not arrived.

The four of us gathered in the large tent wondering if we should go after them. On a radio call from Camp III, at 5:30, Jim Whittaker reported he could see them "probably an hour and a half below your camp, moving slowly." Since John and I had just then got some feeling back in our toes, and Lou and Wick were equally exhausted, it was hard to make the decision to go back out.

"According to Whittaker's estimate," I said, "they should be due any minute. If we don't hear anything in an hour or so, we should go after them."

I dreaded the thought. The wind was blowing, and it was very cold. I was only then getting warm in my sleeping bag. We continued to heat water for cocoa and tea, remembering how necessary fluids are at extreme altitude. We waited. 7:30 passed, then 8:00. It was time to think seriously about suiting up for a rescue. 8:15.

"Did you hear anything?"

"It sounded like someone shouting."

"Could have been the wind, though."

We turned down the stove and listened carefully, ears toward the downhill tent wall. It was a very faint voice, but we all unmistakably heard it: "Help."

Lou and I volunteered to go, but Lou was out the tent several minutes before me because I lingered to warm my brick-hard boots over the stove and to strap on my crampons. Lou left without crampons.

I crawled out of the tent and the cold wind immediately chilled me. Turning off my headlamp, through the blowing spindrift I could see Lou's light in the distance. I turned my lamp back on and headed that direction. Moving quickly, I started to warm.

I found Terry first; Lou was down the slope with Cherie. Terry was on his feet but moving like a robot, stiff-legged, lifting one foot slowly, then the other, and a rope trailed from him down to Cherie. I shined my head-lamp in his face and saw ice frozen in chunks in his beard; his eyes were tired.

"Hypothermic?" I asked.

"Just a little, maybe," he replied slowly but coherently.

"How about frostbite?"

"No, I don't think so."

"Cherie?"

"Worse than I am."

I judged that from the coherency of his speech he was—despite obviously being on the verge of the first stages of hypothermia—able to continue unassisted. I descended to where Lou was propped under Cherie's arm. Terry's assessment was correct: Cherie was worse.

Lou was bracing her, encouraging her to keep stepping upward. Her eyes had a distant, glazed look, and her lips were blue. There was saliva on the corner of her mouth.

"She's hypothermic," Lou said, "but I think she's capable of getting to the tents if we help her along."

"I can make it. I'm O.K."

Her voice had the muffled, barely intelligible sound of someone speaking without moving her lips. I took her hand to help her along, and I was startled by how cold and hard it was. It felt like wood. I feared she was frostbitten. I thought, It has only been dark for a couple of hours, though, and if we can get her on oxygen in time maybe it won't be so bad.

"Come on, Cherie, we'll help you along. Keep making steps. You can make it. We're close now."

"I don't need help. I can walk by myself."

She continued to step forward, awkwardly, but with determination. I knew if she lost that—if we had to try to carry her—it would be difficult to get back. But she gallantly kept on, Lou and me on each side, balancing her.

"My diaphragm hurts. I can't breathe right. It hurts when I breathe."

"Try to breathe steadily, even if it hurts. We'll be there soon."

"I would have made it, but I had to wait for Terry. He took so long."

She spoke with difficulty, mumbling, and the saliva again ran slightly from the corner of her blue lips.

"The weather is so much better there."

"Huh?"

"The weather. When I was a kid back home. So much better. In Australia, you know, where I'm from. Warm there, not like this."

"Keep going. One step. Then another. Now another."

"My diaphragm. Hard to breathe."

She continued, one slow step at a time. We were close now; I could hear

Wick and John shouting, beaconing us with their flashlight—a lighthouse in the spindrift and wind. Cherie made the last steps into camp, still under her own power, and I felt admiration, even pride, witnessing one of my companions muster her last ounce of strength. Cherie stood in front of Wick's and Lou's tent, at attention like a soldier in some war movie reporting in from a hard battle, staring ahead, tears in her eyes, while I worked to untie her harness. Wick put a cup of hot tea to her lips. The harness knot was frozen and I cut the nylon webbing.

"Don't do that," Cherie said. "Don't cut it. I'll need it in the morning."

"Quiet. We've got to get you in the tent."

Lou helped her in, and with her feet out the door, I removed her boots. Wick fed her tea. In the other tent, John was helping Terry into his sleeping bag and feeding him hot broth. He was shaking and very cold, but otherwise undamaged. Lou zipped together two sleeping bags and huddled next to Cherie to transfer his body heat. Wick continued to feed her tea but she couldn't hold it down. I rummaged for an oxygen regulator, and fastening it to a bottle, I cracked the valve and looked at the gauge: 3900 psi, full pressure. We gave Cherie the end of the plastic tube from the regulator—fitting a mask on her face would have been too uncomfortable—and I adjusted the flow rate to two liters a minute. Her shaking stopped, and she seemed to relax. I had inspected her hands when she crawled in the bag, but it was difficult to tell if they were frostbitten; we would know in the morning. I returned to my tent and helped John minister to Terry.

Terry lay in his bag, feeling better. John and I brewed tea and cocoa and rehydrated him. Their call for help had come just as we were preparing our own meal, and I knew I had to try to eat something myself, and drink more liquid, if I was to keep strength for the grueling climb in the morning to Camp VI. It's so slow melting snow to water, then heating it, at high altitude. It takes hours. The stove flame turns weak in the thin oxygen; the cold ambient temperature slows heating.

From the neighboring tent Wick told us Cherie was recovering amazingly well. She had apparently suffered no frostbite, and the oxygen was like a magical, revitalizing potion. Wick reported Cherie was even saying she would be strong enough in the morning to carry to Camp VI.

I thought, That's just the attitude that's going to get her in serious trouble. She was lucky this time.

I finished forcing down chunks of freeze-dried beef stew. Clops of the mixture were still unhydrated; there was no time to even cook the stuff, and we just poured boiling water on it—water that was boiling at a much lower temperature because of reduced atmospheric pressure—and ate the results. I washed it down with a welcome mug of tea, then crawled in my bag.

I thought, We'll need an early start. We should wake up about four-thirty.

I felt so tired. I asked John the time. "Twelve-fifteen," he said. A long, long day.

September 3. 3:30 A.M. I AWOKE FROM A FOGGY dream, my head aching. I was used to headaches; at Camp IV they weren't too bad, but at Camp V and above it was something you simply lived with. At that altitude, at night, your body's involuntary rate of breathing is insufficient to keep an adequate oxygen supply, and you awake continually short of breath, claustrophobic. In the most extreme cases you awake with panic, as if drowning, and you start breathing so fast you fatigue, slowing down, thereby becoming hypoxic, and having to again start breathing fast, starting a wicked cycle medically known as Cheyne-Stokes breathing. Even if you don't Cheyne-Stokes, at high altitude you almost always awake with a headache, and often nausea.

I had to pee. But I didn't want to crawl out of my bag. I was so warm and secure, comforted in the loft of goose down. For a few minutes I lay quiet, breathing regularly and feeling the increased oxygen flow begin to ease my headache. My slight nausea was also disappearing, and I rummaged along the side of my sleeping bag for my water bottle. To ensure an early start we had melted enough water before going to sleep to fill our bottles—two liters to each person—and then we laid them next to our bags where sufficient heat would prevent freezing. I took a swig and knew I had no choice then but to pee. But I put it off, wondering if somehow I could hold out another hour until I had to get up anyway to help prepare breakfast.

Suddenly I was swept again with that nauseated feeling; something was wrong, very wrong. I panicked for a second, and felt a tight grip in my stomach. I was on one side of the tent, John was on the other side, Terry in the middle. Both of them seemed to be breathing irregularly, which was normal at this altitude, and I didn't sense any problem. But something was wrong. I sat up and zipped open the window. Before I looked out, I knew what it was. I thought, No, God, not now. It can't be. Not this late, not after all we've been through, not this close to the end.

But it was. They were there again, in the black, starless predawn, those big, cold snowflakes silently drifting down.

IT IS TOO BAD we couldn't somehow have gone up in a hot air balloon to about forty thousand feet, where we could have seen the entire region. All across the great Karakoram clouds that had gathered during the night—condensed from vapor still present from the last storm—had formed over the highest peaks. There was a big one, a solitary one, over K2, just hanging there from top to bottom, and all of us climbers in that cloud had no way of knowing that over China, and the other way over Pakistan, the big high-pressure cell was still growing, and soon the clouds would melt away to an Indian summer spell of perfect weather that sometimes arrives late in the season in the Karakoram. But down on the mountain, covered by our own cloud and obscured from the world around us, we awoke that morning to profound depression; for most of us it was the lowest our morale had sunk since we had started the ascent of K2, fifty-nine days before. I noted in my journal:

> **September 3.** Woke up early this morning with excitement and hope of moving to Camp VI. But almost unbelievably it is snowing. It is too much to take; if the walls of this tent weren't so soft I would bash my head against them. We only need two days—just two days of reasonably good weather. It doesn't have to be perfect, just clear enough to see where we're going. Only two days, God.
>
> After all this work, all the days and weeks and months and years, we keep being pushed up and down by fickle weather. I've never been on a mountain with so many storms. Today is another day on our backs, staring again at checkered rip-stop walls. I spent the last hour trying to estimate how many of those eighth-inch squares are in the whole tent—anything to keep my mind off the thought.
>
> We only have two days of food here at Camp V. Terry and Cherie will move back to Camp IV in the morning to conserve food. There are hardly any supplies there, either.
>
> Will we make the top? Who knows. It's so frustrating, so incredibly frustrating. John and I have both agreed to not go down, no matter what, until we have made every last effort to reach the top. We will eat what food remains, and if the weather doesn't clear, we try anyway. We climb no matter what. What else is there to do?

The bad weather was in one way welcome relief for Terry and Cherie. Although they wanted as much as any of us to move up to Camp VI, and realized as much as any of us the urgency caused by our diminished supplies, they were that morning exhausted from the previous night's ordeal. Both of them, however, had recovered remarkably, particularly Cherie. She was again her testy self, and she insisted that as soon as the weather broke she would carry to Abruzzi VI, with Lou and Wick, and if possible try for the top. If that weather break didn't occur the next day, however, she and Terry would have to drop back to Camp IV. Although we didn't openly voice it, the four of us on the summit team felt there was little chance Cherie would have it in her to get much above Camp VI; we all knew the climb up the snow dome into Camp V was nothing compared to the effort that would be needed to reach the summit.

But all the speculation, the planning, the different scenarios of who climbed with whom and on what route, seemed hollow, pointless. I sank in despair, thinking it would be difficult to ever again get the desire to return to the Himalaya and try to climb one of the giants. It had been such a long dream. After the work and effort, to be turned back again by storm, without even getting a chance to push, with all our effort, toward the top . . . . I went to sleep that evening, defeated.

September 4. DIRECT MORNING SUN ON YELlow and orange tent fabric. Biting, bitter cold, wind, thirty below zero—eighty below wind chill factor?—and a sky as clear as blue ice. Excited movement in camp. Electric excitement. Freezing fingers strapping cold steel crampons to boots; flesh welding to steel. Freezing toes, nausea, headache. The gasping of people starved for oxygen, the sound of coughing, and a feeling of absolute thrill; the joy of prayers answered.

"You got the oxygen wrench?"

"Yeah."

"Your regulator?"

"Got mine. Make sure your mask is packed."

"I've got stove and cartridges. Seven-mill rope? We won't need any more fixed line than that."

"All packed."

"Finished in the tent?"

"Yeah. Close it. Let's get moving. Starting to freeze."

"Ready. Let's go."

We marched out of Camp V, John and I in the lead, Lou and Wick behind, Cherie and Terry following them. Six figures in a line punching steps down the backside of the snow dome toward the enormous summit pyramid that loomed directly before us, brilliant and glistening in the morning sun, a great rampart against which all our effort and strength would soon be pitted. I could see the route John and I would take to the summit, and rock buttress where we would place our Camp VI later that day, the big snowfield to the right of the campsite that rose up and up, getting steeper, finally ending in an ice cliff that from our estimates would be almost vertical for perhaps a hundred feet or more. Above that the angle lessened slightly, but then near the top, at 27,800 feet or so, we would have to traverse a rock band, laced with snow, that would be steep and difficult. The thrill of that challenge spread through me; the thought of climbing near-vertical ice at such extreme altitude released a rush of adrenaline that sent a warm flush through my body.

Just ahead I could see a rock at the base of the backside of the snow dome; I estimated that would be the place our teams would split. John and I would continue straight ahead, up the ever steepening direct finish of the summit pyramid. Lou and Wick, assisted in a carry from Terry and

Cherie, would begin the traverse to the Abruzzi, where they would establish their Camp VI.

"Hold up," Lou yelled.

I turned around and saw that Cherie had dropped back. She had been slow leaving camp that morning and a short distance beyond the tents had been sick to her stomach. Now she could go no farther. She removed her pack and Lou, Wick, and Terry divided her load. For Cherie, it was the end of the climb. She had pushed herself as far as her body would permit. As we shouldered our packs and continued, I glanced back and saw her still standing, staring at us, not moving. She was too far to see, but I knew she was quietly crying, and I felt a great poignancy. Despite our differences, despite the arguments, Cherie had given her all until the last to help the expedition reach the summit of K2. Lou would later write of that moment:

> She realized she had reached the limit of her endurance and turned back. She had never hesitated during the expedition to carry the same loads as men nearly twice her weight, but had not recovered from becoming extremely hypothermic on the long carry to Camp V. Watching her return to Camp V after setting an Australian altitude record, we were struck by the tragic dichotomy between willpower, which would have carried her anywhere, and her body, which was made of the same weak flesh as the rest of us.

AS I REACHED the rock and sat down to wait for the others, I thought how the mountain had lowered our numbers to the five people then gathering in the bright Karakoram sun at 25,300 feet. The effort was in our hands. Cherie had disappeared back over the dome to await Terry's return in Camp V, but I still held that image of her standing alone, watching us slowly walk away. She stood there, stripped of pretensions, her final dreams dissolving before her eyes, and like the rest of us, at that final hour of the expedition, naked before the mountain.

Lou arrived and sat next to John and me. Wick was slowly coming, thirty feet away, then twenty. He had the comical look of an itinerant pot and pan salesman pulling his clanking cart. That morning the joints of the fiberglass poles of his two-person tent had frozen together, and unable to break them down, his only choice had been to partially collapse the tent and strap the unwieldy package, at least four feet by seven, across the top of his pack. Now he looked more like a dust-bowl farmer en route to California than an expert climber heading for the highest camp on K2.

We rested together, sharing lemonade, our last union before parting ways.

"You could still go with us," John said to Lou and Wick. "It's not too late."

But it was clear they wanted to cut left and traverse toward the

Abruzzi. The wind had calmed, and it was becoming a warm, brilliant day. Lethargy spread through our bodies and we knew we had to get up and move; the longer we waited, the harder it would be. We stood, shook hands, then hugged each other. We all wondered what would be the others' fate.

"See you guys on top," I said. "We'll probably descend your route and join you in Abruzzi Six."

"We'll have a big reunion party," Wick said with his open-mouthed, determined grin. He had the buoyancy of a man whose dreams were about to be realized.

John and I continued ahead, slowly punching steps up the continually steepening slope, mindlessly moving one foot in front of the other. Little skill was needed to trudge up the snow slope, but at over twenty-five thousand feet, with fifty or more pounds in our packs, it was very slow and hard work. I lost track of time, hypnotized, and then thought to look back and see how Lou, Wick, and Terry were doing on their traverse—maybe even make a final farewell wave. I turned around, but all I saw was tracks disappearing around a bulge in the snowfield, toward the Abruzzi Ridge.

TWENTY-SIX THOUSAND FEET. DEEP, DEEP snow, accumulated from the last storm. I thought, The wind must have come from a different direction during this last storm and deposited more snow on this face than when Lou and Wick plunged their way up a week earlier. Snow above our waists, even to our shoulders.

Talking to myself, I fell into a trance: *Hard to breathe. Now only two hundred yards to go, even less, to Camp VI. John just behind me. I have fifty more feet, then it will be his turn. Take my ice axe and push in the snow, pack the snow, push it down with the shaft of the axe, then lift a leg, struggle to lift it, push it into the formless soft white and push up. The leg goes down and I gain what? Six inches, maybe. Then the next foot, a little higher, maybe another six inches, and now I have to beat the snow down again with the axe shaft and then lean forward and press with my body weight, forming a channel up the steep snow slope, a swath through the snow, ready to lift my leg again, but wait. I can't. No oxygen. I have to stop and breathe, so many times, keep breathing until that dizziness goes away and I feel enough strength to lift the next foot. O.K., keep going up until a few more inches become a few more feet become a few more yards and breathe, breathe, breathe again and again. Dizzy; no energy; must rest. Hearing things, too, distant voices.*

"John, Rick. John, Rick."

I looked down. John was just below me, and he too was peering down the slope, back toward the snow dome and Camp V. We could see Wick near the confluence of our two trails, and we knew right away things had not gone well. John waved his arms, acknowledging that we could hear him.

Wick yelled, his hoarse voice barely carrying up the slope. "Soft snow. Turned back. Cannot make Abruzzi. Will join you in morning."

John again waved acknowledgment, and turned and climbed to me while I rested.

"Looks bad," John said.

"I had my fingers crossed they would find better conditions around the corner," I said. "If the snow is this soft above Camp Six, we've had it. I've got enough trouble down here at twenty-six thousand feet, but at twenty-seven or twenty-eight, even without this load, I couldn't climb fast enough to make the top."

"All we can do is try," John said. "It's up to us now."

"At least we'll have Lou and Wick up here to help."

"Yeah, but I'm afraid of avalanche conditions. It's bad enough here, but on that slope above Six, under the ice cliff—it looks real bad."

He paused, then said, "Let me take it for a while. I think I can break the rest of the way."

John and I had originally hoped to be able to arrive at Camp VI early enough to pitch the tent, then continue above, stomping the trail at least several hundred feet higher and perhaps even fix rope on the steepest sections to allow us the next day—with any luck—to make it all the way to the top. But the unexpected deep snow, deposited in the last storm, changed everything. Now our chances of success seemed as uncertain as ever, and the disappointment of learning of Wick's and Lou's failure to reach the Abruzzi added to our despair.

It took another full hour to reach the site of Camp VI—the same place used by the Poles in 1976. There was no sign of their short occupation of this lonely bench of snow below the awesome rock buttress on the summit pyramid. There was also no sign of the gear Wick and Lou had cached a week earlier. We absolutely needed those supplies. Without the fuel cartridges for the stove, buried somewhere under what must have been a snowslide off the buttress above, we could melt no snow, and without water we would be forced to abandon the summit attempt.

Wick had spelled out careful coordinates to locate the cache; he had assumed the gear would be covered by snow and had located it under a feature in the rock he thought would signpost the cache. We traced the coordinates and started to dig. Two feet, three feet, four feet. We worked sideways, expanding the hole. When that failed, we probed other directions. Half an hour passed, then an hour. It was five o'clock—it would be dark in a little over an hour—and we were so weary from the day's climb, and the subsequent digging, I wondered how we would find energy to continue the next day, even if we did locate the gear. We were also very cold, and we were worried about frostbite, especially John, whose feet had lost feeling.

"I'm going to pitch the tent and set up camp," he said. "My feet are going—I've got to get them warmed."

"I'll keep digging," I said, despair in my voice.

We had called Wick and Lou on the radio to ask for any further information that might help locate the cache, but they hadn't been able to give us any more detail than we already had. Their radio's batteries were also running down, and their transmission was garbled. It looked like we would soon lose radio contact.

John had the tent pitched and unpacked our gear.

"Rick, my feet are bad. I'm afraid they're going. Could you warm them?"

I stopped digging and wearily looked over to the tent. John was inside, removing his boots. I had also lost feeling in my feet, and worse, my torso was quivering—my body temperature was dropping. There seemed little chance we could locate the cache.

"Sure," I said.

John put his iced toes against my belly. The ends of some of his toes were already missing, amputated from frostbite suffered on Dhaulagiri, and his feet were therefore more sensitive and susceptible to cold.

"Wish we had a hot drink—any kind of liquid," I said. I was already feeling the enervation of dehydration, and I felt like the caricature of the man in rags, dying of thirst, crawling across the desert—a desert of ice.

"We can't make it tomorrow if we don't rehydrate."

"I know," John said.

I was still shaking, but I managed to partially cover with my parka, and I put my legs in my sleeping bag while still keeping John's feet on my belly. Wick called again, his voice broken by the failing radio.

"We still have not located the cache," we reported.

"Five feet . . . end of rock point . . . point sticks out . . . go out five feet."

"We're in the right place, I think," John said to me. "Maybe we just have to go deeper. There was a lot of snow that last storm. It could be buried deep."

"Maybe," I said despondently. I had nearly given up; there seemed so many things conspiring against us—Wick's and Lou's failure to reach the Abruzzi, the soft snow, avalanche danger, and now no cache.

"I'm going out to look again," he said. He took his feet off my stomach, pulled on his socks, and worked into his cold boots. It was admirable determination.

I was just beginning to warm, but I felt too guilty to stay in the tent. It was nearly dark; we had ten or fifteen minutes of light remaining. I got out of my sleeping bag, put on my boots, and was just ready to crawl out of the tent.

"Got it!" John yelled. "Here's a cartridge, and another. And a food bag."

"Thank God," I said. John handed me fuel cartridges and food from the deep hole, and I carried them back to the tent. By the time we were back in our bags it was dark, but now we had new hope. And we had hot liquid.

We took the first hot water and divided it between drinks and a hot bottle to place inside John's bag, next to his feet. He was still worried about frostbite, but the warm water quickly restored feeling and he thought he hadn't suffered any tissue damage.

We continued the hours-long job of melting snow for drinks, and we managed to force down a dehydrated dinner. At 8000 meters the water was not hot enough to properly rehydrate the meal, and we had neither time nor fuel to cook the food. Somehow John managed to finish his; I could only get halfway through.

It was so cold, so bitterly cold. The night was brilliant, though, and the weather looked better than it had in weeks. If only the snow were firm above, we might be able to do it.

The flame from the stove cast a blue light in the tent. There was no moon. Deep shadows outlined our gear—the sleeping bags and parkas, the boots, crampons, mittens, overboots, miscellaneously scattered and heaped.

"Another brew ready," I said.

"Thanks."

"Two more liters and we can fill our bottles, then get some sleep."

John propped on his arm and drank his cocoa. We continued to melt snow. I was frequently forgetting to breathe fast enough, and I would have to take several rapid, deep breaths to overcome the claustrophobia of hypoxia. We were in such an alien place, such a hostile environment. I thought, We are bedded down at the highest camp, Camp VI, eight thousand meters. The magic number; the no-man's-land of extreme altitude where you have so short a time to survive. We have entered, I thought, the place known to climbers as the death zone.

"We've got to start early," I said. "We should get the stove going at one-thirty."

"I'll let you know when it gets that time," John said.

"What time is it now?"

John looked at his watch. "Twelve-thirty," he said.

"ONE-THIRTY," JOHN SAID.

"O.K."

I WASN'T ASLEEP, BUT MORE IN A MENTAL limbo, a subliminal twilight between conscious and subconscious, and slowly my brain closed whatever synapses were necessary to bring my awareness back to the reality of preparing myself to leave the tent and climb to the top of K2. I didn't want to. It was too cold. I knew if I went out there, in the predawn, my fingers and my toes would freeze and they would be amputated.

I lay quiet. I knew John was wondering if I would start the stove. We had slept heads at opposite ends, and the stove, and the snow for melting, were at my end. It was my duty; I had to do it.

I propped up and fumbled for the lighter, located the stove, and ignited the hissing butane. Even the few seconds needed for that simple procedure had numbed my fingers, and I eagerly warmed them over the flame. I had a headache and felt the nausea, and I did not have to pee. We were de-hydrated already.

With the water heating, I lay back down and thought about what was to come. It seemed such a slim chance we could do it. Perhaps with this ex-treme cold, perhaps the snow conditions would be more firm above, perhaps in the direct sun yesterday the snow had melted, and now was frozen solid. Who could say? We would soon find out.

The weary job of heating water, warming boots and mittens, drinking brews, and nibbling food—candy bars and an Instant Breakfast—took until nearly dawn. I knew we were taking too long. Somehow there was not enough spark to drive us faster; somehow I knew, although I tried not to admit it, we were defeated. John felt the same, but also did not admit it. We had to go through the motions.

We crawled out of the tent at 6:15—much, much too late. It took another thirty minutes to unravel the seven-millimeter rope—a task we should have done the day before. Without words we packed ice screws, pickets, deadmen, pitons. John tied into the climbing rope, and I took the other end and did the same.

"I'll lead the first pitch," he said.

"Sure."

I sat on my pack, braced against a snow bank, and belayed the rope while John climbed around the big serac under which we had pitched our tent. Around the serac we would have our first close look at the steep snow and ice fields leading up the direct finish. John slowly plowed through the deep drift at the base of the serac and disappeared around the corner. I waited, paying out rope. Then he yelled:

"Take in the slack."

He came back around the corner.

"No good. Extreme avalanche condition, and the snow is too deep at any rate to make headway."

The despair I felt all morning jelled to the realization we would now fail to climb K2. It seemed too overpowering to grasp.

"Let me look."

I climbed out around the corner and continued past John's swath in the soft snow several yards. The angle of the upper slope was ideal for avalanches; the deep snow seemed ready to break loose. John was right. Still, I couldn't accept it. Should we try to force our way up? Even though we knew there was no chance of making it and we would be taking extreme risk? It didn't make much sense. I climbed back to John.

We untied and went back in the tent, saying nothing. John picked up the radio for the 8:00 A.M. call.

"Too risky," he reported. "It's not worth the risk."

We could hear Rob Schaller's voice from Camp I, nine thousand feet below.

"We saw an avalanche come down the big snowfield above Camp Six," he reported, confirming our suspicions of unstable conditions.

Jim Whittaker, monitoring the call at Camp III where he was still waiting with Dianne, came on the air. In a solemn, weary voice he said, "Well, I guess that's it. We gave it a hell of a try."

10

At the Edge

SEPTEMBER 5. CAMP V, 5:45 A.M.

The small butane stove hissed and its blue flame—a lonely island of heat in a sea of cold—warmed the water that, once brought to steam, was then mixed with cocoa powder. Lou Reichardt drank the hot potion quickly, then mixed another cup of the steaming water with a package of Instant Breakfast. With a candy bar, a few sticks of beef jerky, and a small portion of granola with freeze-dried blueberries, Lou finished breakfast. It was the most food he would eat at any one time for the next two days: the major sustenance that would fuel the most difficult physical effort of his life.

At that moment, though, Lou still had no idea he would get a chance to make that effort, and certainly neither did his two tent companions, Jim Wickwire and Terry Bech. The previous night at Camp V—following their failure to cross to the Abruzzi—had for all three of them been extremely depressing. The chances of reaching the summit, they realized, were more distant than ever; still, they couldn't give up; they would make one more try. They had two options: either try once more to cross to the Abruzzi, despite the waist-deep snow, or climb up and join John and me on the direct finish. Both options, however, seemed grim.

After we had parted ways the previous morning—John and I continuing up toward the direct finish, the other three splitting direction to the Abruzzi—Lou had started in the lead and encountered the same deep snow John and I had battled all that day. It was slow, very slow. Finally

234

Wick took over, and waded up to his waist. They rested, and Lou again took over, but floundered in the bottomless, wet snow. It was nearly four o'clock—too late to possibly reach Camp VI Abruzzi, at their slow rate still hours away.

"If we could just reach the end of that ice cliff it might be better from there," Lou said, indicating a long wall of ice under which they had been traversing.

They wondered, soft snow notwithstanding, if there was even a passage around the ice cliff, beyond where they could see. It seemed likely, but they couldn't be certain. Once they reached the shoulder above the Abruzzi Ridge, they would be on territory previously explored by other climbers, and from having read their accounts, Lou and Wick would have a reasonably accurate idea where the final route would go. But on the traverse Lou, Wick, and Terry were crossing the only true virgin ground we would explore on our expedition, and the connection of the northeast and the Abruzzi shoulder of K2 would be our claim to routefinding.

"Yeah, I think we'll join the Abruzzi just around that corner," Wick agreed, "assuming we can find a passage through. But I don't see how we can get there before dark at this rate. And if the snow isn't any better around the corner . . ."

"Maybe we should go back and join John and Rick."

"Maybe."

There was no choice but to turn back. In silence the three returned to the fork where our two tracks parted, and from there they could see John and me still struggling to reach Camp VI Direct. That was when Wick yelled to us, telling us of their defeat.

"Let's leave the tent, oxygen, and food here," Lou said. "We can pick them up in the morning."

They returned to Camp V, and there was some talk of going up and joining John and me at Camp VI that afternoon, but they realized they were too tired from the day's effort to make another carry, even if we had a good trail stomped in the snow. It was a depressing evening; everything seemed grim. There was only one more day's food remaining at Camp V. The weather had clouded again that afternoon, and it seemed possible it might worsen. John and I had radioed we could not find the cache, and without it we would have to abandon our attempt. Cherie was still in Camp V suffering from a cough and was in constant violent paroxysms. That evening Wick noted in his journal:

> We are so close, yet so far. Deep snow, cold, lack of support from below. Tonight depressed about our chances. We are way out on a limb.

The following morning, after a brief breakfast on slim rations, the three prepared to leave Camp V still undecided whether to join John and me or to once again attempt to break through to the Abruzzi. Looking up to the summit pyramid to see if they could spot John and me working above our Camp VI (we were only then leaving our camp for our halfhearted attempt on the upper snowfields), they saw a big avalanche sweep part of our route. They knew then there was no choice; they had to try to cross to the Abruzzi. Lou led off, telling Wick and Terry to follow in an hour or so.

He arrived at the cache of food and gear, but instead of loading his pack decided to go empty. Without the heavy weight on his back, he could more easily forge the trail the remaining distance. Even though it meant returning for the gear, he felt in the long run it might be faster.

Wick and Terry arrived at the fork and waited for Lou's report. Looking up toward the direct route, they saw two more avalanches scour the gullies. It was unfortunate their radio was malfunctioning; otherwise they would have been able to report the avalanches, and John and I would have abandoned our attempt then and there. Fortunately, the snow was so deep just out of Camp VI Direct that John and I were floundering; otherwise, we might have made enough progress to climb into the path of the big avalanches.

Without his heavy pack, Lou made rapid progress across his previous tracks, even though they were partially filled with new spindrift, and in a few hours he was back at the junction where Wick and Terry waited.

"I got a little farther than yesterday," he reported, "and I think if the guy leading breaks trail without a pack, we can get around that key corner. With any luck, from there it will be easy."

The three shouldered their loads and climbed back to the end of their tracks. Terry was in the middle—never doing any trail kicking—for the important reason that he was carrying the heaviest load. Whereas Lou and Wick carried mostly personal gear, plus a few camp odd and ends, Terry had a very heavy load of two oxygen bottles, a nine-pound food bag, eleven gas cartridges and stove: a payload weighing nearly fifty pounds, considerable weight at nearly twenty-six thousand feet. His effort carrying the pack was even more impressive considering it was not for himself, but rather in support of two companions. Terry, as well as anyone, knew that if Lou and Wick were successful, all the ballyhoo after the expedition would be for them. On big climbs the spotlight shines on those who reach the summit; the often comparable efforts of those who work so hard to put them there usually goes unnoticed. If there was any one of us on the 1978 American K2 Expedition who lived up to the pledge months before we left the United States "to work as hard as possible to get somebody—anybody —to the top of K2," it was Terry making that heavy carry to support Lou and Wick.

Wick continued the lead, first working up untrodden snow still carrying his pack, but then leaving it behind. Like Lou he would break trail unladen and come back for his pack later. Wick looked up and thought they were perhaps only a hundred yards from the key corner. As he con-

tinued punching steps, slow in the thin air, he realized the distance was
closer to two hundred yards. It took until late afternoon, but finally he
arrived at the corner. Not knowing whether the view a few feet farther
would show only a cul-de-sac under the ice wall or, as he hoped, a passage
to the broad snow and ice field of the Abruzzi shoulder under the summit
pyramid, Wick made the last steps and with anticipation looked around
the corner. Above was a wide-open slope, about forty-five degrees in
angle, leading to the Abruzzi. Moving quickly, he climbed a few more feet
to test the snow conditions. He swung his axe and the pick stuck in the
hard snow, the kind of snow ideal for climbing.

"Looks good," Wick called back. "Hard snow, even some ice. It should
go."

Lou and Terry climbed around the corner, and while they continued
up, making slow but steady progress, Wick traversed back across for his
pack. Returning quickly, he caught Lou and Terry as they climbed over
the shoulder to easier slopes above.

Lou and Wick had originally hoped to place their Camp VI as high on
the Abruzzi shoulder as possible; they knew, for example, that the Italians
in 1954 and the Japanese in 1977 (the only other two teams to ever climb
K2) had established their camp at the highest possible place below the
summit pyramid. That minimized the distance required to reach the
summit the next day, and consequently increased the chance of returning
to the high camp before dark and avoiding bivouac. But the hour was
late; it would soon be dark. There seemed little chance of making the ideal
site, so instead, they would have to settle for a location much lower. About
five-thirty, as the shadows of Broad Peak and the Gasherbrums cast long
across the Godwin-Austen Glacier ten thousand feet below, they found a
narrow but reasonably flat spot, at the base of an offset crevasse that split
the middle of the Abruzzi shoulder. With only a small amount of chopping
and shaping, it would just accommodate their tiny two-person tent. The site
had the additional advantage, since the crevasse was offset and therefore
had a "back wall," of offering some protection from potential avalanche.
A thousand feet above, on the summit pyramid, several seracs loomed
giant in the twilight; they knew that realistically the small ice wall behind
their tent would provide little armor to shield them if one of those big
blocks broke off. The site was also seven hundred feet below the location
used by the Italians and the Japanese, seven hundred additional feet they
would have to climb when they began the long, long assault on the summit
in the blackness of the predawn, then only hours away.

Wick set down his pack and unstrapped the unwieldy tent while Lou
began chopping the platform. Of the three, Terry, having carried the
heaviest pack, was the most exhausted. It was dark when they finally had
the tent pitched, and the three jammed inside for what would be a difficult night without sleep. It was early—seven o'clock—the altitude 25,750
feet.

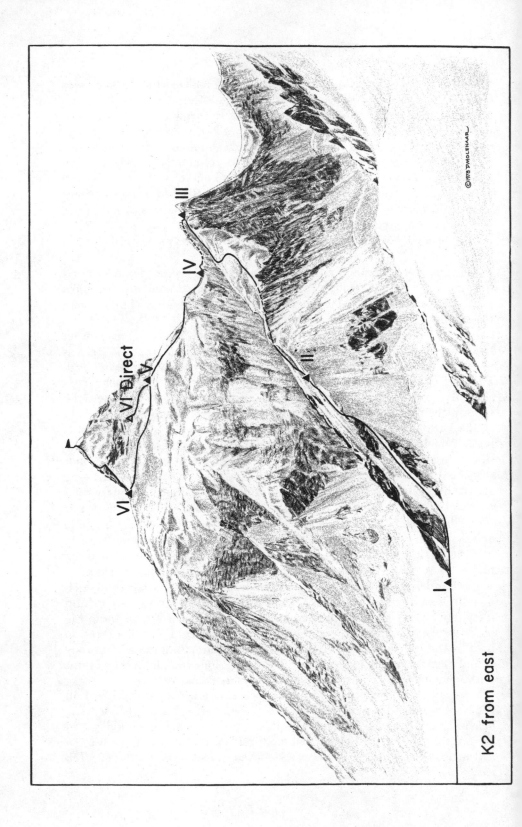

K2 from east

VI Direct

© 1978 P. MOLENAAR

"I'll sleep in the middle," Wick said, "with my head down at the other end. Give us more room that way."

Wick, having the most space at his end of the tent, got the job of cooking, and soon the billy pot packed with snow was balanced on the narrow grill of the small butane stove. Patiently the trio waited for their drinks; it was now of utmost importance to hydrate fully for the summit assault.

It was difficult to feel elation. They were so exhausted from the push to Camp VI, so fatigued from the lack of oxygen. It was difficult to think of anything other than immediate duties: melting snow, arranging gear for the morning, being careful not to doze too late. It was difficult to appreciate that after sixty-two days on the mountain, after the weeks and months of struggling through snow, of climbing across steep ice, of carrying load after load to higher camps; that after six storms and the days and days spent holed up in tents; that after so many frustrations followed by reborn hopes buried by still more disappointments and new frustrations, they were now poised to be, after forty years of questing, the first Americans to make that last step to the summit of K2.

It was still not certain, by any means, that they would succeed. Others had been where they were, and failed. Wiessner, in 1939, was turned back at a point hundreds of feet above where they then were camped. Would they find more impassible soft snow above? That was the possibility that would most likely prevent success. At least the weather seemed, at long last, to have given the expedition a long-awaited reprieve. Although the temperature had dropped dramatically in the last week as winter neared, the sky that night was cloudless, and despite gusting winds, promised a good summit day.

"Damn it," Wick cursed, jerking up.

He had dozed, one hand steadying the pot full of water, and the billy tipped, spilling part of the water on his parka and his half-bag. He had intended to take both parka and half-bag with him to the summit, in case he had to bivouac, but now that they were wet, and in only minutes the water would change to ice, he knew he would leave the useless garments behind. That small incident of spilled water would nearly cost him his life, but at the moment, all that bothered him was losing valuable water and wasting precious time and fuel.

He refilled the pot and patiently waited for the water to heat. He served more drinks. It was near to midnight. Filled with expectation, there was no use trying to sleep. It made more sense to stay up and continue melting snow, to continue hydrating. Wick knew the ultimate test was then only hours away.

SEPTEMBER 6. CAMP VI ABRUZZI. 1:30 A.M.

"Not again, Wickwire, what's wrong with you," Wick groaned, chastizing himself.

"What happened?" Lou asked, lifting his head at the other end of the tent.

"Fell asleep and knocked over the pot again. Now I'm really soaked. No use taking any of this wet stuff along."

Wick looked at his half-bag, flattened and limp, already sheeted with ice from the previous spill.

"We should start getting ready soon," Lou said. "It would be good to get started by three-thirty or four."

"I'll melt more water," Wick said.

The hour arrived; it was time to begin dressing. Awkwardly the two men struggled in the confines of the small tent to fit their clothing and push into their frozen boots. They could only guess the temperature. The nearest thermometer, with Jim and Dianne at Camp III, registered twenty below, and it was probably about thirty below where they were, three thousand feet higher. They knew they would soon be out in the wind, too, then buffeting the sides of the tent, and the chill factor would add even more bite to the low temperature. Wick was concerned about frostbite; in the last spill he had also soaked his pile mittens, and now he would have to use his backup pair of single-layer Dachstein wool mittens, covered with only a thin nylon outer shell.

Time sped as the two continued seemingly in slow motion to finish preparations. Lou, then Wick, crawled from the tent at 4:00 A.M. and pulled their packs behind them through the narrow tent door. It was later than the time they had hoped to leave. Terry crawled out to help them off. Something fell out of Wick's parka; he had stored his water bottle in his parka to keep it warm, and now he and Terry heard it skid down the ice, out of sight, into the black. A small error, and one that would add to the severity of the grueling trial ahead.

The two men each placed an oxygen cylinder in their packs. They planned to climb as high as they could, perhaps 26,500 feet, before using the gas, since they had only one cylinder each and would have to make it last until the summit. Terry watched with blighted hope as Wick loaded his cylinder; he still wanted to help them carry their oxygen higher, until the point they would begin to use it, but Wick had understood that Terry—worried about frostbite—didn't want to go any higher. It was a poignant scene—a misunderstanding at 25,750 feet.

Not saying anything, Terry realized that Camp VI was, for him, the high point. He helped Wick shoulder his pack, and then, as the two climbers tied into their rope and left Camp VI in a blustery wind at 4:30 A.M. he crawled back in the tent and waited for the morning sun. His only remaining desire was to return to Camp V and join Cherie. But their purpose was not finished: They would yet help four climbers crawl off the mountain in a desperate descent and a race against death.

Lou immediately set a fast pace, trying to burn energy and heat his body. Wick struggled to keep up, breathing fast, staring intently at the snow under his feet, being careful not to stumble in the darkness. Already he knew his fingers had frozen. There was no feeling; the fingers felt hard and lifeless. If a few fingers were to be the price to climb K2, he thought, so be it. The snow surface continued hard, and the wind had tortured the ground to small sastrugi. The slope was steeper than Wick remembered from studying accounts and photographs of previous climbs. The pair continued at a good pace, heads lowered against the icy wind, fighting for enough oxygen. At 5:45 the first light tinted the sky across the great Karakoram and slowly filled the deep shadows below them. A hundred miles of mountains spread before the two men. But they could not enjoy the panorama; in the hostility of the cold, thin air, they could barely acknowledge the dawn. For Wick it was the beginning of the day when he would realize the most ambitious mountaineering goal of his life, but the profundity of that moment escaped him. He had already entered the other-worldly somnambulism of those who climb in the death zone.

SEPTEMBER 6. CAMP I, 18,400 FEET. 5:30 A.M.

Rob Schaller slowly drifted to consciousness. In the yellow nylon walls he could see a hue of first dawn. Although the tent was still dark, he nevertheless knew the position of every item inside; it was as familiar as his bedroom back home in Seattle. Without searching he knew where to find his pants, his pile jacket, his red, white, and blue balaclava embroidered with emblems his wife Joanne had sewn on, his medicine and hospital supplies stored along the back wall. Near his head he kept his journal and writing supplies and a stack of letters from his wife. The tent had been pitched in the same place so long the glacial ice around it, melting faster in direct sun, had left him perched on a pedestal three feet above the surrounding terrain.

Rob recalled the events of the previous three days, and the disappointment to everyone in Camp I. They had listened on the radio when John and I reported deep snow, and that we didn't think we could reach the top via the direct finish; they had witnessed, through a telescope, the avalanches down the gully above Camp VI Direct that confirmed what John and I had said; they had watched the only remaining hope for success dissolve when Lou, Terry, and Wick had failed to cross to the Abruzzi. But they thought they had seen them finally make it the next day so that now, Rob thought, there was an outside chance they might be able to try for the summit that morning.

In the cold first light, he crawled out of his tent and in his down booties walked to where the telescope was mounted on a tripod. Everyone else was still asleep. There was already enough light on the upper mountain to distinguish detail in the rock and ice features. He carefully studied the Abruzzi Ridge, the big snow shoulder below the summit pyramid, the ice cliffs above the rock band, and the narrow snow gully that would be the route—the route, that is, if anyone up there was capable of reaching the top.

He fixed his attention on the slope just below the couloir. There were dozens of black dots on the snow—rocks protruding from the ice—and he gazed at them intensely. Something looked different. His eyes fixed on two of the rocks. Could it be? He wasn't sure. He watched, stared, and then he saw it. He saw one of the rocks move, then the other. The two rocks were moving slowly, very slowly, but there was no doubt. He stared, transfixed, realizing even more than the two rocks themselves the full import of the scene.

"I've got them," he shouted. "Lou and Wick. I can see them. It's Lou and Wick. They're on their way to the summit."

SEPTEMBER 6. CAMP VI, DIRECT. 26,200 FEET. 7:00 A.M.

"It really doesn't make much sense."

"Not much."

"But we've got to try. We just can't go back without giving it everything we can."

"O.K. But only once. We'll try to get across the slope, and if we make it we'll push for the summit, but I won't go up, fix ropes and come down, and go up again. It's just too dangerous to cross more than once. Even then I'm not sure it is worth the risk. I don't see how we can get to the top anyway."

John was more certain than I that the slope above Camp VI Direct was like a sprung trap ready to avalanche. As it turned out he was right; had either of us known that morning of the avalanches those below had witnessed, we would have deserted immediately.

As it was, we had decided instead to make one last attempt to reach the summit. Again, we started preparations at 1:30 A.M. It was our second night at eight thousand meters, and our second night without sleep. It had taken even more willpower to get started that morning, and to leave the tent, because we knew in our hearts it was futile. We did not get away until 7:00—a very late start if we realistically hoped to reach the top. While John belayed from near the tent, I led around the corner, out of his sight, retracing the steps from the morning before to their end, and then slowly, slowly wading up virgin snow. Half an hour passed, then an hour. I hadn't even covered the distance of a rope-length. I was working to gain a serac block, hoping it would have a more solid base, but then I exposed a crevasse hidden in the loose snow, and I searched for a bridge to span it. It seemed hopeless; even if I got across I knew the snow was still deep, nearly to my shoulders. I was determined to try, though, to climb as high as possible.

I saw John come around the corner; he had left his belay stance and climbed to within shouting distance. I knew what he was going to say; I knew he wanted to bag it, to go down, and I knew he was right. It was futile and senseless to go farther. But he didn't say what I expected:

"I just got a call on the radio from Rob at Camp One. Lou and Wick are going for the summit. They can see them through the telescope."

I stared at John. So Lou and Wick had done it, I thought; they had managed to force a route to the Abruzzi, and now they were on their way to the top. All the futility cleared as I realized there was hope our expedition would still be successful.

"Rob says they're moving pretty well. Slow, but steady. Obviously they've got better conditions than we do."

I looked back above me. I could see the snowfield going up five hundred or six hundred more feet, then bearing left out of sight. Just as it disappeared I could see the corner of the vertical ice cliff we would have to scale. Above, I knew there would be another snowfield—in all probability more deep snow—and past that a traverse across a rock buttress. In these conditions, it seemed impossible.

I thought a moment, then added, "There's no way we can get up this."

"Then let's bag it."

"And go down?"

"Hell no. We'll pack up this camp and head over to the Abruzzi, then follow Wick and Lou to the top tomorrow."

I thought about John's proposal and considered the words, "pack up our camp." The words were simple, but not the reality: a two-person tent, food, fuel, stove, sleeping bags, pads, parka, camera, climbing hardware, two oxygen bottles and regulators—at least sixty pounds each. We would carry the load from one side of K2 to the other, traversing an altitude close to eight thousand meters. Then go to the summit after our third night in a row in the death zone. I realized, though, there was no alternative.

"O.K.," I said. "Let's go."

We moved quickly to break camp and load our packs. I hefted mine to test the weight; carrying the load to the Abruzzi would be close to my limit of endurance. We still had the rope and climbing hardware to consider.

"We can leave part of this hardware," I said. There was a large assortment of pitons, carabiners, ice screws, deadmen, and pickets. I thought how futile to have worked so hard to carry it that high, and now propose to leave it.

"We can leave it all here," John said. "We don't need to belay any of the pitches on the Abruzzi."

Although the climbing would be steep, I knew he was right. If we had any hope of reaching the top in one day, we had to forego the luxury of protecting the steep sections with the safety of a belay.

"If we're not going to belay, this rope won't do much good either."

"We'll leave it at the junction—get it on the way back. We'll climb to the summit unroped."

I packed the rope on top so I could easily get it out and cache it at the junction near Camp V. I thought, A little farther out on the limb. To the summit—unroped.

SEPTEMBER 6. SUMMIT PYRAMID, ABRUZZI FINISH. 26,500 FEET. 7:30 A.M.

The direct morning sun lit the rock to his left, and feeling evermore in a dream world, Wick slowly, step by slow step, worked toward a small flat spot on that ridge. Lou was already there, sitting, resting. Making the last steps, Wick unloaded his pack and looked around. To his suprise, he found more than just rock, ice, and snow. On the lonely shelf at 26,500 feet, in the heart of Central Asia, he also discovered a high-altitude garbage dump: an empty fuel canister and a fragment of aluminum wrapper from a drink mix, or possibly a soup package. He wasn't certain which since the label was in Japanese. They had stopped at the site of the Camp VI of the 1977 Japanese K2 Expedition.

Wick decided to start using oxygen; Lou was going to wait until a bit higher, until the narrow couloir they could see above them. Opening the top flap of his pack, Wick exposed the yellow fiberglass-wrapped aluminum bottle, and with his fingers unscrewed the brass cap protecting the valve opening. He had made certain, before leaving camp, the cap was only finger-tight; we had all been wary of carrying our oxygen bottle a total of 9500 vertical feet (the altitude distance to Base Camp) only to find a cap that couldn't be removed without a wrench. He next screwed the regulator into the fitting and tightened it with a wing nut designed to operate with mittened hands. He cracked the valve and looked at the gauge, then looked again. At first he couldn't believe it, then he tried to imagine how it had happened, how he could have hauled the bottle that far without knowing it was only partially full. The gauge read 2700 psi, well below the 3900 to 4100 psi of a full-pressure bottle. Somehow, precious gas had leaked. Despite the extreme altitude, Wick was still thinking clearly enough to realize that to make the summit before the bottle emptied he would have to climb with a slow flow rate of one liter a minute. That would be far less than the two- to four-liter rate climbers normally use at comparable altitudes on Everest.

With the mask fitted and the rubber bladder-reservoir ballooned in front of his face, he signaled to Lou he was ready. Lou led out, but just before the bottleneck in the couloir, where it became the steepest, Wick took the lead and worked up, carefully placing his crampons on the ice-covered rock and making sure the pick of his axe was securely in the ice before making each move. He realized his thoughts were slowing, and he knew he had to think through each move carefully, but he was feeling more strength—the benefit of the oxygen.

At the top of the couloir Wick stopped and pulled the rope up, and Lou followed. Despite not yet using his oxygen, Lou was keeping up with Wick. In the narrowest and steepest part, one of Lou's crampons suddenly popped off as the icehold under his boot gave way, and he just caught himself. He had to breathe rapidly before he felt his oxygen-starved body regain strength sufficient to try again. He wondered if he could make the move with the weight on his back. But he did—he had to—and together he and Wick studied the next obstacle.

Straight above them loomed the enormous ice cliffs of the summit pyramid. To overcome the obstacle they would be forced to traverse left over rock covered with loose snow and some ice. It looked spooky. Above the narrow catwalk was vertical ice; below, a ten-thousand-foot drop down the south face to Base Camp.

"You should probably use your oxygen," Wick said.

"O.K."

Lou removed his pack to screw on the regulator, then fitted the mask. Shouldering the pack, he slowly led across the traverse. He gingerly made each crampon-step, trying to keep the metal points off the rock where they would more easily pop off. Wick belayed the rope around his ice axe, but they both knew the anchor might not hold a fall.

Making the moves across the traverse was hard enough, but it was even more difficult because Lou was having trouble with his oxygen apparatus. It didn't seem to be delivering any gas; his bladder was limp and only partially inflated. Balancing with one hand on his axe and his feet carefully placed on the ice-covered rock, he removed the mask with the other hand, took several breaths of ambient air, replaced the mask, and made several more steps, only to be forced to do the same thing. He fiddled with the flow rate, opening it to a maximum eight liters a minute. Even then the bladder remained deflated. Something wasn't working; it had been easier climbing without the mask.

He finished his pitch and belayed the rope as Wick crossed. He enviously noted Wick's bladder puffed like a tight balloon, and knew without doubt he either had an obstruction or a leak. Wick climbed past and Lou followed, continuing to fiddle with the apparatus. He mentally rummaged through his pack for something to jury-rig a leak.

Adhesive tape, he thought, but I don't have any.

Then he realized it was hopeless. He looked up and saw a rock above, the next "goal," and knew he couldn't possibly reach that, much less the summit, carrying a seventeen-pound security blanket that wasn't even working. He stopped, removed the mask, and examined the rubber tube leading to the bladder. There were several holes, possibly caused by a crampon puncture while being transported in the pack lower on the mountain. He removed his pack and set everything—mask, cylinder, even the pack—in the snow and continued to catch up with Wick.

Wick had been slowly punching steps up a long snow slope beyond the end of the ice cliff, realizing the most technically difficult sections were now behind him. From there it would be a long, slow trudge to the top. It was already past noon and they had some twelve hundred vertical feet to go. Much time had been lost while Lou worked with his faulty regulator. It would be all-important to keep a steady pace, and there would be no time for rests.

The snow had once again softened in bright noon sun, and Wick struggled to maintain his pace. He looked behind to check on Lou and was amazed to see him take off his oxygen mask, set his pack in the snow, unrope, and continue, leaving everything behind. Without the weight of his pack, Lou was much faster, and Wick waited for him to catch up.

Wick thought, Is Lou going back down? What's up?

Before Lou arrived, Wick made up his mind to continue, even if Lou was planning to descend, alone to the summit.

"What are you doing?" Wick asked when Lou arrived.

"I'm going without oxygen. My oxygen set wouldn't work. There was a leak or something. It's a gamble, but there's no choice."

Lou was concerned; he didn't know what his body's reaction would be at twenty-eight thousand feet without oxygen, and he feared it might dangerously impair his judgment. Recalling stories of previous climbs to the earth's highest summits where climbers had gotten in trouble when their oxygen ran out, Lou's subconscious notified him it was time to be careful and not to expect his judgment to be sound.

"Watch me, and tell me if I exhibit any bizarre behavior," he said to Wick.

"O.K. I'll talk to you every so often, and that way tell if you start to act weird," Wick said, then added, "You realize, though, I'm going to the top regardless?"

"Yes," Lou replied.

Wick continued slowly. His hopes for better snow conditions dissolved as his feet, calves, and then thighs disappeared in the mushy snow. Another hour passed. He traded leads with Lou, then switched back. One foot, then another, then breathe several times. Wick looked behind to see that Lou had started an angled traverse toward the ridge to their left, and Wick realized he was searching for better snow. Both men forged separate paths for another hour until finally Lou reached the ridge and appeared to have better footing. Wick began to traverse to merge with Lou's tracks. By the time he was in them, Lou was some distance above.

Wick tried to catch up, but it was all he could do to match Lou's pace.

Maybe something's wrong with my oxygen, he thought. He checked the flow rate, looked at the bladder. It was puffed full, still pressurized, still delivering gas. But he couldn't understand why Lou was maintaining distance. Wasn't he, the one with oxygen, supposed to be faster than Lou—the one without?

As they climbed to even more extreme altitudes, Wick slowly closed the distance, then passed Lou. It was like a crossing of the performance curves, if you could have graphed the trade-off of going with or without oxygen. Lower on the slope, Lou had been able to maintain his lead on

Wick who, while breathing oxygen, was nevertheless handicapped by the seventeen-pound bottle and other equipment in his pack. As they approached twenty-eight thousand feet, though, the benefit of the oxygen exceeded the difficulty of the added weight, and Wick slowly worked ahead.

Other than a few sips from Lou's bottle, they had climbed all day without water. The small matter of the water bottle lost from Wick's parka was having its effect. Lou, in leaving his pack behind, had also left his parka, and he was starting to shiver in the increasing cold. The sun dropped behind the summit ridge, and the cold intensified. It was 4:30 P.M. Above, they could see the silhouetted, nearly horizontal ridge. Would the summit be there, or some distance beyond? They would make it, there was no going back, but it would be late.

It seemed deceptively close, yet it receded with each footstep. Wick continued in the slow, steady pace. Neither of them had rested for more than a minute or two since Lou had set down his pack. With each step Wick thought of his family, his wife, his children, his mother and father— all who had given such support to his quest for this summit. He thought of several of the earlier climbers who, except for the vagaries of bad weather and bad luck, might have been the first Americans to walk those last steps. He thought of Dusan and Al and Leif.

There were only a few more steps to the ridge crest. Excited, Wick picked up his pace and made the final moves up the steepening snow face. Suddenly he stepped onto the ridge crest tinted gold in late afternoon alpenglow. He was gasping for air; he thought he had somehow pinched off the supply of oxygen, then realized it was because he had made several rapid steps. He fell on one knee, exhausted.

His head down, he slowly looked to his right, hoping he would see the summit only a few feet away. Instead, the ridge continued level, then seemed to drop away into China. He could see the burnt Sinkiang hills before the setting sun. He looked the other direction. To his surprise, Lou was only inches away, making the final steps up the ridge crest. For Lou, increasingly cold without parka, the psychological warmth of the direct sun rays—then so low on the horizon—seemed to raise the temperature thirty degrees.

Wick looked past Lou, and now the ridge gently arched up, wider than he expected. The snow was gold. Seventy-five feet away he could see the ridge round off, then descend toward the west. It was a little larger than he expected, but still no bigger than a large dining table. He was in no way disappointed. He stood up and said to Lou:

"We've come this far. Let's make the last step together."

Arm in arm, they walked to the summit of K2.

THE SECOND HIGHEST point on the surface of the planet. The summit of his dreams. Wick stared across the mountains stretching endlessly below him, summit after summit painted gold. They were all below him. The world curved away, in all directions, falling away, below his feet.

For Lou it was an even more remarkable victory. He was the first man to climb K2 without oxygen. The magnitude of his feat was measured in his blue lips, in the ice frozen thick in his beard. Although the moment seemed dreamlike, he was still thinking coherently, and unlike Wick, one thought predominated: Get Down. It was 5:15 P.M. Ninety minutes until total darkness. There would be no moon. Lou had no parka. He was fiercely cold. He knew he could not survive a bivouac.

When the pair had crested the summit ridge a few minutes before, Lou had said, "I'm going to walk to the top, then turn around and come right down."

"You've got to at least stay there long enough for me to take a picture of you," Wick had replied.

There was a tacit agreement that Wick intended to stay longer and Lou would descend. But first there were several things to do, and Lou waited impatiently while Wick rummaged in his pack for the American and Pakistani flags, for an eagle feather we had promised the United Tribes of All Indians Foundation, who had helped the expedition raise funds, we would carry to the summit. There was also the microfilmed list of all who had contributed $20 or more. Wick handed Lou the flags and the feather and took several photos. Wick then handed Lou his camera, since Lou had forgotten his own when he abandoned his pack, and Lou took a duty shot of Wick.

"Let's go."

"I want to get a panorama first," Wick said. "But I've got to change film. Go ahead. I'll be along in a minute."

Lou was cold. It was nearly 5:30, and the sun was dropping below the horizon. The first stars emerged in the blackening sky. Without hesitation, he turned and began to descend rapidly. Wick fumbled to change film. He had to remove his mittens, then work quickly to open the camera and thread the film. It was too cold to work for more than a few seconds before replacing his mittens. He waited for his fingers to warm. The wind was blowing harder, and he had to be careful not to let spindrift in the camera. He concentrated on the task; he hadn't been using oxygen since reaching the summit, and everything seemed so weird, so hard to do. He took his hands from the mittens, worked, put them back in. Finally the camera was loaded, but then he noticed the lens had iced, and he gave up.

He studied the terrain around him. He could see down the west side, to where he had tried to climb in 1975. He noted the Savoia peaks to the west. All the peaks of the Karakoram and especially the Baltoro dotted the horizon. He followed the horizon 360 degrees, trying to identify each peak. He was impressed by the brownness of China. All the peaks basked in gold light; the sky was nearly cloudless. Finally he thought to look at his watch. It was 6:10. He had stayed too long; he had to move fast.

Shouldering his pack he descended the summit ridge, then glanced down the route. A thousand feet below he could see Lou nearing his pack. It was then Wick first knew he could not make it down; he knew he would have to bivouac, alone, without sleeping bag, without tent, just below the summit. The wind began to pick up, and already it was fiercely cold.

SEPTEMBER 6. CAMP I, 18,400 FEET. 5:25 P.M.

It had been an exciting day. After Rob shouted, "They're on their way to the summit," that morning, everyone awoke immediately, looking bleary-eyed out their tents toward the summit and, without exception, jubilant. It was a very cold morning—the thermometer in Camp I read ten below zero Fahrenheit, but it was windless. They could see there was no wind on top, either, and it looked like a perfect summit day. Clear and crisp.

It was easy to watch the progress through the telescope. They could distinguish Lou from Wick. They studied their slow progress, watching them make four or five steps, then lean on their axes exhausted. They knew the snow was deep; they could even see the trail as they postholed up the soft snow in the gully leading to the summit slopes. It was painfully slow, but they followed the two each step.

Spirits were very high. There was relief that all the work and toil was paying off. Each person had played a crucial role in the drama they were witnessing; every person on the team was in no small way a player integrally part of that final scene. Whatever rancor had existed, whatever disappointments and disillusionments had divided the team, dissolved with each step that placed Lou and Wick that much closer to the summit.

Concern mounted as shadows fell across the face at 3:30, and the two were still some distance below the top. Finally, about 5:15, they watched Lou and Wick crest the summit ridge. The mountain was backlit as the wind picked up, and a plume of snow blew off the ridge. The dots moved antlike the last yards to the summit. Then, at twenty feet from the top, they disappeared behind the crest. Everyone realized the true summit was out of their view, but there was no doubt. Jim Wickwire and Lou Reichardt had reached the top.

People cheered, bear-hugged, slapped backs. The moment of victory was theirs. There was still concern, however, about the late hour. Rob continued glued to the telescope. Five minutes after they had disappeared. He saw a figure bound off the summit ridge. He could tell it was Lou; he had studied each of them so carefully all day, he could distinguish their idiosyncracies. He waited. Where was Wick? Lou continued with much haste down the slope, as if panicked. Had something happened to Wick? Why was Lou almost at a run? The cheering stopped, and quiet came over them. They waited. One minute, two minutes, three minutes. Each had the same thought: He should have appeared by now. Something has gone wrong.

They quietly discussed the possibilities. Five minutes, six, seven. It was getting dark. Wick would not stay on top this late because he wouldn't be able to get back to high camp before total darkness. They watched Lou continue his rapid descent. He was several hundred feet down the snow slope below the summit. Ten minutes, eleven, twelve.

Diana Jagersky was forced to sit down. Emotions swept through her, spinning dizzily, spiraling to a vortex and precipitating to a crystal realization: Something had happened to Wick, on the summit, at the culmination of the climb of his dreams. Wick had been one of Dusan's closest friends. Dusan had died on the summit; Wick was now on the summit of Dusan's dreams as well. The irony overcame her.

She gripped the rock on which she sat. Scenes whirled before her: She was sitting on the patio of a restaurant in Glacier Bay, Alaska, only a little more than a year before (my God, was it that long ago?) with Wick. She was eating breakfast, slowly, and Wick was not saying anything. She was thinking that there was no way it could be true. There was no way Dusan could be dead. He was too much alive; he was too strong. Nothing could have killed him. It was simply not possible, and she refused to believe it. Dusan was going to come back.

Wick wanted to say something; he wanted to comfort Diana. He too felt Dusan's presence, even at the breakfast table, but he had been there only a few days before when he heard the slip, the rattle of pitons on the shoulder rack, and he turned to see the fall, then only empty sky and blank snow, and the still, eternal silence. He knew Dusan was not coming back.

He paused, "I'm thankful I can be here and talk to you." He paused. "I know if it had been the reverse, Dusan would be here, at this moment, talking to Mary Lou."

No, Diana thought, it can't be happening. A feeling of panic, then helplessness, swept over her. Rob was still glued to the telescope, but there was no sign of Wick. The others talked in low voices. They sensed the great tide of emotions sweeping over Diana, but there was nothing they could say or do to help.

There must be something, she thought, there must be something that can be done. How can we stop this? How can the mountain do this? How can something so beautiful and powerful take still another life? The life of the man who loved the mountain the most?

She steadied on the rock. The scenes flashed before her, so real, so palpable. She was with Dusan, on a climb only a few weeks before he left for Alaska. The weather had been so perfect, everything so beautiful. The rock and snow, the early summer sun and the first alpine flowers, the heather crunching under climbing boots...

Fifteen minutes, sixteen, seventeen. Lou was over five hundred feet below the summit.

"It could have been a summit cornice," Bill speculated.

"Is there a cornice on this summit?"

"I don't know. I don't remember reading about one."

"It's not uncommon. Remember Bruce Carson on Trisul. He was on the summit, peeking over the edge, and didn't realize he was on a cornice. It broke off."

"There could even be a crevasse. Like the Japanese who just died on the summit over on Gasherbrum."

It was unusual to have a crevasse on a summit, but it was not unusual to have a cornice. Bill's speculation and fear was based on several case histories.

Diana listened. A cornice could have broke. The scene crystalized before her: the breaking snow, the falling body, plummeting, hitting rock, bouncing, smashing, limbs limp like a rag doll. Every detail, every foot of the fall reeled before her in vivid detail. The climber... it wasn't Wick falling, it was Dusan. He was falling, falling... he was dead.

Not again, Diana thought; there has got to be some way to change it. We can't sit here and watch and wait.

A void came over her, like an ether that permeated everything, and left her floating in space. She looked up at the great mountain. The high snows were hued the red colors of day's end, the alpenglow. It was so beautiful. She had the urge to leave camp and to walk out on the glacier and begin climbing the mountain, alone, forever, keep climbing and going and somehow nestling into its bosom. It was not a wish of death. It was, instead, a desire to join the mountain and share its secret, and know why it chose to deal men's lives such a game of irony. The thought of joining the mountain gave her comfort.

Twenty minutes, twenty five. There seemed little doubt something had happened to Wick.

Diana's thoughts jumped from extreme to extreme. One moment she felt the desire to join the mountain, to be one with the white eternity, then she flashed again to that late spring climb, just before Dusan left, then to the patio of the restaurant in Glacier Bay with the icebergs floating, reflecting white in the azure water, then to the cornice breaking and to the fall, and now she could see it was not Dusan falling, but Wick, and she again felt so helpless.

Thirty-five minutes. Lou was now a thousand feet down, nearing the place where that morning they had watched him inexplicably leave his pack. Forty minutes...

"There he is!"

Everyone bolted up, staring hard at the darkened face and the still backlighted ridge crest.

"I can see him," Rob said, fixed to the telescope. "He seems to be O.K."

Suddenly everyone went crazy, hugging, cheering, dancing. Wick was alive. For some reason he had stayed longer on the summit, but he was on his way down. Diana also felt the relief, the joy. It hadn't happened again; once had been enough for one lifetime. The mountain had given a reprieve, and dealt a second hand. But she still felt as in a vacuum, as though someone had socked her stomach and taken her breath. She still held the image of Dusan. For the first time she could accept the fact; she knew. Thank God Wick, at least, was coming back.

"But it's late," someone said. "He can't make it back to Camp Six before dark."

"And there's no moon. He probably can't downclimb without moonlight."

The cheering quieted as everyone realized the implications. Above, the last light disappeared, the plume off the summit crest grew with the mountain wind. Already, in Camp I, it was much below zero. Ten thousand feet higher it had to be incomparably worse. They had made the summit, and Wick was alive—there was much relief in that—but everyone knew the real fight was just beginning. Rob Schaller walked slowly back to his tent. As the team's chief physician, his most important and demanding duty still lay ahead.

SEPTEMBER 6. CAMP VI ABRUZZI, 25,750 FEET. 6:30 P.M.

"I apologize for being so hard to get along with these last couple of days. Must be the altitude."

"Don't worry about it," John said. "I haven't been so easy to live with myself. This is our third day at eight thousand meters, and our second night without sleep. What do you expect?"

I lay my head back down on my boot—I used it each night as a pillow—and smiled.

"Yeah, I guess you're right. I'm pretty bushed. But I'll try and be a little more even-tempered"

Actually, I was completely exhausted, more than at any time on the expedition. After leaving Camp VI Direct that morning we had descended only two hundred feet when we took off our packs, tied a line on them, and started dragging them, thinking it was easier to sled the heavy loads than to shoulder them. We passed Terry on his way down and learned that Lou and Wick had gotten an early start. We reached Camp VI Abruzzi about three o'clock; the last hundred feet with those heavy loads had brought me close to my limit.

As soon as we arrived John complained that his feet were frozen again, so we crawled into Wick's and Lou's tent and for the third day in a row he put his feet on my chest. I decided I might as well do the same, so we lay there for nearly an hour, feet up each other's parkas, and I blew warm air down my jacket as much to warm my chest as John's feet. I wanted so much to lie back and fall asleep, but I couldn't. There was still so much to do. About four I put my boots back on and went out to dig a platform for our tent.

"My toes are still numb," John said. "I'd better stay in and warm them."

"Yeah, you'd better stay inside," I said with deliberate irony. "Relax. I'll dig the platform."

The last two days I had been very irritable, downright crabby. Every little thing seemed to rub me wrong. Normally little inconveniences don't bother me much, but of late I had been short with John, and he noticed it. Each time he wanted me to defrost his feet seemed like a major sacrifice of my time. It was as though the altitude was changing my personality; as though I couldn't remember all the times he had gone out to shovel snow off the tent while I lay in the sack, or all the mornings he was up first to start breakfast, or all the times he took over and did most of the postholing to break trail.

Now he couldn't help me with the tent just because his feet were frozen. Cursing under my breath I madly hacked away at the snow with my ice axe, working with what little reserve of energy I had left to level a spot and pitch the tent before dark. After an hour I could see I might not make the sundown deadline. I was getting very cold and starting to shiver.

"I'll come out in a minute," John said. "Let me get my boots on."

"Thanks."

By dark we had the tent pitched. I crawled in my bag but continued to shiver for some time. As soon as I got a hot brew down me, I warmed up and was able to laugh at myself and apologize to John. We put a hot water bottle down John's bag to warm his toes, and soon he felt better too. We still had a couple of hours of melting snow and cooking, but we looked forward to a few hours' sleep before again getting up about one o'clock to prepare for our own summit bid.

We received a garbled radio call from Camp I and managed to decipher that Wick and Lou had reached the summit. The expedition was a success. Now we only hoped they made it back without bivouacking. The wind had been picking up all evening, and the sides of the tent were flapping with increasing pitch.

By eight we were worried. It was very dark. We had a policeman's whistle along for just such an emergency, and leaning out the tent door, we blew it while flashing a headlamp beam, hoping to beacon them in. Another hour passed.

"Did you hear something?"

"Blow the whistle again."

We listened carefully. Above the wind we distinctly heard Lou's voice. We looked at each other, smiled, and grabbed the light to signal them in.

Lou had overshot our camp in the dark and was a hundred yards below the tents when he spotted our light. He had nearly given up finding camp and was hoping instead for a crevasse suitable for bivouac. When he saw the light all the strain of the last several hours gave way and the tension flowed out, as he realized he was safe. Consequently, he had an extremely difficult time climbing back to the tent. When he finally arrived he was shaking with cold, drained, on the edge of collapse. Few men would have been equal to the physical endurance of Lou that day.

We heard him arrive outside our tent, but before we could get out to help him he jammed his head through the vestibule door. I knew the hour was late, that Lou had been climbing at extreme altitude all day without stop, that he had been through a superhuman ordeal, and that all this would no doubt read in his face, but I was not prepared for the apparition that met me eye to eye.

"Good God," John said.

"Jesus," I confirmed.

His face was frozen, looking like a specter raised from a frozen underworld. Large clumps of ice were frozen in his beard—not just snow, or spindrift, but heavy pieces of blue ice. There was a large icicle hanging from his nose. His lips were puffed, red and split from the ordeal. But his eyes still glowed with life; there was no hiding there the joy he felt to be in our tent.

We pulled him in, careful not to upset the stove, and helped him off with his crampons and boots. While John did that I mixed a brew of hot Gatorade. Lou was shaking and had difficulty speaking.

"Just a minute. You can tell us all about it in a second. First get this down you."

I held the cup to his lips, but was aghast to discover so much ice in his beard I couldn't get the rim of the cup to his lips. I set down the cup and tried to remove the ice. I pulled and yanked, and finally a big hunk broke loose and with it a clump of hair. Lou said nothing, oblivious to what I was doing, still shaking. With the larger ice hunks gone, he was able to drink the hot liquid. Wearily he leaned against John, and appeared almost to fall asleep.

"We made the summit," he said, a quiver in his voice.

"Yes, we know," we said, excitement in our voices.

"I made the summit without oxygen."

John and I looked at each other, realizing the magnitude of Lou's words. He said it simply, but with pride.

"Where's Wick?" we asked. "Is he behind you?"

"I don't know."

"What do you mean, you don't know?"

"I'm not sure where he is."

"Where did you last see him?"

"On the summit. I think he's bivouacking."

John and I looked at each other again, but this time with grave expressions. The wind was worse than ever, and it was already extremely cold.* For a moment, none of us said anything.

"Maybe he's still coming down."

"I don't think so. It's very dark, and I think he had it in his mind to

---

*By estimates based on a thermometer reading at Camp III, where it registered thirty below zero, it was approximately forty-below that night at eight thousand meters. Accounting the chill factor for an estimated fifty-knot wind, about 115 below zero, Fahrenheit.

bivouac; it was something he almost anticipated."

"No headlamp?"

"It was in my pack."

"If he has his half-bag and parka, it might not be too bad."

"He doesn't. The half-bag got soaked this morning when he spilled water. He left it behind. He's got a pair of down pants he borrowed from Cherie. Just that and his sixty/forty parka."

"Are there any crevasses up there to bivvy in?"

"I don't think so."

We continued to melt water and feed Lou steaming drinks. He stopped shivering, and with the ice out of his beard he looked not nearly as frightful as when he first poked his head through the tent. He still leaned against John. He was weary and extremely tired, nearly asleep.

"You feel rehydrated?"

"Yeah. A lot better."

"Let's get you in your bag."

"Thanks. I can't tell you what it felt like to find you guys here, with hot drinks ready."

We all smiled, and John and I patted Lou's shoulder as he crawled out to move to his own tent. There was an unspoken feeling—more than just camaraderie (that word doesn't quite describe it), more perhaps a feeling of fraternity—of men sharing a common stress and hardship, a common danger, and together achieving a common victory. If only we could be with Wick to see him through his ordeal.

On his way out Lou uprooted one of our tent's guy lines, and John went out to fix it. He quickly came back in, already shaking.

"It's cold out there. As cold as it's been."

"Let's make sure we're ready. Go over everything: mask, regulator, tank packed; water bottles ready for the morning brew, lunch packed, goggles, sunscreen, face mask."

"Should we take a bivvy sack?"

"No—we've got to stay as light as possible."

"Leave the stove, then?"

"Yeah. Keep it light."

"And no rope 'cause we ain't got one."

We turned off the stove and snuggled in our bags. In the warmth I felt safe, secure, and aware that at that moment Wick was struggling for his survival. I listened to the wind, gusting perhaps to forty knots, and felt the cold air on my face. That survival, I thought, would be marginal.

"What time is it?"

"A little after midnight."

"We'd better get ready again about one-thirty."

"I'll let you know when it's time."

"What do you think Wick's chances are?"

"Pretty grim."

"So do I. I think in the morning we're as likely to be on rescue mission, or a body detail, as a summit attempt."

John did not answer. We both lay quiet, listening to the wind, waiting for the hour to pass until we would make preparations. I did not look forward to climbing into the cold blackness.

SEPTEMBER 6 OR 7. SUMMIT PYRAMID, ABRUZZI FINISH. A LITTLE LESS THAN 28,000 FEET. AROUND MIDNIGHT.

I am slipping, slowly, closer to the dropoff. Inch by inch, my bivouac sack slides down the icy slope. I dig in my boot heels, trying to jam them through the thin nylon sack that I am huddled in. I still slide. The wind is blowing hard, it is so cold. I cannot stop the slipping. It must be the empty oxygen bottle in the sack, and the empty stove. They are both empty. I wonder why they are still in there? Why haven't I thrown them away?

I only wish the stove was still working. I had it going for a while, but the fuel ran out. I thought to bring an extra cartridge, but something happened. I think the rubber O-ring, the gasket, fell off. Something like that. Anyway, the gas all hissed out of the new cartridge when I screwed it down. I threw the thing in the corner of my bag, in disgust. I went easy on my oxygen. Wanted it to last. Took only a few sucks now and then. But there was not much left after using it all the way to the summit. It ran out awhile ago. About 11:00, I think. I'm not sure when, really.

I still have the cylinder in my sack. I wonder why?

I am still slipping. I chopped a platform up higher. I was going to bivouac there. Then the sack started slipping. It still is.

It is so cold. So windy. I am shivering. I cannot control the shivering. I move my hands and feet, my arms and legs, constantly. I must maintain circulation; I must avoid as much frostbite as possible. I must survive.

O.K. You got this far. You made the summit so you must get down. You can't come this far and not get down. You will survive.

I am still slipping. Wait. Isn't there a ten-thousand-foot dropoff here? Ten thousand feet. The thought makes me laugh. That is a long way, ten thousand feet.

It is too dark to see. And so cold. When will it end? When will this be over? Every second creeps by.

You had better do something, Wickwire. You might be close to the edge. The edge, Wickwire. You are at the edge.

I must do something. I do not want to get out of this sack. I have to. I pull down the opening, and crawl out. I seem so stiff. The wind is so strong. I am out, and I start pushing the sack back up the hill. It is a long way, Ten feet, then twenty, then thirty. There, I find the platform I chopped earlier. I put the sack back on it.

Now what is to keep me from sliding again? I have an idea. No, under these conditions, it is an inspiration. In one corner of the bivvy sack I take my ice axe and jam it through the fabric, pinning it to the snow. I do the same to the other corner, using my ice hammer. Then back inside the sack to escape the wind. But not the cold. Good thinking, Wickwire. Not bad under these conditions. Now you won't slide anymore. You do not have to worry about that ten thousand feet.

Now you can concentrate on staying alive until dawn. It will not be easy. You are shaking with no control. The first stage of hypothermia. Your toes no longer have feeling. Keep wiggling though; keep moving them inside your boots. Maybe it will not be as bad, that way. Keep tensing, keep moving, keep circulation going. Survive, Wickwire. You know you can make it until dawn. You have done this kind of thing before. Cold nights in crevasses bivouacking on Mount Rainier.

But this is not Rainier. This is not fourteen thousand feet. This is K2, and this is twenty-eight thousand feet.

But you will survive. You have made the summit. You have gone this far. It is all downhill from here. It is that simple. Keep moving your toes, your fingers. Shift your arms, your legs. Keep the circulation going. The night will end. The sunlight will return. You will survive.

11

No Conquerors— Only Survivors

SEPTEMBER 7. SUMMIT PYRAMID, ABRUZZI FINISH. ABOUT 26,200 FEET. 4:30 A.M.

Hard snow, wind-tortured to small crescents like the surface of the sea frozen, and a sense of time in slow motion. The sound of crampons biting hard snow, squeaking, and the sound of quick, conscious breathing. Dark. Wind. Cold. Extreme cold. The feel of fingers frozen, hard and lifeless, and a momentary fear from the imagery of missing digits. Other imagery, other fears: a companion lost, or worse, near death, and us helpless to save him.

John was ten feet away, and together we climbed, at a slow, even pace, the steepening snowfield above Camp VI, the base of the summit pyramid. It was black and moonless, but in the rarefied atmosphere starlight was sufficient to see above us the major features of the upper mountain: the enormous ice cliffs like ramparts guarding the summit fortress, and below the cliffs, the constricting couloir through the rock band. A ground blizzard blew spindrift over our boots, and studied care was necessary to place each step on the crescent sastrugi that patterned the hard snow surface. I was conscious, in the dark, of the absolute necessity for precise footwork because we had no rope.

Despite the heavy oxygen, the extreme cold, and the altitude—eight thousand meters—I felt strong. We planned to go on oxygen above the couloir, and without it I was surprised at the fast pace we kept. I felt much stronger than I had at the same altitude on Everest two years before, and it

260

confirmed my hope that my difficulties at that altitude had been a result of pulmonary congestion and not a physiological limit of the altitude to which my body could adapt. It was our fourth day at eight thousand meters, and our third night with little or no sleep, but nevertheless I felt I had sufficient strength to reach the summit. I also thought there was only a chance we would reach it; it seemed more likely our duty would be to rescue Wick.

Silent speculation on Wick's chance of survival had overshadowed our preparations. We had started the stove at 1:30, first warming water, then our boots and mittens. We tried to drink as much hot liquid as we could, but it was not possible to hold the warm mug of cocoa—the heat so comforting to cold fingers—without thinking how desperately Wick was in need of that cocoa. Was he still alive? Was he, somehow, to survive the forty-below-zero temperature and the fierce wind that was buffeting our tent? With no sleeping bag or parka we expected to find him that morning, if alive, at least seriously damaged by the ordeal.

At 3:30 we crawled out of the tent, packed the last items in our rucksacks, and left Camp VI.

"Good luck, you guys," Lou called from the next tent. "I have a feeling Wick will be O.K."

Lou had felt more confidence than either John or me. He thought that Wick had been mentally prepared for a bivouac, and that even without bag or parka he would be able to see it through without serious injury. Lou thought that perhaps Wick had found a site to dig a snow cave. The night had been so fierce, however, it was hard to share Lou's optimism.

We immediately set a fast pace as much to warm our bodies as to make quick progress, so that by 4:30 we were several hundred feet above camp. I climbed just a few steps behind John in a zigzagging route up the slope. I was thankful for each switchback because I moved my ice axe (always held uphill) from one hand to the other, that way thawing my fingers frozen from gripping the metal tool. The fingers were still numb, but I felt with enough care—enough moving them inside the mitten, enough flicking my wrists to force blood to the fingertips, enough alternating of the axe between hands—I could prevent frostbite.

OUR FIRST REST came at the site of Japanese Camp VI. We sat on our parkas and picked through the refuse preserved in amber ice, and watched dawn over the Karakoram. We were at the same altitude as the summit of Broad Peak, across the valley of the Godwin-Austen Glacier and the closest mountain to the Abruzzi Ridge.

"There's enough light to see," I said. "Wick might be moving by now."

"I hope so."

"God knows what kind of condition he's in. We're going to have trouble getting him down if he's in bad shape. Especially with no rope."

"If he's bad, I don't think we could get him down."

We sat still, silent, staring. The dawn filled the shadows in the lee of the great peaks. New mountains rose on the horizon, not visible from lesser altitudes. The glaciers so far below flowed inexorably in their timeless path to the sea. We hoped Wick was also witness to such grandeur.

SEPTEMBER 7. SUMMIT PYRAMID, A LITTLE LESS THAN 28,000 FEET. FIRST DAWN.

You have to remember, Wickwire, to keep moving your toes. You forget to do that too often. There's no feeling left in them. Your fingers are gone, too. Maybe it won't make any difference whether you move them or not. No, you've got to try. You know it will help in the end.

This night has to end sometime. This would be so much easier if somebody else were here with you. Somebody to talk to. Remember how Ed Boulton helped when just the two of us bivvied on Rainier's Willis Wall. We sort of bouyed each other—when one was down, the other was up. Then you survived that night alone on the south face of McKinley. This is certainly higher, maybe colder, but you know you can survive this night. You must.

Wiggle your toes and fingers.

It will get light outside. No sense looking, though. Keep covered inside this sack. You'll know when it's light. You can see it though the nylon.

Wiggle your toes.

Shaking uncontrollably.

The night will end.

It must.

You are the highest man in the world right now. Somewhere around twenty-eight thousand feet—there is certainly no one else on earth right now standing anywhere higher than you are. Alone. Surviving this awful night.

Wiggle your toes.

Shaking so bad. So cold.

Wish the shaking would stop. No, that would mean you are freezing.

How much time has passed? Who knows? It will be over sometime.

Remember, there is no way you can come this far and then not make it. You have been to the summit. You are on your way home. This whole thing will soon be over. You must survive the night.

Getting rummy. Not thinking right. So cold.

It's finally going to end, isn't it?

The walls of the sack are getting lighter. It must be light outside. It must be dawn.

No sense going anywhere. Wait for that sun. The night is over.

It is so cold. It is dawn. Maybe you should look out. There. Still clear—another good day. Only those small clouds so far away. Everything looks surreal. Sunshine on Broad Peak. Almost like you could touch it. And the glacier moving down to Concordia. So far below. Remember when you camped there on the way in. It was Fourth of July, and we slept under the stars and played Handel's Royal Fireworks *on Rick's little cassette machine. So long ago, like another life.*

You have to go down.

What a place this would be to spend an eternity. Frozen up here forever on the summit of K2. The highest man in the world. That's kind of funny . . . . But you should go down. Even if it's harder to do that. It would be so easy just to stay. There is plenty of time. Stay inside the bivvy sack. Plenty of time.

There is still no warmth. So cold. Remember how warm it was on the approach march. One day it was 126 in the shade.

Maybe you should think about moving. That means you will have to crawl out of this magnificent bivvy sack. What a way to spend the night, huh. Covered with a piece of half-ounce rip-stop in a full gale at twenty-eight thousand feet. This is going to be one to tell stories about.

Probably be ice this morning. There was some yesterday; guess that means there will be some today. You should put your crampons on. Let's see, they are outside the bivvy sack here somewhere. Yeah, here they are. Now get out of the sack and put your crampons on. O.K., ol' crampon, there you go on the boot. Now lace the strap through the eye here, then it goes over the boot and crosses to this loop, then back again. Now buckle it down and make sure it is fastened. O.K. One crampon on. Sun feels good, but it is still so cold. My fingers are awfully hard. I wonder how the toes are doing inside that boot. Wait a minute, Wickwire. Look at your boot. The crampon is loose. Two steps with that rig and it would pop off and so would you. A long fall. All the way to Base Camp.

Ha, ha. That's funny.

Who needs crampons anyway. Just lie back and relax. You can go down later. Put the crampons on later. You probably don't need them anyway.

Feel the sun. Things seem so strange.

Relax.

What a magnificent view, huh. There are the four Gasherbrums, then Broad Peak, and farther to the right Chogolisa and Masherbrum. And the summit, just up above, an easy walk.

Look how ridiculously close I bivouacked to the cornice. Might have fallen through. So far down the south face.

Go down later.

Mary Lou?

Mary Lou and our five wonderful children. I can see all of you so clearly. Going to the airport and the rest of the team is getting off the plane, but where is Wick? Where is Dad? Mom, isn't Dad going to come home?

Sit up, Wickwire. Focus. You're in bad shape, now straighten up. Snap out of it. Concentrate, Wickwire, concentrate. Strap the crampon tight.

Put the other one on. Tighten it. Keep warming your fingers. Keep moving them. Double-check the crampons. They look better, now. That will work.

I'm coming home. I love you.

Stand up. Careful. Awfully stiff. Get your axe. Put the bivvy sack in your pack—keep it around as a souvenir. O.K. Ready? Maybe you should go down facing in. No. You're not that bad, and it is not that steep. Not right here, but be careful at the traverse. Now start moving. Keep thinking. Concentrate. You'll loosen up in a minute. Remember, most accidents happen on descent. Be careful.

You'll be down soon.

I'm coming home, Mary Lou.

I love you.

SEPTEMBER 7. SUMMIT PYRAMID, THE NARROW COULOIR ABOUT 27,000 FEET. 7:30 A.M.

I thought, *Check that it is a solid hold, frozen in the blue ice. O.K., looks good. Lift your leg, high—it's difficult to lift your leg with the first layer of angora wool underwear, the two layers of pile wool over that, followed by the nylon jumpsuit. Kind of binds. There. Now place your crampons carefully on the rock. Put your axe through the shoulder strap on your pack, get it out of the way. You need both hands for these next moves. Dust snow from the handholds, look for edges on the rock. Keep your balance, move slowly, make each move count. Do not waste energy because you have none to spare. Altitude about twenty-seven thousand feet. You can go on oxygen once above this steep section.*

John was only a few feet above me when we started through the narrows of the couloir, and I looked directly into the teeth of his crampons. Only his front points were on the ice and rock so that the remaining sharpened steel points—ten on the bottom of each boot—poised above me like an executioner's axe. I did not want John to slip.

I waited for him to make the several moves necessary to pass the steep bottleneck; then he was above the difficulties and it was my turn. I found two good handholds, and using my arms to balance, I leg-pressed my body up, moved my hands to higher holds, and lifted the next foot. Between my legs I could see the couloir fall away steeply to the Abruzzi Shoulder, to Camp VI, and ten thousand feet below that, to the Godwin-Austen Glacier.

Remember, I told myself, you cannot make a mistake. You have no rope.

Wind continued in gusts, lifing spindrift in swirls—small snow devils—backlighted by morning sun. The wind seemed to be lessening, however, and the sky, cloudless and clear to crystal visibility, boded a magnificent summit day—if Wickwire were in good shape.

It was about seven-thirty. I wondered, Where will we find Wickwire? Did he make it down this far before bivouacking, or was he still higher? What if he tried last night to climb down. It was black. This is very steep climbing, he would have been solo, very tired; he could have fallen. We would never learn what became of him.

Dark thoughts, fuzzy scenarios, disjointed images, dreams from a high-altitude opium den. I thought, I feel no emotion. Wick may be dead, he may be above me frozen, he may be ten thousand feet below me, crumbled on the glacier, yet I feel nothing. Last night there was alarm, there was that feeling of possible tragedy, of possible loss, that feeling of emptiness. Now I feel nothing. I recognize that Wick may be in trouble. Beyond that, no other feelings, no other thoughts except how to make the next move up this steep couloir.

I must breathe evenly, coordinate my breathing to my footwork. That will save energy. I must move with precision. There is a beauty in what I do, isn't there. Despite the extreme altitude, the weight of this oxygen bottle, I can still be coordinated, I can still move with grace and economy. I can still dance.

I have two more moves, and then I will be out of the couloir. Lift the leg, carefully place the crampon, test the handholds, pressure the leg muscles, move up. Always up, one more step higher, one more step toward the top. I am above the gully. Where to from here? There will still be some kind of traverse to turn the ice cliff above me that will lead to the snow gully and eventually to the summit snowfield. How far is John? Look up, I should see him now, he should be just around the corner. There he is, but wait. I stare at the scene before me mesmerized; I am not prepared for what I see: Twisting swirls of ground spindrift. Rainbow red, blue, and violet flashes—refractions of a million crystal eyes and the fathomless indigo of rarefied sky. Brilliant white. Ice cliffs, shining with wet, sensuous smoothness. Extreme altitude and vertigo. A feeling of no time: no beginning, no end. Frozen in the scene two figures. One, below the other, blue-suited and moving slowly—John. The second, standing above, no apparent movement, legs slightly spread, arms down, a scarecrow figure yet also godlike, still not moving—frozen solid? Jim Wickwire.

I watched John climb the last few feet to Wick, who stood, not moving, in his scarecrow stance. Was Wick alive? Motionless, he stood staring down at us. Then he raised his arm—a greeting. He was alive; he had survived. I could see they were talking to each other.

I looked down to the snow and ice in front of me to concentrate on the climbing until I reached the more level stance where Wick and John were resting. As I neared, I could hear their conversation:

"I was on a small flat spot a little below the summit. Pretty cold."

"Frostbite?"

"I think so. It's hard to tell."

"Can you make it down the rest of the way by yourself?"

"Yeah. I'm doing O.K. I've got the hard part behind—that traverse over here to the gully."

Wick indicated with his ice axe. I climbed up and joined the conversation. Wick looked haggard, of course, ice in his beard, eyes sunken and tired but still with a sparkle, a determination. It looked to us as if he had suffered no serious damage, but it was impossible for us, or for Wick, for that matter, to then realize the extent of his injuries. We continued to talk, joking, making light of an ordeal John and I—emotions obscured in the anesthesia of twenty-seven thousand feet—could in no way share.

"Good luck, you guys. I'll see you back in Camp Six."

"Be careful, Wick. You still have the couloir to get down. Move slow."

"Don't worry. I'll be O.K."

Wick climbed past us, and John patted him affectionately on his cap. A simple gesture, and neither John nor I had any way of knowing it brought Wick close to tears. It was the first human contact in fourteen hours— fourteen hours of which he had counted each minute. It was a small gesture of affection of one human for another that Wick, for the rest of his life, would not forget. Wick climbed slowly to the top of the gully, turned inward, and began his descent.

Watching him, I thought, Not now Wick, not after what you've been through. Not after victory. Be careful, go slow, make no mistakes.

Wick's movements were mechanical and stiff, like the Tin Man of Oz with no oil. There was no way, without rope, we could assist him. We only crossed our fingers.

John called to him, "Wick, when we get back remind me to enroll you in my climbing school. You could use a few lessons."

Wick looked up and smiled that open but closed-teeth smile that meant he felt confident. I knew he could make it, and John and I turned to our next task—the summit.

"LET'S GO ON OXYGEN from here up," I said.

We looked at our next climbing obstacle—a steep rock and ice traverse —and it seemed like a good idea to cross it with the benefit of oxygen. We unshouldered our packs, carefully balancing them on the steep slope. John removed his bottle and pushed it into the snow, then set his regulator and mask alongside. He then strapped on his pack.

"What are you doing?"

"Leaving the oxygen. I'm going without it."

I paused, looked at my own twenty-pound apparatus, and considered the option.

"There's no way I'm hauling that thing to the top," he said, pointing to the bottle. "I know I can get up without it."

I suspected John was right; *he* could get to the top, but I was less certain about myself. True, Lou had made it without oxygen, but I considered both him and John physically stronger than me. I did not want to risk getting this close and not being able to make it because of a last-minute decision to leave my oxygen—especially since I had carried it all that way. To leave the bottle, jammed into the snow at twenty-seven thousand feet, with an untapped 3,900 psi supply of pure oxygen, seemed absurd.

"I'm going to use mine."

"O.K."

John waited while I removed the regulator—carefully wrapped in plastic to protect against moisture—screwed it on the bottle, and opened the valve. Full pressure—no leaks. Next I fitted a cloth skullcap to which straps from the aviator-type mask would fit. I had to shoulder the pack, bottle inside, then secure the second-stage selector valve to a drawstring I had earlier sewn on my parka. I had practiced this procedure many times, in the lower camps waiting out storms, adjusting the straps and snaps, checking the regulator, with soapy water, for leaks, making certain I would arrive at the point where I would begin using oxygen with a problem-free apparatus.

But even after all that, something was wrong. My mask would not seal around my face. Its straps seemed to lead to the snaps on my skullcap at the wrong angle, and without a tight fit I would leak valuable oxygen. John watched with growing impatience as I removed the skullcap and re-fitted it. Again, the mask pulled askew. Again, I removed the skullcap. John lost patience.

"I'm going. See you up there."

"I'll be along as soon as I get this thing straightened out."

John started the traverse, obviously finding it easier without the weight of his oxygen. He moved across the snow laced with rocks, crossing legs and placing his crampons on rock with expert precision, movements automated by subconscious accumulation of years of experience. He held his axe with one hand on the shaft, the other on the adze, placing the pick in the ice between the rocks. He reminded me of the old sepia photographs of Armand Charlet, the great French alpinist famous for ballet precision when climbing ice. Below John's feet the rock and ice angled abruptly, disappearing to empty space, and all I could see was the zebra stripes of the glacier about two miles down. John moved in perfect balance, made more dramatic because he had no rope. Not bad, I thought, for over twenty-seven thousand feet.

I continued to hassle with my oxygen apparatus. John disappeared around a corner, and my frustration mounted. I once again removed the mask, and the skullcap, and studied them. I rerouted the fastening straps through loops on the mask and fitted the skullcap at a different angle. It was worse, the mask dropping hopelessly from my face. I tried a different lacing, but it too failed. My fingers were freezing. The more I studied the puzzle, the more it bewildered me.

I thought, *Damn it, this is crazy. I had this thing adjusted days ago.*

Everything was ready. Now study it, Ridgeway; think. Imagine what my IQ score would be right now. Even a half-wit chimpanzee could do better than this. John's probably halfway up the snow gully by now, on his way to the summit snowfield. How long have I been fiddling with this contraption? Five minutes? Twenty minutes? This is like being loaded on dope. Can't think right. Don't even know how much time has passed. Too bad my watch broke. Don't let my mind wander; focus on this problem. O.K. It's simple: It worked before, when I tested it in the tent, so therefore it has to work now. Try putting the strap through the other loop, around the nose piece on the mask, then back through the bottom loop. That doesn't look right, either. John must be halfway to the top by now. If I don't hurry, I'll never make it. He climbs faster than I do anyway. Maybe I'll just end up staying here all day, fiddling with this mask, while he climbs to the summit. The thought of that chimpanzee comes to mind again. Remember a picture I once saw of a chimp wearing eyeglasses, sitting and staring confoundedly at a book. The same thought now, only it's me, Rick Ridgeway, sitting just like the chimp, staring confoundedly at my oxygen mask. O.K., now don't let my mind wander; focus on this mask. Let's see, what else can I do?

Try to climb K2 without oxygen?

Can I do it?

I had been performing satisfactorily up to that point, without oxygen, carrying the dead weight of the cylinder. Without that hindrance it would be even easier. But there were over a thousand feet to go. What would it be like at twenty-eight thousand? Would it be possible for me? I considered the danger of pulmonary edema. If that happened, there would be no hope. My lungs would fill with blood, and I would die.

I had to make some decision fast. I was quickly losing body temperature, starting to shiver. I needed to move to regain warmth. The wind was still dropping, but even the direct sun failed to warm. I looked again at my regulator, and the chance that I could correctly adjust the straps seemed remote.

What about brain damage? I knew there was that risk; it was a real concern. Brain cells do not replace themselves; cerebral damage from hypoxia is a clinical fact. I had another whimsical thought: If I had any brains to begin with, I wouldn't be up here at over twenty-seven thousand feet on K2 freezing to death, so what have I got to lose?

I chuckled at the thought.

I realized I was getting dingy.

I was very, very cold.

I set the mask and regulator in the snow, removed the bottle from the pack. Putting on the near-empty pack, I grabbed my axe and started across the traverse. I would climb without oxygen, and I would put every ounce of energy remaining in my body into reaching the summit. I thought, I might just be able to make it.

SEPTEMBER 7. SUMMIT PYRAMID, ABOUT 28,000 FEET. 2:30 P.M.
*There are only two hundred more feet at the most even though I'm not
sure I can lift my foot and then the next foot and the next until I get to the
top. Not after coming this far. Not this close.*

*So up goes my boot and crampon. There, that's better, now breathe a
few times, and think about that next step. This will be over soon, and the
sooner I lift the next foot, the sooner it will be over. Keep thinking: I've
come this far, I have to make it.*

*I can't lift the foot. I can't move up any higher. Have to rest, have to
rest, have to rest.*

No. I cannot.

*John is ahead of me. Look up at him. See, he's still moving, and moving
faster than me. He has been breaking most of the trail. I can't let him do
all the work. I have to do my share. So lift my foot and catch up and help
break trail. There. That's better. Now think about the next foot.*

When will it end?

*John is stopping to rest. He is hunkering over his axe, head down, facing
the slope. I must catch him. If I can make ten more steps I can reach him,
and then rest, but not before. That is it: Ten steps, then rest. O.K., now
up with the foot, breathe, breathe, breathe, and another step. No good,
can't make it. Have to stop for a minute, getting dizzy again. John is still
resting. Only four or five steps and I can rest too. Lift a foot. Now only
three more steps, now one more step and I can rest. Careful, don't
collapse, don't slide down the slope. Rest on my axe.*

"You O.K.?"

"Slow. Hard to breathe. Forcing each step. Sorry I'm not breaking
more trail."

"Can you lead a little?"

"I'll try. Need to rest first."

"We're close—maybe a hundred fifty feet."

"If that is the summit. If not, if it is farther behind the ridge, don't
know if I can make it . . ."

"Don't worry, we've got it now."

*John is right. We have it now, keep remembering that. We are too close
not to make it.*

*I must get up; I must move on. This will soon be over. No more getting
up at 3:00 A.M., no more freezing in predawn starts. I can sit in a hot bath
and feel the steaming water on my skin. Never again for the rest of my life
will I take a bath and not think of this moment I wanted to soak in
steaming water, so get going and soon I can have that bath.*

Lift a foot.

*Carefully place my crampons. This surface is irregular, small crescent
patterns in the ice, and my ankles hurt from twisting to the angle of the
slope.*

Lift a foot.

Noise and voices. Like there are many people around me, like on a crowded train with everyone talking. Echoes, noises, voices. A din like a million voices. But that's crazy, there is no one around.

Lift a foot.

Fingers are so hard. There is no doubt this time they are frozen. It's strange, like my fingers are made of a foreign material. Must be what artificial limbs are like. It's my right hand, mostly, because that is the hand I've been holding my axe in. I should switch hands. But then my left hand would freeze, and since my right is already frozen, why freeze my left too. Does that make sense? I guess so, keep the axe in my right hand.

Lift a foot.

Look at the slope, scimitar-shaped, arching upward brilliant white against purple sky. The left side of the summit slope drops away, and I can see a steep rock ridge joining the summit slope near the top. Is that the finish to Bonington's route? It would be too hard to climb that the way I feel now. Could anyone do it? Maybe a future generation of climbers? Poor Nick Estcourt, down there somewhere buried in ice.

Lift a foot.

How nice it would be to sit on a warm beach. A tropical beach with white sand and palm trees. It's easy to imagine, look there, in front of me, I can even see a palm tree now, in the sand, growing there, in the snow. Lift a foot.

John is just behind me. I've been leading now for some time, but I've only come, what?—twenty feet since I rested. It seems so far, though. There is a slightly offset edge in the ice surface—a convenient mark—about another twenty feet in front. Focus on it. Begin stepping until I get there. Think of nothing else.

Lift a foot.

Breathe, breathe, breathe, gasp hard, even then I can't get enough air. Lift a foot, another, another, keep going to the mark.

It's close. Keep going.

Getting dizzy, head pounding, noises—the voices, the voices. Keep going, force it out from somewhere, somehow force out the will to step, to lift the foot, the mark is close, one more step.

I made it.

Breathe, breathe, breathe. Getting dizzy again, spinning, can't get enough air. Can't breathe fast enough. Don't panic, keep control, breathe fast. Feel like I'm drowning, will my lungs explode?—don't panic. Lean on my axe. Breathe fast. There, the dizziness is starting to go away, but the voices, the voices.

"You O.K.?"

"Have to rest. Tried to go too fast. Hallucinating."

"I'll take the lead."

Rest while John climbs. He is stronger than I am. How can he do it? He is doing most of the step-kicking. I can't do my share. Not enough strength. But we are close now. Maybe fifty feet to the summit ridge. Hope to God the summit is close behind the ridge. If it's farther . . .

Get up, follow John. It's so much easier following in his steps. Sections of the ice are hard and it doesn't matter who leads, but sometimes the crust breaks, and that is when John's job is hardest.

Lift a foot.

It's not bad the first few steps after I've rested. But then each one starts getting harder. My body is screaming for oxygen. Each step harder, need to breathe more. The farther away from the last rest, the harder, but I can't rest again. Not now.

Lift a foot.

So close. Soon it will be over. John is maybe fifteen feet ahead, now maybe twenty. He is climbing faster. He is making the last steps to the summit ridge. His head is even with the ridge, now he is on it.

What does he see? How far is the summit? He isn't saying anything. Is it farther behind? Do we still have more to go? How can I do it?

Lift a foot.

Catch up to John. He is resting on the top of the ridge. Close now, only a few more feet. He isn't saying anything. But I can't talk to him because I have to breathe fast.

Stop. He is ten feet away. Look at him. He is looking down at me. Breathe a few times so I can talk.

"Can you see it? How far? How far to the top?"

John is looking at me. Now he is smiling. Is it good news?

"Fifty feet. A fifty-foot walk up a gentle slope and we're on the summit."

SEPTEMBER 7. THE SUMMIT OF K2, 28,250 FEET. 3:30 P.M.

No wind. No clouds. Cerulean sky, brilliant sun, and at once a feeling of warmth through the thick parka, and also a strange cold. Nothing quite real, the feeling of dream. Below, a world falling in all directions. Snow peaks too numerous to identify, and glaciers traveling to distant horizon. Quiet, but an inner noise, a ringing in the ear. A thought: As an old man I will often recall this moment; I must try to remember it. It must be important. But there is failure to feel much emotion. The only feeling is absolute fatigue.

We were on the summit. We had made the last few steps together, arm in arm. From the summit ridge it was an easy walk to the highest point, but just short of it John had stopped.

"It may be corniced. Summits usually are. I'm not going up there."

He spoke with much finality. Neither of us seemed to remember Lou and Wick had been there the day before and had reported no cornice. But we were beyond remembering, beyond rational thinking, operating only on instinct. I thought, It may be corniced, but we've come too far not to reach the very pinnacle.

I volunteered to belly-crawl up to the highest point. John stood back, holding my ankles. I eased up to the edge, and peered over. There was solid snow under me, and the south face dropped down so steeply, about twelve thousand feet, I had a euphoric sense of flying. John crawled up behind me, and together we sat on top, holding each other, too exhausted to speak.

I told myself several times, Remember this moment. Remember what it is like. Later in my life, years from now, I will look back, many times, on this scene; this day will stand above all.

But I could not appreciate it. I was only thankful at the moment to rest, to breathe and lessen the dizziness, and if I felt anything akin to elation, it was from the realization I no longer had to go up. This was it; there was no higher place to climb.

We rested. The sky was calm; at 28,250 feet there was no breath of wind, and the sun shone through cloudless atmosphere. We could see to the curve of the earth. To the north and east, two distant peaks somewhere in the wild vastness of Chinese Turkestan; to the west the peaks of Hunza, Shangri-La, the secret valley, to the west and south the great Karakoram—a turbulent sea of endless summits and glaciers. Away to the south the singular Nanga Parbat. Closer, the Gasherbrums, and below us the summit of Broad Peak, a flat, wide strip like an airplane landing field. Broad Peak, the first eight-thousand-meter peak to be climbed without oxygen in 1957, and now, in 1978, we, also without oxygen, looked down on its summit. To the east the brown hills of Sinkiang, and far, far off, at places distant and mysterious, occasional glacier-covered summits.

Twenty feet below the summit, toward the northwest, there was a flat rock bench, and we climbed down to rest. The rock was warm and I lay back and my breathing eased and I closed my eyes and drifted to half-consciousness. I had few coherent thoughts, just images of boots and crampons and snow and endless steps. I opened my eyes.

I thought, Remember where I am. I am on the second highest point on earth. I must remember that. Think how hard I have worked to get here.

I had the idea that to better remember the summit I would take some of it with me. I got out of my climbing hammer and started pounding on the rock. John looked over.

"What are you doing?"

"Souvenirs. Take a few pieces of rock back. Christmas isn't far off, and they'll make great presents."

"Good idea."

Soon John and I were sitting on the rock beating on it with our hammers, prying small chips of stone.

"We should take some photographs, too," John said.

"Yeah, I forgot about that."

I lay back on the rock, propped on one arm, while John took my photograph.

"We've been up here almost an hour," he said.

"An hour?"

"We should take a couple of pics on the summit and head down."

We climbed back to the high point on the snow ridge and took a few photographs of one another. I recalled the way summit photographs normally looked: The climber stands, ice axe above head in victory, chest puffed out, flags waving like a sale at a used car lot. That was not at all how I felt. I had no feeling of having conquered anything. I thought of something Barry Bishop said after he climbed Everest: "There are no conquerors—only survivors." It was true. We were two small humans on top of an awesome mountain that was indifferent to our climb. I stood on the high point, dropped my arms, and held the axe across my waist. I could not wave my arms; I could not grin in victory; I could only stare across the empty space below me. John took the photo, and we began our descent.

SEPTEMBER 7. CAMP VI ABRUZZI. 25,750 FEET. ABOUT 5:00 P.M.
Hard as he tried, Wick could not sleep. He had arrived back in Camp VI, after passing John and me on our way to the top, about nine that morning, and was greeted with warm drinks and warm hugs by his summit companion. Lou was much relieved to see that Wick had weathered his ordeal, apparently suffering only a few frostbitten fingers and toes. Lou had been uncomfortable with his decision to leave Wick on the summit, although at the time it seemed the logical thing to do: Lou had been, without parka, extremely cold, it had been very late in the day, Wick had said he intended to leave the summit just behind Lou. Nevertheless Lou knew if Wick had had any major problem on his bivouac—if he had not been able to survive the night—he would have had to live with his decision the rest of his life. It was with that thought heavy on his soul that Lou had seen Wick's weathered face appear that morning in the tent door.

Other than an hour spent shoveling drifted snow off the tent walls, and a few more minutes lowering Lou into a crevasse (Wick holding Lou's ankles) to retrieve an ice axe he had somehow dropped, they passed the day in sleeping bags. They were languid, physically spent, but not able to sleep—only to lie in an indolent dreaminess as the hours melted together. It was about five when John arrived, an hour ahead of my much slower descent.

They offered John hot lemonade, which he drank with enthusiasm. John crawled in the tent he and I shared, and in the last twilight I arrived. It had taken all my inner resources to make the last steps to Camp VI. Just above camp, I had slipped, sliding about twenty feet before digging my axe into the hard snow. I had barely acknowledged the mishap that normally would have caused sharp self-reprimand to be more careful; as it was, I was so exhausted I hardly recognized the ease with which such a slip could have resulted in fatality.

When I arrived Lou and Wick had more hot lemonade. I savored first the feeling of the mug on my hard fingers (the ends were too numb to feel even the hot liquid), and then the tangy, steaming drink washing my mouth, heating my throat, then my stomach, and finally spreading to my body. Other than rest, and a fuzzy hope to soon be off the mountain—to be safe in Base Camp with this ordeal behind—hot liquid was the only desire left to me.

Finishing the hot lemonade, I made my way to our neighboring tent and crawled in to join John. Light had disappeared, and the stars were sharp in clear, black sky. I wanted badly only to find my sleeping bag and crawl in. Nothing else mattered.

"Why don't you sleep in the Denali," John offered. "I'll take the McKinley tonight."

The Denali is a warmer and consequently heavier bag than the less substantial McKinley model. John and I had chosen to take the lighter bag, intending originally to use it for bivouac on the direct finish, but since plans had altered we were then sleeping one in the warm bag and one in the much colder bag. For three nights I had used the light bag, and for three nights I had been cold. John's offering to switch bags agreed with my desire to get warm as fast as possible. Also, since for three nights there had been only an hour, or two hours at the most, in which we had been able to *try* to sleep, the thought of a night with no 1:30 wake-up, combined with warm bag, seemed a full and just reward for the day's effort.

"Thanks, buddy," I said.

It took several minutes to remove my boots. My breathing was heavy and labored; it seemed the congestion my lungs suffered on Everest was returning, and for a moment I thought it could be pulmonary edema. I considered the symptoms: There was no gurgling in my lungs—the telltale of edema—and consequently I supposed I most likely had a bronchial congestion compounding the already difficult task of breathing at such high altitudes. With my boots off, I removed my parka and jumpsuit, and clothed only in wool underwear, I quickly slipped into the thick down bag before my shivering became more violent. For several minutes I lay fetus-style, shaking, but slowly gaining warmth and slowing my breathing. There were no thoughts in my mind.

"We should drink more liquid," John said.

I did not acknowledge. He was right, of course, but there was no way I had the energy necessary to start the stove and melt the snow to prepare drinks.

"I'll get the stove going," he said.

"Thanks, John. I'm too out of gas to help."

I thought, And only yesterday I was upset at John because I thought he wasn't doing his share digging the tent platform. It's so easy to lose patience under the strain of altitude.

Warmth slowly returned to my body, and my shivering stopped. I lay listening to the stove hissing, feeling pleasure from the Pavlovian recognition that we would soon have hot brews. John was fiddling with another stove, apparently changing fuel cartridges, but I paid no attention. I was thankful he had the discipline necessary to melt snow; I knew even with a major dredging for possible remaining energy I could not help him. I was so exhausted it took over a full second to respond to the deep, airsucking explosion.

"Out of the tent," John screamed.

I opened my eyes. Flames were everywhere, covering everything. My hair was burning, the tent walls were burning, and my sleeping bag was in flames. The stove had exploded. I had an instant flash—a panic—of being burned alive, and then I felt the claustrophobia from not being able to breath. The next second I had only one, dominant thought: Escape the tent. Which entrance? I could see the shape of John's body already half out the main door; that left me to bolt through the opposite end, the vestibule. In a continuous motion I slipped out of my bag and through the drawstring back entrance of our flaming tent.

Outside I could see John already reaching through the gaping holes in the tent walls to save boots and climbing clothing—the loss of which would jeopardize our ability to descend. I pulled my bag out—still burning. It was nearly destroyed, and without thinking I threw it down the slope. It appeared to have been the major fuel to the fire, and with the emergency under control John and I turned to see the bag, still aflame, roll hundreds of feet down the Abruzzi Shoulder and disappear over the ten-thousand-foot drop to the glacier. It reminded me of when as a child I watched the firefall display in Yosemite.

"You guys O.K.?" Lou yelled.

"Yeah, but the tent's gone. Some of the other gear is probably damaged too, but we won't know until morning."

I was again starting to shiver. Our predicament seemed ludicrous: There I was, in only my wool underwear, exhausted, at night at 25,750 feet with the temperature about thirty below zero, dehydrated and coughing and barely able to breathe, with only one pair of wool socks on my feet—now rapidly freezing—staring at the charred remains of our tent, where only moments before I had been cuddled blissfully in a warm bag. And it had been my night for the Denali bag, too. It didn't seem fair.

"Rick's bag burned up," John reported to Lou and Wick. There was no response from them as they realized the import of this information.

"There's no choice," he continued. "We're going to have to crawl in with you guys."

Two days before when Lou and Wick had, with Terry, established Camp VI Abruzzi, the three had sandwiched into the tent designed to house, with no luxury, two people. It was a difficult night. Now, with our physical condition further deteriorated, Wick and Lou contemplated the nearly uncontemplable thought of four in the tent.

"It might not be possible to fit us all in here," Wick said.

"No choice," John replied. "Otherwise we'll freeze with only one bag— the McKinley at that."

John rummaged in the remains of our tent for the reasonably undamaged McKinley bag, and I found my parka. That was enough goosedown to get us through the night, and since we would be packed so tightly in the other tent, being short one bag might cause discomfort but not injury. Pulling out our remaining bag, John handed it to me.

"You'd better get in this," he said. "It looks like you're pretty cold."

Despite my now uncontrollable shaking, I felt a warm camaraderie for my summit partner who was willing to give up his sleeping bag that he had all rights to claim. With some feeling of humbleness at his gesture, I accepted the offer.

"Thanks, pal. That's nice."

I crawled in first, squeezing against Wick, who was sandwiched against the tent wall. I bent my limbs and torso trying to dovetail with the shape of Wick's contorted figure. John crawled in. It was impossible not to over-lap limbs and torsos. We squirmed, trying to find a reasonably comfort-able position for everyone.

"I've got to move my shoulder."

"Wait, then. I've got to move my arm first."

"Then I'll have to move mine, too. Hold on, my leg is jammed."

Eventually we reached, at least for a while, equilibrium. It was immensely uncomfortable. My head was under Wick's arm; my chest jammed against John's back. Again, the claustrophobic feeling returned. My lungs were congesting, and I breathed faster—gasping rapidly—to get enough oxygen. I had the feeling of drowning. Phlegm stuck in my throat, and I thought I might black out. Panic. In desperation, I forced my torso out the tent door, upsetting the bodies interlocked like pieces of a puzzle, and hung my head outside, gasping. The others squirmed to regain positions.

"You O.K., Rick?" Wick asked. "Think it might be edema?"

"Don't know. Congestion. Can't breathe. Coughing up junk."

I was getting worried. I was starting to cough up hard nodules covered with blood. My lungs ached; my body cried for water.

"Any water left?"

"No," Wick said. "We'll have to wait till morning."

I squirmed back inside, and again we jockeyed about, unavoidably elbowing and kneeing each other. Eventually we regained temporary equilibrium. No one could sleep. We lay quiet, wishing the hours speed through the night. John, without bag, was cold but complained little. He was in a very contorted position, too, and he tried to force the discomfort from his mind. But it was no good. Sometime in the middle of the night he could no longer stand it.

"I've got to change," he said.

"What?"

"I've got to move to the other side of the tent. This is killing me, and I'm freezing."

John started to crawl over me to trade places with Wick. There was a jumble of arms and legs and down gear, and the panic of claustrophobia returned. Again, I could not breathe. With two bodies draped over me, I struggled to sit up and get my head higher to clear phlegm from my throat. I tried to get my head out the tent door.

"What the hell. Wait a minute, Ridgeway."

"Can't breathe. Got to get out."

"Can't you guys get in one place and stay there?" Lou complained, losing patience.

I hung my head out the tent, gasping, and then John and I changed positions. The tiny tent stretched and bulged as bodies pressured against the sides. John found a position that at least he could force himself to maintain. I stayed half out the door, coughing nasty stuff out of my lungs. My head and shoulders were getting cold, and my thirst was awful. I told myself over and over, be patient. The night will end. We can start the stove in the morning and make a gallon of lemonade. A full, complete U.S. gallon. Be patient.

Despite my difficulty breathing, the cold forced me back in the tent. I tried to lie still, to overcome my claustrophobia, to not think about my dehydration, to wait patiently for the dawn. It was our fourth night without sleep, our fourth night in the death zone. I began counting the hundreds of minutes until dawn, when we could crawl out and stretch and make drinks and then begin our escape. I only hoped I could find strength to get down; I hoped whatever was causing the blood I coughed up became no worse. I didn't want to burden the others who I knew would be taxed to their limits getting themselves down. Of the four of us, it seemed I was in the worst shape. In the cold predawn I thought how four of us had reached the summit, how the expedition was now a success, but also how much room was left for mistake, how easy it would be to quickly trade that victory for tragedy.

SEPTEMBER 8. CAMP VI, 25,750 FEET. ABOUT 11:00 A.M.
On the warm insulating pad spread on the floor of the tent, with full sun shining through the large holes in the burned-out tent walls, I lay half-conscious. I was dressed in wool underwear, in which I had passed the dreadful night, and my jumpsuit. My head lay on my parka, and on my feet I had only one boot. The other was next to my hand, tongue pulled open, but at the last minute I had lost the desire necessary to continue dressing, and had collapsed on my parka. That the day was relentlessly passing—that it was nearly noon—and we were still not prepared to begin our long descent, seemed in no way important.

I was consumed by total torpor; my mind and body melted in the warm sun. John lay next to me, apparently asleep. We were surrounded by the wreckage of our charred tent. Luckily, the gear needed for our descent had not burned, but it had taken some time to sort the debris, and the job was not yet finished. Wick and Lou had managed, meanwhile, to melt snow for nearly two liters of water, and I had drunk my ration with religious thanksgiving. Wick and Lou were presumably also asleep, or, like me, half-conscious; there was no voice from their tent.

Earlier that morning, waiting for the sun to heat the air sufficiently for us to crawl wearily from our tomblike tent, we had acknowledged the importance of descending rapidly, given our deteriorating condition and the uncertainty of how long the good weather would hold. We made plans to drop that day to Camp IV, and then the following day to Camp II, or perhaps even to Camp I. It would depend, in part, on where the others were positioned to assist our descent; their help breaking trail down would speed our escape.

Now, despite acknowledging the importance of rapid descent, we told ourselves that if we left before noon, there still would be sufficient time to get to Camp IV. It was not sound thinking, but rather giving in to our greater need for rest.

The sun shone on my face and I felt my skin burn. My lips were already cracked and bleeding, my neck peeling, and I knew I should apply protection lotion, but I had not the energy to search it out; I simply let the sun burn. My breathing seemed more regular, and my coughing and the choking phlegm also decreased. I thought I should try again to put on the other boot, but I could not bring myself to the task. I dozed, warm in bright sun, thankful for the absence of wind, and I dreamed of faraway places and of tropical sun.

"We'd better get moving soon. It's almost noon."

It was Lou's voice, and it sounded as though he and Wick were preparing to get under way. Lifting one hand, I pushed my goggles over my eyes, then dropped the hand. I opened my eyes. John was not moving. I wondered if I could find the energy to fit my other boot. I knew I must; I knew we had to start down. But the langour was all-consuming. I felt drugged.

I finally mustered the will to sit up and slowly lace my boot. I found my crampons and fitted them over the thick, insulated overboot.

"Time to go?" John asked.

"Yeah, we'd better get under way, I guess."

John sat up wearily and started lacing his crampons. I was still very thirsty and longed for another drink, but there was no time to melt snow. We would have to wait until evening, at Camp IV. With crampons fitted, I forced myself to stand and shake off the lassitude. I located my pack and sorted what to take and what to leave. Extra pile pants—leave. Camera—take. Extra mittens—leave. Sack of summit rocks—take. Stove and cookware—leave. I found the oxygen regulator I had picked up yesterday on the descent. It cost six hundred dollars. It also weighed several pounds—leave.

With packs shouldered, we wearily stepped out of camp, leaving behind the tents and miscellaneous gear to the gods of the mountain and also, no doubt, to the goraks who would most likely fly even that high to scavenge our jetsam. The sky was limpid and cloudless, and we descended with the summits of Broad Peak and the Gasherbrums to our right. The valley of Godwin-Austen was formed of ice and rock walls, and the flutings on the ice faces were furrows in a vertical field of whiteness. One face was cut by a sharp line marking the fracture of a slab avalanche. I thought of Nick Estcourt.

The descent was slow and mindless and required little care until we arrived at a steep drop of hard ice before the corner marking the beginning of the traverse to the snow dome on which Camp V was situated. We faced into the ice and carefully downclimbed, kicking our front points and placing the picks of our ice axes. We were all conscious of not wearing a rope. We were conscious of our exhaustion, and the need to keep reminding ourselves to be careful, to keep telling ourselves that after all we had been through it would be unthinkable to face tragedy. With these thoughts, we inched down the ice. When I made the final move to the more secure and less steep snow, I realized the last hard section of unroped climbing was behind me, and I was that much closer to safety.

It was easier hiking the remaining distance to Camp V, but we were reminded, nevertheless, that we still held space on the roulette wheel. We traversed a fifty-yard-wide swath of avalanche debris from a big serac that had broken from the hanging glacier sometime during the last few days. We picked our way through the jumble of ice blocks knowing had we been there during the avalanche there would have been no chance of survival.

We were at a crawl. John led, breaking through the soft snow. Lou followed, then Wick, and finally me. I was slowest. We came to a small rise that we knew was the back of the snow dome. Camp V was a hundred feet farther. At the tents Wick turned around, and with dismay he watched me trying to make the last uphill distance to camp. I could not walk. I was on hands and knees, crawling.

"John, look at Ridgeway," Wick said. "Can you believe that. He's crawling."

"Don't worry," John said. "He's come this far. He'll make it."

FROM WICK'S JOURNAL

September 8. Camp V. Difficulty in writing. Fingers frostbitten. Back at Camp V with Lou, John, and Rick. Getting down today from Camp VI was an ordeal. We walked like zombies—like sleepwalkers—during the three hours it took us. We were to have descended to Camp IV this afternoon, but

Rick and I both suffer frostbite, and we did not want to risk further damage by descending the shaded face below Camp V. We are all exhausted, but John and Lou have more strength than Rick and me. Details later as I am absolutely without strength.

September 10. Camp III. Storm. A new, violent storm has hit us following the long Indian summer that enabled us to climb K2 and retreat this far, but our attempts to now descend to Camp I are frustrated. We have not been able to locate the fixed ropes below Camp III. They are buried somewhere in deep snow. We need them as guidelines down the mountain. There is no visibility. John and Terry are out trying to locate the rope now.

Yesterday was long. We descended from Camp V to here with a brief stop at Camp IV to brew up. Still very weak. John, with more energy than the rest of us, led down, following the trail Terry and Cherie had made the day before. We arrived late afternoon. Warm greetings from the Bechs, waiting for us in Camp III (everyone else was in Camp I). Drinks, rehydration.

1:20 P.M. John and Terry just returned. No luck on the rope. Appears we are pinned here at least until tomorrow. Jim and Rob (on the radio in Camp I) were strong in urging us to come down. We told them impossible in these conditions. They worried we are deteriorating physically and mentally. Actually we are recovering strength compared to what we went through above. But we need to get off the mountain to ultimately recover. Jim and Rob seem pessimistic about the projected length of the new storm. Seven days. Tomorrow, notwithstanding the weather, we will descend with or without the fixed ropes. We'll get down tomorrow. We must.

SEPTEMBER 11. THE SLOPES BELOW CAMP III. 22,500 FEET. ABOUT 10:00 A.M.

Bitter cold wind out of the east. Mist and cloud. My companions just visible although less than a rope length distant. Spindrift carrying rapidly across my legs. Feet buried in deep, white powder. Exhaustion; the continuing task to force on, to make new steps. My body deteriorated, skinny with loss of muscle tissue. Sore lungs, difficulty breathing. Fingers now turning gray and black. The longing, the desire, for it all to end.

I THOUGHT, IF ONLY the weather had lasted one more day, we would now be off the mountain. As it was, we had been forced to hole up one day in Camp III, and now despite the continuing storm, we were pushing down. We had never located the fixed rope just below Camp III; and therefore we needed a climbing rope. Terry and I had spent several hours yesterday climbing back toward Camp IV and cutting two lengths out of the fixed rope (that line was not buried because no snow accumulated on the much steeper knife-edge ridge). With that line we had roped up, and we were now feeling our way down, scouting through the thick, blowing clouds, probing our memories to identify familiar landmarks. We must get down.

It had been a feeling of warm homecoming to find Terry and Cherie waiting, in Camp III, for our arrival. There was a mug of hot cocoa when we entered camp, and many embraces. To have someone simply to melt snow for brew water was great assistance, and Terry's and Cherie's faces held much sympathy for our haggard condition.

Actually, our condition seemed improved from the two previous days; yesterday's convalescence in Camp III was welcome rest. Wick and I were easily the worst, and it had been mostly up to John, with help from Lou, to break trail down to Camp IV and then across to Camp III. During the two nights since we had begun our descent, I had slept on oxygen, and the gas had improved my lung congestion remarkably. Breathing was easier, although still painful. My fingers were turning mottled gray and black, but I think the oxygen also mitigated the damage of the frostbite. And I had had a nasty abcess—which smelled of infection and made each step across the traverse a trial—that Cherie had nursed in Camp III: it was now less painful. It had been an embarrassment to ask her to clean the infection—more because of the wound's septicity than from my nakedness. But she had dismissed my concern with a nurse's indulgent laugh, and her ministrations gave me a warmness toward both her and Terry who, despite their disappointments, and their own weakened condition, had stayed high on the mountain to assist our descent.

Wick now seemed in worse shape. He had used no oxygen during sleep, and that morning he awoke with pain in his left side and difficulty breathing. He said it felt like broken ribs, but since he had not fallen, or bashed himself, Cherie thought it was more likely pneumonia. It was hard with Wick to judge whether the pain was serious, because he was stoical and not given to complaint.

We were in two teams, Lou, Wick, and John on one rope, leading and cutting a swath through the deep snow, and Terry and Cherie and me following on another rope. No one spoke. We silently trod downward, each of us alone with our thoughts. Lower on the ridge, at Camp II, there had been less snowfall, and we easily recovered the fixed rope. Untying from our climbing rope, we each descended at our own pace, and I chose to go last. I realized it was my last trip down the ropes; I was leaving places filled with so many memories, with so much emotion, that I wanted the time alone.

While I waited for the others to open distance down the ropes, I rested in one of the abandoned tents, nibbling what snacks I could find in the rifled food bags: a pepperoni stick, a few Corn Nuts, a piece of beef jerky. The beef jerky caused me to remember an incident from the Everest expedition two years earlier. Just before leaving for Nepal, we discovered our shipping invoice listed forty-five pounds of beef jerky. It is against the law to import beef products into Nepal, and with no time to retype the entire 240-page invoice, we had the idea simply to erase all the f's in beef and retype in t's, so we were importing forty-five pounds of beet jerky.

The thought brought a grin. Memories. Everest, K2—all behind, all memories. I crawled out of the tent, secured my brake system to the rope, and began the dramatic descent to the glacier, slowly rappelling rope length after rope length. I thought how Lou and I had fixed these ropes so many weeks before (I could count the time in months, too). The cloud cover had in some places opened to blue sky.

At the steepest place in the descent I stopped, secured the rope, and hung off it, silently studying the geography. Across the back of the glacier the familiar features of Skyang Kangri were colored subtle pastels of green and purple and light browns. The rock face divided into two monolithic intrusions, one light gray stone, a source of sun, of things positive, the Yang; the other dark stone, the color of earth and moon, the Yin. Both sides were cut with long linear dikes of still other stone, knife-sharp in contrast. Snow from the latest storm delicately laced the rock walls. The mountain rose boldly against a sky piebald of grays and browns, with patches of cerulean blue. Skyang Kangri's northeast ridge descended to Windy Gap, the pass to Shaksgam, and over the pass I could see the needle summits of lesser peaks, the last disturbance of the Karakoram before giving way to the endless brown hills of China. Memories.

I thought, My companions will be arriving in Camp I by now. There will be the joy of reunion, the hugs, the congratulations, the tears. The relief. Yes, there will be much relief.

I looked up the ropes, up the snow gully, then down to the glacier. It was time to go. The others would be concerned if I did not arrive soon. But I had to wait a few more minutes before releasing the rope and continuing my rappel. It was the thought of the relief, that we had done it. We were all down alive. It was behind us, we had climbed to the summit, and now we were all down alive. We had been climbing on K2 for sixty-seven days. We were all going to make it. That was the relief. That was what caused the tears coming down my cheeks, tears I had to wipe away before continuing into camp. I didn't want my companions to see me in tears.

12

The Griffon

LEGS WEAK AND NEAR COLLAPSE, JIM WICK-
wire wished, nevertheless, to remain standing. Rob Schaller supported one
arm and Saleem Khan, the liaison officer, natty in khaki fatigues and
black field boots and looking trim from the months in Base Camp,
supported the other. Wick was about to address the over one hundred Balti
porters standing before them. He was giving his farewell; that afternoon a
rescue helicopter would pluck him from near the snout of the glacier and
carry him from the thirteenth to the twentieth century, the first step from
the inner sanctum of the Karakoram to the surgery room of a hospital in
Seattle.

Wick could not have chosen a more dramatic amphitheater. He was at
Liliwa, a stopping place of about an acre of flat bench on the littoral of the
Baltoro Glacier, and by custom, an established campsite. The back
periphery of the sandy bench is a brown wall of some hundred feet of con-
glomerate mud and wash stone (which threatened to avalanche on the
temporary rock and plastic sheet shanties the porters had built under it).
In the other direction the bench looked across the vista of the Baltoro and
bordering peaks—over the stone debris hitching a ride on the ice moving
down-valley—to the Lopsang and Trango Towers, and Paiju Peak.

Wick could not address the porters directly, and his was not merely the
problem of translation. He could not talk above a whisper. His vocal cords
were paralyzed, and he was capable only of a harsh, aspirated whisper.
Saleem, still affecting much bombast, translated to the porters.

"Tell them," Wick said in a weak frog voice, "I am sorry I cannot accompany them all the way out. Tell them I want to visit their villages, and join the celebration, but I am sick and must leave by helicopter."

Saleem translated, and the porters acknowledged Wick's request with cheers of support. The porters remembered Wick from the approach march: the short, sturdy man who always carried heavy, who always was one of the first to arrive in camp, who remembered many of them from the 1975 expedition and who had greeted them with the embrace of parted brothers. That this man was standing before them—weak, coughing blood, frostbitten, unable to talk, breathing in loud rasps, near death—and thanking them for all they had done to help, they knew was a gesture of the heart.

"Tell them," Wick said, "I enjoyed listening to them play music and sing last night. I was very sick in my tent, but I still listened, and I still enjoyed it. It was the best Balti music I have ever heard."

Again, they cheered.

"Most of all," Wick continued, "I have to thank them for all they've done for me in the last five days. I know they have gone without food because I have been slow, and it has taken them twice as many days to hike out as they brought food for. Tell them . . ."

Wick stopped in a paroxysm of low, deep, slow coughing—more a rasp, from the depths of his clogged lungs. He lowered his head and tried to clear the bloody spittle from his throat, and his face grimaced in pain. The porters watched in silence.

"Tell them I most want to thank them for helping carry me down, for bearing the stretcher to Concordia. I was very touched by their help, and I want them to know I think they are fine human beings, close brothers."

Saleem finished the translation, and the hundred porters began, in unison, to pray to Allah. They asked Allah to grant reprieve to this man, to allow him to live.

For Wick, it was the last day of the grueling hike from Base Camp to an altitude low enough for the Pakistan Army helicopter to land and rescue him. Since the day we had rappelled the last ropes and arrived safely in Camp I, six days before, Wick's condition had been steadily worsening. Then, we had been delivered safe from the mountain to the teary-eyed greetings of our teammates. There was much embracing, and our companions quickly set us in the cook tent to what seemed a great feast of leftover freeze-dried dinners. To the untrained eye it would have appeared a toss-up which of us looked the worst from the ordeal, but Rob Schaller quickly singled out Wick for immediate attention. He noted Wick was cyanotic—his fingernails and lips were bluer than anyone's. His cough was also the worst, and obviously painful. Rob escorted Wick to his medical tent to listen to his lungs. There were all the classical indications of pneumonia, but to his relief Rob detected no friction, or rawls, that would have indicated pleurisy (that would come later).

286 / THE LAST STEP

Rob considered putting him on oxygen and decided against it, fearing it might deacclimatize him and make him dependent on it. It was a double-edged sword: Wick might have immediate benefit from oxygen, but the long-term effects could have been worse. Rob placed him on intravenous fluids and antibiotics.

The next day, with support from the two HAPS, Gohar and Honar, Wick had had enough strength to walk the long distance down the Godwin-Austen Glacier to Base Camp. He arrived, accompanied by Jim, Dianne, and Rob, late in the afternoon to the merrymaking of the porters, beating on empty fuel cans, cheering the safe arrival off the mountain of the last sahibs. But Wick had been in no mood for celebrating. His condition deteriorated rapidly, and the next day, when we abandoned Base Camp, Wick was transported on a litter jury-rigged by several team members from tent poles and rope. Leaving in the morning, Wick and an entourage of porters and team members had not arrived in Concordia until nine that night.

By then Rob was concerned for Wick's life, and by the time we reached Urdukas we decided to request, using our single-sideband radio, an evacuation helicopter. Wick was coughing up quantities of blood. Rob concluded that his pneumonia was becoming complicated with pleurisy, and that he had formed dangerous pulmonary emboli. In addition, Wick's left vocal cord and diaphragm were paralzyed—which Rob considered the result of a further viral infection—and several of his toes were badly frost-bitten. All Wick's problems resulted from a general physical collapse related to the stress of the summit climb, the bivouac at nearly twenty-eight thousand feet, the long descent, the prolonged dehydration and mal-nutrition. The one ordeal Wick suffered that was spared the rest of us summit climbers—the bivouac—was probably the final blow.

There are no bacteria, of course, at twenty-eight thousand feet, so how could Wick have contracted pneumonia and a viral infection? Rob spec-ulated it occurred during bivouac or descent, and was the result of aspirated spittle. Rob postulated Wick had carried the bacteria in his body and coughed them up, then aspirated them into his lungs. Normally the body's defense system would shut off the larynx to avoid such aspiration, but in Wick's condition the night of the bivouac, or on descent, he was so physically exhausted, out of oxygen and dehydrated, his normal defense systems were broken.

Amazingly, despite sedation, lack of sleep and malnutrition, Wick forced himself to continue his entries in his journals.

> **September 14.** Today, to avoid the torture and slowness of the litter, I walked with the team. Extremely hard work. Bad lung had not only cut back strength, but also general body dehy-dration and malnutrition. Haven't eaten much since summit on September 6. We are apparently short of food. Took seven hours to reach same campsite used on way in July 3.

Tomorrow to Urdukas. Last view today of K2. No emotion. Totally drained.

September 15. Urdukas. Took nearly eight hours to reach here. Rob, Gohar, Sanger Jan, and I, along with a few porters to carry our gear, were the last of the caravan to arrive. Today was easier footing, slightly shorter in distance, yet physically more demanding because I felt weaker. I had the hand of Gohar Shah, who walked at my side, supporting me virtually the entire way. So weak I lacked normal balance. As we walked into Urdukas and hit the level dirt trail, I thanked Gohar, walked a hundred feet, and fell off the trail. Back came Gohar to support me for the remaining short distance.

September 16. Liliwa. This is not a normal stopover coming down the Baltoro—most groups make a long double stage to Paiju, but to accommodate my illness we camped here. Still the most strenuous single stage of the entire route. Left in light snowstorm. On I-V fluids all night. Helped dehydration, but nevertheless a damn long day. Gohar and Honar were principal aides. Turned out to be a beautiful fall day as clouds finally broke, revealing the orange-tinted flanks of the Grand Cathedral and the Trangos. In the scene, however, I was a robot moving, swaying, clinking, and every so often, for the doctors' and presumably my benefit, coughing up globs of blood.

Wick was very much moved by the sight of a hundred ragamuffin men kneeling before him, praying to God for his safe deliverance. He had never been the recipient of the collective goodwill of so many people. When they finished the prayers, Saleem thanked them again for their support and hard work, and with a great simultaneous cheer, the Baltis hefted their loads, strapped their goat-hair harnesses over their shoulders, and began the trek down the glacier to Paiju Camp.

For many of us the hike out, although nothing compared to Wick's ordeal, was painful. Of the four summit climbers, John appeared strongest, although he suffered minor frostbite and was in pain walking. I was very weak and frequently dizzy and was forced to sit down and rest. The ends of most of my fingers were turning coal black, accompanied by razor jabs of pain. I still had an infection, my skin was breaking out in a rash, and boils formed inside my mouth—all, the doctors felt, a result of general physical weakness. I had lost over thirty pounds. Normally I can come nowhere close to pinching my fingers around my biceps; now they wrapped easily around.

It would have been easy to complain, to try to elicit sympathy from my companions, but in view of Wick's troubles, it would have been petty sniveling. Lou was also suffering, stoically, as we had learned that morning leaving Liliwa. He had mentioned having a frostbitten toe that pained him when he walked, and he thought perhaps Rob should have a look. He removed his boot and sock, and aghast, we stared at his big toe.

All the skin had sloughed off, and the entire toe was exposed muscle tissue. Rob bandaged the toe, and without comment Lou turned to the day's hike.

I found myself frequently walking alone, no doubt partly because I was slower than most, in my weakened state, and also because of a propensity to silence. I noticed that several of the others seemed to share this inclination, and I suspected many of us spent much time in reverie over imminent reunion with parents and wives and children and lovers. Other than the satisfaction of having successfully climbed the mountain, the most common sentiment shared by team members, not surprisingly, was relief: Finally the expedition was at an end; the storms, the monotonous food, the endless carries to higher camps, were at last over.

Now we were on our way home; now it would be only a couple of weeks until we arrived back in the United States. We hiked toward Paiju, a scraggly lot, haggard, limping, coughing, skinny, and without bath for almost a hundred days, strung a mile over the stone trail covering the Baltoro ice. About noon the trail descended the terminus of the glacier, and I hiked the last miles to Paiju Camp on the easier footing along the alluvial bench bordering the Braldu River. In the distance I could hear the unmistakable Thumpf! Thumpf! Thumpf! of the helicopter.

It turned out to be two helicopters—the Pakistani Army had a safety policy of always flying the back country with escort. I watched, puzzled, as the two French-built Alouettes continued past us, up the Baltoro to Concordia. It seemed unlikely, but apparently they had missed our long caravan. In a few minutes they returned, this time spotting several of our team on a sand bar at the river's edge near the snout of the glacier. They set down, and in a few minutes Wick's party arrived; they had hiked madly the last half mile, after hearing the helicopters, to get to the landing spot. Wick was nearly in collapse. With him and Rob loaded in one, they took off and in a few minutes set down on a gravel bar in front of Paiju Camp. The rest of the team quickly gathered.

With two machines there was now available space for four passengers, and we had to decide who to pick for evacuation. It was essential that Rob accompany Wick, and Lou was next in line with his raw toe. That left John or me. We both had frostbitten feet. My hands were certainly more frostbitten, but that was no hindrance in walking.

"Go ahead," John said.

I was reluctant to accept, thinking he had as much right as I did, and also harboring a desire to stay the distance with the team, despite the pain of hiking.

"Let's flip for it," I whispered to John, winking. We decided to keep our decision-making secret from Jim, thinking he might not approve such a haphazard technique. Rob was standing nearby, and we asked him to pick a number between one and ten. I lost.

"Sure you don't want to go?" John said.

"See you back home," I replied, smiling. The helicopters were idling, ready to go, waiting for John. I gave him a hug, and he climbed in. The team gathered around and waved to Wick, Rob, Lou, and John. The blades revved; the birds lifted off and sped down the Baltoro. We stood silently and watched as the machines grew small among the peaks, then rounded a turn in the deep valley. There was much relief in seeing Wick delivered to the safety of hospital care, and when the helicopters disappeared the sight filled me with an odd, mixed feeling, a kind of happy melancholy.

AHEAD JIM WHITTAKER HIKED THE TRAIL, steeply switchbacking a ridge we had to climb up, then down, to detour an hour-glass constriction in the river gorge. It had been four days since the helicopter had evacuated the others; ahead we still had another three days of walking. Behind a short distance followed Dianne Roberts, and a group of Baltis carrying their personal gear. Jim's tall frame was gaunt, testimony to the many weeks of hard work at altitude, but his face was at ease, contented. He had no regrets; he had led the first successful American ascent of K2, and for Jim the expedition had been a ratification of the creed he lived.

Following our last retreat to Camp IV during the final storm, Jim and Dianne had descended to Camp III and waited there the next several days while we reached the summit. Before abandoning that camp to make room for our arrival, and also to conserve meager food and fuel, Jim had made a solo carry to Camp IV with extra supplies in case, for some reason, we were delayed on our descent. (Had the storm that pinned us in Camp III arrived a day earlier, Jim's precaution would have been vital to our survival.) His trail through that new snow also aided Cherie's and Terry's descent, and consequently made our own escape easier. Jim had performed remarkably well for a man a few weeks from his fiftieth birthday.

Upon abandoning Camp III, Jim and Dianne had written several messages with a marking pen on the tent walls conveying their hearty congratulations for our successful ascent, and also a selection of their favorite quotes and aphorisms. Now, watching Jim hike ahead of me, I thought back to the graffiti walls and realized the writing on the tent was a pithy representation of the creed of the man who had led our expedition:

"Whatever you can do, or dream you can, begin it. Boldness has genius, power and magic."

"Victory is sweetest to those who have known defeat."

Jim had every right to be proud, for what he did took courage. To be sure, Jim made mistakes. It would have been better, for example, had he at times been more authoritarian, and left less to democratic consensus.

But his reasons for so doing were valid, based on lessons from the dismal failure of the 1975 expedition. He had gambled high going back to K2 in 1978. He easily could have rested on the laurels of the Everest climb the rest of his life. Even fifteen years after being the first American to climb the highest mountain in the world, Jim was very much the hero in the public's eye. It was a role he regarded seriously. He had strong ideas about the function of heroes in society; he regarded it as no small tragedy that young kids worshipped lacquered, larger-than-life heroes of popular TV drama or rock 'n' roll stars elevated to the position of demigods, instead of men and women of real-life flesh and blood accomplishment. He never turned down a request to speak to a grade school or give a slide show to a Boy Scout troop. But Jim had wanted a confirmation of his mettle as a man of deeds, and now, having gone back and led a successful ascent of K2, he had every justification to believe he was made of the stuff that was his public image.

To Jim's friends, it was also a confirmation of this mettle, an affirmation that Jim embodied the ideal of the man who picks a goal and strives, not giving up, until that goal is reached. When we had arrived in Base Camp, safe from the ascent, a series of telegrams had been relayed to us over the radio. The first to arrive at the U.S Embassy in Islamabad read simply, "Congratulations to you and your team. Ted and Joan."*

Jim continued to hike slowly up the trail, followed closely by Saleem. Jim pulled over to the side and let Saleem pass while he waited for Dianne to catch up.

Unlike Jim, the expedition for Dianne was less a reaffirmation of a previously formed creed than the maturation of new ideals and, consequently, an increased confidence. It had been a quantum leap from Calgary to Hyannisport and Dianne was now a little less "the wife of Jim Whittaker" and a little more the woman who fought storm and delivered a load to 25,300 feet. The experience was fodder for her growing self-confidence, something she had struggled for years to develop.

---

*Ted Kennedy was absolutely sincere in his admiration. On flying back to the United States after the climb, I stopped in Washington, D.C., and thought to give his office a call and leave a note thanking him for his support of our expedition. The secretary asked me to hold, and in a minute Kennedy came on the phone. "You're in town? Have you got a minute? Good, come over, I'd like to meet you." I caught a taxi, and in a few minutes he was giving me a guided tour of the Senate building. We walked to the Senate floor, and I waited outside while he gathered several senator friends who came out to meet me.

"Can you believe that?" he asked them, after relating the climb. He held my hand to show my fingers still black with frostbite. "Without oxygen, to twenty-eight thousand feet," he said with great enthusiasm.

I was a little embarrassed. "All we did was climb to the top of a mountain—that's nothing to what you guys do here every day," I said.

"Oh no," he replied, beaming. "I think it's one of the most incredible things I've heard anyone doing."

In a letter written in August to her friend Susanne, Dianne mentioned other insights:

> A long climbing expedition is one of the few situations in modern life when you have the opportunity of really living on the edge, of pushing to your physical and mental limits. Most of the time we are not required to come anywhere near those limits, and even if we want to, there are so many comforts and temptations forcing us into an easier style, so we never really learn where they are. There is value in knowing your limits, I mean *really* knowing from actual experience. For one thing, it eliminates a lot of guesswork. I *know* I can survive in conditions that are marginal. I may never have to after this expedition, but having done it once, I know I can probably do it again. That knowledge eliminates a lot of low-level anxiety. If someone dumped me in the street in the clothes I'm wearing, I could somehow survive.
>
> It also makes *normal* life easier. Relative to laying your life on the line getting down a mountain in a snowstorm, a case of the flu is pretty insignificant. After melting snow for water over dirty kerosene stoves that won't work half the time, turning a faucet is a damn miracle.
>
> I think most people's limits are a lot farther on than they believe. Consequently, they live life holding themselves back for fear of sailing off the earth. Once you realize this—that you have more reserves than you'd imagined you're free to explore and experiment, to take risks—emotional, mental, and physical—that you'd never dreamed of taking before. You're free to laugh at yourself when you fail (because in most of life, failure is not life-threatening, merely a learning experience) and relish the simplest of pleasures.
>
> I don't advocate everybody packing off to the Himalaya but I think it is good to do *something* that involves risk— preferably mental as well as physical—to push yourself beyond what is comfortable. To hell with the mentality that would build fences around every cliff, outlaw hang-gliding, put a hard-hat on every cyclist. Life itself is less precious than the ability and freedom to live life to its fullest.

Dianne caught up to Jim.

"Hello, luv," he said in a voice mushy with romance.

"Hello, luv," she replied. They put their arms around each other, and gazed across the valley, and down to the line of porters zigzagging up the steep trail.

"It's such a beautiful place," she said to Jim, "I kind of hate to leave it." Pausing, she added, "Well, maybe not *that* beautiful."

They both laughed, and holding hands, walked up the trail.

DIANA JAGERSKY AND I SAT ALONE ON A ROCK
beside the trail, about a mile from the village of Askole. The weather was
again clear. After so many months in the high mountains there was glory
in beholding flowers in the sun, or walking along shady lanes of tall
Lombardy poplar and listening to irrigation water purl in canals beside
the trail.

It had been necessary for me to rest several times that day, and during
our stops Diana and I had reminisced about the expedition. Now we talked
of the arguments and fights we had suffered.

"They were inevitable," I said. "You can't have a group this size in a
confined place for that long under so much stress without arguing."

Diana agreed, and then expanded the idea: "On a climb like this there
are none of the distractions people usually have in their environment.
They normally have to interact with telephones and traffic, they are
constantly bombarded with TV advertisement—it's a complex and
distracting culture. But up here there's none of that. Just us—forced to
face each other every day. I don't think people were used to that."

I said, "But even in the old days before TV or telephones there were
plenty of fights on the long expeditions. They just never wrote about them;
to read their accounts those trips sounded like perfect Victorian picnics.
Look at the 1902 K2 Expedition, the first attempt to climb the mountain.
The arguments got so heated Aleister Crowley pulled a gun at twenty
thousand feet and threatened to blow the head off another climber."

"Yeah, but you can't compare anybody to Crowley," Diana said. Then
she added, "Although we did have some pretty offbeat characters on this
climb. I guess this sport never has attracted too many regular people."

We both laughed. We lay back on the rock, staring at the valley walls
and clear sky, desert brown against cobalt blue.

"We'll soon forget all the bad stuff, anyway," Diana said, "and there
will only be the good memories."

"I already feel good about it overall. There's a lot of satisfaction
knowing we stuck it out to the end, held on until we made it. It looked
pretty grim there several times."

I continued, "But it's easy for me to say—I got to the top. I know how
frustrating it is for the others. I felt the same way on Everest when I didn't
make it. You work so somebody else gets up, and then after the climb,
when you're back in the city, you stand around in a corner at the celebration parties while the summit guys answer everybody's questions. You tell
yourself you don't climb mountains just so you get your back slapped, but
you still feel bad when nobody realizes what a collaborative effort these
things are. Especially this one. We came so close to failing that without
support of even one of the team, we probably wouldn't have made it."

"I think everybody knows that," Diana said.

"There are still a few people disappointed."

"Or homesick," she said. "Like Bill, Craig, and Skip."

While it is neither possible nor fair to say Bill, Craig, and Skip felt the separation from their wives and children more than the others, they did seem outwardly more affected, more homesick. Perhaps it was because they realized earlier than most there was little chance that they personally would reach the summit. For Lou, Wick, John, and me, the goal of the summit was our carrot on a stick to carry us forward. And Jim and Dianne, and Terry and Cherie, had the companionship of their spouses. But for Bill, Craig, and Skip, the last days of the expedition as they marked time in Camp I, despite the excitement of the final push to the summit, were a trial of waiting. What mattered most to them was to reunite, as soon as possible, with those they loved the most.

There is something consummately lonely in long mountain climbs in the Himalaya. It is no doubt the long waiting out of storms in small tents, the attrition of high altitude, the trial of constant danger, that causes one to think often of those left behind, and to wait expectantly for the mail runner with the satchel of letters stamped with months-old postmarks. Much of one's journal entries are devoted to love letters promising never again to go away for such long times, entries claiming to be able to see, from the rarefied atmosphere of twenty thousand feet, new dimensions in relationships.

Skip was lucky. His wife, Sandy, had flown to Pakistan and was at that moment hiking in to rendezvous with him, and the only desire left him was to be back with her. For Skip, the expedition had been an emotional strain. He is not the type of person given to competition, especially among friends. At the beginning of the expedition he had a notion that anybody who wanted to might get a chance to try for the top, but as the weeks wore on he realized that expectation was naive, based on not knowing the nature of big expeditions, and big mountains. When he realized he had no chance of making it, the principal reason for being there evaporated, and it had taken all his patience to remain those last days in Camp I.

For Craig, the expedition had also been too long, but nevertheless, he felt it had been very much a worthwhile experience. Even before leaving the United States, he had had doubts whether he could reach the summit, and he had even decided it would probably be too risky—and not fair to his wife and children to attempt the final climb to the summit. The most rewarding aspect of the trip was the three or four new friendships, especially his bond to Skip and Bill. Of lesser importance, but nevertheless of personal satisfaction, was knowing he had pushed the limits of his climbing ability. While he thought he never again wanted to participate in a big expedition to the Himalaya, with all the attending hassles, he had no regrets.

It was more difficult to decipher the inner feelings of Bill Sumner. He was so quiet, so introspective. He seemed, though, in his passive manner, disappointed.

Initially one of the expedition's big attractions for Bill was the chance to accompany his good friend Dusan. At about the same time Dusan died, Bill was married, and these two events caused him to seriously consider dropping out. After our first team meeting in Seattle, a year before the trip, Bill decided to stay on. He had been impressed by our commitment to work together, "to get somebody to the top of K2."

By the end of the expedition that commitment seemed to Bill to belong to mythology. He felt the expedition was, strictly speaking, a success; he considered the near alpine-style ascent to the summit from Camp IV an impressive feat. But as an experience of people working together—or as Bill called it, a "family experience"—he felt we had been a failure. "K2 was the distillation," he would later say, "of life in a crowded society."

Part of his feeling was no doubt from the severe dysentery he had suffered the last part of the expedition: On the march out he had had the worst stomach cramps—the worst pain—he had ever endured. But even with illness and all the other disappointments, Bill could still count some memorable experiences. He left the trip with several new friends—especially Craig, whom he had not known before; he had gazed on the most impressive mountain scenery on earth; he had learned much from the Hunzas and the Balti porters. Nevertheless, now Bill wanted only to return to his cabin in the mountains, and like Skip and Craig, he had no further desire for big expeditions.

I SUPPOSE THE ONES most disappointed are Terry, Chris, and Cherie," I said to Diana.

"I still can't figure them out," she said.

"I'm not sure I can either. I feel bad about it. I think they still blame John and me for most of what happened."

"Cherie really wanted to get to the top."

"I know. She admits, though, she ran out of gas just above Camp Five. I'll never forget that day she turned back after the last storm when we left for the top, and for a long time she just stood there, watching us walk away. She was such a lonely figure."

"Terry really wanted her to get to the top, too," Diana said. It was the most important thing to him, more important than whether he made it."

"There's still something bothering him. Even more than just being disappointed."

"He's really on edge lately. That scene at the river crossing, for example."

The Dumordo River, which on the approach march we had rigged with a Tyrolean rope bridge, and for two days had ferried across porters and supplies, was low enough on the trek out to force our way across it. It was nevertheless risky, and we had crossed in groups of four to six, arms locked, to prevent being swept downstream in swift, chest-deep water. It was wide, and glacial cold. One porter broke from his companion's grip and swept down, eyes wide with panic, fifty yards before one of our

Hunzas waded from the far bank and rescued him. On the far side, the porters built fires over which to warm, and to brew tea.

Most of us, weak from the climb, before crossing had divided our loads among the stronger porters. Terry, however, had tried to cross with a pack weighing over fifty pounds, and halfway he was in trouble. Unable to maintain footing, he partially submerged and the porters with him struggled to keep a grip on his arm. Another Hunza rushed into the water and rescued him. His legs were bruised and bleeding and he was blue with cold.

He tried to warm over a porter's fire, but he chose one used for heating tea water and cooking chapatties, and the porters asked meekly if he could move to a fire used for warming. Terry flushed with rage, eyes wild and brimstony. He hurled a string of abuse at the porters, who cowered surprised and uncertain what to do.

"Something is bothering him," I said to Diana, still sitting with me on the rock. "He normally wouldn't have blown up. I asked Cherie about it, but she said she didn't know, or she wouldn't tell me."

None of us knew, at the time, the extent of Terry's frustration. It had increased even on the march out, to the point he no longer wanted to see anyone, even Cherie. He was emotionally as taut as the strings on his viola. He had been so utterly disappointed, and he felt used. He seemed, more than any of us, the victim of misconstrued intentions, and he felt victimized by what he saw as a conspiracy to prevent Chris and Cherie—and by association, himself—from reaching the summit. Even the last days of the climb, when he had helped Lou and Wick reach Camp VI, had been a bitter letdown based on yet another misunderstanding. Terry had thought both Lou and Wick understood his desire to accompany them as high as he could on the morning they left for the summit; it had been *their* understanding, however, that Terry wanted to return to Camp V. When Terry realized the mistake, as Lou and Wick were preparing in the blackness to leave, he was too exhausted, too drained, to say anything. It was only another in a long string of disappointments. By the march out, his frustrations had exceeded all his patience, even for the porters.

"HOW ARE YOU getting along with Chris?" Diana asked.

"I still feel strange around him. We never have talked like we should. There's this distance; I feel it most when he's with Cherie. He thinks I betrayed him."

We sat in silence, tossing small stones. Nearby the pink flowers of wild rose added color to the otherwise drab desert. Overhead a large griffon (or was it the lammergeier?) turned in widening gyres, carried aloft on morning updraft.

"It's too bad he quit," Diana said. "All he did was go to Base Camp and wait until the end of the expedition. He could have made it to the top, you know."

"I have mixed feelings," I said. "I feel satisfied getting to the top— that's what I came for—but it was at a cost. It was a trade-off. I don't know, maybe these big climbs are like that. Only room for a few at the top, and you've got to elbow your way up."

I leaned back, staring at the sky, and thought about it. It seemed that each of the people who began with many doubts or hesitations failed to fulfill his ambitions. I went down the list: Craig had been skeptical of his own ability at the outset; Skip had been the last person invited to join the team, and considered himself in a weak position; Bill had made a hard decision whether to come at all. Chris was looking for an escape, for a vacation from his personal problems, more than for the trial of a difficult ascent.

Because there was limited space on the summit team, the jockeying for position had left those with any doubts, any hesitations, behind. It had left Cherie, whose will exceeded her strength, behind. Bill was right—the expedition was a microcosm of life in a crowded society.

I felt the regrets from my failure to live up to my friendship with Chris. I had made several mistakes; I had suffered several shortcomings. But we all had. Each of us was weakened by stress, danger, long exposure to altitude. At one time or another we had all been stripped naked, we had all stood exposed, our human foibles bared.

I asked myself if on this expedition there were any heroes, and I realized the answer was no. We had no gallant knights conquering new worlds. Instead we had fourteen people overcoming their all-too-human frailties to achieve a goal. In that sense maybe we were heroes—modern-day ones— anti-heroes. Not larger than life, but ordinary people with ordinary weaknesses.

WE WERE QUIET AGAIN, and staring up I watched the griffon sailing higher on uplifts. After several minutes Diana said, "Wick should be getting close to Seattle by now. I was relieved to see him choppered out. It was about as much as I could take seeing him in pain, coughing and wheezing and not able to talk. It was hard to believe he was the same guy who hiked in here three months ago. He was so skinny, his eyes so sunken."

I said, "They still had the sparkle, though. If he had lost that, I would have worried."

We watched the griffon in a growing gyre.

"You and Wick seemed to have stayed close."

"We're good buddies. He was Dusan's best friend."

Another silence, then, "You know, Diana, Wick said he could feel Dusan up there, near the summit. I wish he had had a radio on top. He could have called down and told you he knew Dusan's spirit was up there."

We watched the griffon.

"Dusan probably would have been pleased you came on this trip," I said.

"No doubt about it. The trip gave me something to strive for, to fill the time—more than that. I guess that's why I worked so hard, cooking meals and carrying loads. I felt closer to him that way."

She hesitated. The griffon carried higher, smaller and smaller, wheeling in widening gyres.

Then I said, "Thank God we all came back. There were so many places something could have gone wrong. We're lucky."

"There was that time, though, we didn't seem so lucky, when Wick disappeared on the summit. I guess you and John didn't know about it at Camp Six, but at Camp One we feared the worst. It seemed certain that something had happened to Wick."

Diana told me about the forty minutes during which Wick had disappeared, and about the thoughts that flashed before her: the breakfast with Wick in Glacier Bay after the accident, the late summer climb before Dusan left for Alaska, the image of him falling.

"After Wick showed up, and we realized he had only stayed up longer— we didn't know then it was to change film—I still felt hollow, like there was nothing left of me but skin; I felt like there was a vacuum inside. When we thought he might have died, it was like an incredible deja vu, a feeling the whole nightmare was repeating, that now Dusan's best friend had also died in the exact same way. I was completely defeated. It just ran over me, left me blank."

She paused, and for a moment, neither of us spoke.

Then she finished, "I had been fighting it, but with Wick up there, gone too, I had to accept it. When you lose somebody close to you, you refuse to think about it, to accept it. You force it out of your mind. But I could no longer do that. I think it was the image of Dusan falling, but for the first time I knew he was not going to come back; for the first time I knew he was dead."

The griffon was a distant dot against the cerulean sky. Diana shouldered her light load (I was carrying nothing) and we continued hiking under the shade of the poplars. Finches bounded in the branches of the nearby apricot, chirping morning songs, and sunlight spilled through the leaves highlighting the trail before us. For Diana, it was more than just the trail home, but the trail to the rest of her life. The past was still many warm memories, and still many quiet evenings occasionally filled with tears, but it was behind; she was ready to continue forward.

I thought, Dusan would have liked it this way. I looked up. The griffon was gone.

FROM THE JOURNAL OF JIM WICKWIRE, SEPTEMBER 22.

A little more than an hour from Seattle. The final leg homeward. One hundred and two days of separation from Mary Lou, Annie, Cathy, Susy, Bobby, and David. In an hour we'll be together, even if briefly before I go in the hospital. All of my efforts for the past two weeks have pointed to this reunion today. They were out in front, as a goal during that endless journey down the Baltoro, through the long nights of little or no sleep. I am indeed a man of great good fortune to be able to return to the persons I cherish more than anything in this world.

I should be on a terrible binge of euphoria now, but I am not. I have a cerebral satisfaction about the achievement. But gutwise, deep in my emotional side, there is no spark. This I attribute to the bivouac at 27,800 feet, and to my illness. Both have drained me, and have cut sharply into the joy of standing on that high, isolated summit.

My old life resumes; a new life begins. Nearly thirty years later, Maurice Herzog's words still shine with meaning: "There are other Annapurnas in the lives of men." Ahead lies the task of identifying and surmounting these other Annapurnas.

MARY LOU WICKWIRE STOOD WAITING IN International Arrivals at Seattle-Tacoma Airport. She knew she was at the right gate—there were the several TV cameras, the large lights poised to be turned on as soon as the passengers cleared customs, the dozens of TV, radio, and newspaper reporters. They had somehow learned that part of the K2 Expedition, including at least a couple of the summit team, was to land that afternoon. Mary Lou avoided talking to them. She had hoped they wouldn't be there; she had wanted the moment to herself.

She was nervous. Her children, however, were excited—not only was Dad coming home, but they would be on television, too. To Mary Lou, it seemed like it was taking forever to clear customs. She wasn't certain what to expect, and she didn't know exactly what shape Wick would be in. There had been little information. A week earlier she had received a telegram from Skardu:

NOW IN SKARDU. HELICOPTER BROUGHT HERE FROM BALTORO SNOUT. HAVE PNEUMONIA. DON'T WORRY. IN ROB'S CARE. SHOULD BE HOME BEFORE END OF MONTH. MUCH LOVE. JIM.

Then, only the day before, Joanne Schaller had called. Rob had phoned her from London; he and Wick were on the next flight to Seattle. Wick would be in a wheelchair, and he would have to enter a hospital for a checkup shortly after arriving.

Joanne had been surprised at Mary Lou's apparent nonchalance on hearing this news. Mary Lou, however, was hiding her real feelings. She didn't want to alarm the children, but she was very anxious to learn just how sick her husband was. There had been nothing to suggest to her, though, the ordeals that lay ahead: the major surgery, the removal of a small part of his left lung, the amputation of the end of his big toe.

This last expedition had seemed more drawn out than the ones before—even longer than the 1975 K2 expedition. Maybe it was because this time she had had few illusions about her husband's climbing. In 1975 she had been more naive about the danger. She had had no doubts, then, that Jim would return, and in one piece. After all, he had been climbing mountains for the entire sixteen years they had been married and nothing had happened to him. When they married in 1962, she had been skeptical and decided to accompany him on one of his rock climbs and watch from the ground. She saw that he was careful, and she concluded that he would never put himself in a dangerous situation.

So she had happily bid him God's speed in 1975. The time passed quickly, and he was home and soon involved in another expedition to go back to K2 in 1978. If Mary Lou felt any resentment, it was that the preparations took so much of her husband's time. She felt often, as the time of the climb neared, that he would begin to focus his thinking on that goal and shut himself off once more from his family. She also was mildly jealous of the men with whom he climbed: There was an intimacy of common adventure that she would never share, and she felt, simply, left out.

But she also knew climbing was an absolutely necessary part of Wick's life, and she was supportive of his desire to go back to K2, to reach the summit of his dreams. Overall, she had good feelings about his return to K2. Good feelings until that day in June 1977, when she learned that Al and Dusan, climbing with Wick in Alaska, had been killed.

She was brought up short; her illusions were shattered. There was no hiding it—it could happen to him next. When finally he left for K2, she steeled herself. She had thought it through; she knew it was a possibility; she knew if it happened it would be a great responsibility with the kids; she wasn't sure it was completely fair, but she accepted it.

It had been a long summer. She found time passed more quickly if she stayed busy. She was house-sitting for Jim Whittaker and Dianne Roberts, so she spent many days in the garden or entertaining friends, or taking care of the kids as she patiently waited for word from Pakistan. The mail was horribly slow; the most updated news was the newspaper stories radioed in from Base Camp and relayed by wire to the States. Mary Lou grew impatient with the endless phone calls, wanting news of the climb.

"Read the papers," she said, "and you'll know as much as I do."

She remembered most vividly the afternoon of August 25. It was their anniversary. She was across the street, in a blackberry patch picking fruit for pie and thinking of Wick. She saw the Western Union man arrive and with blackberry juice still on her fingers, she tore open the telegram. The news was good: The climb was progressing, despite the storms, and there was yet a chance they might reach the top. And happy sixteenth, he had said. What she remembered most, though, was the last line, which had been garbled in its transmission over the international wire. It read: WEEP MIMMS ON ICE. She read it several times, thought of different interpretations, substituted letters in the words, finally deciphered the message, and laughed and laughed. Every year, for their anniversary,she and Wick had celebrated with champagne, saving the corks. Wick's message intended to say: KEEP MUMMS ON ICE.

She waited, anxiously reading the newspapers and listening to the radio. Finally the news broke: Jim Wickwire and Lou Reichardt had reached the summit. The hordes of friends and well-wishers were surprised how cool she was to hear the news. She showed little elation. To Mary Lou, it was not yet time to celebrate. She remembered too vividly that Al's and Dusan's accident was on the descent. She waited. No news came, and she interpreted that to mean the descent had gone without incident. Then came the cryptic telegram about helicopters and pneumonia and finally Joanne's message from Rob. Wick was sick, although apparently not seriously. All she really wanted at that point was to have him, as soon as possible, in her arms.

Mary Lou prayed, too—every night, and several times a day. She felt it had worked and in the next few weeks, when she learned more of the details of Wick's bivouac alone at nearly twenty-eight thousand feet, and his subsequent struggle to live through the hike out, she became more and more certain her prayers had been answered.

But waiting at the airport's arrival gate, she as yet had no clue to the trials her husband had suffered. All she knew was that he was supposed to enter a hospital for a checkup. She thought perhaps they could do that in the morning. All that really mattered was that he would be home and she could hold him.

Finally, after an eternity, the passengers started emerging from the door. They must have been surprised to be greeted by bright lights, TV cameras, and news reporters. Mary Lou thought how the passengers must have thought they had unwittingly been on the same flight as some political bigwig. She first saw the flag—one of those ridiculous little orange pennants attached to a tall wand they always have on airport wheelchairs. The lights were on—so bright and hot—and the cameras and newsmen seemed intrusive. She hadn't wanted it that way; she had hoped it would be intimate. The kids pushed through first, and then she saw him.

Mary Lou saw him and she froze. She stared. She looked at her husband, and their eyes held. The kids rushed to hug and kiss their Dad, but Mary Lou stayed back, paralyzed. She could not go forward to greet her husband.

He was there, sitting in the wheelchair, not the man who had left her four months before. He was too small. He was too shrunken. She looked at his black beard, flecked with gray, his sunken face. She could see he was trying to talk to her children, but he could make no voice, only a gasping, harsh sound. She thought, He couldn't be so small, he couldn't have shrunk. He was so solid and strong.

Joanne Schaller, standing behind Mary Lou, lightly pushed her forward.

"Go on, what are you waiting for?"

Mary Lou only later realized, when watching television, that she cried as she gently bent over to hug her husband. All she remembered was touching him, again and again, to make certain it was him, and she kept wondering how he could be so small. She cried for a long time. It was only then she knew, in full, just what it was he had been through, and what it had taken for her husband to climb to the summit of the mountain K2.

Epilogue

IN THE FALL OF 1998, TWENTY YEARS AND A month after we arrived home from K2, the Mazamas mountaineering club of Portland hosted a reunion not only for our expedition but for other K2 climbers as well. Charlie Houston and Bob Bates of the 1938 and 1953 American K2 expeditions attended; Bob Craig, George Bell, Tony Streather, and Dee Molenaar, also of the 1953 attempt were there; Greg Child, who climbed the north ridge in 1990, perhaps the greatest ridge-climb on earth, attended; and all of us from the 1978 climb were there, except for Lou Reichardt and Cherie Bech, who couldn't make it, Terry Bech and Diana Jagersky, who now live in Europe, and Chris Chandler, who died of cerebral edema during a 1985 attempt on Kanchenjunga.

A few wrinkles and some gray hair notwithstanding, we had aged well. Perhaps more important to the occasion, we all got along well. It wasn't that anyone's personality had changed, but I do think the years had healed our differences, and there was genuine conviviality. That's not to say that had our reunion been on a ship that sank and cast us adrift together in a lifeboat, differences might not have resurfaced, but it is to say, as in most reunions, we enjoyed catching up with what had happened to us in the intervening twenty years.

Craig Anderson showed up with his wife, Anne, and all four of their children. The two oldest had been young kids during our climb, and it was only now, at the reunion, as a parent myself, that I understood how much Craig must have missed them during the long months we were away, and also why he

303

climbed as cautiously as he did on K2. "I got what I was looking for out of our climb," he said. "It satisfied a hunger that drove me to high adventure in my younger years and left me free to focus on the more important challenge of my life, raising our four children."

Bill Sumner still owned his endearing Einstein countenance, and he was still passionate about theoretical physics, mountain equipment design, and mountain adventures. With a twinkle in his eye he told me he discovered that "quantum wave functions evolve with space-time geometry, which means that the universe is now collapsing!" At Mountain Safety Research, where he has been for years, he designed the WhisperLite stove that so many of us use and love. After K2 he led many trips to the Soviet Union and lived for awhile in Uzbekistan with his wife, Flura Zhirnova, a champion Soviet rock climber. He and Flura have a new son, Sasha, and they now live in Eastern Washington where, as Bill put it, "I'm seriously toying with the idea of building a real house and maybe even settling down."

Skip Edmonds has spent the last twenty years "juggling family, career, and recreation: pick any two, because you can't do all three well." But he's done a good job trying. He is happily remarried, gets away climbing with his seventeen-year-old son when he can, and continues his career in medicine. In addition to keeping up his climbing, Skip is also an avid ski-mountaineer.

The K2 climb was a turning point for **John Roskelley,** but more because it steered him away from big expeditions to smaller teams attempting extreme alpine routes on smaller Himalayan peaks, and harder new routes on larger ones. Over the next ten years he became the most accomplished Himalayan climber in the United States, and one of the best in the world. "But it was self-indulgent," he told me recently, "and along the way I metamorphosed into someone more concerned with long-term environmental, community, and social issues. It was not a hard transition." In 1995 he ran for and won a seat as county commissioner in his hometown of Spokane, a position he was re-elected to and continues to hold today.

Lou Riechardt returned to the big mountains, making the first ascent of Everest's Kangshung Face in 1983, and at the same time becoming the first American to climb both Everest and K2. Just as impressive—or perhaps even more impressive—he continues as a professor at the University of California San Francisco, where he is on the cutting edge of his discipline, studying molecules that regulate the early development of the nervous system, determining, among other things, which ones live, or die (he doesn't think he lost any molecules on either Everest or K2). He and his wife have four children, three of whom are either in or have graduated from college.

After arriving at the Seattle airport in a wheelchair, **Jim Wickwire** underwent lung surgery at a local hospital. He made a remarkable recovery and went on to climb Denali again, made three expeditions to Everest, as well as expeditions to Kanchenjunga and Menlungtse. Wickwire continues to practice law with his Seattle firm, and Anne, the oldest of his five children has now given him and Mary Lou twin granddaughters. Grandpa Wickwire continues to climb, and, as recently as 1995, he put up a new route on Sarmiento, a remote peak in windswept Tierra del Fuego.

Jim Whittaker and **Dianne Roberts** left Seattle in 1985 and moved to Port Townsend, where the two of them built a beautiful log house looking out over the Straits of Juan de Fuca and pursued their passion for sailing. In 1990 Jim again reached the summit of Everest as the leader of a joint expedition of climbers from the United States, the Soviet Union, and China. The expedition was known as the Peace Climb, and its intent was to demonstrate the desire of the common citizen for a more peaceful world. Two years ago Jim and Dianne sold the house, bought another boat, and set sail. They were at the reunion having left the *Impossible* anchored in Mooloolaba, Australia. Once the younger of their two sons finishes his school term, and Jim completes his autobiography, they intend to return to the *Impossible* and complete their circumnavigation.

In 1988 **Rob Schaller** remarried and had three more children, including one named Sierra, which means *high mountain*. "K2 still means a lot to me," he said at the reunion. "It was one of the last of the old-style expeditions, before GPS and FAX and satellite up-link, and we were there on our own." He continues to climb, and a couple of years ago, when he was sixty-two, ascended Mera, a 21,000-foot peak near Everest. He and his family live on a ten-acre farm in the Cascade foothills, and Rob is professor of surgery at the University of Washington, and a very active and accomplished pediatric surgeon as well. Referring to his work, he said, "I would buy tickets to do what I do. I love my work and I love my life." He and his wife Teresa also volunteer their services to preserve old-growth forest in Washington State.

As for myself, like Wickwire and Roskelley, I continued to climb in the remote ranges although I took a hiatus—after nearly dying in 1980 in an avalanche on a remote peak in eastern Tibet—to reconfirm that the rewards of mountaineering outweighed the risks. I also married during that time, and my wife Jennifer and I have three children. I continue to make my living from a combination of endeavors related to climbing and adventure: I have a line of packs, sleeping bags, and tents called *Ridgeway by Kelty*, I make documentary films, and I continue to write books.

After the K2 climb, I traveled to Seattle to see **Chris Chandler,** to try and repair our friendship. I was writing *The Last Step* at the time, and Chris told me he didn't want me to refer to his friendship with **Cherie Bech.** I told him it was so central to everything that happened on the mountain that I didn't know how I could avoid referring to it, or even avoid making it one of the central themes of the story. That didn't mollify Chris, and, of course, I wrote the book, and Chris never really talked to me again after that. **Terry Bech,** who eventually moved to Europe to take a job playing the viola for a Dutch symphony, felt the same as Chris about including any reference to the affair in the book and even threatened to sue me (although he never did).

Later Cherie wrote about the affair, and about her deep love for Chris, in her own book, *Living on the Edge*. Opposite the title page there is a wonderful photograph of Chris, his long blond hair as wild as any Norseman's, his broad smile enough to stop any woman in her tracks. He was one of the most handsome men I've ever known. In her book, Cherie tells how she and Chris sailed his 34-foot ferro-cement ketch *Laylah* on voyages in the Northwest and the North Pacific. They also continued climbing, attempting a satellite peak of Kanchenjunga, then returning in December 1984 to attempt what would have been the first winter ascent of the third highest mountain in the world. In a snow cave at their high camp, Chris quite suddenly was blinded with cerebral edema. Cherie and one Nepali struggled to get him down, but he died the next day, and she had no choice but to leave him where he lay. Cherie just escaped with her own life, losing all of her fingers and toes to severe frostbite.

When I learned of Chris's death, I went for a long walk on the beach, and among many other issues, I once more wrestled with the question whether or not the rewards of serious mountaineering outweigh the risks. Although I continue to go abroad on a climbing expedition about once a year, and although I now favor smaller peaks in obscure places, each time I still must weigh one side of that balance beam against the other. As for my children, I am hopeful they will stick to backpacking.

Rick Ridgeway
Ojai, California
February 1999